Second Language Learning and Teaching

Series editor

Mirosław Pawlak, Kalisz, Poland

About the Series

The series brings together volumes dealing with different aspects of learning and teaching second and foreign languages. The titles included are both monographs and edited collections focusing on a variety of topics ranging from the processes underlying second language acquisition, through various aspects of language learning in instructed and non-instructed settings, to different facets of the teaching process, including syllabus choice, materials design, classroom practices and evaluation. The publications reflect state-of-the-art developments in those areas, they adopt a wide range of theoretical perspectives and follow diverse research paradigms. The intended audience are all those who are interested in naturalistic and classroom second language acquisition, including researchers, methodologists, curriculum and materials designers, teachers and undergraduate and graduate students undertaking empirical investigations of how second languages are learnt and taught.

More information about this series at http://www.springer.com/series/10129

Mirosław Pawlak · Anna Mystkowska-Wiertelak
Editors

Challenges of Second and Foreign Language Education in a Globalized World

Studies in Honor of Krystyna
Droździał-Szelest

 Springer

Editors
Mirosław Pawlak
Faculty of Pedagogy and Fine Arts
Adam Mickiewicz University
Kalisz
Poland

Anna Mystkowska-Wiertelak
Faculty of Pedagogy and Fine Arts
Adam Mickiewicz University
Kalisz
Poland

ISSN 2193-7648   ISSN 2193-7656   (electronic)
Second Language Learning and Teaching
ISBN 978-3-319-88356-4   ISBN 978-3-319-66975-5   (eBook)
DOI 10.1007/978-3-319-66975-5

Printed on acid-free paper

This Springer imprint is published by Springer Nature
The registered company is Springer International Publishing AG
The registered company address is: Gewerbestrasse 11, 6330 Cham, Switzerland

Preface

Although I have edited or co-edited a number of volumes over the past 15 years, including those published in honor of distinguished friends and colleagues in the fields of second-language acquisition and applied linguistics, none of them has been as special and personal as the present collection of papers, dedicated to Prof. Krystyna Droździał-Szelest. The reason for this is that I have had the privilege to get to know her in so many different roles over the past 25 years since I became a student of English philology at the start of the 1990s at the School of English of Adam Mickiewicz University, Poznań, Poland. At the outset, she taught a course in foreign language methodology that I attended, then she supervised my M.A. thesis and doctoral dissertation, and, finally, she acted in the capacity of the reviewer of the monograph that I wrote as a requirement for my postdoctoral degree. In a word, she was my unquestionable mentor, a source of inspiration, and someone from whom I was able to learn a great deal. She has never ceased to perform these roles but has also assumed several new ones, that of a colleague, with whom I have had a chance to work, cooperate on a number of projects, attend conferences and serve on the board of the Modern Language Association of Poland, but also a close friend with whom I have talked about things that could not be more unrelated to foreign language teaching and learning. Most importantly, though, all of this has by no means been only my experience because Krystyna Droździał-Szelest has performed some or all of these roles to tens, or should I say hundreds, of those involved in research on foreign language pedagogy and teacher training in Poland and other countries. On the academic level, her contribution to research on language learning strategies, particularly her book published in 1997, can hardly be overestimated. On the pedagogic level, she has always been a devoted, enthusiastic and inspiring teacher, respected and cherished by her students, someone who has tirelessly spent hours reading and commenting on homework assignments, B.A. and M.A. papers and chapters of Ph.D. theses. What surely speaks for itself is the fact that over the course of her academic career Krystyna Droździał-Szelest has successfully supervised 20 doctoral dissertations and that number is bound to grow in the near future, a feat that very few scholars would be able to match, let alone surpass. Finally, and perhaps most importantly, on the personal level, she has always been an affable, approachable, friendly, ingenious, smart, and witty person, endowed with a great sense of humor, a true live wire and someone who is always fun to be with. It is perhaps all of those qualities combined but first and foremost the high esteem in which she is held in the academia that accounts for the fact that so many eminent scholars but also her colleagues and former doctoral students have agreed, with little deliberation, to contribute chapters to this edited collection.

The outcome is truly impressive, a monograph comprising 19 excellent papers, both theoretical- and research-based, which address the ways in which the challenges of second and foreign language education in the present-day globalized word can be confronted. The book has been divided into three parts, each including contributions that are linked by a common thread. Part I, *Challenges of language teaching and learning*, is the most extensive but also the most general in nature, bringing together nine contributions devoted to the concept of mission in English language teaching, the need for applications in our field, language instruction in non-specialist departments in universities, the role of emotions, gestures and creativity in language learning, the use of simulation in the development of intercultural communicative competence, teaching business English, and a comparison of aspects of language education in Norway and Poland. Part II, titled *Challenges of researching language classrooms,* comprises six papers reporting the results of original research projects focusing on the use of think-aloud protocols in translation tasks, the link between ambiguity tolerance and willingness to communicate in a second language, the application of retrodictive qualitative modeling in the study of motivation, learners' awareness of the role of their mother tongue in learning second and third languages, the impact of instruction in affective learning strategies on anxiety levels, as well as universal characteristics of effective language teachers. Part III, *Challenges of teacher education and development*, includes four chapters concerning such issues as the contribution of metaphor to the development of knowledge about language teaching methodology, the pitfalls of adopting neoliberal policies in teacher education, long-term development of teacher identity, and the role of international experience in shaping future teachers' beliefs about the need to foster intercultural communicative competence. I am confident that all the papers included in this collection will, on the one hand, constitute important signposts for those researching the processes of second and foreign language teaching and learning, providing food for thought and a source of ideas for future empirical investigations, and, on the other, serve as well as an important impulse for teachers who are willing to engage in professional reflection and are constantly on the lookout for ways in which their classroom practices could be enhanced.

I would also like to express my profound gratitude to all to contributors to this volume, who, without any hesitation, not only consented to write up their chapters on very short notice, but also agreed to offer invaluable feedback on each other's papers, and instantaneously reacted to all the requests for missing sources or other revisions that had to be made almost overnight. I believe that I am speaking also on their behalf in declaring that the endeavor was definitely worth the effort as there are few things that are more rewarding in the academic world than putting together a collection of papers in honor of such a distinguished scholar, a valued colleague, and an exceptional person as Prof. Krystyna Droździał-Szelest.

Kalisz, Poland   Mirosław Pawlak

Contents

About the Editors and Contributors

About the Editors

Mirosław Pawlak is Professor of English at the Faculty of Philology, State University of Applied Sciences, Konin, Poland, and the Department of English Studies, Faculty of Pedagogy and Fine Arts in Kalisz, Adam Mickiewicz University, Kalisz, Poland. He received his doctoral and postdoctoral degrees as well as his full professorship from Adam Mickiewicz University, Poznań, Poland. His main areas of interest are SLA theory and research, form-focused instruction, corrective feedback, classroom discourse, learner autonomy, learning strategies, grammar learning strategies, motivation, willingness to communicate, and pronunciation teaching. His recent publications include *The place of form-focused instruction in the foreign language classroom* (2006, Adam Mickiewicz University Press), *Production-oriented and comprehension-based grammar teaching in the foreign language classroom* (co-authored with Anna Mystkowska-Wiertelak, 2012, Springer), *Error correction in the foreign language classroom: Reconsidering the issues* (2014, Springer), *Applying cognitive grammar in the foreign language classroom: Teaching English tense and aspect* (co-authored with Jakub Bielak, 2013, Springer), *Willingness to communicate in instructed second language acquisition: Combining a macro- and micro-perspective* (co-authored with Anna Mystkowska-Wiertelak, 2017, Multilingual Matters), and numerous edited collections. Mirosław Pawlak is the Editor-in-Chief of the journals *Studies in Second Language Learning and Teaching*, *Konin Language Studies*, and the book series *Second Language Learning and Teaching*. e-mail: pawlakmi@amu.edu.pl

Anna Mystkowska-Wiertelak is Assistant Professor at the Department of English Studies of the Faculty of Pedagogy and Fine Arts of Adam Mickiewicz University, Poznań/Kalisz, Poland as well as Senior Lecturer at the Faculty of Philology of State University of Applied Sciences, Konin, Poland. Her main interests comprise, apart from teacher education, second-language acquisition theory and research, language learning strategies, learner autonomy, form-focused instruction, willingness to communicate, and motivation. Her recent publications include *Production-oriented and comprehension-based grammar teaching in the foreign language classroom* (with Mirosław Pawlak, Springer, 2012) and *Willingness to communicate in instructed second language acquisition* (with Mirosław Pawlak, Multilingual Matters, 2017). e-mail: mystkows@amu.edu.pl

Contributors

Jakub Bielak Adam Mickiewicz University, Poznań, Kalisz, Poland; State University of Applied Sciences, Konin, Poland

Anna Czura University of Wrocław, Wrocław, Poland

Maria Dakowska University of Warsaw, Warsaw, Poland

Marek Derenowski State University of Applied Sciences, Konin, Poland

Anna Domińska Adam Mickiewicz University, Poznań, Poland

Małgorzata Ekiert Pomeranian University, Słupsk, Poland

Danuta Gabryś-Barker University of Silesia, Katowice, Poland

May Olaug Horverak Agder University, Kristiansand, Norway

Hanna Komorowska SWPS University of Social Sciences and Humanities, Warsaw, Poland

Mariusz Kruk University of Zielona Góra, Zielona Góra, Poland

Hadrian Lankiewicz University of Gdańsk, Gdańsk, Poland

Anna Michońska-Stadnik University of Wrocław, Wrocław, Poland

Anna Niżegorodcew Jagiellonian University, Kraków, Poland

Rebecca L. Oxford University of Maryland, College Park, USA

Liliana Piasecka University of Opole, Opole, Poland

Ewa Piechurska-Kuciel University of Opole, Opole, Poland

Paweł Scheffler Adam Mickiewicz University, Poznań, Poland

Teresa Siek-Piskozub Adam Mickiewicz University, Poznań, Poland

Paweł Sobkowiak Adam Mickiewicz University, Poznań, Poland

Aleksandra Wach Adam Mickiewicz University, Poznań, Poland

Dorota Werbińska Pomeranian University, Słupsk, Poland

Joanna Zawodniak University of Zielona Góra, Zielona Góra, Poland

Anna Mystkowska-Wiertelak Adam Mickiewicz University, Kalisz, Poland

Mirosław Pawlak Adam Mickiewicz University, Kalisz, Poland

Part I
Challenges of Language Teaching and Learning

Mission in English Language Teaching: Why and Why Not?

Anna Niżegorodcew

Abstract The purpose of this chapter, written for the volume in honor of a colleague in the field of applied linguistics and English Language Teaching (ELT) is to view through personal lenses the "missionary" aspect of ideas and behavior of English as a Foreign Language (EFL) teachers and teacher trainers. The inspiration for this paper has been drawn from Bill Johnston's recent book *English teaching and evangelical mission* (2017). However, while Johnston uses the term *mission* in a literal religious sense of the word, I am using it more metaphorically, as the imposition of one's ideas and practices upon one's colleagues. This chapter is a case study based on a few accounts of encounters with native and non-native ELT professionals, which serve as illustrations of "missionary" approaches in our field. It focuses, firstly, on the perceived "missionary" approaches of ELT activities of the British Council in Poland in the 1990s, secondly, on the inherent "missionary" aspects of an intercultural EFL project carried out by this author in Ukraine and, finally, on a recent cooperative ELT to senior students project, in which we have liberated ourselves from the "missionary" approach.

Keywords English language teaching · Linguistic imperialism · Third-age learners · Intercultural projects

1 Introduction

The purpose of this chapter, written for the volume in honor of a colleague in the field of applied linguistics and English Language Teaching (ELT) is to view through personal lenses the "missionary" aspect of ideas and behavior of English as a Foreign Language (EFL) teachers and teacher trainers. As the head of a university foreign language teacher training college (1990–1997), I was not only one of those deeply involved in the Poland of the 1990s in receiving British Council (BC) guidance and

A. Niżegorodcew (✉)
Jagiellonian University, Kraków, Poland
e-mail: annanizegorodcew@gmail.com

© Springer International Publishing AG 2018
M. Pawlak and A. Mystkowska-Wiertelak (eds.), *Challenges of Second and Foreign Language Education in a Globalized World*, Second Language Learning and Teaching, DOI 10.1007/978-3-319-66975-5_1

aid in ELT and language teacher training, but also in the subsequent years, I acted as a manager and disseminator of western standards in setting up an intercultural EFL teacher training project in Ukraine. Finally, in recent years I have been disseminating modern approaches to ELT in teaching senior students. In all three contexts, I have cooperated with EFL teachers and teacher trainers, both native British and non-native Ukrainian and Polish. I began to realize in the 1990s and I fully realize at present that their and our ideas and activities in the first two cases had a "missionary" aspect to them. The inspiration for this paper has been drawn from Bill Johnston's recent book *English teaching and evangelical mission* (2017). However, while Johnston uses the term *mission* in a literal religious sense of the word, I am using it more metaphorically, as the imposition of one's ideas and practices upon one's colleagues. My approach is retrospective since I base my account on memories of my professional past as well as on my present professional experiences bound with this aspect of ELT.

2 Three Cases

Since the publication of the seminal book by Robert Phillipson *Linguistic imperialism* (1992), in the sociolinguistic and sociocultural approaches to ELT in the Third World countries and in post-communist countries, teaching English has been identified with a domineering and patronizing attitudes of the native or near-native ELT organizations and individuals towards local non-native EFL teachers and local educational institutions, as well as with imposing a globalized western culture upon local communities and cultures (cf. Canagarajah, 1999). Firstly, reflecting back on the position of Polish EFL teachers in the changing landscape of teaching English in Poland in the 1990s, I must admit that Polish EFL teachers and teacher trainers were objects of what I call in this paper the "missionary" actions implemented by the BC and its representatives in Polish English language teacher training colleges. Secondly, reflecting on my mind-child intercultural project, I realize now that my ideas and western editorial standards were to some extent imposed upon Ukrainian EFL teachers and teacher trainers. Finally, reflecting on my own and my Polish colleagues' present initiatives in teaching English to senior students, I come to the conclusion that our success in teaching this age group consists partly in refraining from imposing anything on one another. Having written that, I would like to stress that the "missionary" insistence on imposing ideas, standards and procedures does not mean that those ideas, standards and procedures are wrong in themselves. It rather implies that the people who are their recipients are not sufficiently prepared to receive them and/or are not treated as partners by the "missionary" teacher trainers. For obvious reasons. the names of the described native and non-native teachers and teacher trainers' have been changed.

I do not uncritically adopt Phillipson's radical views, according to which the promotion of teaching English in the so-called "peripheries" serves a neo-colonial policy of the so-called "core" English-speaking countries to maintain their hegemony. We must distinguish two layers in the very concept of ELT as a form of "linguistic imperialism": a layer of particular cultures (e.g., West vs. East-European) and a layer of ELT ideas, standards and procedures as they are implemented in a given local context, which is treated as a "periphery" and is dominated by institutions and individuals representing the dominating "core". The so-called "linguistic imperialism" or neo-colonialism in such sociolinguistic views refers more to the methods of implementation than to the cultural content. However, in ELT, more than in any other field, the methods of teaching cannot be separated from the content of teaching. A good example of such a mistaken implementation of the dominating "core" method of teaching English in the 1990s was the Communicative Approach. It stemmed from multilingual English as a second language (ESL) classrooms taught by native English-speaking teachers. Its transfer and use in monolingual EFL classrooms taught by non-native teachers in "periphery" countries of Eastern Europe and elsewhere resulted in confusion, misunderstandings and finally, in the lowering of EFL teacher training standards (cf. Niżegorodcew, 1995). The question arises to what extent in the first two cases described in the following parts of this paper, ELT ideas, standards and procedures were imposed upon, firstly, Polish and, secondly, Ukrainian teachers and teacher trainers. It befits to briefly introduce those cases to try to answer the question from the "missionary" perspective.

In the first case, in the early 1990s, under the changed socio-political situation, the BC was invited by the Polish Ministry of Education to help organize a network of English teacher training colleges throughout Poland. The BC was considered to be the best partner, having not only the material resources but also the required expertise in the field of EFL teacher training. The BC native teacher trainers played the role of mentors placed in Polish university teacher training colleges responsible for other colleges in the regional clusters. Apart from native advisors who stayed in Poland, Polish heads of university colleges or English departments were supposed to coordinate the training of the Polish college staff by British teacher trainers. My retrospective account will describe two native teacher trainers, who imposed their ideas of EFL teacher training upon Polish staff, although, admittedly, one of them seemed to do it for the sake of the trainees, while the other was clearly patronizing and arrogant. The first teacher trainer played the role of the BC permanent mentor at a university teacher training college. Her "missionary" zeal was evident and her exaggerated involvement was criticized by Polish staff members, who were not prepared to work as enthusiastically as she did. The other teacher trainer was a native professional responsible for training Polish staff during a short intensive workshop. His approach was unanimously assessed by the Polish staff as unprofessional and arrogant. In Phillipson's terms, he acted as a neo-colonial "master" imposing his ideas on the local staff, contrary to their wishes. In consequence, the Polish college staff opposed the native trainer's behavior, which resulted in his dismissal. Let me call the former trainer Sue, and the latter Geoff.

In the second case, in the first decade of this century, I was responsible for the conceptualization of the Polish-Ukrainian intercultural project. The project was conceptualized as partner cooperation between staff and students of two English departments, one in Poland and the other one in Ukraine. From my present perspective, I must admit that I acted on the basis of my expectations rather than reality. My objective was to compile a research-based book of texts for students of English on aspects of Polish and Ukrainian culture. However, the idea of student cooperation in researching both cultures failed and, finally, the Ukrainian staff members became responsible for finding suitable texts on culture and designing accompanying tasks, whereas the Polish students managed to carry out research and write original texts on its basis. It became clear at a later stage that the project was too ambitious for the Ukrainian students, who had no previous experience in research. I and my Polish colleague involved in the project realized that the collaborating student groups could not be treated as equal for objective reasons stemming from their different education and age since Ukrainian students were two years younger than Polish ones. Striving to complete the project, we changed our roles from those of equal partners to the mentors of the Ukrainians, both in terms of the content of their chapters and of their formal features in the editorial process. Towards the end of the project our "mission" was to manage the publication of the book according to western standards, notwithstanding Ukrainian publishing customs. In the following parts of this paper I will focus on two Ukrainian staff members: a Ukrainian head of the English Studies Department who collaborated in the editing process and another Ukrainian senior teacher trainer. The former to some extent resisted our dominance in the project, while his ideas were frequently unacceptable to us. Nevertheless, his aim was clearly to bring our common project to completion. The latter acted in a quiet and professional way as our partner. She compiled an interesting chapter with tasks for students and carried out research among Ukrainian students based on Polish students' chapters. Let me call them, respectively, Oleg and Liza.

As has been said above, the third case does not have a hidden "missionary" agenda. EFL courses for senior students as they were taught recently by a Polish colleague and myself were taught together but also separately and independently. Alongside the development of EFL skills and teaching grammar and vocabulary, our aim was to socialize senior students through the introduction of varied personalized group activities and stimulating content. We did not, however, patronize each other or impose anything on each other. It seems that the main reason why we were successful in such an approach was our familiarity with each other and similar educational and cultural background. Our approach was based on trust in our professionalism and mutual respect. Let me call my colleague Dorota.

Contrary to that, different cultural backgrounds and unequal distribution of power tend to create situations conducive to imposition and dominance of a more powerful party over the other. Johnston (2017) claims that there is a significant colonial dimension in relations between North American evangelicals and Polish Catholics. Such a claim does not seem justified in terms of asymmetrical relations of power. Evangelical EFL native teachers as described by Johnston were more "powerful" only in the sense of their native English language competence but not in the sense of their greater religious involvement. The fact that they talked more freely than Polish Catholics about their faith stemmed more from their evangelical training and North American openness than from their spiritual superiority. In fact, some fragments of the classroom discourse cited by the author provide evidence of Polish Catholics' equal status in discussing moral issues in spite of their lower language competence.

Searching for the possible colonial dimensions in the described first two cases, it is easier to find them in the first case. When it was created in 1934 as a British official institution to propagate British culture and the English language, the BC was to some extent following the imperial tradition of the British Empire in its colonies. Although Poland had never been a British colony, due to its history of subjugation by Russia, Prussia and Austria at the end of the 18th century and partitions of the country, which lasted until 1918, as well as due to its status of a satellite country of the Soviet Union (1945–1989), in the early 1990s the BC may have treated Poland as a post-colonial country and may have underestimated Polish EFL teachers' and teacher trainers' level of education and expertise. Nobody admitted it openly, yet tensions between some of the BC representatives and Polish senior university staff indicated that the former considered themselves superior in education and expertise. In the following years, owing to numerous contacts, British underestimation of the Polish teachers and teacher trainers was positively modified.

I am more knowledgeable of the second of the described cases as the initiator of the intercultural project. Originally, I believed that the Polish and Ukrainian teacher trainers, EFL teachers and students would represent more or less equal levels of English language proficiency and of intercultural competence. Additionally, originally, my colleague and I did not realize that editorial standards in Ukraine were different from those in Poland. Since our co-authored book was to be published in Poland, we had to persuade our Ukrainian partners to accept Polish, that is, international editorial standards. There is a fine line between persuasion and imposition. To the best of my present knowledge, we refrained from outright imposition but in some most blatant cases, we refused to approve of our partners' ideas and editing ways, and we imposed our ideas and editorial standards upon them. On the other hand, in the final stages of the editorial process one of our Ukrainian partners openly resisted some of our suggestions, which he must have treated as impositions. At that stage our contacts became less cordial. However, since our Polish-Ukrainian project had a common goal to publish a co-authored book and our group of co-workers could be characterized as a "community of practice" (cf. Lave & Wenger, 1991; Wenger, 1998), both sides did not break the rules of politeness in mutual contacts.

At a deeper historical and psychological level, I am asking myself why I embarked on the intercultural project in the first place. In this respect, a semi-colonial dimension could be traced back to the history of present Western Ukraine. It used to be part of pre-war Poland with a large Polish population, displaced during and after the Second World War. Their descendants living in Poland and elsewhere in the world treat Lvov, Stanislavov (at present Ivano-Frankivsk) and other towns in which they ancestors used to live with the kind of nostalgia that the former West European colonists could have felt after having left African and Asian colonies. The semi-colonial dimension may be seen in the present treatment of Ukrainians by the Polish people. It seems that, apart from nostalgic feelings towards the land of our ancestors, we cherish a kind of patronizing approach towards Ukrainians. The more their socio-political situation becomes difficult, the more certain we are that they would have been much better off if they had followed our advice and, indeed, had not opposed us. Economic imbalance between Poland and Ukraine may have also increased the Polish feelings of superiority. Although we, as ELT professionals, tried to disregard those sentiments in the intercultural project, they may have contributed to our "missionary" zeal in carrying out our project.

Finally, I would like to emphasize that what I have written is a case study based on a few accounts of encounters with native and non-native ELT professionals, which serve as illustrations of "missionary" approaches in our field. I do not wish to generalize my observations of those particular cases to other ELT professionals. However, I believe that our and our partners' approaches and actions may have had much in common with other native and non-native professionals in similar situations. In describing particular cases, I have not drawn on any single sociocultural and sociolinguistic theory; rather, I have combined some theoretical threads from theoretical approaches accounting for negative and positive aspects of cultural encounters in contact situations. On the one hand, "linguistic imperialism" (Phillipson, 1992) with its focus on the unequal distribution of power may interpret the encounters in terms of neo-colonialism; on the other hand, however, the above-mentioned model of the "communities of practice" (Wenger, 1998) focuses on the positive sides of common intercultural projects which support cooperation and interpenetration of cultures.

3 Playing the Roles of ELT "Missionaries"

3.1 Sue: An Enthusiastic "Missionary"

Sue was the most enthusiastic teacher trainer I have ever met. She arrived at our university teacher training college in the early 1990s with a set of deeply ingrained ideas what EFL teacher training should look like and she did not waver in her approach during the whole year she spent with us. Finally, however, after only one year, she was substituted by another native mentor. I wondered if she was considered too enthusiastic not only by us, her local colleagues, but also by her BC employers. Her ways were straightforward and she did not hesitate a moment to present and later to implement her teacher training ideas.

As the head of the college, at first I liked her openness and sincerity and I did not suffer as much as my other colleagues due to her transgressions of their privacy. For instance, a colleague was once woken up at 8 a.m. on a Sunday morning because Sue did not see anything inappropriate in finding her colleagues in their homes and summoning them to work extra hours at her "school-within-a-school" place. In itself "school-within-a-school" was an excellent idea but due to Sue's abrupt way of acting it was totally unprepared. At first, Sue advertised in neighborhood churches free weekend EFL courses for children and in this way she organized free teaching practice for our college trainees. At weekends children with their parents swarmed from morning till late afternoon in our modest college building and paired teacher trainees took shifts to teach them. The only supervisor of the whole enterprise was Sue because other staff members refused to work overtime during weekends. I visited Sue's weekend school from time to time and I had rather mixed feelings. On the one hand, I was deeply impressed by Sue's dedication in providing our trainees with genuine teaching experience; on the other, I realized that the experience was like "putting the cart before the horse" since the trainees had not had any teacher training before they started their weekend courses. Finally, I had to radically cut the weekend school experiment for safety reasons after I noticed some children sitting on the window sill in an open second floor window. I believe that if anybody had been hurt, I would have been the first person to blame.

Sue had other fascinating ideas she immediately implemented, helped by the trainees and parents. For instance, she organized a Christmas Party for the whole college, including staff, trainees, children and their parents from the weekend school. The party started in the main square of the city where all of us were supposed to light candles and to follow a hired cab with Santa Claus who was throwing sweets all around. We walked with candles for half an hour to reach a community center, where Sue with trainees and parents organized performances, carol singing and refreshments. The event was a great success, except for a small incident when some real evangelical missionaries, who must have joined the pageant, started preaching from the stage. I managed to persuade them to leave us to enjoy the Christmas Party.

Another successful event was a weekend training workshop for our trainees with the children from the weekend school and their parents, organized at a holiday center in the country. What Sue failed to implement was to be a more ambitious continuation of the workshop. She planned to have a summer training camp for the trainees combined with a summer camp for children. The camp was to be run by the parents. Finally, however, sanitary and safety regulations prevented Sue from organizing it. It seems that being disappointed with her colleagues' lack of enthusiasm for her initiatives, Sue enlisted the support of parents. Her failure to continue with some of her excellent teacher training ideas seemed to lie in her uncompromising character and her disregard for local rules and customs. I met Sue in Britain a few years after she left our college. She was as enthusiastic as ever and we spent a pleasant afternoon on talking about our professional and private lives.

3.2 Geoff: An Arrogant "Missionary"

Geoff was the most arrogant teacher trainer I have ever met. He did not take any notice of the wishes and preferences of our college staff. He represented a British university and was employed by the BC to run a series of short intensive workshops for college staff. Since I was the head of the college, Geoff invited me in the first place to visit the British ELT Department where he worked. For private reasons, I could not leave Poland at that time and I suggested that a colleague of mine substitute me. Indeed, she visited Geoff's department and reported to us on the visit, which was very interesting for her. The department itself had a good reputation as a teacher training research center. I did not expect at that time that Geoff could have held a grudge about my failing to visit his department. Apart from my feeling that Geoff, whom I had met briefly before, seemed to be a person with an oversized ego, there was nothing in the air to indicate the future training disaster. To give Geoff some guidance on what areas of training he should or should not focus on during his visit to Poland, I wrote to him that the only area the Polish staff did not need any training in is English grammar since we were all graduates of English Studies and had completed extensive courses on historical and modern English grammar.

An intensive training workshop with Geoff as our mentor was to cover a few days and was organized at a hotel in a holiday resort. Our trainees were excused from attending classes and the whole college staff went with Geoff and his colleague to the workshop site. On the first day, Geoff started his workshop by writing an English clause on the board and underlining nouns in it. Then he asked us if we could possibly guess what the function of the underlined words was. Such an activity may be appropriate for the fourth grade of primary school. That was apparently too much, especially for some younger and more outgoing staff members, who started to giggle and share little notes about the poor quality of the workshop. Geoff grew red in the face and left the room slamming the door. I tried to mitigate but he refused to run the workshop and for the remaining time left it to his colleague. On our departure from the place, I tried to make it up with him but he was deeply offended and refused to shake hands with me, claiming that I was the instigator of the ridicule.

The situation after the incident became serious because Geoff in a report to the BC accused me and all college staff members of offensive behavior which disrupted his workshop. Luckily, those present at the workshop unanimously supported my reply to the BC, rejecting Geoff's accusations and describing his behavior as blatantly unprofessional and arrogant. In consequence, he was dismissed by the BC from his position and our college was linked with another British university. Geoff's behavior could be interpreted following the neo-colonial model of linguistic imperialism as a drastic case of imposition of one's own ideas in the most arrogant way. However, it could also be accounted for by male chauvinism, since all staff members to be trained were women. Certainly, Geoff represented the most extreme case among representatives of British universities who had been appointed to train Polish college staff and whose cooperation with staff in other Polish teacher colleges, as I learned, was unproblematic. Unluckily, Geoff was delegated to train our college staff.

4 Coping with ELT "Missionaries"

4.1 Oleg: Co-operation with Resistance

Let me describe a Ukrainian teacher trainer whom I met in the late 2000s. Oleg was the head of the English Studies Department at a university in Western Ukraine. For the reasons I hinted at before, I tried to link our English Studies Department, and specifically, as its head, the Section of Applied Linguistics and EFL Teacher Training with a Ukrainian English Studies Department. With a Polish colleague we drew up a plan of Polish and Ukrainian students' co-operation in researching cultural topics and compiling on their basis an intercultural reader with tasks, preceded by a few theoretical chapters on intercultural issues, written by Polish and Ukrainian staff members. I met Oleg for the first time in his Rector's office. He seemed to be easy-going and quick to grasp my ideas of co-operation. Later we talked without working out a precise plan of cooperation but with an understanding that it could be specified in the future. I also met the Ukrainian students and staff of the English Studies Department who volunteered to participate in the intercultural project. I can recollect my feelings of satisfaction and even pride after those first meetings that my mind-child project was so well received by our Ukrainian partners.

I did not realize then that for Oleg my proposal was, first of all, an opportunity to publish a co-authored book in Poland, which for him, as for many other Ukrainians, was considered part of "Europe", that is, the prestigious "West". He strongly opposed my suggestion that the book could be more easily published in Ukraine. He also cared for his students' proficiency in English and at first intended to include in it a very great number of reading comprehension exercises, which were to follow the compiled texts. After we had agreed that the book would be published in Poland, the publication had to comply with international standards in terms of a style sheet and referencing. To the best of my knowledge, Oleg managed to per-suade his colleagues that those standards constituted an indispensable condition for the book to be published at all. He may have introduced the necessary corrections himself. Apparently, he was a skillful head and manager. He also conceded when my colleague and I to some extent imposed on him cutting the number of exercises at least by half in view of focusing in them on intercultural rather than purely lexical and reading comprehension tasks.

I must admit in retrospect that Oleg and I cooperated on a partnership basis as far as sharing ideas, drafts of the compiled texts and their revised versions was con-cerned. The first serious misunderstanding occurred when I and my Polish col-league drafted an introductory chapter, in which we wished, among other things, to describe the process of conceptualization and editing of the book as an example of challenges in intercultural projects. The draft was consulted with an American researcher of Ukrainian origin, who approved of the ideas included in it. However, after receiving the draft, Oleg expressed his indignation and he strongly protested against a public disclosure of any problems in our collaboration. He insisted on a standard introduction, with only a description of the content of the book and acknowledgements. While we argued that the editing process might be interesting for the readers, Oleg bluntly stated that nobody would be interested in the process, and that what matters would be only the product, that is the completed book.

I remember quite well my response to Oleg's reservations, where I disagreed with his objections but I said that our co-authored book must have an introduction both parties would agree upon. In consequence, we discarded the detailed description of the conceptualization and editing process, leaving only very general statements about our cooperative project. In other words, the decorum Oleg insisted on prevailed over our "naughty" version of the introduction. In that case, Oleg successfully coped with our "missionary" approach and he made the co-authored book closer to Ukrainian than to western standards of what is appropriate to disclose to the public. As has been said before, our relations became less cordial after that. I believe that Oleg must have felt a sense of satisfaction after the book was published, although, apart from sharing mutual congratulations on the completion of our project, he never wrote a word about the book and its reception by colleagues and students. I hope that he considered our co-authored book also his own. We still exchange Christmas and Easter greetings.

4.2   Liza: Co-operation with Dignity

Liza was a senior EFL teacher and teacher trainer at the same department as Oleg. She was a co-author (with Oleg) of the first chapter in the part of the book devoted to texts on Ukrainian culture, which presented fragments of traditional folk stories and modern Ukrainian literature, followed by the corresponding tasks. Both the literary texts and tasks were perfectly chosen and my Polish colleague and I had no objections to Liza and Oleg's chapter. In fact, Liza seemed to have been fully responsible for the co-authored chapter but she never admitted it. She was a quiet person, full of dignity and subdued self-assurance. She spoke very little and never expressed her opinions about the co-authored book and its content. It seemed as if she fully trusted Oleg or as if she had been dominated by him.

In this respect, Liza can be considered a representative of other female staff members who compiled the remaining chapters in the part of the book focused on Ukrainian culture. Some of them were more talkative than Liza but, similarly to her, none of them tried to contact me during my visits to their university or by e-mail to discuss their chapters, as if they had left the whole responsibility for the book to Oleg. Indeed, the English Department we collaborated with had a very clear hierarchical structure and resembled a high school with its patronizing head, subordinated subject teachers and well-behaved students. Although Oleg was much younger than Liza and some other female staff, he seemed to enjoy the unquestionable superiority of a male leader.

Thus, our "missionary" attempts to trigger a wider debate among particular authors on differences between Ukrainian and Polish cultures were doomed to failure. Moreover, as has been said before, Polish students who researched aspects of Polish culture did not have counterparts in Ukrainian students. In spite of it, after the publication of the book, some of our students' chapters were read and discussed in Ukrainian classes. One of the teachers who used our book in class was Liza. Not only did she use the book but also she sent us her students' insightful comments. In comparison with Sue, Geoff and Oleg, Liza does not stay in my memory due to extraordinary behavior, arrogance or frequent contacts. I remember her, first of all, because her collaboration in the project gave me a sense of its meaningfulness not only to us in Poland but also to teachers and students of English in Ukraine. Having described our involvement in the project as "semi-missionary", I believe that Liza's collaboration enabled us to preserve a sense of partnership and created a space for our common "community of practice".

5 Liberating Ourselves from the "Missionary" Approach in ELT

I would like to juxtapose the described cases of "missionary" and patronizing approaches, in which EFL teachers and teacher trainers from one country tried to impose their ways of teaching and teacher training on teachers and teacher trainers from another country, to my colleague's and my own approach in teaching together EFL to senior students, in which we did not impose anything on each other.

Dorota and I conducted together an intensive one-week EFL course for two groups of senior students at the A2/B1 and B2 level. Each of us taught 180 min per day and we both organized evening activities in English. Additionally, we were both responsible for using English and making students use English throughout the course. Some of the students had been attending my courses at a Third Age University before (75 min-classes once a week). Our cooperation started when I asked Dorota to join me in conducting the course and she readily agreed. Both of us had had a long professional history of EFL teaching and teacher training in Poland, although I have been rather an academic and Dorota—a practitioner. I had known her for a long time and we liked each other.

We did not try to create a common syllabus or to introduce similar teaching techniques. We knew each other well enough to realize that we were both convinced of our professionalism and mutual trust. Before the course we only informed each other of some of the proposed activities and of the teaching materials we were to use. Final performances staged by our students were directed separately by Dorota and myself. In other words, our roles in the course were independent and we were fully autonomous. The assessment of the course by our students was very positive. The students I had taught before congratulated me on finding Dorota as the other course teacher. After we had finished teaching, we shared our feelings of satisfaction and made plans for the next similar course. The question arises what contributed to our and our students' satisfaction. I believe it was, first of all, our professionalism. Additionally, it could have been our mutual trust and respect, which did not leave space for a "missionary" and patronizing approach in our contacts. Neither of us, consciously or subconsciously, felt superior to the other. My academic expertise was definitely counterbalanced by Dorota's practical experience. As far as I can judge, we were real partners.

6 Conclusion

The "missionary" approach described in this chapter on the part of the British native teacher trainers and on the Polish side in relation to the Ukrainians may be frequent in intercultural contacts due to unequal distribution of "power", both in the economic and linguistic sense, as well as due to unrealistic expectations of the more "powerful" party concerning the other party's knowledge and competence. However, as the described cases indicate, each person in the role of a "missionary" or that coping with a "missionary" attitude may act differently. People have different levels of emotional intelligence, empathy and ability to learn from experience. The actual Evangelical missionaries described by Johnston (2017) also acted differently, being more or less empathetic towards Polish Catholic students in their classes.

The two described cases of British teacher trainers, Sue and Geoff, who definitely imposed their ideas on Polish teacher trainers, were not representative of all British trainers who I met and who collaborated with us at the time when the BC actively supported EFL teacher training in Poland. I have decided to describe them because they stayed so vividly in my memory as extreme rather than as average cases. As has been said before, I observed a positive modification of the approaches of British native teacher trainers towards Polish trainers as the mutual contacts became more frequent. I even heard a British teacher trainer addressing his Polish counterpart, saying that there was nothing more he could possibly teach her in the future. It might have been a compliment but it also showed a certain development from the "missionary" to the partner approach.

In the case of Liza, a Ukrainian teacher and teacher trainer, our "missionary" approach was not necessary; indeed, her ideas and her behavior identified her clearly as a partner co-author. Other Ukrainian colleagues may have provoked our patronizing attitudes when they avoided direct contacts and discussion on their proposed chapters, in view of our determination to have the co-authored book published. Oleg played two roles, one of the head and representative of the remaining staff and the other of an author himself. His blunt resistance to our version of the introduction indicated that he may have treated it as an imposition of the Polish cultural standards upon the Ukrainian ones and disregarding the Ukrainian point of view concerning their public image.

Finally, I would like to try to answer the question that I posed in the title of this chapter: Why (and when) is the "missionary" approach frequently combined with ELT and why (and when) is it unacceptable? First of all, EFL teaching and teacher training empowers teachers and trainers even more than subject teaching and teacher training. They are more knowledgeable not only as far as the subject matter is concerned but also in terms of the language of communication. If they are native or near-native speakers, they are treated and they treat themselves as natural representatives of the target language and its culture and their roles usually become more prestigious than those of non-native target language teachers. There is usually only one step from such a privileged position to being convinced that it is their "mission" to tell others how they should teach, learn and use EFL. Sometimes teachers and teacher trainers have to impose their ideas on other teachers and trainers, particularly in the case of joint intercultural projects, where international standards and procedures have to be followed. However, imposition should be the last resort after discussion and persuasion have failed. In conflict situations, the "missionary" approach should give way to compromise. There is probably nothing equally counterproductive in EFL teaching and teacher training as enforcing one's ideas upon other teachers and trainers who do not accept them. Thus, the tentative answer to the above question about the "missionary" approach in ELT could be: While such an approach is frequently the case, particularly in intercultural projects, EFL teachers and teacher trainers should attempt to refrain from imposing their ideas on others since the best results are achieved when co-workers are autonomous and respect one another. Admittedly, such ideal conditions of partnership may not be attainable for a number of reasons. If, however, a teacher or a teacher trainer has to impose his or her ideas on others, he or she should at least do it in a civilized way.

The two theoretical models I mentioned before which could refer to the "missionary" aspect of ELT, the linguistic imperialism model and the community of practice model, may both partly account for the observed phenomena. The linguistic imperialism model may explain teachers' and teacher trainers' impositions of their own ideas and their patronizing and arrogant behavior in contact situations, in particular in intercultural contexts. On the other hand, the community of practice model may account for partnership and mitigating behavior in view of achieving a common goal by a group of collaborating people. Both models may be valid, probably depending on external and internal factors, such as cultural distance, available time, frequency of contacts, significance for the participants, empathy and emotional intelligence. My account has been based only on my memories referring to particular cases of more or less "missionary" approaches in ELT. It is not a study in the strict sense of the word. That is why the above conclusion could be only speculative. My hope is that in spite of it, it might be interesting for those involved in the past or at present in ELT, but most of all, it is for my colleague Krystyna.

References

Canagarajah, S. (1999). *Resisting linguistic imperialism in English teaching.* Oxford: Oxford University Press.

Johnston, B. (2017). *English teaching and evangelical mission: The case of Lighthouse School.* Bristol: Multilingual Matters.

Lave, J., & Wenger, F. (1991). *Situated learning: Legitimate peripheral participation.* Cambridge: Cambridge University Press.

Niżegorodcew, A. (1995). The communicative approach in the polish context: Strengths and weaknesses. In I. Przemecka & Z. Mazur (Eds.), *Studies in English and American literature and language* (pp. 271–278). Kraków: Universitas.

Phillipson, R. (1992). *Linguistic imperialism.* Oxford: Oxford University Press.

Wenger, F. (1998). *Communities of practice: Learning, meaning and identity.* Cambridge: Cambridge University Press.

Author Biography

Anna Niżegorodcew graduated from the English and the Psychology Departments of Jagiellonian University of Kraków, Poland. She took her Ph.D. at the Philosophical Faculty of the same university. She is Professor Emerita in Applied Linguistics. She taught for 40 years at the English Department of Jagiellonian University. She was Head of the Applied Linguistics Section of the English Department and Head of Jagiellonian University Teacher Training College. She has published a number of books and articles in the areas of teaching English, second language acquisition and second and foreign language teacher education. Her present interests cover teaching English to third-age students, and teaching English for intercultural communication and international understanding.

How to Deal with Applications in Foreign Language Learning and Teaching (FLLT)

Maria Dakowska

Abstract As a technical term, applications are understood as results of pure research useful in optimizing the phenomenon under investigation. The sources and strategies of deriving useful, that is, applicable, knowledge in the field of FLLT are a serious challenge at present in view of the fact that English is a global language taught professionally in our educational system on a mass scale. Professional activity on a mass scale must have solid, that is, scientific bases. So far, although the problem of applications in the field of FLLT has a fairly long history, satisfactory solutions have yet to be developed. The manner in which the problem has been posed or contextualized, conceptualized and addressed, has evolved in the past decades. Characteristically, both the nature of the relationship between the providers and the recipients of applications as well as their status have changed. In the chapter, I highlight the main stages in this development and argue that at present a qualitatively different approach to applications in FLLT is needed.

Keywords Applied linguistics · Applications in foreign language learning and teaching · Empirical discipline

1 Introduction

First, I briefly outline how views on the nature of applications in the field of FLLT have evolved. They were initially conceptualized in the context of strong ties between practical language teaching and descriptive linguistics, treated as its source discipline. Next, these bonds were redefined as a less direct relationship, mediated by an interface called *applied linguistics* where linguistic ideas were modified "somehow" to inform practical language teaching. This mediating level was introduced not only for the sake of foreign language teaching, but also for other language-related fields. More recently, as a result of their dynamic growth and

M. Dakowska (✉)
University of Warsaw, Warsaw, Poland
e-mail: m.b.dakowska@uw.edu.pl

© Springer International Publishing AG 2018
M. Pawlak and A. Mystkowska-Wiertelak (eds.), *Challenges of Second and Foreign Language Education in a Globalized World*, Second Language Learning and Teaching, DOI 10.1007/978-3-319-66975-5_2

specialization, these fields, including FLLT and second language acquisition research (SLAR) have become disciplines in their own right. As a result, applied linguistics is regarded as an alliance of various language sciences rather than an interface between linguistic theory and practical activities. Second language acquisition research, for example, without breaking its ties with applied linguistics, follows its own research agenda and, rather than seek applications for second language teaching in linguistics, it develops its own contributions to language teaching, called *language pedagogy*.

Applications as a technical term can be understood as the discipline's ability to generate, rather than derive, knowledge which is useful in influencing, controlling, regulating, reinstating, cultivating, meliorating or otherwise rationalizing the phenomenon it investigates. Therefore, the question arises: Can the problem of applications in the field of FLLT be moved to a more systematic level? It is argued in this chapter that applications may be elaborated as a result of this discipline's incorporation of a number of constraints in its own science format. These constraints bring to bear on representing "language" as the discipline's subject matter, defining the goals of scientific research which distinguish between basic and applied research. This discipline's feasibility of generating its own applications (being applicable) is inseparable from constituting itself as an empirical discipline, that is, a discipline which has material basis to communicate with the real world rather than a discipline which investigates the abstract construct of language as a self-contained system. An empirical discipline targets language use by human beings. As a result, to have systematic applications, the field of FLLT must elaborate them within its own confines, with reference to its own empirical phenomenon under investigation in the real world rather than import them from an even closely related field of investigation.

2   The Nature of the Problem

In any discipline, producing applicable information is a noble goal: Nobody takes pride in generating useless knowledge. The trademark of real knowledge is the ability to do something with it. In the field of FLLT, however, this issue still remains a complex, ill-defined problem with various, sometimes conflicting ideas dominating literature on the subject. Following Hayes (1978), a complex problem is characterized by such a vast problem space that neither a systematic nor an unsystematic method for solution search is useful. While well-defined problems offer solutions which are the same for all problem-solvers, ill-defined problems involve specifying the problem itself. The solver is actively involved in defining its nature and structure or filling the missing elements in his or her categorization of the problem space. Since people make selective use of various sources and types of knowledge which they see relevant, there is a clear possibility of reaching different solutions to the same question, depending on the individual contribution of problem solvers to its definition. Evolving conceptions of applications in the field of FLLT illustrate this point very well:

1. First, applications in foreign language teaching were understood as the top-down flow of information from the science of linguistics to practical language teaching, especially the use of linguistic concepts, terms, ideas and theories in order to format the uncultivated area of practice with linguistic infrastructure.
2. Next, following some negative feedback from the practical activity of foreign language teaching, the top-down flow of information had to give way to a more cautious attitude to the influences from linguistics. As a result, there was a growing awareness of the qualitative difference between the linguist's angle on language and the learner's one, which spurred a growing recognition of its own identity on the part of the representatives of foreign language teaching.
3. The need was also voiced for a less direct relationship between linguistics and foreign language teaching so that applications could be elaborated at a level between linguistics and other more practically, or should we say, empirically, oriented language fields, including foreign language teaching; this mediating level was called applied linguistics.
4. More recently, as a result of strong demands for research on language in the real world, applied linguistics has gradually become an alliance of language-related fields rather than a mediating platform for developing linguistic applications; members of the alliance continually grow as academic disciplines in their own right.

Yet the problem of applications in FLLT persists as a major challenge at present in view of the fact that English is a global language, professionally taught in our educational system on a mass scale. Professional knowledge for language teaching on a mass scale must have solid bases in scientific understanding of the phenomenon in question.

3 Linguistics as an Authority in Language Teaching

It is generally recognized that the field of foreign language learning and teaching in the middle of the 20th century was revolutionized by the influence of more mature disciplines such as linguistics (and psychology). At the time, the idea of modernizing foreign language teaching was understood as the import of scientific foundations from linguistics (and psychology) in order to construct effective methods of language teaching some of which became the success of the Army Specialized Training Program developed in the United States (Moulton, 1962).

A significant aspect of this impact is the participation of linguists, for example Fries (1945) and Lado (1957, 1964), in designing materials and formulating teaching principles for foreign languages in the United States. Their active role had a lasting effect on the relationship of foreign language teaching and linguistics for years to come. In contrast to the earlier period, influenced by traditional grammar, there was a growing awareness of the complexity of language teaching and of the need to support it with more solid bases. Therefore, it was assumed for quite some time that linguistic and psychological theories had the power to optimize foreign language teaching by virtue of being scientific (Rivers, 1964, 1982); they were automatically treated as the theories of foreign language teaching. It seemed so natural and obvious that specialists did not even attempt to justify this idea, so that this attitude to linguistics was called a "complete dependence position" by Krohn (1970).

The influences of linguistics (and psychology) in this "early colonization" stage run fairly deep, stimulating the field's internal specialization; linguistics as a source of applications impacts not only global but also specific issues in the field of foreign language teaching, such as methods of teaching, teacher training and testing, criteria of difficulty and syllabus design, the role of the native language, the priorities in the development of the four language skills, the nature of the teaching materials and classroom techniques, the form and role of grammar, the function of language rules, error correction policy and lesson planning (Dakowska, 1987). These influences are more profound than just applications: They format, that is, give structure and content to the whole area of foreign language teaching. However, as some of us recall, Newmark and Reibel (1968, p. 149) questioned this logic, pointing to the main problem in this bond between linguistics and language teaching:

> The logical flaw arises when the linguist attempts to draw simple and direct conclusions about the manner of acquisition of language from his knowledge of the abstract structure of language and claims that the success or failure of language teaching programs depends to a large extent on the degree to which the language course writer or language teacher orders his pedagogical material to reflect a theoretically sound description of the native and target languages.

3.1 Cracks in the Relationship

The predominantly uncritical attitude of the field of foreign language teaching to linguistics was put to the test when Transformational Generative Grammar (TGG) and cognitive psychology emerged as new schools of thought in the source disciplines and started their career by criticizing their predecessors. In this context, language teaching specialists felt that their theoretical carpet had been pulled out from under their feet, and, willy-nilly, they had to choose between the older schools and the more recent, equally, or even more "scientific" ones. The fact that there were options in the linguistic offer meant that they had to formulate some criteria for choosing one school of thought over the other. Moreover, the whole situation evoked a wave of disappointment with, and skepticism towards, the source disciplines, first and foremost linguistics.

Many articles appeared at that time questioning linguistic influences in language teaching (e.g., Bolinger, 1972; Brown, 1970; Carroll, 1971; Cooper, 1970; Gefen, 1966; Hill, 1967; Johnson, 1969; Kandiah, 1970). In this regard, Lamendella (1969) and Oller (1973) argued that, undoubtedly, what TGG offers was scientific and probably linguistically more adequate than the structural linguistic description, but it referred to language as a self-contained system depicting relationships between forms. In the structural descriptive view, language is disconnected from the human being it is living in (see Engels, 1973), that is, the psychological processes which make it possible for us to acquire, store and use language knowledge. Therefore, it is irrelevant to the field of foreign language learning and teaching, in which a psycholinguistic description is needed. A cognitive theory describes people, not languages in the sense of abstract representations of an autonomous system of forms with the human subject factored out. As Mackey (1973, p. 6) puts it: "Linguistics is not language learning". Oller (1973) emphasized that a theory which aspires to adequacy must take the communicative function of language into account.

However, this critical, criteria-oriented attitude toward linguistic and psychological transfer of conceptions into the field of language teaching, and fine discriminations between various perspectives of language should not overshadow the fact that the impact of linguistics as a source of applications remained very strong: Its influence went right into the core of the field, into the definition of its subject matter, which represented three entities each individually illuminated by the respective source discipline. Linguistics provided conceptions of language, psychology defined learning, and pedagogy defined teaching. Although the view of language was different from the early audiolingual one, the subject matter was still envisaged as a sum of three parts rather than a coherent whole, a system of factors. Language learning and teaching was treated as an art or a practical activity informed by linguistics as a source of applications.

3.2 Signs of Change

Difficulties in the relationship between linguistics and the field of teaching had positive consequences for our understanding of the nature and status of linguistic descriptions of language in the field of foreign language learning and teaching. The growing number of linguistic schools which emerged and seemed relevant necessitated a qualitative change in the manner in which the potential and real linguistic influences were viewed. They were no longer perceived as adequate or inadequate, scientific or not, but as different models, that is, representations of language, reflecting a specific perspective of its functioning and specific goals of linguistic research. This was a fundamental leap in the direction of distinguishing language "as such" from its approximate, scientific representations.

Leontiev (1963) explained the nature of modeling a language as constructing an object, real or imaginary, that is isomorphic with the object it represents in certain essential features, for example, in that it captures its governing principles.

Subsequent empirical research demonstrates to what extent the model reflects the real patterning or structure of the phenomenon in question. An absolute model of linguistic description is neither feasible nor necessary because each model is determined by the purpose for which it is constructed. Widdowson (1979) stressed that a model which aspires to being useful must focus on the language user. The following quote comes from his article "The partiality and relevance of linguistic descriptions" (1979, p. 232):

> It is a common assumption among language teachers that their subject should somehow be defined by reference to models of linguistic description devised by linguistics. This does not mean that they try to transfer such models directly into the pedagogic domain (although such attempts are not unknown): there is usually a recognition that they have to be modified in one way or another to suit a teaching purpose. But the basic theoretical orientation is retained. The same assumption dominates applied linguistics. The very name is a procla-mation of dependence (...). In this paper I want to question this common assumption, axiomatic in its force, that a linguistic model of language must of necessity serve as the underlying frame of reference for language teaching.

Widdowson objects to the notion expressed by Halliday, McIntosh, and Strevens (1964) that the contribution of linguistics to language teaching is to provide good descriptions of the language being taught. He sees no evidence for the assertion that the best description of language is derived from linguistics. It is a kind of propa-ganda, a declaration of faith. Widdowson (1979, p. 244) concludes:

> It is this kind of description, participant rather than observer oriented, deriving from the beliefs and behavior of learners as users and not as analysts of language, that I believe applied linguistics needs to develop as relevant to its concerns (...). Such a description will be necessarily partial, and it will probably not meet the approval of others with different axes to grind. This should not trouble us. We have our own conditions of relevance to meet and our own independent way to make in the world.

Widdowson's point of view is interesting, but it is progressive and misleading at the same time. It is progressive in stressing that the status of description provided by applied linguistics, which is the theoretical level of language teaching, is one of many possible descriptions so, to be accepted, it must be relevant to our concerns. It must focus on the language user, the participant, and his or her perspective on language. However, Widdowson's position is misleading in that it supports the *status quo* whereby the field of language teaching is merely practical (e.g., Widdowson, 1979, 1990, 2003). While foreign language teaching as a practical activity is very strongly anchored in the empirical reality, what is misleading in his idea is that without the benefit of a coordinating view of language learning as an empirical phenomenon required by scientific research agenda there is no chance of formulating these criteria of relevance. In his conception, there is certainly no place for constructing a coherent model of the domain in which practitioners operate, or seek explanations of this phenomenon at some level of generality. The real catch in this program, deceptive in its simplicity, is that if we make a point of saying nothing systematic about something, nothing systematic will be said, with all the ensuing consequences.

To sum up the ideas on the role of linguistics as a source of applications, it must be reiterated that this field serves as authority for language teaching, either with or without the mediation of applied linguistics. Linguistics provides a description of language, which must "somehow" be incorporated into teaching. The recognition of the plurality of language models calls for the criteria of their relevance for the purposes of teaching, especially their focus on language users as opposed to formal descriptions produced for the sake of linguistic analysis. All told, however, the field of foreign language teaching is still perceived as a practical matter or art illuminated by linguistics.

As has been pointed out, the initially submissive attitude of language teaching toward the related fields resulted from the scarcity of relevant knowledge about language learning and teaching available to specialists. This information shortage attracted various tenets from the academically more advanced neighbors. However, the whole relationship was challenged when the sophistication of these theories grew beyond the point of supposedly easy, one-way flow of the source findings to the field of foreign language learning and teaching.

4 Applied Linguistics as a Mediator

Interesting ideas were elaborated to convert the direct impact of linguistics into an indirect one. Of our interest here is the notion of applied linguistics mediating between theoretical linguistics and the practical activity of language teaching, responsible for converting linguistic ideas into more specific recommendations for the classroom. It had many followers, but while inserting a connecting level between the two fields, it sanctioned the *status quo* in the area of language teaching (Brown, 1970; Corder, 1971, 1973a, b; Roulet, 1975; Wardhaugh, 1974; Wardhaugh & Brown, 1976; Widdowson, 1979). At that time, foreign language teaching was not regarded as a discipline in its own right, but as a "special" field, partly practical, partly an art, subordinated to applied linguistics. The view of linguistics, or even macro-linguistics, as the provider of theories for foreign language teaching puts the latter into the position of a consumer of these theories, precluding systematic focus on its own concerns (e.g., Cook & Seidlhofer, 1995; Davies & Elder, 2004; Ewert, 2013, Grabe, 2002; McCarthy, 2001; Schmitt, 2002; Widdowson, 1990). This conception is clearly conducive to developing a variety of connecting paths between the two areas, mostly leading from linguistics to the field of teaching rather than a representation of the phenomenon of non-primary language learning and teaching as the field's subject matter, a unique research territory of an autonomous discipline within language sciences. Grabe (2002) admits that applied linguistics has emerged as a genuine problem-solving enterprise, a discipline that addresses real-world language-based problems rather than theoretical explorations based on the recognition that no one discipline can provide all the tools and resources needed to deal with these real-world problems. He goes on to say (2002, pp. 4–5):

By the close of the 1980s, a common trend was to view applied linguistics as incorporating many subfields (as indicated earlier) and as drawing on many supporting disciplines in addition to linguistics (e.g., psychology, education, anthropology, sociology, political science, policy studies, and public administration, and English studies, including composition, rhetoric, and literary studies). Combined with these two foundations (subfields and supporting disciplines) was the view of applied linguistics as problem-driven and real-world based rather than theory driven and disconnected from the real language use.

Nowadays applied linguistics incorporates such fields as first language literacy research, language processing, neurolinguistics of verbal communication, second language acquisition, second language reading and writing research, forensic linguistics, language testing, corpus linguistics, lexicography and lexicology, translation theory and translation studies, speech pathology, bilingualism, language policy, and so on. These research areas grow, mature and become increasingly specialized and sophisticated. Among them foreign language teaching is no longer seen as an art or a practical endeavor but a fully-fledged academic discipline in its own right.

5   SLA and Language Pedagogy

It may be tempting for the foreign language teaching specialists to replace the former linguistic authority and a source of applications with a new one, the vibrant and dynamically developing field of study called *second language acquisition research*, which separated itself from the concerns of foreign language teaching in the 1980s. Central to this split was a shift of interest from language teaching to language learning, or acquisition, linked with the idea that learner language should be investigated as a linguistic system in its own right, and it should first and foremost be described and explained; this idea initiated the field of SLAR (e.g., Corder, 1981; Davies & Elder, 2004; Gass & Madden, 1985; Ritchie, 1978; Richie & Bhatia, 1996; Seliger & Long, 1983; Selinker, 1972, 1992).

Corder (1981) and Selinker (1972) were instrumental in forging the view of learner language as a system which develops according to its built-in syllabus. Within the past decades, SLAR has developed dynamically both in terms of empirical and theoretical research increasing our understanding of non-primary language learning and providing vast evidence for countless research questions (e.g., DeKeyser, 2007; Dörnyei, 2005, 2009; Doughty & Williams, 1998; Doughty & Long, 2003; Ellis, 1985, 1994; Larsen-Freeman & Long, 1991; Long, 2007, 2012; Long & Doughty, 2009). It seems clear that the main point of interest of SLA researchers is to describe invariant developmental processes of second language acquisition in order to develop explanatory theories (Crookes, 1992; Gregg, 1993; Gregg, Long, Jordan, & Beretta, 1997; Jordan, 2004; Long, 1990, 2004, 2007). It would be a mistake, therefore, to expect that all the solutions for foreign language teaching would come from SLAR because, despite a considerable overlap, there is an important difference between the two fields. SLAR investigates classroom processes in addition to language learning in the field. From the point of view of SLA researchers, teaching is a form of intervention into what is called "naturalistic" acquisition; classroom teaching provides only some of the language learning opportunities, but not all of them. In the case of foreign language teaching, the classroom is the only language learning environment and this environment, to echo Newmark and Reibel (1968), must provide all the necessary and sufficient conditions for successful foreign language learning. Therefore, the perspective and understanding of language learning for the purposes of foreign language teaching must be convertible into teaching guidelines as opposed to being an intervention into an ongoing process; that is, it must be sufficiently specific as to enable us to make foreign language learning happen solely in the educational environment. The process has nowhere else to develop.

Moreover, SLAR's clearly expressed goals, namely, to develop explanatory theories of non-primary language acquisition, do not necessarily include obligations to deliver applications, that is, knowledge useful to the language teacher. As Long (2004, p. 4) comments:

> Most SLA theories, and most SLA theorists, are not primarily interested in language teaching, and in some cases not at all interested. So, while SLA theories may be evaluated in absolute terms and comparatively in a variety of ways – parsimony, empirical adequacy, problem-solving ability and so on – it makes no sense to judge them solely, as some have suggested, or in some cases at all, on the basis of how useful they are for the classroom or how meaningful they are for the classroom teachers.

Although Long himself makes claims to contribute not only to second but also to foreign language teaching with his task-based language teaching (Long, 2016), this statement is a fairly accurate portrayal of the situation in SLAR.

6 Emancipation of Foreign Language Teaching

As each of the disciplines produced increasingly advanced ideas and theories, the field of foreign language teaching also grew and matured to judge these source findings more rationally, that is, from the point of view of its own aims and priorities. By way of analogy with human development, the first stage of this stormy relationship can be regarded as the time of compliance on the part of language teaching, marked by identifying itself with the source disciplines. The second, much more demanding stage of defiance, was characterized by the strong rejection of their influence. Finally, the natural third stage of the field's maturation is its movement away from subordination toward academic autonomy.

An autonomous field defines its subject matter as an empirical phenomenon of foreign language learning, namely, a spatiotemporal system (Wójcicki, 1977). This system is derived from its elementary event or episode (Kotarbińska, 1977), that is, language use, which is central to my present investigation. Such a representation is not a sum of conceptions accepted from other authoritative fields, no matter how carefully or skillfully integrated. Instead, it is constructed "from scratch", as a representation of the empirical phenomenon of interest, an occurrence in space and time, in line with the constraints relevant to foreign language didactics. Cognitive subordination, on the other hand, admits conceptions and perspectives of the source disciplines as components, which, even when integrated, cannot provide a uniform representation of an empirical (human social) phenomenon with its vital energy flows, that is, communicative interactions among people, but clusters of factors chosen as relevant by the source disciplines and stitched together.

6.1   Focus on the Specific Phenomenon in Question

In contrast to its natural counterpart, namely, second language acquisition, foreign language learning takes place when we recreate the relevant conditions in the educational system and try to make it happen by teaching. In most neutral terms, foreign language teaching can be understood as the construction of the learner's educational environment and experience, that is, input, interaction and feedback, conducive to language learning. In this broad sense, although the process taps our natural human propensities to some extent, it is always sensitive to various socio-cultural and political factors, not to mention material and intellectual resources, as well as social values and expectations regarding foreign language proficiency (for a recent account, see Phillipson & Skutnabb-Kangas, 2009). In other words, it is a cultivated phenomenon *par excellence*. As in the case of any other cultivated phenomenon, people in charge of foreign language education are designers who make choices, that is, follow strategies based on their understanding and resources. Second languages are usually acquired both naturally, via social interaction in the field, and in the classroom environment, while being taught.

Both language acquisition and foreign language learning are treated as equally real and available for investigation in the empirical reality, that is, as empirical phenomena. For analytical purposes, however, we should keep in mind that foreign language learning and teaching are shaped by someone's implicit or explicit understanding of the whole process, reflected in the construction of learning environment and resources, as well as in teaching behaviors. The extent to which these ideas result from, are congruent with, or interfere with the mechanism and processes of language learning is open to investigation. In an attempt to understand the mechanism and the processes of language learning, its natural instances certainly provide a more solid point of reference and evidence than the cultivated ones because the latter are, of necessity, stained by our partial or approximate understanding.

However, the difference between second and foreign languages is considerable: second language learning takes place in the educational setting where the language is taught, as well as outside, in the broader social environment where it is used for communication; the learner has extensive input and interaction opportunities outside the classroom. The ultimate attainment is attributed to both sources, that is, language use "in the field" and in the educational setting. A foreign language, on the other hand, is not used for communication by the speech community at large; it is learned principally while being taught, within the confines of the educational system (on the distinction between naturalistic and instructed learners, see Ortega, 2009). This has important consequences for constructing the process: the classroom must provide sufficient conditions in the form of input, interaction and feedback opportunities to evoke foreign language learning. Mitchell and Myles (1998, p. 1) use the collective term "non-primary languages", within which they distinguish second from foreign languages. I use my terms in the same way:

> (...) 'second languages' are any languages other than the learner's 'native language' or 'mother tongue'. They encompass both languages of wider communication encountered within the local region or community (e.g., at the workplace, or in the media), and truly foreign languages, which have no immediate local uses or speakers.

Cook (2010) rightly points out that the notions of "native language", "second language" and "foreign language" refer to dynamic phenomena and require much finer distinctions than has been the case so far. Nevertheless, the level of specificity he suggests is not absolutely necessary for our purposes at this point. Foreign language teaching is the domain of deliberate human activities aimed at reconstructing the phenomenon of language learning in the educational environment, in other words, instituting it from scratch, in the absence of this language being used by the community at large. This reconstruction takes the form of language experience, materials and resources, based on our conception of the respective phenomenon. Its reconstruction, cultivation and melioration in the educational context, however, can be effective only to the extent to which it is understood as a real occurrence, a phenomenon in time and space.

FLLT, therefore, has quite a different focus of investigation from language pedagogy. "Pedagogy" is used in various accounts of the relationship between SLAR and the practice of second language teaching (Crookes, 1997; Eckman, Highland, Lee, Mileham, & Weber, 1995; Ellis, 1991, 1994, 1997, 2010; Ellis & Shintani, 2014; Gass, 1993; Gass & Mackey, 2012; Nassaji, 2012; van Compernolle & Williams, 2013), but from the point of view of FLLT, this label is not precise in that it deemphasizes the unique specificity of language. Technically, the term "pedagogy" classifies the field as a study of upbringing, whereas the primary concern in FLLT is not upbringing in general, but the unique dispersal of language data in language use and learning along the life-span. FLLT stands out among other disciplines, such as pedagogy or didactics of various content subjects as well as other language sciences, because its focus on (non-primary) language learning as a human phenomenon is specific enough to provide guidelines on foreign language teaching. The study of upbringing in general does not and cannot provide such guidelines. For the purpose of converting insights on language learning into expertise of foreign language teaching in the educational system, the most fundamental and elementary concept of language learning is language use. I strongly endorse the view that language learning is language use (Wolff, 2002), most importantly, language use as verbal communication in speech and writing anchored in our cognitive system along the life-span. This perspective provides a unique dispersal of language data reflecting the incremental time-and-space, attentional and procedural nature of non-primary language learning.

The term "pedagogy" does not even begin to do justice to this unique specificity emphasizing the general area of upbringing instead. It is significant that leading SLA researchers do not target language use as their focus of investigations, but deliberately choose acquisition (for a collection of reprinted articles on the lively acquisition/use controversy in SLA, see Seidlehofer, 2003; Sect. 4). Gass (2003, p. 221) is explicit about this issue: "the emphasis in input and interaction studies is on *language* used and not on the act of communication".

7   Applications in Their Technical Meaning

The ultimate justification for any discipline is its ability to provide explanations whereas feasibility to generate applications is the ultimate testing ground of an empirical as opposed to formal scientific discipline. As Pitt (1988, p. 7) points out, explanations:

> are supposed to tell us how things work, and knowing how things work gives us the power to manipulate our environment to achieve our own ends, (…) science is supposed to be our best means of generating explanations which satisfy the criterion of providing the means to accomplish our goals. All the research in the world counts as nothing if it fails to generate explanations of the domain under investigation (…). Whatever knowledge may be, its hallmark is the ability to do something with it. In the case of scientific knowledge this means offering an explanation for some phenomenon or other. If it can't successfully be used in some such fashion then it doesn't qualify as knowledge.

This conviction is significant for one important reason: the program of a "normal" academic discipline is called upon here (for the sake of posing and solving the problems of foreign language teaching) because it offers the most promising route to understanding non-primary language learning as an empirical phenomenon, that is, as episodes or events involving human operations and interactions in space and time. An understanding of non-primary language learning as an empirical phenomenon can be the source of inferences about the conditions and events promoting non-primary, namely, foreign language learning in the educational (cultured) setting. Essentially, such inferred conditions and interactions are foreign language teaching behaviors. This point of view is completely neutral with regard to knowledge for its own sake in other language disciplines, which may see themselves as formal and/or purely explanatory. What follows from the above is that in contrast to borrowings, transplantations or inspirations, applications are not developed in a top-down manner as by-products in another field. In their technical sense, applications result from the incorporation of a network of relevant constraints on the subject matter within the format of an empirical discipline. These internal, discipline-specific constraints enable researchers to communicate with the empirical phenomenon, identify significant relationships among the factors and derive applicative inferences, or conclusions, from them. Under no circumstances can applications in "normal" science be regarded as just surplus ideas discharged by related fields, floating around and waiting to be utilized.

Typically, language sciences are divided into *theoretical* and *applied* (Kaplan, 2002). However, I prefer the distinction between *basic* and *applied research* levels within one discipline, keeping in mind that a rigid division cannot be made. "Pure" research provides evidence for a question with a view to theory construction, while "applied" research does all of the above as well as offers findings which can influence, control, regulate, reinstate, cultivate, meliorate or otherwise rationalize the phenomenon in the real world. Applications are legitimately elaborated within the scope of the field's subject matter (McLaughlin, 1987) and their successful export to another field is an extra benefit. Descriptive linguistics investigating phonology and syntax in the past decades did not provide the field of foreign language learning and teaching with applications, but ideas, conceptions, terms, definitions and taxonomies referring to the linguistic nature of language as a synchronic formal system. Benefits of this relationship should not be underestimated: Linguistics provided external descriptions of the language subsystems which, from the learner's point of view, must become internalized, that is, acquired functionally. This relationship spurred the field of foreign language learning and teaching toward emancipation, that is, toward identifying its own perspective of language: the phenomenon of language learning in time and space inextricable from the human learner. At the same time, there is no denying that language teachers must be thoroughly educated in linguistics in the broadest and deepest sense of the word (Kaplan, 2002).

All told, the goal of scientific disciplines is to enable us to understand. Therefore, each discipline investigating a given phenomenon must sooner or later provide this understanding in the form of an explanatory theory. Theoretical knowledge is abstract and abstract knowledge is characterized by being relatively independent of concrete situations from which it is derived. Therefore, it can be transferred, that is, applied, to new ones provided they belong to the same category of phenomena. Applications are derived from our understanding of the phenomena under investigation, especially the relationships and interactions among the factors singled out in the subject matter of enquiry. To reiterate, applications are primarily derived from various relationships among the factors of the empirical system rather than developed in a top-down manner across two different disciplines. Understanding a given phenomenon in the empirical reality inevitably produces potentially useful knowledge, that is, knowledge which can be applied in reconstructing and cultivating the phenomenon which has been the source of understanding in the same discipline to begin with.

8   Conclusions

In light of the above, how can applications become feasible? In foreign language learning and teaching, applications in their technical sense are not to be seen as directives based on the abstract notion of language as a formal system, or language learning as the acquisition of grammar, transformed into teaching guidelines by way of adjustments or concretizations, but as logical inferences drawn from our understanding of the functioning of language use, learning and teaching as a phenomenon. It would be realistic to see applications as guidelines for constructing relevant conditions for language learning and removing any hurdles therein. The top-down flow of reasoning by way of concretization is a dubious path for developing applications because: (a) it is, of necessity, limited by the source ideas which are too abstract as representations of the empirical phenomenon at hand (this is why they have to be concretized to begin with), and (b) such "applications" are elaborated unsystematically, by intuitively restoring some, but not all of the relevant elements to reconstruct the empirical phenomenon. However, representing an empirical phenomenon by way of idealization, a bottom-up process, gives us a chance of capturing the relevant factors in a coherent system, factors which are at play in reconstructing and stimulating the phenomenon under investigation.

References

Bolinger, D. (1972). The influences of linguistics: Plus and minus. *TESOL Quarterly, 6*(2), 107–120.

Brown, D. (1970). The psychological reality of "grammar" in the ESL classroom. *TESOL Quarterly, 6*(3), 263–269.

Carroll, J. B. (1971). Current issues in psycholinguistics and second language teaching. *TESOL Quarterly, 5*(2), 101–114.

Cook, G., & Seidlhofer, B. (1995). An applied linguist in principle and practice. In G. Cook & B. Seidlhofer (Eds.), *Principle and practice in applied linguistics. Studies in honor of H. G. Widdowson* (pp. 1-26). Oxford: Oxford University Press.

Cook, V. (2010). Prolegomena to second language learning. In P. Seedhouse, S. Walsh, & Ch. Jenks (Eds.), *Conceptualizing 'learning' in applied linguistics* (pp. 6–22). Basingstoke: Palgrave Macmillan.

Cooper, R. L. (1970). What do we learn when we learn a language? *TESOL Quarterly, 4*(4), 303–314.

Corder, P. S. (1971). *Applied linguistics: Various interpretations and practices.* Strasbourg: Council of Europe.

Corder, P. S. (1973a). *Introducing applied linguistics.* Harmondworth: Penguin Books.

Corder, P. S. (1973b). Applied linguistics and language teaching. In J. P. B. Allen & P. S. Corder (Eds.), *Readings for applied linguistics. The Edinburgh course in applied linguistics* (Vol. 1, pp. 1–15). Oxford: Oxford University Press.

Corder, P. S. (1981). *Error analysis and interlanguage.* Oxford: Oxford University Press.

Crookes, G. (1992). Theory format and SLA theory. *Studies in Second Language Acquisition, 14,* 425–449.

Crookes, G. (1997). SLA and language pedagogy. A socioeducational perspective. *Studies in Second Language Acquisition, 19,* 93–116.

Davies, A., & Elder, C. (Eds.). (2004). *The handbook of applied linguistics*. Oxford: Blackwell.
Dakowska, M. (1987). *Funkcje lingwistyki w modelach i procesach glottodydaktycznych*. Warszawa: PWN.
DeKeyser, R. (Ed.). (2007). *Practice in a second language: Perspectives from applied linguistics and cognitive psychology*. Cambridge: Cambridge University Press.
Dörnyei, Z. (2005). *The psychology of the language learner: Individual differences in second language acquisition*. Mahwah, NJ: Lawrence Erlbaum.
Dörnyei, Z. (2009). *The psychology of second language acquisition*. Oxford: Oxford University Press.
Doughty, C. J., & Long, M. H. (Eds.). (2003). *The handbook of second language acquisition*. Oxford: Blackwell.
Doughty, C. J., & Williams, J. (Eds.). (1998). *Focus on form in classroom second language acquisition*. Cambridge: Cambridge University Press.
Eckman, F., Highland, D., Lee, P. W., Mileham, J., & Weber, R. R. (Eds.). (1995). *Second language acquisition theory and pedagogy*. Mahwah, New Jersey: Lawrence Erlbaum.
Ellis, R. (1985). *Understanding second language acquisition*. Oxford: Oxford University Press.
Ellis, R. (1991). *Second language acquisition and language pedagogy*. Clevedon: Multilingual Matters.
Ellis, R. (1994). *The study of second language acquisition*. Oxford: Oxford University Press.
Ellis, R. (1997). SLA and language pedagogy. *Studies in Second Language Acquisition, 19*, 69–92.
Ellis, R. (2010). Theoretical pluralism in SLA: A way forward? In P. Seedhouse, S. Walsh, & Ch. Jenks (Eds.), *Conceptualizing 'learning' in applied linguistics* (pp. 23–51). Basingstoke: Pelgrave Macmillan.
Ellis, R., & Shintani, N. (2014). *Exploring language pedagogy through second language acquisition*. London: Routledge.
Engels, L. K. (1973). Linguistic versus psycholinguistic models in teaching foreign languages to university level students. In K. R. Jankovsky (Ed.), *Georgetown University roundtable on languages and linguistics* (pp. 1–9). Georgetown: Georgetown University Press.
Ewert, A. (2013). Research traditions in Applied Linguistics. In D. Gabryś-Barker, E. Piechurska-Kuciel, & J. Zybert (Eds.), *Investigations in teaching and learning languages. Studies in honour of Hanna Komorowska* (pp. 9–18). Heidelberg: Springer.
Fries, C. C. (1945). *Teaching and learning English as a foreign language*. Ann Arbor: University of Michigan Press.
Gass, S. M. (1993). Editorial: Second language acquisition. Cross-disciplinary perspectives and second language acquisition: Past, present and future. *Second Language Research, 9*(2), 95–177.
Gass, S. M. (2003). Apples or oranges: Or, why apples are not oranges and don't need to be. A response to Firth and Wagner. In B. Seidlhofer (Ed.), *Controversies in applied linguistics* (pp. 220–231). Oxford: Oxford University Press.
Gass, S. M., & Madden, C. (Eds.). (1985). Input in second language acquisition. Rowley, MA: Newbury House.
Gass, S. M., & Mackey, A. (Eds.). (2012). *The Routledge handbook of second language acquisition*. London: Routledge.
Gefen, R. (1966). Theoretical prerequisites for second language teaching. *IRAL, IV*(4), 227–233.
Grabe, W. (2002). Applied linguistics: An emerging discipline for the twenty-first century. In R. B. Kaplan (Ed.), *The Oxford handbook of applied linguistics* (pp. 3–12). Oxford: Oxford University Press.
Gregg, K. (1993). Taking explanation seriously, or, let a couple of flowers bloom. *Applied Linguistics, 14*(3), 276–294.
Gregg, K., Long, M. H., Jordan, G., & Beretta, A. (1997). Rationality and its discontents in SLA. *Applied Linguistics, 18*(4), 538–557.
Halliday, M. A. K., McIntosh, A., & Strevens, P. (1964). *The linguistic sciences and language teaching*. London: Longman.
Hayes, J. R. (1978). *Cognitive psychology. Thinking and creating*. Homewood, IL: The Dorsey Press.

Hill, A. A. (1967). The promises and limitations of the newest type of grammatical analysis. *TESOL Quarterly, 1*(2), 19–22.

Johnson, F. (1969). The failure of the discipline of linguistics in language teaching. *Language Learning, XIX*(3&4), 235–244.

Jordan, G. (2004). *Theory construction in second language acquisition.* Amsterdam: John Benjamins Publishing Company.

Kandiah, T. (1970). The transformational challenge and the teacher of English. *Language Learning, XX*(2), 151–182.

Kaplan, R. B. (Ed.). (2002). *The Oxford handbook of applied linguistics.* Oxford: Oxford University Press.

Kotarbińska, J. (1977). On ostensive definitions. In M. Przełęcki & R. Wójcicki (Eds.), *Twenty years of logical methodology in Poland* (pp. 233–260). Warszawa: PWN and Dordreht: Reidel.

Krohn, R. (1970). The role of linguistics in TEFL methodology. *Language Learning, XX*(1), 103–108.

Lado, R. (1957). *Linguistics across cultures.* Ann Arbor: University of Michigan Press.

Lado, R. (1964). *Language teaching. A scientific approach.* New York: McGraw-Hill Inc.

Lamendella, J. T. (1969). On the irrelevance of transformational grammar to second language pedagogy. *Language Learning, XIX,* 255–270.

Larsen-Freeman, D., & Long, M. (1991). *An introduction to second language acquisition research.* London: Longman.

Leontiev, A. A. (1963). The plurality of language models and the problems of teaching languages and grammar. *IRAL, I*(3 & 4), 211–222.

Long, M. H. (1990). The least a second language acquisition theory needs to explain. *TESOL Quarterly, 17,* 359–382.

Long, M. H. (2004). Second language acquisition theories. In M. Byram (Ed.), *Routledge encyclopedia of language teaching and learning* (pp. 527–534). London: Routledge.

Long, M. H. (2007). *Problems in SLA.* Mahwah, NJ: Lawrence Erlbaum Ass.

Long, M. H. (2012). Current trends in SLA research and directions for future development. *Chinese Journal of Applied Linguistics, 35*(2), 135–152.

Long, M. H. (2016). In defense of tasks and TBLT: Nonissues and real issues. *Annual Review of Applied Linguistics, 36,* 5–33.

Long, M. H., & Doughty, C. J. (Eds.). (2009). *The handbook of language teaching.* Chichester: Wiley-Blackwell.

Mackey, W. F. (1973). Language didactics and applied linguistics. In J. W. Oller & J. Richards (Eds.). *Focus on the learner. Pragmatic perspectives for the language teacher* (pp. 4–28). Rowley, MA: Newbury House.

McCarthy, M. (2001). *Issues in applied linguistics.* Cambridge: Cambridge University Press.

McLaughlin, B. (1987). *Theories of second language acquisition.* London: Edward Arnold.

Mitchell, R., & Myles, F. (1998). *Second language learning theories.* London: Edward Arnold.

Moulton, W. G. (1962). Linguistics and language teaching in the United States 1940–1960. In C. Mohrmann, A. Sommerfelt, & J. Whatmough (Eds.), *Trends in European and American linguistics 1930–1960* (pp. 82–109). Utrecht: Spectrum.

Nassaji, H. (2012). The relationship between SLA research and language pedagogy: Teachers' perspectives. *Language Teaching Research, 16*(3), 337–365.

Newmark, L., & Reibel, D. A. (1968). Necessity and sufficiency in language learning. *IRAL, VI*(2), 145–164.

Oller, J. W. (1973). Some psycholinguistic controversies. In J. W. Oller & J. Richards (Eds.), *Focus on the learner. Pragmatic perspectives for the language teacher* (pp. 50–54). Rowley, MA: Newbury House.

Ortega, L. (2009). *Understanding second language acquisition.* London: Hodder Education.

Pitt, J. C. (1988). Introduction. In J. C. Pitt (Ed.), *Theories of explanation* (pp. 3–8). New York: Oxford University Press.

Phillipson, R., & Skutnabb-Kangas, T. (2009). The politics and policies of language and language teaching. In M. H. Long & C. J. Doughty (Eds.), *The handbook of language teaching* (pp. 26–41). Chichester: Wiley-Blackwell.

Ritchie, W. C. (Ed.). (1978). *Second language acquisition research*. New York: Academic Press.

Ritchie, W. C., & Bhatia, T. K. (Eds.). (1996). *Handbook of second language acquisition*. San Diego: Academic Press.

Rivers, W. M. (1964). *The psychologist and the foreign-language teacher*. Chicago: The University of Chicago Press.

Rivers, W. M. (1982). Psychology, linguistics and language teaching. *English Teaching Forum, XX*(2), 2–9.

Roulet, E. (1975). *Linguistic theory, linguistic description and language teaching*. London: Longman.

Schmitt, N. (Ed.). (2002). *An introduction to applied linguistics*. London: Edward Arnold.

Seidlhofer, B. (Ed.). (2003). *Controversies in applied linguistics*. Oxford: Oxford University Press.

Seliger, H., & Long, M. H. (Eds.). (1983). *Classroom oriented research in second language acquisition*. Rowley, MA: Newbury House.

Selinker, L. (1972). Interlanguage. *IRAL, 10*(3), 209–231.

Selinker, L. (1992). *Rediscovering interlanguage*. London: Longman.

Van Compernolle, R. A., & Williams, L. (2013). Sociocultural theory and second language pedagogy. *Language Teaching Research, 17*(3), 277–281.

Wardhaugh, R. (1974). *Topics in applied linguistics*. Rowley, MA: Newbury House.

Wardhaugh, R., & Brown, D. H. (Eds.). (1976). *A survey of applied linguistics*. Ann Arbor: University of Chicago Press.

Widdowson, H. G. (1979). *Explorations in applied linguistics* (Vols. 1–2). Oxford: Oxford University Press.

Widdowson, H. G. (1990). *Aspects of language teaching*. Oxford: Oxford University Press.

Widdowson, H. G. (2003). *Defining issues in English language teaching*. Oxford: Oxford University Press.

Wolff, D. (2002). *Fremdsprachenlernen als Konstruktion. Grundlagen fur eine konstruktivistische Fremdsprachendidaktik*. Frankfurt am Main: Peter Lang.

Wójcicki, R. (1977). Basic concepts of formal methodology of empirical sciences. In M. Przełęcki & R. Wójcicki, (Eds.). *Twenty years of logical methodology in Poland* (pp. 681-708). Warszawa: PWN and Dordreht: Reidel.

Author Biography

Maria Dakowska has been affiliated with the University of Warsaw, first Institute of Applied Linguistics and later Institute of English Studies, where she works with students of English at the M.A. and Ph.D. level, designing and teaching courses addressed to teacher trainees of English as a foreign language. She has visited various leading research centers in Europe, studied at American Universities and participated in international conferences. Her academic interests and publications focus on the scientific constitution of second/foreign language learning and teaching, especially its maturation as an academic discipline, as well as the cognitive psycholinguistic foundations of modeling language use and learning with focus on English as a international language. She has written numerous articles and six monographs on these topics, most recently *In search of processes of language use in foreign language didactics*, published by Peter Lang. Since April 2015 she has served as the Dean of the Faculty of Modern Languages, University of Warsaw, Poland.

Evaluating Language Courses at Foreign Language University Centers

Danuta Gabryś-Barker

Abstract The background to the empirical study presented in this chapter discusses European Union (EU) policies of promoting language education by elaborating on the major recommendations proposed, demonstrating the engagement of the EU in educational mobility programs. It also discusses EU engagement in foreign language (FL) teacher training through various programs, documents and organizational activities. The chapter demonstrates how these recommendations are implemented in foreign language instruction in foreign language courses run at the tertiary level in the form of the so-called *lektoraty*. The study carried out is part of an on-going discussion on what an optimal form of teaching FLs should be and how the present situation needs to be changed, amended or straightforwardly revolutionized. Some of the dimensions of the problem obviously relate to teaching itself but inevitably they also relate to the institutionalized policies employed that express FLs' roles in present-day education and the demands created by the job market and by effective functioning in life in general. The study presented here aims to portray the situation of foreign language teaching at the University of Silesia, through the eyes of both students and their teachers (*lektorzy*). It demonstrates the positive side of FL courses in their various aspects, from the organizational to the didactic, and crucially points to the defects in their functioning. In the concluding part, ways of improving the situation are proposed for the particular context described.

Keywords European Union educational policies · Challenges · Foreign language instruction · Non-language university departments · Levels of satisfaction

D. Gabryś-Barker (✉)
University of Silesia, Katowice, Poland
e-mail: danuta.gabrys@gmail.com

© Springer International Publishing AG 2018
M. Pawlak and A. Mystkowska-Wiertelak (eds.), *Challenges of Second and Foreign Language Education in a Globalized World*, Second Language Learning and Teaching, DOI 10.1007/978-3-319-66975-5_3

1 Introduction

European Union foreign language policy takes the form of special recommendations embracing the need to adapt FL instruction to the personal and professional
needs of individuals. Thus, it promotes learner-centered approaches and the
development of individual autonomy of a learner, taking into consideration individual learner differences. The latter recommendation implies FL programs that
have been tailored to individual needs and contexts of teaching and learning. The
recommendations are put into force in various documents, programs and activities
carried out by specialist agencies. These policies are juxtaposed here with what
happens in FL instructional practices in reality in a selected foreign languages
teaching context, that is, at a university in non-language departments. The challenges FL instruction faces are reviewed here on the basis of both FL teachers' and
students' responses in a satisfaction questionnaire.

2 European Union Foreign Language Policy Recommendations

The EU recommendations stress the importance of developing multicompetence
and plurilingualism at various levels of advancement and extends traditional
communicative competence by adding interactive, intercultural and mediation
competences as key to successful multilingual communication. Foreign language
learning is to be perceived as a life-long learning process, which captures very well
the need for linguistic education of adults and senior learners of the aging societies
of Europe. The importance of languages in professional life is expressed by the
promotion and encouragement of different models of Content and Language
Integrated Learning (CLIL). The development of technology is strongly endorsed
by EU recommendations for promoting language instruction in a blended-form,
combining online and face-to-face hybrid learning. Also, in terms of assessment,
the EU introduced quite some time ago a standardized grading system, which is
now being extended due to its insufficiency at differentiating levels of competence,
hence the introduction of half-grades (e.g., B2+).

All the above recommendations concerning FL instruction have a bearing on
new approaches to and models of FL teacher education and training. Additionally,
the EU sees the importance of translators and interpreters for its successful functioning as well as for guaranteeing people's professional success internationally. It
therefore promotes different types of translation training programs. These recommendations are expressed in numerous documents and publications, for ease of
access generally available online (Table 1).

As stated elsewhere, teacher training is seen as a critical route to success in
present and future FL instruction. Thus (Gabryś-Barker, 2012, p. 250) (Table 2):

Specific topic focus and other major concerns in pre-service language teacher education, together with ways of enhancing teacher growth, are very significantly highlighted by European Union initiatives in education. Various agencies of the European Union, for example the Council of Europe, have made a significant contribution to the development of

Table 1 EU foreign language policy in documents (selected texts)

Text	Objective
Common European framework of reference for Languages CEFR	Planning, learner autonomy, levels of language competence and their detailed description
European language portfolio	*Language passport* *Language biography* *Dossier*—a tool for reflection and self-assessment
Guide for the development of language policies in Europe	A guide to European language policy (Beacco & Byram, 2007)
Universities and language policy in Europe. Reference document	Objectives, methods and strategies in university language policies

Table 2 References and guidelines for teachers and teacher training (*source* Gabryś-Barker, 2012, p. 250)

Document	Objective
European language portfolio (ELP)	It aims to promote learner-centred approaches to teaching in which self-assessment is central; ELP is a practical tool for learner self-assessment (Little, 2009). After an initial period of piloting, ELP has been adopted by some Polish schools, either by local educational authorities or by individual teachers on their own initiative
Autobiography of intercultural encounters (AIE)	This focuses on the role of intercultural experience, aiming at the development of intercultural communicative competences by developing the language learner's ability to reflect critically on his/her individual cultural experiences in international contacts (www.coe.int/t/gd4)
European profile for language teacher education (EPLTE)	It is a proposal for language teacher education in the 21st century which makes suggestions concerning the "*structure* of educational courses, the *knowledge* and *understanding* central to foreign language teaching, the diversity of teaching and learning *strategies* and *skills* and the kinds of *values* language teaching should encourage and promote" (Kelly, Grenfell, Allan, Kriza, & McEvoy, 2004, p. 1)
The European portoflio for student teachers of languages (EPOSTL)	It is a document intended for students undergoing their initial teacher education which encourages them to reflect on the didactic knowledge and skills necessary to teach languages, helps them to assess their own didactic competences and enables them to monitor their progress and to record their experiences of teaching during the course of their teacher education" (Newby et al., 2007)

educational guidelines and programmes for language learners and language teachers
(Council of Europe, 2001).

Constant restructuring and changes made in educational systems, now and observable across the world, demand that professional training and the development of foreign language instructors is of major concern to educational reformers. Unfortunately, what Goodson (1995) believed some time ago continues to be true today "(...) teachers' work intensifies, as more and more centralized edicts and demands impinge on the teacher's world, the space for reflection and research is progressively squeezed" (p. 62). The study reported in this chapter looks at foreign language teacher reflections and critical comments on how FL instruction works in non-specialist university departments. It also reports on the students' feedback and responses to their learning experiences in the above-mentioned environment.

3   Educational Programmes and Mobility Projects

One of the major achievements of EU focus on education, FL development and teacher training is the establishment of various mobility programs for teachers and students. The main programs such as Erasmus (and Erasmus + in its updated form) develop student and staff mobility through international exchange at the tertiary level, whereas Grundtvig concentrates on mobility and exchange in adult education. Jean Monet promotes European integration and, importantly, Comenius consists of promoting student mobility at earlier stages of education (mainly secondary schools), by supporting school exchange visits. These programs are a powerful tool for the implementation of the language policies of the EU.

Of the above, it is Erasmus that has gained most popularity and funding. Table 3 presents its major forms of activity. In describing Erasmus, the European Commission states that:

> An overriding aim of the programmer is to help create a "European Higher Education Area" and foster innovation throughout Europe. In addition to exchange actions ("trans-national mobility"), ERASMUS helps higher education institutions to work together through

Table 3 Erasmus mobility program (based on Gabryś-Barker, 2011)

Students	Universities/higher education institution staff
Studying abroad Doing a traineeship abroad Linguistic preparation	Teaching abroad Receiving training abroad
Universities/higher education institutions working through	Business
Intensive programmes Academic and structural networks Multilateral projects	Hosting students placements Teaching abroad Participating in university cooperation projects

intensive programs, networks and multilateral projects. Thanks to all these actions, ERASMUS has become a driver in the modernization of higher education institutions and systems in Europe and, in particular, has inspired the establishment of the Bologna Process (http://www.viaa.gov/v/eng/ec_education).

The Erasmus Program in the Polish educational context traditionally embraces: student mobility and exchange, exchange of research and didactic staff, introduction of ECTS to allow flexible mobility between institutions, new programs of studies worked out with partner institutions, for example, joint M.A. programs, organizing intensive courses and participation in Erasmus thematic networks. Participation in Erasmus programs is open not only to language department students but also specialist departments of humanities and sciences and, in fact, what can be observed is that it is the last of these that take the greatest advantage of the program, both at the language development level but also in professional expertise in a given area of study. They additionally become acquainted with other models of content course education. Erasmus has become a critical tool in developing language competence as well as professionally-oriented knowledge in foreign tertiary institutions, offering its participants invaluable experiences, often those of a lifetime. It is essential that students participating in the program are well-prepared to take best advantage of it. One of the areas of preparation is obviously appropriate language competence, which would allow the students to function successfully in tertiary education courses abroad.

4 Foreign Language Instruction in Foreign Language University Centers

The way foreign language instruction at the tertiary level of education is organized and run is the operational object of various organizations and agencies. Internationally, one of them is *The European Confederation of Language Centers in Higher Education—Cercles*, which focuses primarily on the teacher training of *lektors*, the exchange of publications in this area and the exchange of experiences through mobility visits. In Poland, a similar role is performed by *Stowarzyszenie Akademickie Ośrodków Nauczania Języków Obcych (SERMO)* (Association of Foreign Language Academic Centers), which organizes various seminars, workshops and conferences for lektors. As foreign language instruction in Poland is also extensively engaged in by the private sector, there is an organization concerned with quality of language instruction working in close collaboration mainly with private language schools. It is *Polskie Stowarzyszenie na Rzecz Jakości w Nauczaniu Języków Obcych* (Polish Association for Standards in English).

There are also many initiatives undertaken by tertiary education institutions such as universities and polytechnics that aim at introducing new and improved practices into foreign language instruction. One of them is the project of Warsaw Polytechnic (www.spj.pw.edu.pl), which was awarded the *European Language Label* in 2007 for its quality in FL instruction. The aim of the project was to introduce a more coherent and quality-focused FL instruction in tertiary education. It embraced the following dimensions:

1. The main objective was the promotion of quality language instruction by:

   - introducing the system of quality assessment consisting in the implementation of teacher training and support programs;
   - support for student learning (more effective strategies);
   - monitoring teacher development and teacher assessment.

2. Changes in syllabuses and system of instruction:

   - standardized syllabuses based on *Common European framework of reference for languages* scales;
   - standardized language examinations.

3. Training seminars and workshops on:

   - quality in teaching foreign languages;
   - implementation of work contracts with students (groups);
   - use of student portfolios;
   - motivation in teaching and learning;
   - language testing;
   - voice emission (use);
   - learner autonomy;
   - use of questionnaires and surveys.

4. Tools used in quality assessment:

   - checklist for teachers (regulations, information packets for students concerning language instruction);
   - vademecum (guidelines) for a novice teacher;
   - self-assessment questionnaire for teachers;
   - mid-semester assessment questionnaire;
   - information leaflet for the first year student.

5. Monitoring and teacher assessment:

   - detailed criteria of teacher employment and promotion;
   - periodical assessment by students (a questionnaire);
   - assessment with an observation sheet.

This new system was successfully introduced and can serve as an example of good practice in FL teaching oriented towards quality.

5   Problems and Challenges of Tertiary Level FL Instruction in Poland Using the Example of the University of Silesia: A Study

5.1   Participants, Instruments and Procedure

Concerns with foreign language instruction expressed in the quality improvement project at the Polytechnic of Warsaw were reiterated in a project run by the University of Silesia. As a result of various actions including consultations with other university language centers, foreign language teaching experts, teachers and university authorities, a set of proposals for amending the situation of FL instruction was suggested by the author of this chapter, who acted as a coordinator of foreign language teaching at the University of Silesia (*Stage 1*). This initial discussion at the University of Silesia conducted in a group of interested parties—authorities, policy makers, FL teachers and students—was complemented by a questionnaire for students and teachers (*Stage 2*). Both groups, teachers and students, were asked in a detailed way to assess their degree of satisfaction with FL instruction at the University of Silesia, on a scale from *very satisfied* to *totally not dissatisfied*. A questionnaire was administered to 498 students from various departments and their foreign language teachers ($N = 48$) to assess the situation in the academic year 2014/2015 (Gabryś-Barker & Bontko-Jakubiec, 2015). The learner questionnaire (Appendix One) focused on the following aspects of FL instruction:

1. Organization of courses in terms of:

   - availability, completeness and clarity of information concerning language courses;
   - information on the obligatory final examination, online registration into FL groups;
   - length (number of hours) and intensity of the course;
   - physical conditions (rooms, equipment) and timetable (its friendliness for students and teachers).

2. Methods of FL teaching:

   - comprehensible and communicative classes;
   - appropriate pace of teaching;
   - attractiveness of classes;
   - clarity of assessment criteria;
   - availability of teachers for consultations during their office hours;
   - the final examination (its form and content);
   - FL teachers' attitude towards students (openness, friendliness, etc.).

The teacher questionnaire (Appendix Two) required respondents to give feedback on the first part of the learner questionnaire, that is, to comment on the organization of the courses (point 1 above), and also to make an open comment on the needs for resolving problems the teachers face in their daily work and the changes they assume to be necessary to improve the practice of FL instruction at the University of Silesia.

5.2 Results and Discussion

5.2.1 Problem Areas Diagnosed by the Coordinator: Discussion (Stage 1)

The initial discussion of the above-mentioned aspects resulted in the identification of several problem areas which need addressing. In most cases, the aspects pointed out did not come as a surprise but rather they represented the forward thinking of many involved in the process of FL instruction at the University of Silesia. They pointed to:

- insufficient number of contact hours (four semesters of instruction or 120 h— one of the lowest numbers if compared with other tertiary education institutions;
- too narrow a choice of languages for students;
- lack of a standardized system of credits, tests and examinations across different university departments;
- multilevel groups;
- oversized groups, where the bottom limit was set at twenty but there was no upper limit (so groups could consist of well over thirty students);
- insufficient use of e-learning approaches by means of the e-platform *Moodle* (in reference to examinations, tests, sources materials).

What was generally seen as the biggest drawback of the FL teaching system was the very limited number of contact hours of the entire language course. Various models of FL instruction functioning at different universities in Poland, in terms of the number of contact hours, range from as few as 120 h embracing both first level (B. A.) and second level studies (M.A.) at UMCS University in Lublin, the Pedagogical University in Krakow, the University of Silesia, among others, to as many as 240 h at the University of Warsaw, the University of Wrocław or the Jagiellonian University, with some institutions, for example, Szkoła Prawa i Administracji (Law and Administration School) in Przemyśl-Rzeszów and Małopolska Wyższa Szkoła Ekonomiczna (Małopolska Higher School of Economics), with a significantly higher number of hours: 360 and 285 h, respectively (online sources of individual institutions). Obviously, this inadequate number of hours devoted to FL instruction at the University of Silesia is one of the main challenges teachers and students alike have to face in relation to the ministerial requirement for the first level graduate (B.A.) to reach B2 and for the second level graduate (M.A.) to gain FL competence at B2+ levels (according to the accepted scales of the *Common European framework of reference for languages*).

5.2.2 Assessment of FL Instruction from the Teachers' and Students' Perspectives: Data Presentation and Discussion (Stage 2)

The summary of the quantitative data collected from both the students and teachers confirm the problems previously indicated that need to be rethought. On the one hand, what can be observed in the students' assessment is the voicing of high satisfaction with:

- the way the FL teaching process is organized (satisfaction ranging from 70 to 80%);
- the way FLs are taught (satisfaction over 90%, mostly in relation to methods of instruction, teachers' positive attitudes to students, their availability).

On the other hand, the areas assessed at the lowest levels of satisfaction were:

- the number of contact hours and their frequency (2 h a week);
- not enough focus on the development of communicative competence (speaking skills) in a FL and too much grammar-oriented instruction;
- oversized groups in FL classes;
- the offer limited to one FL course only;
- a student-unfriendly system of online registration for a FL course;
- insufficient didactic equipment available in class and not enough access to books in the library.

It seems that all the positive comments registered in the students' assessment give evidence of the good work and expertise of FL instructors, not only in terms of their professional qualifications but also in relation to their positive attitudes towards the students, availability and constant assistance in their FL development.

The teachers participating in the data collection expressed very strong positive attitudes towards the organization of FL classes at the level of administration. The teachers emphasized their full satisfaction with:

- cooperation within the Foreign Language Center (*Studium Praktycznej Nauki Języków Obcych*—SPNJO);
- the availability of information on regulations, procedures for running the courses and course requirements;
- the administrative work of the Center;
- organization of the final examination in FL languages (81.6%).

However, the number of changes and amendments that need to be made, as expressed by the teachers, was very high and related to FL classes and teaching itself, as well as to their own positions as teachers and to their functioning at the university. The respondents believe that:

- the total number of hours of FL instruction at the University of Silesia is not sufficient;
- the language material is too extensive for only four semesters of instruction;
- the groups are oversized, as there is no upper limit;

- there is generally not enough audio-visual equipment for every lecturer and thus availability is limited;
- basic aids such as blackboards are still the major didactic resource; the black-boards used are not at their best and need replacement.

Apart from the critical comments relating to the conditions of work, the teachers were not fully satisfied with:

- the bureaucracy, the many regulations and an overwhelming amount of administrative work each teacher is obliged to do;
- a fairly complex and not always effective registration of students into groups (an online system);
- an insufficient number of language groups at the lower level (A2);
- too rigid a form of the final examination (testing).

Apart from the above, the teachers expressed their concern about the situation they find themselves in in terms of professional promotion, which in many cases is lagging behind (67%) and which, if it happens at all, is given after a very long professional career. According to the respondents, the procedures of promotion should rely more on the learner assessment of each teacher, which is done periodically and could easily be used as a tool for evaluation and, in consequence, further promotion.

As can be seen, both the teachers and the students give high assessment marks to the organization of FL teaching at the level of the Language Center (SPNJO) and the professional expertise of the teachers. The best evidence of this are the results of the final examination in all the departments for the 2014/2015 academic year (Gabryś-Barker, Bontko-Jakubiec, Sikora, 2015, Figs. 1, 2 and 3). The results are presented here in departmental groups to demonstrate the consistency of final scores across all the departments. The scale of assessment used was a university grading system: 5—very good (A), +4—plus good (B), 4—good (C), +3—plus satisfactory (D), 3—satisfactory (E), and 2—unsatisfactory/fail (F).

Fig. 1 Results of the final FL examination at the humanities and social sciences departments (Gabryś-Barker & Kalamarz, 2013)

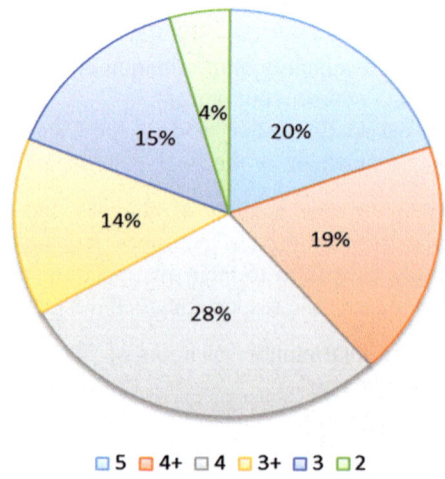

□ 5 □ 4+ □ 4 □ 3+ □ 3 □ 2

Fig. 2 Results of the final FL examination at the sciences and natural sciences departments (Gabryś-Barker & Kalamarz, 2013)

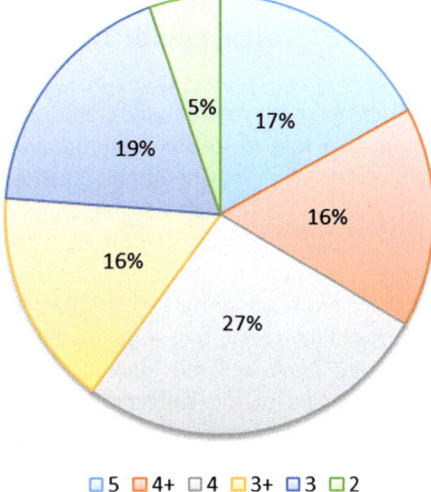

□ 5 ■ 4+ □ 4 □ 3+ □ 3 □ 2

Fig. 3 Results of the final FL examination for all the university departments (Gabryś-Barker & Kalamarz, 2013)

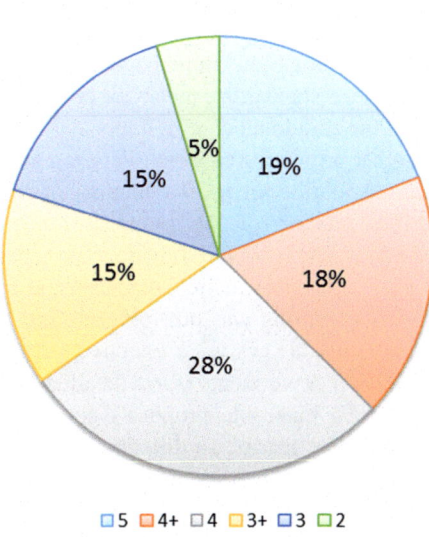

□ 5 ■ 4+ □ 4 □ 3+ □ 3 □ 2

Despite the positive results of the final examinations across all the departments, there is a visible need for improvement in addressing the well-being of students and teachers alike. As can be seen in the data presented above, the areas of dissatisfaction overlap in both groups of respondents. Expressly, they were difficulties in teaching and learning in oversized groups, with deficient (or unavailable) equipment, and 120 h across four semesters to reach the prescribed level of B2 language competence as a wholly inadequate allocation of time. In short, this was felt to be an unattainable goal.

6   Conclusions and Implications: Implementing Changes in FL Instruction at the University of Silesia

The above study results only confirm what was proposed in the 2013/2014 academic year and is still in the process of being implemented. As a result of the cooperation of various bodies involved in FL instruction at the University of Silesia (among them the Foreign Language Center, Rector's Spokesmen for FL instruction, the Quality Assessment Committee and the Education Committee), a proposal for change was put forward to maximize the impact of FL courses on final student achievement (Gabryś-Barker & Kalamarz, 2013). Some of these proposals call for changes in the program of studies, some can be and are implemented by the Foreign Language Center and individual teachers themselves, and some have been approved by the Senate of the University of Silesia. In effect, some changes have been successfully implemented almost immediately and others are still on "the back burner". Unfortunately, there are some which may never be put into practice.

The first and most strongly voiced need has been the change in the number of contact hours at the first level of studies (B.A.) from the present 120–180 h in six semesters, complemented by 180 h of individual student work. Thus far this proposal has not been implemented. However, as advocated in the proposal, it was possible to standardize the so far diverse number of hours at the B.A. level at 180 h. With the additional contact hours at the M.A. level, the number would go up to 240. Another problem area were oversized groups; the proposal suggested that the upper limit should be set at 20 students per group. This was partially realized due to the implementation of the proposal for creating cross-departmental courses (pol. *pasma*), which would function as separate humanities, neo-philological, social sciences, sciences, natural sciences and artistic subjects' paths. A detailed plan for this restructuring was put forward. The paths have indeed been implemented, but they do not always work effectively due to various factors and the functioning of individual departments (for a detailed assessment, see Gabryś-Barker & Kalamarz, 2017). To make the proposals concerning the number of hours and size of FL groups more feasible, a different form of teaching was proposed, adopting blended learning, which had in fact been made obligatory earlier by University regulations, defining the proportion between contact hours (70%) and online instruction, via the *Moodle* platform (30%). This idea has not been received favorably by all the teachers (according to personal communication). The promotion of blended learning was connected directly with a further suggestion of setting up obligatory training for all first year students in the use of the *Moodle* platform. Perhaps it should also be offered to some of the teachers, some of whom are quite reluctant to go online.

To alleviate the problem of the disparity of language proficiency levels in multilevel groups in terms of language competence, which is a common complaint of all FL teachers, it was proposed that a levelling (placement) examination should be used, which was welcomed by the teachers and the learners alike. For those who needed to catch up with their peers, non-obligatory courses were offered by the Language Center and these are successfully functioning at the moment. Also, it was proposed that the final FL examination should be made obligatory for all students and should be standardized across all the departments, which has also been successfully implemented. Students who have passed certified foreign language examinations may be exempted from the obligation to attend a language course. A list of such equivalent certificates will be compiled and published. It was also suggested that the Foreign Language Center should expand its offer of FLs courses. For example, Spanish and Italian should also be taught and thus students should be given a chance or perhaps even obliged to enroll in another FL course, in this case however without the final B2 level requirement.

An important recommendation was made to help emphasize the role of specialist languages in FL university instruction—by enshrining the benefits of their instruction in general university descriptors of the effects of language education (pol. *efekty ksztalcenia*). These were to be part of a generally accepted description of FL instruction effects for the whole university, rather than being presented in great diversity of forms depending on the given department. This proposal has been successfully put into practice.

As mentioned earlier, some of the changes proposed in the academic year 2013/2014 were implemented in 2014/2015, whereas others require more long-term procedures and are directly connected not only with the university policy on FL instruction but also its policy relating, for example, to employment issues. However, it must be conceded that a lot has changed over the past four years at the University of Silesia in this area and that this has stimulated greatly the activity of the Foreign Language Center (for more information, see www.spnjo.us.edu.pl) and our FL instructors. Hopefully, this has also contributed to the growing satisfaction of students. A final benefit is that this has also brought us closer to the generally accepted policies of FL education as put forward in the European Union documents on FL education, mentioned in th introduction to this chapter.

Appendix 1: Student satisfaction questionnaire results: quantitative data (no 498) (translated from Polish) (all the data is given in percentages)

A foreign language learnt: ....
Level: ....
I. *Please define your level of individual satisfaction with your FL course at the University of Silesia.*

No.	Focus	Totally dissatisfied	Hardly satisfied	Fairly satisfied	Satisfied	Very satisfied
Organisation of FL instruction						
1.	Availability of information about courses:					
	– in the Language Center (SPNJO) and online	1.0	3.8	1.8	38.4	38.6
	– in the department	0.8	5.7	8.2	38.4	37.0
2.	Availability of information on the final examination	0.4	2.2	9.4	27.5	60.4
3.	Completeness and clarity of information	0.8	1.4	11.7	30.0	56.1
4.	Online registration for courses	6.3	11.9	28.1	30.9	22.8
5.	The length of a course	2.2	7.7	22.4	34.5	33.3
6.	Conditions (room, equipment)	2.6	0.0	24.1	40.4	28.0
7.	Timetable	0.8	5.6	19.5	38.2	35.8
8.	Availability of materials (coursebooks9	1.2	2.8	15.0	35.6	45.1
Quality of teaching						
9.	Comprehensible and communicative classes	1.0	0.0	3.4	19.1	76.1
10.	Pace of classes and intensity	0.0	1.4	8.0	33.7	56.8
11.	Attractiveness of classes	0.4	1.0	9.2	29.7	59.6
12.	Clarity of assessment criteria	1.2	0.4	3.5	21.4	73.5
13.	Availability of lecturers (office hours)	0.8	0.2	3.8	18.9	76.3
14.	Final examination:					
	a. form	0.8	0.8	6.2	26.5	65.6
	b. content	0.8	0.6	6.0	26.6	66.0
15.	Lecturers' attitude to students, openness and kindness	1.6	0.2	0.6	7.8	89.7

II. *Please comment on what you think should be changed or improved in your foreign language instruction at the University of Silesia.*

....
....
....
....
....
....
....

Appendix 2: Teacher satisfaction questionnaire: quantitative data (no 48) (translated from Polish) (all the data is given in percentages)

Which language do you teach? ....

Please define your level of individual satisfaction with the way FL instruction is organised and managed at the University of Silesia.

No.	Focus	Totally dissatisfied	Hardly satisfied	Fairly satisfied	Satisfied	Very satisfied
1.	Availability of information important for lecturers (e.g. requirements, regulations)	0.0	0.0	8.1	37.8	54.1
2.	Administrative work at the Language Center (SPNJO)	0.0	0.0	13.2	34.2	52.6
3.	Administrative work at the Dean's office	0.0	0.0	29.7	43.2	27.0
4.	Online registration for courses	6.1	15.2	27.3	24.2	27.3
5.	The length of a course (a number of hours)	5.4	67.6	21.6	2.7	2.7
6.	Groups' size	7.9	36.8	42.1	10.5	2.6
7.	Conditions of work (room, equipment)	7.9	31.6	42.1	15.8	2.6
8.	Timetable	0.0	5.3	39.5	39.5	15.8
9.	Availability of materials (coursebooks, supplementary materials)	0.0	5.4	13.5	43.2	37.8

(continued)

(continued)

No.	Focus	Totally dissatisfied	Hardly satisfied	Fairly satisfied	Satisfied	Very satisfied
10.	Availability of: (a) audio-visual equipment (b) rooms with a-v equipment	13.2 13.2	39.5 39.5	23.7 26.3	18.4 15.8	5.3 5.3
11.	Organisation of final examination	0.0	5.3	13.2	55.3	26.3
12.	Opportunities for professional development	10.5	21.1	39.5	28.9	0
13.	Opportunities for promotion	40.5	27.0	21.6	10.8	0
14.	Cooperation between lecturers and the Language Center management	0.0	11.1	13.9	25.0	50
15	Cooperation between the language Center and university departments	2.6	5.3	28.0	50.0	13.2
16.	Cooperation with institutions outside the university	9.7	6.5	45.2	29.0	9.7

II. Diagnose the biggest problems in your work as a FL teacher

....
....
....
....

III. Suggest changes to be implemented in FL teaching at the University of Silesia.

....
....
....
....
....

References

Autobiography of Intercultural Encounters. (n.d.). Retrieved from at www.coe.int/t/gd4.
Beaco, J. C., & Byram, M. (2007). *Guide for the development of language policies in Europe.* Retrieved from www.coe.int/dg4/linguistic/Source/FullGuide-EN.pdf.

Gabryś-Barker, D. (2011). Student mobility as a way of uniting cultures: A case study of an ERASMUS student. In I. Guske & B. Swaffield (Eds.), *Global encounters: Pedagogical paradigms and educational encounters* (pp. 275–289). Cambridge: Cambridge Scholars Publishing.

Gabryś-Barker, D. (2012). *Reflectivity in pre-service teacher education: A survey of theory and practice.* Katowice: University of Silesia Press.

Gabryś-Barker, D., & Bontko-Jakubiec, J. (2015, October). Nauczanie języków obcych na Uniwersytecie Śląskim: Analiza wyników ankiety satysfakcji lektora i studenta [FL instruction at the University of Silesia: Analysis of teacher and learner satisfaction questionnaire]. A report presented at the meeting of Committee of Quality Assessment at the University of Silesia.

Gabryś-Barker, D., Bontko-Jakubiec, J., & Sikora, T. (2015, October). *Ocena wyników końcowych egzaminu z lektoratu, 2014/2015* [The assessment of the final FL examination results, 2014/2015]. An unpublished report presented to the Committee of Quality Assessment at the University of Silesia.

Gabryś-Barker, D., & Kalamarz, R. (2013, April). Propozycje zmian w kształceniu językowym na Uniwersytecie Śląskim [A proposal for changes in FL instruction at the University of Silesia]. A report presented at the meeting of the Commission of Education at the University of Silesia.

Gabryś-Barker, D., & Kalamarz, R. (2017). *Działanie pasm lektoratowych: Wyniki ankiety dla lektorów.* [The analysis of the questionnaire on cross-departmental FL courses. An unpublished report]. Katowice: Uniwersytet Śląski.

Goodson, J. (1995). Studying the teacher's life and work. In J. Smyth (Ed.), *Critical discourse in teacher education* (pp. 55–64). London: Cassell.

Kelly, M., Grenfell, M., Allan, R., Kriza, C., & McEvoy, W. (2004). *European profile for language teacher education—A frame of reference.* A report to the European Commission Directorate General for Education and Culture. Yarmouth: Intercultural Press.

Little, D. (2009). *The European language portfolio: Where pedagogy and assessment meet.* Strasbourg: Council of Europe, 2009. Retrieved from www.coe.int/t/dg4/education/elp/elp-eg/ Source/Publications/ELP_pedagogy_assessment_Little_EN.pdf.

Newby, D., Allan, R., Fenner, A. B., Jones, B., Komorowska, H., & Soghikyan, K. (2007). *The European portfolio for student teachers of languages* (EPOSTL). Retrieved from http://www. ecml.at/mtp2/FTE.

Author Biography

Danuta Gabryś-Barker is Professor of English at the University of Silesia, Katowice, Poland, where she lectures and supervises M.A. and Ph.D. theses in applied linguistics, psycholinguistics and especially in second language acquisition and multilingualism. She has published numerous articles and the books *Aspects of multilingual storage, processing and retrieval* (2005) and *Reflectivity in pre-service teacher education* (2012). She has also edited fifteen volumes, among others for Multilingual Matters, Springer and the University of Silesia Press. Professor Gabryś-Barker has been the Editor-in-Chief of *International Journal of Multilingualism* (Taylor & Francis/Routledge) since 2010 and the co-founder and the Editor-in-Chief of the journal *Theory and Practice of Second Language Acquisition* (University of Silesia Press) since 2015.

Emotion as the Amplifier and the Primary Motive: Some Theories of Emotion with Relevance to Language Learning

Rebecca L. Oxford

Abstract Emotion is crucial to living and learning. The powerful intertwining of emotion and cognition ignites learning within a complex dynamic system, which, as several sections of this paper show, also includes societal and cultural influences. As "the primary human motive" (MacIntyre, 2002a, p. 61), emotion operates as an amplifier, which provides energetic intensity to all human behavior, including language learning. This chapter explains major theories of emotion drawn from positive psychology, social psychology, social constructivism, social constructionism, and existential psychotherapy. It also offers implications for language learning related to understanding and managing emotions; expressing emotions appropriately despite cultural and linguistic differences; viewing emotions as transitory social roles; enhancing positive emotions and developing resilience; and recognizing, perhaps paradoxically, both the negative and the positive aspects of anxiety. The chapter concludes with the statement that language learners can become more agentic in dealing with their emotions. This form of self-regulation can lead to greater success in language learning.

Keywords Language learning · Positive psychological · Social, and existential theories of emotion

1 Introduction

Emotion is "the primary human motive", said MacIntyre (2002a, p. 61). The human brain is an emotional brain (Le Doux, 1998; see also Johnson, 2014; Lewis, Haviland-Jones, & Barrett, 2008). It creates relationships among thought, emotion,

The paper first appeared in *Studies in Second Language Learning and Teaching, 5*, 371–393.

R.L. Oxford (✉)
University of Maryland, College Park, USA
e-mail: rebeccaoxford@gmail.com

53

and motivation in a complex dynamic system in which components interact in complex, nonlinear, organic, and holistic ways (Dörnyei, 2009; Mercer, 2011). Emotion "functions as an amplifier, providing the intensity, urgency, and energy to propel our behavior" in "everything we do" (MacIntyre, 2002a, p. 61). All learning is a powerful combination of cognition and emotion (Lewis, 2005; Piaget, 1981), so Dörnyei (2009) spoke of a "cognition-emotion interface" in language learning.

As a background to my own research with learner histories and as a means of deepening my understanding of learner anxiety and other emotions, I decided to study emotion theories. This article and a prior one (Oxford, 2015) grew from that interest. My aim here is not to provide a review of research on emotions in language learning nor to examine all theories of emotion. Instead, I intend to describe several focused theories of emotion drawn from various branches of psychology, sociology, and philosophy and to explain how those theories apply to language learning. The article addresses theories of emotion in (a) positive psychology, (b) social psychology, (c) social constructivism, (d) social constructionism, and (e) existential psychotherapy.

2   Emotion Theory in Positive Psychology

The goal of positive psychology is to "increase flourishing by increasing positive emotion, engagement, meaning, positive relationships, and accomplishment," said Seligman (2011, p. 12), the father of positive psychology. According to So and Huppert (as cited in Seligman, 2011), "flourishing [is] (...) defined as having high positive emotion, plus being high on any three of the following: self-esteem, optimism, resilience, vitality, self-determination, and positive relationships" (p. 238). Well-being is the operationalization of flourishing.

Some discussion areas in the theory of well-being in positive psychology are particularly germane to understanding emotions. These areas relate to positive emotions, negative emotions, flow, resilience, and emotional intelligence. Though positive psychologists do not tend to refer to a mix of emotions, I include this topic along with positive emotions, because every human life contains a mix of emotions.

2.1   Positive Emotions and a Mix of Emotions

In Seligman's (2011) well-being theory within positive psychology, positive emotion is one of the five key areas, accompanied by engagement, relationships, meaning, and accomplishment, summarized as "PERMA". Seligman (2011) endorsed Frederickson's (2001, 2003, 2004) "broaden-and-build" concept of positive emotions by saying "the positive emotions broaden and build abiding psychological resources that we can call on later in life" (p. 66). The broaden-and-build concept says that positive emotions, such as happiness, curiosity, and interest, broaden the individual's awareness and encourage innovative, diverse thoughts and actions. This broadened range builds skills and resources. For instance, pleasure in interacting with someone else can build up friendship and social skills, joy in childhood's rough-and-tumble play can lead to motor skills, and curiosity can lead to searching skills. Positive emotions (a) "trigger upward spirals toward emotional well-being" (Frederickson & Joiner, 2002, p. 172), (b) broaden the scope of attention (Frederickson & Branigan, 2005), (c) contribute to resilience (Frederickson, Tugade, Waugh, & Larkin, 2003; Waugh, Tugade, & Frederickson, 2008), and (d) speed up recovery from cardiovascular situations related to negative emotions (Frederickson & Levenson, 1998).

Oxford and Cuéllar (2014) and Oxford, Pacheco Acuña, Solís Hernández, and Smith (2014) significantly adapted Seligman's well-being theory (PERMA) to interpret histories of language learners who were selected for the studies because of their record of success and high proficiency. We were interested in capturing a true mix of emotions—both positive and negative ones—and not just concerned about the presence of positive emotions, as Seligman might have been. With these successful learners, we discovered a mix of emotions but realized that positive emotions, such as interest and happiness in learning, were more prevalent than negative emotions, such as sadness and anxiety. We framed the narrative task by asking: "What obstacles did you face in language learning? Were you able to overcome them, and if so, how?" The learners in these studies proved to be resilient in working to overcome their difficulties. We also asked: "What were the peak experiences in your language learning?" We avoided defining a peak experience so that the learners could respond freely. Maslow (1970) described peak experiences as transient but powerful moments of self-actualization. In his view, a peak experience is "a great and mystical experience, a religious experience if you wish —an illumination, a revelation, an insight (…) [leading to] 'the cognition of being', (…) almost, you could say, a technology of happiness (…)" (Maslow, 1971, p. 169). Peak experiences are especially joyous, exciting, ego-transcending moments in life, involving sudden feelings of intense happiness or ecstasy, creativity, meaning, well-being, wonder, awe, love, unity, empathy, limitlessness, and timelessness. Maslow (1971) indicated that "most people, or perhaps all people, have peak experiences, or ecstasies" (p. 168). Peak experiences can never be a goal; they are byproducts of engaging fully in something meaningful. In analyzing language learner histories, Oxford and Cuéllar (2014) and Oxford et al. (2014) found that many of the successful learners had peak experiences gained through interacting with teachers, fellow students, and native speakers in the target language and experiencing the richness of the culture.

In other narrative research that did not apply positive psychology (see Kao & Oxford, 2014; Ma & Oxford, 2014; Oxford, 1996, 2011a, b, 2013, 2014; Oxford, Ehrman, & Lavine, 1991; Oxford, Lavine, Felkins, Hollaway, & Saleh, 1996; Oxford, Massey, & Anand, 2005; Oxford, Meng, Zhou, Sung, & Jain, 2007; Oxford et al., 1998), we allowed learners to talk and write about the negative and positive relationships with teachers and their experiences with language learning as a whole. We opened the door to anything they might want to say. Results showed an array of emotions, connected in various ways with learners' personalities, goals, self-esteem levels, self-concepts, and experiences of crossing linguistic and cultural borders (Pavlenko & Lantolf, 2000), often involving moving to other countries. While some of the emotions, such as anger, shame, guilt, and anxiety, were negative, other emotions experienced by these learners, such as love, confidence, pleasure, pride, contentment, and joy, were highly positive.

2.2 The Roles of Negative Emotions

In contrast to positive emotions, "negative emotions warn us about a specific threat: when we feel fear, it is almost always preceded by a thought of danger" (Seligman, 2011, p. 139), such as sadness being preceded by a thought of loss or anger being preceded by a thought of trespass. Our negative emotional reaction is often disproportional to the actuality of the danger. Negative emotions—"the firefighting emotions" (Seligman, 2011, p. 66)—narrow the individual's response options to survival behaviors (Frederickson, 2001, 2003, 2004). For example, anxiety leads toward the fight-or-flight response.

In other researchers' narrative studies of language learning, multiple emotions were found, most of which were negative and potentially "narrowing" in the sense of Frederickson's theory. In Pavlenko's (2006) investigation, the narratives of bilingual writers who had learned English as a second language displayed "an array of emotions", such as guilt, insecurity, anxiety, worry, sadness, and confusion (p. 5). Japanese women learning English self-identified responses of longing, disappointment, sadness, and powerlessness, but also occasional confidence (Piller & Takahashi, 2006). In her book *Lost in translation*, Hoffman (1990) explained the emotional changes and sense of dispossession that occurred when she moved with her family from Poland to Canada. In *Hunger of memory: The education of Richard Rodriguez*, Rodriguez (1983/2004) portrayed emotional and social alienation from his familial linguistic and cultural identity. One wonders why the emotions were mostly so negative. Did the sociocultural aspects of language learning make the process such a profoundly unsettling psychological experience (Guiora, 1983)? Why was so little positive emotional value found for some of these individuals during a large part of their language learning process?

Research on language anxiety reveals that this frequently found emotion has many negative correlates for learners: (a) worsened cognition and achievement (Gardner, Tremblay, & Masgoret, 1997; Horwitz, 2001, 2007; MacIntyre, 2002a), (b) negative attitudes toward the language (Dewaele, 2005), (c) decisions to drop the language (Dewaele & Thirtle, 2009), (d) less willingness to communicate (MacIntyre, 2002b), and (e) diminished self-confidence, reduced personality, and lowered personal agency and control (Horwitz, 2007; Horwitz & Young, 1991). However, contrary to positive psychology's pessimistic reaction to negative emotions, evidence also exists that language anxiety can occasionally be stimulating and helpful (e.g., Marcos-Llinas & Juan Garau, 2009). The Janus-like (Dewaele & McIntyre, 2014) negative and positive natures of language anxiety can be explained from an existential psychotherapeutic perspective: "Anxiety has a negative expression in angst or anguish and a positive one in excitement and anticipation" (van Deurzen, 2012, p. 153).

Language anxiety (and implicitly other negative emotions) can be managed through particular emotional strategies promoted by positive psychology. For instance, the ABCDE macrostrategy (Seligman, 2006, 2011), drawing on the theory and practice of rational emotive behavior therapy (REBT; Ellis, 2003), contains a set of interlocking strategies. Specifically, the learner must recognize that beliefs, especially irrational beliefs, about adversity cause consequent negative feelings (e.g., anxiety) but disputation, which means presenting counterevidence, results in energization, or a positive change of mind (Seligman, 2006). Within the ABCDE macrostrategy, the strategy of identifying irrational beliefs—"I must/should" (dogmatic demands), "It's terrible" (awfulizing), "I can't stand it" (low frustration tolerance), and "I'm worthless and incompetent" (self/other rating)—is very important, especially for language learning. Many language learners hold dysfunctional, irrational beliefs about their own learning, and this contributes to language anxiety. The strategy of identifying irrational beliefs must always be accompanied by the strategies of (a) identifying counterevidence and (b) creating a new mindset. The ABCDE macrostrategy combats the pessimistic explanatory style (Peterson, Seligman, & Vaillant, 1988), which is often found in anxious learners. Well-being theory notes that "emotions don't follow inexorably from external events but from what you think about those events, and you can actually change what you think" (Seligman, 2011, p. 90). In REBT, the ABCDE macrostrategy is a central focus for personality change, but it can also be deployed to diminish language anxiety specifically (see Cohn & Frederickson, 2010, for predictors and consequences of positive psychology interventions).

2.3 Flow

Csíkszentmihályi (2008) described flow not as passive or relaxing but as occurring when an individual's mind and body are stretched to their limit in a quest to accomplish something worthwhile and difficult. Flow is comprised of complete engagement in an activity, merging of action and awareness without distraction, intrinsic motivation (autotelism, or the desire to do the task for its own sake because it is enjoyable), balance between challenge and skill (task is neither too easy nor too hard), heightened control (security and lack of worry about failure), effortlessness, lack of self-consciousness, and an altered perception of time (slowing down or speeding up) (Csíkszentmihályi, 1998, 2008, 2013; Csíkszentmihályi & Csíkszentmihályi, 2006).

Flow is associated with emotion by means of skill level and challenge. As noted, a state of flow occurs when the tasks' challenge matches the person's skill level. When skill level and challenge are imbalanced, lack of flow is assured and one of the following negative emotional states is likely to emerge: anxiety (higher challenge than skill level), boredom (lower challenge than skill level), or apathy (both challenges and skill levels are low) (Nakamura & Csíkszentmihályi, 2005). Peterson (2006) stated, "the aftermath of the flow experience is invigorating (…) [although] flow in the moment is nonemotional and arguably nonconscious. People describe flow as highly and intrinsically enjoyable, but this is an after-the-fact summary judgment, and joy is not immediately present during the activity itself" (pp. 66–67). Flow can produce emotions such as pleasure, joy, and excitement—but, as Peterson contended, after the experience is over.

2.4 Resilience

Resilience is the ability to successfully spring back from adversity. Language learners need resilience in times of emotional, cognitive, and/or physical stress. Some resilience theories and research studies emphasize "personal strengths (e.g., cognitive, social, emotional, moral/spiritual)" (Truebridge, 2014, p. 15), such as hope, interest, excitement, outgoing personalities, ability to enlist support and develop competence, problem-solving ability, and self-esteem (Masten & Obradovic, 2006; Werner & Smith, 1992). Benard (1991) listed the following personal, individual components of resilience: positivity (e.g., hope for the future, interest, engagement), persistence, hardiness, goal-directedness, achievement orientation, educational aspirations, a sense of anticipation, a sense of purpose, and a sense of coherence. Resilience also involves social factors, such as compassionate relationships, messages that focus on strengths and build positive emotions, and opportunities for responsible participation (Luthar, Cicchetti, & Becker, 2000; Luthar, Sawyer, & Brown, 2006; Truebridge, 2014). Resilience was theoretically linked to "psychological fitness" in the military (Seligman, 2011, pp. 127, 240). The opposite of resilience often involves giving into negative emotions, such as depression or anger, when situations become very difficult.

In a study involving multiple learner histories (Oxford et al., 2007), resilience in language learning emerged as the main theme. In one of these learner histories, a Chinese learner of English overcame her anxiety, embarrassment, and shame about speaking English. To help her teacher, whose instruction was being evaluated by the district education authorities, the student stood up and spoke in English when other students would not. This action saved the teacher's reputation in the eyes of the inspectors and served to make the student feel competent, confident, and resilient. The study contained numerous stories of learner resilience.

2.5   Emotional Intelligence

Goleman's (2005) view of emotional Intelligence (EQ) grew out of prior work on multiple intelligences, empathy, neuro-linguistic programming, and transactional analysis. Goleman asserted that the intelligence quotient (IQ), or traditionally described intelligence, is too narrow to explain variation in human behavior and contended that it was essential to consider emotional intelligence. He identified the domains of emotional intelligence as knowing and managing one's own emotions, motivating oneself, recognizing and understanding other people's emotions, and managing relationships. Emotional intelligence has been shown to reduce stress and anxiety, decrease conflict, improve relationships, and increase stability, self-motivation, social awareness, and harmony (Goleman, 2005). With increased awareness and effort, it is possible to develop new aspects of emotional intelligence in individuals and organizations (Goleman, 2005).

Emotional intelligence theory is useful for understanding differences in the attitudes and behavior of language learners and users. Dewaele, Petrides, and Furnham (2008; see also Dewaele, 2013) found that adult multilinguals with higher emotional intelligence had lower levels of foreign language anxiety in various situations and languages. They discovered that in communication situations such individuals, compared to individuals with lower emotional intelligence, perceived themselves as more capable of (a) gauging the emotions of their interlocutor, (b) controlling their own stress, and (c) feeling confident (and hence less anxious). Other factors in lower anxiety and stronger confidence were younger age of acquisition of the foreign language, stronger socialization in that language, higher self-perceived proficiency, use of the language outside the classroom, communication with a larger network of people, and knowledge of more languages (Dewaele et al., 2008).

As we have seen, emotions and related phenomena (such as flow) play an important role in positive psychology, which therefore has implications for understanding language learners' emotions. In the next few sections, we see that emotions are very social. As is evident in their names, social psychological theory, social constructivist theories, and social constructionist theories all emphasize the social nature of emotions. Existential psychotherapy also suggests the involvement of social relationships in an individual's emotions. I will now outline briefly each theory and its relevance for this discussion.

3   Emotion Theory in Social Psychology

Social psychologists Markus and Kitayama (1991) discussed the influence of culturally-based self-construals on emotional expression. They first described the differences in self-construals between people in collectivist cultures and those in individualist cultures. Collectivist cultures, such as Asian, Latin-American, African,

and some southern European cultures, stress harmony, interdependence, cooperation, long-term relationships, and group loyalty, in contrast with individualist cultures, which view the individual as unique, independent, special, self-reliant,
autonomous, and competitive, with many loosely connected, short relationships.
Markus and Kitayama (1991) contrasted emotional expression in collectivist and
individualist cultures. In collectivist cultures, emotional expression "may or may
not be related directly to the inner feelings [of a person]" because of the desire to
retain interpersonal harmony (Markus & Kitayama 1991, p. 236). Emotional
expression is often "a public instrumental action" (p. 236). Overt expression of
anger and of other intense emotions might threaten the interdependent self and is
typically avoided. In individualist cultures, emotional expression is expected to be a
literal portrayal of an independent person's feelings. For example, overt expression
of anger and grief are seen as acceptable expressions of the independent self. For
further information on the social psychological view of culture, self, and emotion,
see Kitayama, Markus, and Matsumoto (1995).

4   Emotion Theory in Social Constructivism

Social constructivists argue that knowledge and artifacts are socially constructed,
though the degree to which this happens is disputed even among themselves. Some
social constructivists, such as Vygotsky (1978), Palincsar (1998), Brown, Collins,
and Duguid (1989), and von Glasersfeld (1995), have been especially concerned
with the socially constructed way in which learning takes place. Von Glasersfeld
offered the most radical perspective, that is, that the process of constructing
knowledge depends strictly on the individual's subjective experience, not on any
objective or actual "reality".

4.1   Averill's Concept of Transitory Social Roles

Emotion theorist Averill (1980, 1982, 1985, 1986, 1996) took a position that was,
perhaps confusingly, called social constructivist by Dewaele (2006) and social
constructionist by Ratner (1989). Because Averill's work has been cited as social
constructivist in the language learning field, I will include his work in this section
on social constructivism. Averill criticized overly simplified views on emotion,
such as cognitive appraisals or patterns of arousal alone. In his view, emotions are
part of larger sociocultural systems that link culture and cognition and are therefore
socioculturally constructed. He argued that emotions can be analyzed socially,
psychologically, and biologically. Averill (1980) defined an emotion as "a transitory social role (a socially constituted syndrome) that includes an individual's
appraisal of the situation and that is interpreted as a passion rather than as an action"
(p. 312). These transitory social roles or syndromes are generated by social norms

and expectations, which are mentally represented by schemata, or cognitive structures. Although individuals actually choose the roles, they are not aware of this; they perhaps surprisingly interpret their own emotional responses not as active decisions but as passive responses to situations (Averill, 1982; see Johnson, 2014), responses which are shaped by what the culture determines as what, where, when, and how to feel and act.

In Averill's perspective, emotional syndromes or subsystems "are composed of such elements as physiological changes, expressive reactions, instrumental responses, and subjective feelings" (Dewaele, 2006, p. 122). Averill (1982) described syndromes as sets of covarying responses and as subsystems of behavior. A syndrome also includes beliefs about the nature of the stimulus. For instance, grief is a syndrome with many possible grief responses and many potential targets, and it is based partially on beliefs about what conditions should elicit genuine grief. For Averill, emotions echo "the thought of an epoch, the secret of a civilization. It follows that to understand the meaning of an emotion is to understand the relevant aspects of the sociocultural system of which the emotion is a part (subsystem)" (p. 24, as cited in Dewaele, 2006, p. 123).

Dewaele (2006, p. 123) stated that Averill's social constructivist position was "ideally suited" for his own sociolinguistic analyses of emotions of multilingual individuals. Dewaele (2004a) found that the perception of emotional force of swearwords was associated positively with self-rated language proficiency in multilinguals. These individuals generally preferred to swear in their first language, though they sometimes swore in their other languages, depending on the effects on the interlocutor (perlocutionary effects) and the competence of the interlocutor. Dewaele (2006) reported that multilingual study participants used their native language most frequently to communicate anger. However, he found that another language can indeed become the most frequent language of anger expression, depending on socialization in that language. Though not studying personality factors in the 2006 study, he mentioned that such factors might play a role. He had found in an earlier study that extraverts, compared with introverts, were more willing to express strong emotions in their nonnative language (Dewaele, 2004b).

4.2 Linguistic Approaches to Social Constructivism

Cognitive linguists Wierzbicka and Harkins (2001) also took a social constructivist stance, specifically arguing that emotions are socially constructed and that language is crucial in the development and expression of emotions. Though they accepted many neuroscientific advances in studying emotions, they cautioned that brain research on emotion was too generally applied and that such research did not consider people from different cultures and with different languages (see Dewaele, 2006). "[W]hatever the conditions that produce an emotion like anger, whether or not it is visibly expressed, and whatever physiological responses accompany it, it is only through language (if at all) that we can know that what is experienced *is* anger" (Wierzbicka & Harkins, 2001, pp. 2–3). Panayiotou (2006) likewise described emotions as socially constructed through language. She argued "that emotions that seem key in some cultures may be linguistically non-existent in others" (p. 183). The operative word is "linguistically", because Panayiotou depicted emotions as "language dependent", since "the raw of bodily experience of an emotion must be filtered through a cultural meaning making system (…), that is, language, before it can be defined as an emotion" (Panayiotou, 2006, p. 187). Languages "actively construct and reconstruct" emotions (Pavlenko, 2002, p. 209).

Certain emotions may have supposed equivalents in translation, but they are not adequate equivalents due to the contrasting salience in different cultures. For example, the emotion of guilt, that is, feeling criticized for what we have done or a transgression we have committed, and the emotion of shame, that is, feeling criticized for the person we have become (Wollheim, as cited in Panayiotou, 2006) have been differentially applied to various cultures, which have subsequently been called "guilt cultures" and "shame cultures". Panayiotou (2006, p. 188) maintained that "every language contains its own 'naïve picture' of the world, including its own emotionology (Stearns & Stearns, 1988)" and uses its particular emotion words. This shapes the way people in that culture experience emotions.[1] A bilingual person draws upon two "emotional universes" (Panayiotou, 2006, p. 204) that offer certain emotion terms, which are often incongruent, but these universes are intertwined by virtue of the fact that that the bilingual person experiences them.

5   Emotion Theory in Social Constructionism

Like social constructivists, social constructionists contend that knowledge and artifacts are socially constructed. However, following Berger and Luckmann (1967) and Gergen (1999, 2007), their emphasis is often on *what* is socially constructed. This would include the texts, activities, objects, beliefs, emotions, and moral systems that are produced by the group or society and that help shape how each person behaves in the group or society. There are many different social constructionist approaches, not just one position (Harré, 2002; Stam, 2001; Weber, 2012).

Social constructionists adopt a functional framework, suggesting that the transfer of judgments, beliefs, and cultural norms serves the purpose of sustaining cultural values (Armon-Jones, 1985, 1986). Kingston (2011) argued that a contextual approach should look to the cultural continuities of basic beliefs, evaluations, and behavior patterns that help to construct emotional experience, but it should also allow for some degree of personal interpretation of cultural rules.

---

[1]The Greek language has no word for emotion and does not discriminate between feelings and emotion (Panayiotou, 2006).

5.1 Strong and Weak Forms

Social constructionism has different forms. One strong form of social constructionism argues that emotions are of purely social origin, with no emotion existing
naturally outside of our ability to understand and describe it socially through language (see Hacking, 1999 for a critique of such a form of social constructionism).
Some social constructionists' emphasis on language and emotion is reminiscent of
the linguistic approach described earlier by Wierzbicka and Harkins (2001), social
constructivists discussed in the prior section.

A weak form of social constructionism acknowledges an underlying naturalist
impulse in certain situations (i.e., a desire to see emotions as natural rather than
purely social and existing outside of language) but still highlights the fact that the
power of social norms can significantly shape the experience of emotions. All social
constructionism shares the assumption that culture specifies ways to appraise, feel,
and act when experiencing or performing a certain emotion.

5.2 Role of Social Practices in Constructing Emotions

Social constructionists Harré (1986, 1995) and Harré and Finlay-Jones (1986) noted
that cultural aspects such as language and social practices are keenly influential in
the construction of emotions. People develop emotions based on direct or indirect
social experiences. For example, Harré and Finlay-Jones (1986) described the
emotion of *accidie*, which involved "boredom, dejection, and even disgust with
fulfilling one's religious duty" (p. 221) in the Middle Ages. At that time, *accidie*
was felt to be a sin. *Accidie* no longer exists as an emotion because of the shift of
cultural priorities and a different view of the moral order (Harré & Finlay-Jones,
1986).

For social constructionists the purpose of emotions is to support the norms and
values of society. Emotions regulate socially undesirable behavior and promote
attitudes that endorse certain political, aesthetic, social, religious, and moral practices. Envy at someone else's success and guilt over cheating are "both emotions
that have been prescribed by the individual's society so that the individual will take
the appropriate attitude towards success and cheating", stated Johnson (2014) in
explaining the social constructionist perspective of Armon-Jones (1986). If an
emotion violates the norms and values of the majority of the society, Armon-Jones
(1986) insisted that such an emotion is still socially learned, but from a social subset
or peer group whose norms and values the individual identifies with, rather than
from the society at large.

6 Emotion Theory in Existential Psychotherapy

The goal of existential psychotherapy is to help people "gain insight into the unavoidable paradoxes that life presents and to gain strength from that knowledge", rather than to provide "quick pragmatic solutions" (van Deurzen, 2012, p. xiii). Existential psychotherapy puts responsibility on the individual to be authentic and purposeful in life, and it strongly emphasizes the importance of social relationships. Emmy van Deurzen, a major authority in the field of existential psychotherapy, proposed an explanation of a large set of emotions, many of which are related to social interactions. From an existential viewpoint, we might consider that a person's emotions are affected by, and in turn affect, social interactions, as illustrated in Fig. 1.

In Fig. 1, exhilaration and happiness are at the high-tension apex of the "compass" or circle of emotion, while despondency, depression, and sadness are at the low-tension, release-based nadir. The emotions located in between occur in relation to our wanting something important (our value). In the upper right quadrant are pride, jealousy, and anger, which reflect perceived threats to value. These threats can

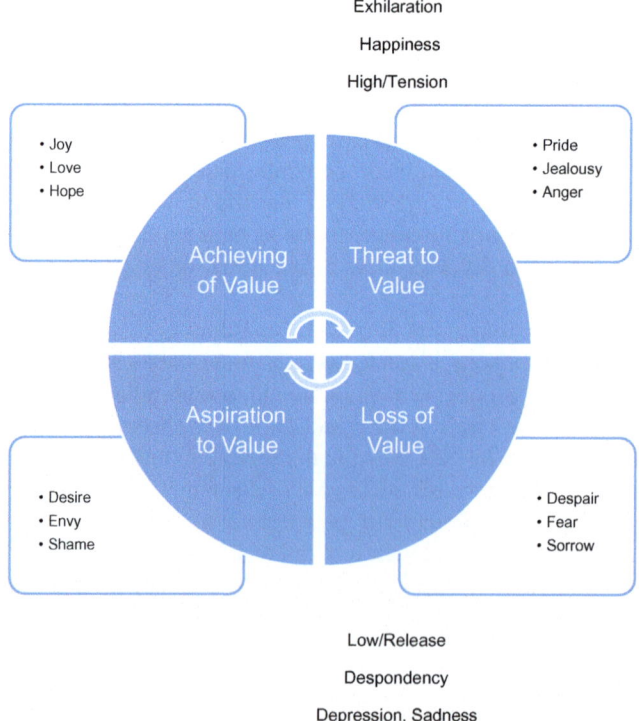

Fig. 1 The compass of emotion; adapted from Figs. 5.1 through 5.7 in van Deurzen (2012, pp. 151–155)

come from other people or situations. Pride occurs when we still feel control of what we value but are perhaps too eager to show it off, suspecting that it might be under threat. Jealousy arises when what we value is being threatened and we feel that it might be taken away. Anger emerges when what we value is deeply threatened and we are making a last-ditch effort to get it back or to keep on grasping it.

Despair, fear, and sorrow are emotions in the lower right quadrant, and they signify the loss of value. Despair occurs when we recognize we might have to give up what we value. Fear is an apprehension that the threat might steal what we value, possibly requiring us to let go. Sorrow arises when we realize that the threat has actually taken what we value, and we have no choice but to let go. At the bottom of the circle we experience general sadness and depression, a sense of being without energy.

The bottom left quadrant contains shame, envy, and desire, which together signify aspiring to what we value when we do not have it. Shame emerges because we feel we are unable to accomplish anything of value. Envy happens when we see what we value being gained by others; we feel we cannot be the same as they are, so we covet what they have. Desire occurs when we start reaching out once more toward what we value.

The upper left quadrant involves hope, love, and joy, which together signify the gaining of value once more (however, in language learning, attaining what the learner values, a personally acceptable degree of proficiency and self-confidence, might occur for the very first time, rather than "once more"). Hope springs forth when we have an inkling that we can actually gain what we value once again. Via love, we participate in committing to what we value and in working toward attaining it. Joy arises when we feel we are finally integrating with what we value. At the top of the circle we experience genuine exhilaration and happiness, reflecting a positive, high tension.

All of the emotions described by van Deurzen can apply to language learners, although the salience and frequency of the emotions will vary across learners and across time. For instance, learners might feel shame if perceiving themselves unable to accomplish anything valuable in learning. They might experience envy if someone else can communicate in the target language more effectively than they. They might experience hope and exhilaration if they believe they might someday be able to use the language effectively. They might experience joy if they attain what they value, which might be any or all of the following: a desired level of proficiency, self-efficacy and confidence to go with it, an ability to communicate easily in the target language and get to know aspects of the target culture intimately, an ability to forge friendships with people from the target culture, and so on.

Anxiety is not specifically shown in Fig. 1. van Deurzen (2012) indicated that anxiety is "a more general and basic experience" (p. 153). As noted earlier, van Deurzen described anxiety as being negatively expressed in anguish and positively expressed in excitement. She also stated: "the emotional cycle swings downwards from possession of something that is deeply valued, and considered essential, to its loss and eventual absence. The emotional cycle swings upwards from the sense of emptiness of existence through a lack of what is valued to an aspiration to obtain what is desired and to fulfillment in its ultimate possession" (van Deurzen, 2012, p. 153).

Figure 1 and its explanation imply that language learners who experience negative emotions, such as despair, fear, sorrow, shame, and envy, can hope to experience positive emotions, which are part of the same cycle. There is a "potential for transformation of destructive emotional experience to constructive emotional experience" (van Deurzen, p. 153). Van Deurzen cautioned that loss and gain are not the same as failure and success and that letting go is as important as building up. She disparaged positive psychology's tools, which she considered to be overly simplistic techniques and one-sided solutions. Nevertheless, I contend that some positive psychology strategies, including REBT and aspects of resilience and emotional intelligence, might help struggling language learners transform negative emotions to positive ones.

7 Implications for Language Learners

This paper has presented a number of theories of emotion drawn from positive psychology, social psychology, social constructivism, social constructionism, and existential psychotherapy. The discussion so far leads to the following implications:

1. Managing emotions is a critical part of emotional intelligence (Goleman, 2005). Positive psychology offers readily teachable techniques for managing emotions (Seligman, 2011), and research on language learning strategies (Oxford, 1990, 2011b) highlights affective strategies for doing the same. These are very important and readily sharable techniques and strategies. In teaching them, language teachers can help learners develop their emotion management capabilities.
2. Resilience involves both personal factors, including emotions and problem-solving skills, and social factors, such as a supportive environment (Truebridge, 2014). Teachers and learners can work together to strengthen the resilience of all involved in the language learning process.
3. Expressing emotions might be useful in some settings and not in others. Cultural individualism and collectivism influence whether it is wise to express an emotion publicly (Markus & Kitayama, 1991). Teachers can help learners identify their emotions and decide whether and how to express them in different settings.
4. Cultural and linguistic differences make it difficult to understand all the subtleties of emotional communication in another culture and language (Dewaele, 2004a, b, 2006), and, indeed, some emotions and emotion words do not have translations in some languages. Teachers and native informants can help learners understand the complexities of emotion across cultures.

5. Averill (1980) asserted that emotions are transitory social roles that language learners—and all other individuals—actively accept, though they do not usually understand that they are literally taking on roles. If teachers help learners understand that both positive and negative emotions are transitory social roles, learners might feel motivated to take on positive ones when possible and might feel relieved to know that any negative emotions are only transitory.

6. Moreover, if emotions are socially and linguistically created, as argued by many social constructivists and social constructionists, teachers might enable learners to develop social and linguistic techniques for dealing with negative emotions and enhancing positive emotions.

7. According to van Deurzen (2012), existential psychotherapy suggests that anxiety can have positive or negative expression. Existential psychotherapy also implies that language learners who experience negative or destructive emotions, such as despair, fear, sorrow, shame, and envy, can expect or hope to experience positive or constructive emotions at some point in the cycle. Thus, we might say that no learner is doomed.

Knowing that emotions can be managed, controlled, shaped, and transformed makes the learner less of a purely passive recipient and more of an agent in the emotion game. Recent research (e.g., Kao & Oxford, 2014; Ma & Oxford, 2014; Oxford & Cuéllar, 2014; Oxford et al., 2014) reveals that some successful language learners already grasp this important truth.

References

Armon-Jones, C. (1985). Prescription, explication and the social construction of emotion. *Journal for the Theory of Social Behaviour, 15,* 1–22.

Armon-Jones, C. (1986). The social functions of emotion. In R. Harré (Ed.), *The social construction of emotions* (pp. 57–82). Oxford: Blackwell.

Averill, J. (1982). *Anger and aggression: An essay on emotion.* New York: Springer.

Averill, J. (1985). The social construction of emotion with special reference to love. In K. Gergen & K. Davis (Eds.), *The social construction of the person* (pp. 173–195). New York: Springer.

Averill, J. (1996). Intellectual emotions. In R. Harré & G. Parrott (Eds.), *The emotions: Social, cultural, and biological dimensions* (pp. 24–39). London: Sage.

Averill, J. R. (1980). A constructivist view of emotion. In R. Plutchik & H. Kellerman (Eds.), *Emotion: Theory, research, and experience* (pp. 305–339). New York: Academic Press.

Averill, J. R. (1986). The acquisition of emotions during adulthood. In R. Harré (Ed.), *The social construction of emotions* (pp. 98–118). Oxford: Blackwell.

Berger, P. L., & Luckmann, T. (1967). *The social construction of reality: A treatise in the sociology of knowledge.* New York: Anchor.

Benard, B. (1991). *Fostering resiliency in kids: Protective factors in the family, school, and community.* San Francisco: Western Regional Center for Drug Free Schools and Communities, Far West Laboratory.

Brown, J. S., Collins, A., & Duguid, P. (1989). Situated cognition and the culture of learning. *Educational Researcher, 18,* 32–42.

Cohn, M. A., & Fredrickson, B. L. (2010). In search of durable positive psychology interventions: Predictors and consequences of long-term positive behavior change. *Journal of Positive Psychology, 5,* 355–366.

Csikszentmihályi, M. (1998). *Finding flow: The psychology of engagement with everyday life.* New York: Basic.

Csíkszentmihályi, M. (2008). *Flow: The psychology of optimal experience* (2nd ed.). New York: Harper.

Csikszentmihályi, M. (2013). *Creativity: Flow and the psychology of discovery and invention.* New York: Harper Collins.

Csíkszentmihályi, I. S., & Csíkszentmihályi, M. (Eds.). (2006). *A life worth living: Contributions to positive psychology.* New York: Oxford University Press.

Dewaele, J.-M. (2004a). The emotional force of swearwords and taboo words in the speech of multilinguals. *Journal of Multilingual and Multicultural Development, 25,* 204–222.

Dewaele, J.-M. (2004b). Perceived language dominance and language preference for emotional speech: The implications of attrition research. In M. S. Schmid, B. Köpke, M. Kejser, & L. Weilemar (Eds.), *First language attrition: Interdisciplinary perspectives on methodological issues* (pp. 81–104). Amsterdam: John Benjamins.

Dewaele, J.-M. (2005). Sociodemographic, psychological, and politico-cultural correlates in Flemish students' attitudes toward French and English. *Journal of Multilingual and Multicultural Development, 26,* 118–137.

Dewaele, J.-M. (2006). Expressing anger in multiple languages. In A. Pavlenko (Ed.), *Bilingual minds: Emotional experience, expression, and representation* (pp. 118–151). Clevedon: Multilingual Matters.

Dewaele, J.-M. (2013). Emotions and language learning. In M. Byram & A. Hu (Eds.), *Routledge encyclopedia of language teaching and learning* (2nd ed., pp. 217–220). London: Routledge.

Dewaele, J.-M., & MacIntyre, P. (2014). Two faces of Janus? Anxiety and enjoyment in the foreign language classroom. *Studies in Second Language Learning and Teaching, 4,* 237–274.

Dewaele, J.-M., Petrides, K. V., & Furnham, A. (2008). The effects of trait emotional intelligence and sociobiographical variables on communicative anxiety and foreign language anxiety among adult multilinguals: A review and empirical investigation. *Language Learning, 58,* 911–960.

Dewaele, J.-M., & Thirtle, H. (2009). Why do some young learners drop foreign languages? A focus on learner-internal variables. *International Journal of Bilingual Education and Bilingualism, 12,* 635–649.

Dörnyei, Z. (2009). *The psychology of second language acquisition.* Oxford: Oxford University Press.

Ellis, A. (2003). Early theories and practices of rational emotive behavior theory and how they have been augmented and revised during the last three decades. *Journal of Rational-Emotive & Cognitive-Behavior Therapy, 21,* 219–243.

Frederickson, B. L. (2001). The role of positive emotions in positive psychology: The broaden-and-build theory of positive emotions. *American Psychologist, 56,* 218–226.

Frederickson, B. L. (2003). The value of positive emotions: The emerging science of positive psychology looks into why it's good to feel good. *American Scientist, 91,* 330–335.

Frederickson, B. L. (2004). The broaden-and-build theory of positive emotions. *Philosophical Transactions of the Royal Society of London (Biological Sciences), 359,* 1367–1377.

Frederickson, B. L., & Branigan, C. (2005). Positive emotions broaden the scope of attention and thought-action repertoires. *Cognition and Emotion, 19,* 313–332.

Frederickson, B. L., & Joiner, T. (2002). Positive emotions trigger upward spirals toward emotional well-being. *Psychological Science, 13,* 172–175.

Frederickson, B. L., & Levenson, R. W. (1998). Positive emotions speed recovery from the cardiovascular sequelae of negative emotions. *Cognition and Emotion, 12,* 191–220.

Frederickson, B. L., Tugade, M. M., Waugh, C. E., & Larkin, G. (2003). What good are positive emotions in crises? A prospective study of resilience and emotions following the terrorist attacks on the United States on September 11, 2001. *Journal of Personality and Social Psychology, 84,* 365–376.

Gardner, R., Tremblay, P., & Masgoret, A. (1997). Towards a full model of second language learning: An empirical investigation. *Modern Language Journal, 81,* 344–362.

Gergen, K. J. (1999). *An invitation to social constructionism*. London: Sage.

Gergen, K. J. (2007). *Relational being*. New York: Oxford University Press.

Goleman, D. (2005). *Emotional intelligence: Why it can matter more than IQ* (2nd ed.). New York: Bantam.

Guoira, A. Z. (1983). Introduction: An epistemology for the language sciences. *Language Learning, 33*, 6–11.

Hacking, I. (1999). *Social construction of what?*. Cambridge: Harvard University Press.

Harré, R. (1986). An outline of the social constructionist viewpoint. In R. Harré (Ed.), *The social construction of emotions* (pp. 2–14). Oxford: Blackwell.

Harré, R. (1995). Emotion and memory: The second cognitive revolution. In A. P. Griffiths (Ed.), *Philosophy, psychology, and psychiatry* (pp. 25–40). New York: Cambridge University Press.

Harré, R. (2002). Public sources of the personal mind: Social constructionism in context. *Theory and Psychology, 12*, 611–623.

Harré, R., & Finlay-Jones, R. (1986). Emotion talk across times. In R. Harré (Ed.), *The social construction of emotions* (pp. 220–233). Oxford: Blackwell.

Hoffman, E. (1990). *Lost in translation*. Harmondsworth: Penguin.

Horwitz, E. (2001). Language anxiety and achievement. *Annual Review of Applied Linguistics, 21*, 112–126.

Horwitz, E. (2007). *Words fail me: Foreign language anxiety crippling for some students. E. Horwitz interviewed by K. Randall. University of Texas at Austin feature story*. Retrieved from http://www.utexas.edu/features/2007/language.

Horwitz, E., & Young, D. J. (Eds.). (1991). *Language anxiety: From theory and research to classroom implications*. Englewood Cliffs, NJ: Prentice Hall.

Johnson, G. (2014). Theories of emotion. In *The Internet encyclopedia of philosophy*. Retrieved from http://www.iep.utm.edu/emotion/#H4.

Kao, T.-A., & Oxford, R. L. (2014). Learning language through music: A strategy for building inspiration and motivation. *System, 43*, 114–120.

Kingston, R. (2011). *Public passion: Rethinking the grounds for political justice*. Montreal: McGill-Queen's.

Kitayama, S., Markus, H., & Matsumoto, H. (1995). Culture, self, and emotion: A cultural perspective to "self-conscious" emotions. In J. Tangney & K. Fischer (Eds.), *Self-conscious emotions: The psychology of shame, guilt, embarrassment, and pride* (pp. 274–301). New York: Guilford.

Le Doux, J. (1998). *The emotional brain: The mysterious underpinnings of emotional life*. New York: Simon & Schuster.

Lewis, M. (2005). Bridging emotion theory and neurobiology through dynamic systems modeling. *Behavior and Brain Science, 28*, 169–245.

Lewis, M., Haviland-Jones, J. M., & Barrett, L. F. (2008). *Handbook of emotions* (3rd ed.). New York: Guilford.

Luthar, S., Cicchetti, D., & Becker, B. (2000). The construct of resilience: A critical evaluation and guidelines for future research. *Child Development, 71*, 543–562.

Luthar, S., Sawyer, J. A., & Brown, P. J. (2006). Conceptual issues in studies of resilience: Past, present, and future research. In B. M. Lester, A. S. Masten, & B. McEwen (Eds.), *Annals of the New York Academy of Sciences* (Vol. 1094, pp. 105–115)., Resilience in children Malden, MA: Blackwell.

Ma, R., & Oxford, R. L. (2014). A diary study focusing on listening and speaking: The evolving interaction of learning styles and learning strategies in a motivated, advanced ESL learner. *System, 43*, 101–113.

MacIntyre, P. D. (2002a). Motivation, anxiety, and emotion in second language acquisition. In P. Robinson (Ed.), *Individual differences and instructed language learning* (pp. 45–68). Amsterdam: John Benjamins.

MacIntyre, P. D. (2002b). Willingness to communicate, anxiety, perceived competence, and motivation among junior high school French immersion students. *Language Learning, 52*, 537–564.

Marcos-Llinas, M., & Juan Garau, M. (2009). Effects of language anxiety on three proficiency-level courses of Spanish as a foreign language. *Foreign Language Annals, 42,* 94–111.

Markus, H. R., & Kitayama, S. (1991). Culture and the self: Implications for cognition, emotion, and motivation. *Psychological Review, 98,* 224–253.

Maslow, A. H. (1970). *Motivation and personality* (Rev. ed.). New York: Harper & Row.

Maslow, A. H. (1971). *The farther reaches of human nature.* New York: Penguin Compass.

Masten, A. S., & Obradovic, J. (2006). Competence and resilience in development. In B. M. Lester, A. S. Masten, & B. McEwen (Eds.), *Annals of the New York Academy of Sciences* (Vol. 1094, pp. 1–12)., Resilience in children Malden, MA: Blackwell.

Mercer, S. (2011). The self as a complex dynamic system. *Studies in Second Language Learning and Teaching, 1,* 57–82.

Nakamura, J., & Csíkszentmihályi, M. (2005). The concept of flow. In C. R. Snyder & S. Lopez (Eds.), *Handbook of positive psychology* (pp. 89–105). Oxford: Oxford University Press.

Oxford, R. L. (1990). *Language learning strategies: What every teacher should know.* Boston: Heinle.

Oxford, R. L. (1996). When emotion meets (meta)cognition in language learning histories. *International Journal of Educational Research, 23*(7), 581–594.

Oxford, R. L. (2011a). Meaning-making, border crossings, complexity, and new interpretive techniques: Expanding our understanding of learner narratives. *Zeitschrift für Fremdsprachenforschung (Journal of Foreign Language Research), 22,* 221–241.

Oxford, R. L. (2011b). *Teaching and researching language learning strategies.* Harlow: Pearson Longman.

Oxford, R. L. (2013). Understanding language learner narratives. In J. Arnold & T. Murphey (Eds.), *Meaningful action: Earl Stevick's influence on language teaching* (pp. 95–110). Cambridge: Cambridge University Press.

Oxford, R. L. (2014). What we can learn about strategies, language learning, and life from two extreme cases. *Studies in Second Language Learning and Teaching, 4,* 593–615.

Oxford, R. L. (2015). How language learners can improve their emotional functioning: Important psychological and psychospiritual theories. *Applied Language Learning, 25,* 1–15.

Oxford, R. L., & Cuéllar, L. (2014). Positive psychology in cross-cultural narratives: Mexican students discover themselves while learning Chinese. *Studies in Second Language Learning and Teaching, 2,* 173–204.

Oxford, R. L., Ehrman, M. E., & Lavine, R. Z. (1991). Style wars: Teacher-student style conflicts in the language classroom. In S. S. Magnan (Ed.), *Challenges for the 1990s for college language programs* (pp. 1–25). Boston: Heinle/Thomson Learning.

Oxford, R. L., Lavine, R. Z., Felkins, G., Hollaway, M. E., & Saleh, A. (1996). Telling their stories: Language students use diaries and recollection. In R. L. Oxford (Ed.), *Language learning strategies around the world: Cross-cultural perspectives* (pp. 19–34). Honolulu: University of Hawaii, Second Language Teaching and Curriculum Center.

Oxford, R. L., Massey, K. R., & Anand, S. (2005). Transforming teacher-student style relationships: Toward a more welcoming and diverse classroom discourse. In C. Holten & J. Frodesen (Eds.), *The power of discourse in language learning and teaching* (pp. 249–266). Boston: Heinle & Heinle.

Oxford, R. L., Meng, Y., Zhou, Y., Sung, J., & Jain, R. (2007). Uses of adversity: Moving beyond language learning crises. In A. Barfield & S. Brown (Eds.), *Reconstructing autonomy in language education: Inquiry and innovation* (pp. 131–142). London: Palgrave Macmillan.

Oxford, R. L., Pacheco Acuña, G., Solís Hernández, M., & Smith, A. L. (2014, June). *Positive psychology in action: Social and psychological themes reflected in first-person learner histories of bilingual adults.* Paper presented at the International Conference on Language and Social Psychology, Honolulu, Hawai'I, USA.

Oxford, R. L., Tomlinson, S., Barcelos, A., Harrington, C., Lavine, R., Saleh, A., & Longhini, A. (1998). Clashing metaphors about classroom teachers: Toward a systematic typology for the language teaching field. *System: An International Journal of Educational Technology and Applied Linguistics, 26*(1), 3–51.

Palinscar, A. S. (1998). Social constructivist perspective on teaching and learning. *Annual Review of Psychology, 49,* 345–375.

Panayiotou, A. (2006). Translating guilt: An endeavor of shame in the Mediterranean? In A. Pavlenko (Ed.), *Bilingual minds: Emotional experience, expression, and representation* (pp. 183–208). Clevedon: Multilingual Matters.

Pavlenko, A. (2002). Emotions and the body in Russian and English. *Pragmatics & Cognition, 10,* 207–241.

Pavlenko, A. (2006). Bilingual selves. In A. Pavlenko (Ed.), *Bilingual minds: Emotional experience, expression, and representation* (pp. 1–33). Clevedon: Multilingual Matters.

Pavlenko, A., & Lantolf, J. P. (2000). Second language learning as participation and the (re)construction of selves. In J. P. Lantolf (Ed.), *Sociocultural theory and second language learning* (pp. 155–177). New York: Oxford University Press.

Peterson, C. (2006). *A primer in positive psychology.* New York: Oxford University Press.

Peterson, C., Seligman, M. E. P., & Vaillant, G. E. (1988). Pessimistic explanatory style is a risk factor for physical illness: A thirty-five-year longitudinal study. *Journal of Personality and Social Psychology, 55,* 23–27.

Piaget, J. (1981). *Intelligence and affectivity: Their relationship during child development.* Palo Alto: Annual Reviews.

Piller, I., & Takahashi, K. (2006). A passion for English: Desire and the language market. In A. Pavlenko (Ed.), *Bilingual minds: Emotional experience, expression and representation* (pp. 59–83). Clevedon: Multilingual Matters.

Ratner, C. (1989). A social constructionist critique of naturalistic theories of emotion. *Journal of Mind and Behavior, 10,* 211–230.

Rodriguez, R. (1983/2004). *Hunger of memory* (2nd ed.). New York: Dial/Random House.

Seligman, M. (2006). *Learned optimism: How to change your mind and your life.* New York: Vintage.

Seligman, M. (2011). *Flourish: A visionary new understanding of happiness and well-being.* New York: Atria/Simon & Schuster.

Stam, H. J. (2001). Introduction: Social construction and its critiques. *Theory and Psychology, 11,* 291–296.

Stearns, C. Z., & Stearns, P. N. (Eds.). (1988). *Emotion and social change: Toward a new psychohistory.* New York: Holmes & Meier.

Truebridge, S. (2014). *Resilience begins with beliefs: Building on student strengths for success in school.* New York: Teachers College Press.

van Deurzen, E. (2012). *Existential counselling and psychotherapy in practice* (3rd ed.). London: Sage.

von Glasersfeld, E. (1995). *Radical constructivism: A way of knowing and learning.* London: Routledge Falmer.

Vygotsky, L. (1978). *Mind in society.* Cambridge: Harvard University Press.

Waugh, C. E., Tugade, M. M., & Fredrickson, B. L. (2008). Psychophysiology of stress and resilience. In B. Lukey & V. Tepe (Eds.), *Biobehavioral resilience to stress* (pp. 117–138). Boca Raton, FL: CRC Press.

Weber, H. (2012). What is a social in a social constructionist view on emotion? *Emotion Review, 4* (3), 234–235.

Werner, E., & Smith, R. (1992). *Overcoming the odds: High-risk children from birth to adulthood.* Ithaca, NY: Cornell University Press.

Wierzbicka, A., & Harkins, J. (2001). Introduction. In J. Harkins & A. Wierzbicka (Eds.), *Emotions in cross-linguistic perspective* (pp. 1–34). Berlin: Mouton de Gruyter.

Author Biography

Rebecca L. Oxford, Ph.D. received a Lifetime Achievement Award for "changing the way the world teaches languages" through learning strategy research. As a language teacher educator and psychologist, Dr. Oxford published 14 books, 260 chapters and articles, three book series, and nine journal special issues (including one co-edited with dr. Mirosław Pawlak). She made presentations in 43 countries. She holds two degrees in languages and two in educational psychology. At the University of Alabama, she led language teacher education programs, taught languages, was Associate Dean, and received faculty honors. At the University of Maryland, she directed a language teacher education program and received key honors, including the Distinguished Scholar-Teacher Award. She served as a Fulbright Fellow (Costa Rica); U.S. State Department Specialist (Cambodia, Baltic States, and Russia); Director, Macedonia-U.S. Language Teacher Exchange; and long-term academic expert for two universities in China.

Speech and Its Silent Partner: Gesture in Communication and Language Learning

Hanna Komorowska

Abstract Speaking is inherently connected with silence and gesture. The chapter looks into the evolutionary processes operating during the emergence of language in order to identify types of mutual relationships between gesture and speech with special emphasis on approaches to gesture in the history of research on non-verbal and verbal communication as well as on the implications of gestural hypotheses for present-day views on interaction. Types of gestures as well as their role in communicating affiliation or disaffiliation and in fulfilling persuasive functions are also analyzed with a view to resolving the dilemma of whether it is justified to explicitly teach non-verbal behaviour in the language classroom. Implications for designing tasks aiming to encourage non-verbal signals and raise learners' awareness of the way they engage in interactive activities are sought.

Keywords Language teaching · Language learning · Speaking · Gesture · Gestural hypothesis · Communication · FL classroom

1 Introduction

Non-verbal behavior, however important in human communication, has not received sufficient attention in applied linguistics and second language teaching. Although in the last decades interesting research has been conducted on gesture and eye-contact (Argyle, 1988; Argyle & Cook, 1976; Burgoon, Guerrero, & Floyd, 2016; Efron, 1941/1972; Feldman & Rimé, 1991; Kendon, 2004; McNeill, 2000; Mehrabian, 1972), recently its focus has been mostly on neurolinguistic and psycholinguistic aspects with less frequent excursions into the realm of second language acquisition and interaction analysis (Gullberg, 2008; McCafferty & Stam, 2008; Sidnell & Stivers, 2014; Sueyoshi & Hardison, 2005). Foreign language teaching and learning contexts have attracted the attention of relatively more

H. Komorowska (✉)
SWPS University of Social Sciences and Humanities, Warsaw, Poland
e-mail: hannakomo@data.pl

© Springer International Publishing AG 2018
M. Pawlak and A. Mystkowska-Wiertelak (eds.), *Challenges of Second and Foreign Language Education in a Globalized World*, Second Language Learning and Teaching, DOI 10.1007/978-3-319-66975-5_5

researchers interested in the function of silence and turn-taking in the classroom (Jaworski & Sachdev, 2004; King, 2013), while the first attempts at comprehensive presentations of gesture, posture, facial expression, eye behavior and touch have occurred as recently as the current year (Gregersen & MacIntyre, 2017). Language teachers held accountable for the development of their students' speaking skills now face a dilemma whether to ignore non-verbal behaviour with gesture as its most conspicuous component or to raise awareness of its significance in individual contacts, perhaps even explicitly teaching it. To clarify this issue it seems helpful to reflect on the nature of gesture, and its role in the development of cooperative communication as well as to analyze the function it plays in expressing affiliation and disaffiliation.

2 Gesture: What Is It and How Does It Develop During a Lifetime?

Gesture is by no means an obvious concept and its diverse definitions are extremely controversial. Although most researchers tend to agree on the approach defining gesture as bodily movement expressing emotion or thought, some narrow the definition down to hand movements (McNeill, 2012), while others extend its scope to face and eye (Kendon, 2004). Broad definitions reach out to articulatory movements, considering speech "a mouth gesture", an important part of the communicative activity, its gestural nature evidenced by human skills of lip-reading (Hewes, 1973; Liberman & Mattingly, 2000).

In the narrower definitions of gesture its types can be presented on a continuum ranging from gesticulation through hand movements replacing individual words, language slotted gestures replacing grammatical slots, to pantomime and sign languages. Gesticulation includes beats, iconic, metaphoric and deictic gestures (McNeill, 2012). Its power was also used by Kasimir Malevitch (1879–1935) in his naturalistic *Self-portrait* (1933), with a hand gesture demonstrating empty space in the shape of his *Black square* (1915), an example of abstract artwork forbidden by communist authorities (Néret, 2003).

Controversy also arises over the role of intentionality in human communication. Some researchers define gestures as movements produced intentionally, addressed to the interactant, devoid of mechanical consequences, aiming at the elicitation of a response and persistent if the response does not come. They view gestures as field-independent, that is, ready to be used to achieve a variety of aims, but also implying audience-checking and response-waiting. Gestures carrying one, shared intentional meaning are often referred to as emblems (Tomasello, 2008; Żywiczyński & Wacewicz, 2015). Other approaches include unintentional movements in the definition of gestures. For example, Paul Ekman in a series of his famous research projects on non-verbal behavior talks about unintentional, subconsciously produced facial gestures also called micro-expressions (Ekman, 2001).

The inclusion of unintentional movements has been adopted in research on child cognitive and linguistic development. Smiling, a type of body movement also qualified as a face gesture, appears very early in an individual's development and later undergoes differentiation into qualifier smiles reducing the power of criticism, compliance smiles signaling acceptance, coordination smiles accompanying collaborative tasks and listener smiles functioning as attention signals (Ekman, 2001; Foster, 2013). Rhythmical hand movements accompany cooing and babbling. Combinations of words and gestures appear together from the beginning of an infant's speech, although certain concepts such as, for example, those related to quantity, are represented in gestures earlier than they are in speech (Goldin-Meadow, 2003). For that reason hand gestures received most of the researchers' attention.

The development of gestural activity depends on personality characteristics—for example, extroverts tend to use more gestures than introverts—and also on the individual conversational style, but it is also strongly influenced by the culture of the community in which the individual is raised (Efron, 1941/1972; Komorowska, 2016; Monaghan, Goodman, & Robinson, 2012). Later in life hand movements can reach exceptional speed and precision of which the achievements of famous surgeons operating with no technological support can serve as convincing examples. Dominique Jean Larrey (1766–1842), as a Surgeon-in-Chief during the Napoleonic campaigns was the organizer of *ambulances volantes*, flying ambulances that helped to quickly transport wounded soldiers from the battlefield, gained fame not only by effective signaling the presence of medical aids, but also for his surgical skills, performing 200 indispensable amputations within 24 h after the Battle of Borodino. His skills went hand in hand with his morality as he operated on patients in the order of medical emergency, irrespective of their nationality or rank, and tended to soldiers from both sides of the military conflict. His noble attitude was rewarded after he fell into Prussian captivity during the Battle of Waterloo; thanks to his role in saving the son of the Field Marshal Gebhard von Blücher, the Prussian leader stopped his execution (Richardson, 2000).

3 The Role of Gesture in the Origins of Speech and Cooperative Communication

To understand the role gesture plays in human communication it is useful to take a mental trip to the origins of language. In the process of evolution speech developed on the basis of a number of preadaptations (Tallerman, 2005). The most important was the change from quadrupedal to bipedal movement. As quadrupedal movement exposes the body to shock resulting from harsh contact with the ground, huge amounts of air are needed to cushion it. Bipedalism results in the loss of big air sacs, descent of the laryngeal cavity and the formation of a double resonator system, a special vocal tract anatomy with a two-tube configuration and right angle bend

(McMahon & McMahon, 2013). Changes in the voice channel allow more precision in discriminating vowels at the cost of resonance, but also conscious control over phonation enabled by new nervous connections between vocal folds and neocortex. Better breath control, considerably increased auditory acuity and highly developed skills of imitation soon made possible the momentous step from animal to human communication (Dor, Knight, & Lewis, 2014; Fitch, 2000; Żywiczyński & Wacewicz, 2015).

The move from quadrupedalism to bipedalism gave writers and philosophers food for thought. Literary intuitions connected with verticality are worth recalling as they tend to have a great explanatory power and, what is more, last much longer than today's increasingly ephemeral academic publications. According to Georges Bataille, one of the intellectuals on the list of surrealists excluded by André Breton, it is the big toe that should be granted the status of the most human and thus most noble of all body parts. In opposition to the leader of the surrealist movement, who looked for the beginnings of humanity in the unconscious, Bataille argues that anatomy gave rise to human achievements. In *Le Gros Orteil*, his brilliant essay of 1929, which Roland Barthes in his text written 44 years later labelled referential, reverential, parodic and subversive, Bataille points out (Bataille & Barthes, 2006) that due to the toe's change from an abducted to adducted position and from its flexibility needed to swing on vines to the rigidity indispensable for erect posture, the stable toe, drawn inwards, helped to form the main base on which human beings could stand and thus allowed for their verticality. His poetic image of humans with their heads raised to heavens and their feet in the mud explained the human potential for participating in both spheres: that of *sacrum* and that of *profanum*. Batailles' essay, beautifully illustrated by Jacques-André Boiffard, Man Ray's assistant photographer, continues to inspire contemporary researchers interested in cultural anthropology and art (Ades & Baker, 2006; Barthes, 1980; Beaumont, 2015; Kraus, 1985).

Whichever approach to the origins of language we take, the one based on scientific hypotheses or the one based on literary intuitions, it is the evolution of the human body that explains the transfer of predispositions from generation to generation. The role our genetic endowment plays in the process is demonstrated with examples of changes in the FOXP2 gene causing specific language impairment, such as genetic Developmental Verbal Dyspraxia (DVD), resulting in problems with generalisations of grammar rules related to past tenses and plurals (Gopnik, 1990) or the Williams syndrome, characterized by difficulties with reading and writing, which, however, paradoxically coexist with fluent, poetic oral production (Gorzelańczyk, 2003).

A question often asked in relation to the origins of language is: What contributed to speech development: vocal organs or brain? Recent research on chimps and baboons demonstrates that production of vowels and consonants lies technically within their bodily possibilities (Boë, Berthommier, Legou, Captier, Kemp, & Sawallis, 2017). Yet they do not speak; therefore, it is believed that speech must depend on cognitive functions which neither in Old World monkeys nor in great apes have developed well enough to enable the development of verbal communication. Humans on the other hand can speak thanks to the development of cognitive and executive functions helped by their gestural activity (Goldin-Meadow, 2003; Kita, 2000). This skill would not be possible without certain cognitive preadaptations such as the Encephalization Quotient (EQ), that is, the ratio of actual brain to brain size expected on the basis of weight and the speed of physiological processes. EQ is 7.4–7.8 in humans, but only 4.14 in dolphins, 1.2 in dogs, and 1 in cats (Donald, 2001; Roth & Dicke, 2005). This is not the only preadaptation that allowed humans to develop speech. An equally important one is mimesis, intentional representations allowing parsing and coding motor sequences. Mimetic control over body movements makes autocuing possible, thus triggering the development of verbal and non-verbal communication (Donald, 2001).

The origins of speech do not fully explain another step: the birth of cooperative communication. Yet it is cooperation that can tell us more about the role of gesture and speech in the development of human interaction. Its beginnings are traced back to communicating danger and signaling the proximity of food. Like speech we owe cooperative communication to bipedalism which made it difficult to engage in various activities while holding a child and thus paved the way for alloparenting. Cooperative breeding helped adult individuals to cope with problems caused by the extended period of dependency of the child and the weight of the human infant (Hrdy, 2009). Alloparenting promoted prosociality as parents tended to work in groups. This in turn led to shared intentionality (Tomasello, 2008; Tomasello, Hare, Lehmann, & Call, 2012) and later to cooperative communication based on multi-modality in the use of eye-contact, musical vocalisations and gesture (Corballis, 2002). The role of gesture is especially interesting here, as bipedalism "would have left the hands free for communicative gesturing" (McMahon & McMahon, 2013, p. 115). Distance, making vocal communication difficult, also encourages the multimodal use of voice and gesture.

It should be noted that there are certain specific features of human cooperation. Non-humans engage in dyadic cooperativeness, for example, addressing signals directly to another individual. Humans, however, engage in triadic cooperativeness: infants demonstrate motivation to spontaneously point to objects in order to achieve joint attention (Tomasello, 2008, 2009). Predispositions for cooperative commu-nication can be found in human anatomy. Cooperative eye hypothesis (Kobayashi & Koshima, 2001) explains that thanks to *sclera*, the white of the eye, it is possible to assess in which direction our conversational partner is looking. Lacking *sclera*, great apes rely on head direction only, while human infants use eye direction for communicative purposes (Brooks & Meltzoff, 2005; Tomasello, Hare, Lehmann, & Call, 2007). Because vocal communication does not engage hands, it is known to be more effective in the course of cooperative activity in the darkness and, what is more, it makes it possible to communicate "displaced" meanings. This is extremely important for the safety of interactants in the evolutionary process, yet the secrecy of gesture is much greater than the secrecy of vocal communication and proves to be life-saving in dangerous circumstances (Żywiczyński & Wacewicz, 2015). Cooperation is consolidated by several phenomena: relatedness resulting in the work in kin groups, reciprocity based on mutual gratifications, retribution as its negative mirror image and reputation as a fundament of trust and a source of social capital. To promote reciprocity and reputation in a group, the development of episodic memory was needed. This type of memory enabled abstract thinking and allowed for the liberation from the *here and now* (Deacon, 2004; Hurford, 2007) making mental time travel possible (Corballis, 2002). Due to these gains, humanity is believed to have developed the theory of mind.

4   The Gestural Primacy Hypothesis

An interesting controversy has been going on over the nature and origins of speech and especially over the role of gesture in this process. In the history of human interest in gesture and speech, the possibility that language emerged from gestures rather than vocalisation was first signaled by three 18th century authors: Bernard de Mandeville (1670–1733) in *The fable of the bees* (Bristow, 2011), Ètienne Bonnot de Condillac (1715–1780), his follower and Diderot's friend, in *Essai sur l'origine des connaissances* (Falkenstein, 2010) and also by another even more famous of Diderot's friends, Jean-Jacques Rousseau (1712–1778) in *L'Essai sur l'origine des langues* (Bertrand, 2012). They all maintained that in the phases of human communication the coexistence of two categories of signals developed. Rousseau believed that the later growth of the status of the vocal channel in human communication, leading to the increasing dominance of speech over gesture, was a result of the increasing density of population.

Soon Helvétius (1715–1771) joined this group of authors in suggesting the gestural origin of speech (Bristow, 2011), but the strongest influence in promoting language's gestural origins was exerted by Giambattista Vico (1668–1744), who to this day holds a prominent place in the history of philosophy and art. In *Scienza Nuova* (1744/1968) he claimed that language was preceded by gesture and that communication developed through three stages: in the era of gods iconic gestures were used in rituals, in the era of heroes communication moved to the language of metaphor and poetry, while in the era of humans it became conventionalized and started using arbitrary signals. As often happens, those early intuitions were later reflected in research on child development. Fahey (2009), for instance, identifies the following three stages in child development: a stage based on perception, a stage based on identification with persons and roles, as well as a stage based on abstraction.

A century after Vico, reflection on the beginnings of language was stopped in 1866 by the statutory regulation of the Linguistic Society of Paris, soon followed by a similar decision of the Philological Society of London, both taken on the grounds of the unscientific character of writings on the subject. These bans, however, did not stop reflection on the origins of speech for long. Several years later a new hypothesis was set forth, this time stressing the role of sound. Darwin in his *On the origin of man* (1871) claimed that foundations of speech should be traced back to vocalisations and tunes expressing emotions (Ekman, 2006). Even today music-based origins of speech or at least of some of its components continue to be advocated (Mithen, 2005), and comparisons of music and speech continue to be drawn (Fitch, 2010; Jackendoff, 2002).

With time more and more often attention was being turned to gestural hypotheses. In their account of the 19th century developments in the field, Żywiczyński and Wacewicz (2015) state that around that time Alfred Wallace's (1823–1913) concept of oral-facial gestures as our primary form of communication became popular. The theory was elaborated by Wilhelm Wundt (1832-1920) in *Die Sprache* and later also by R. A. S. Paget (1869–1955) in *Nature et origine du langage humain.* They both considered oral-facial gestures to be an echo of those of the hand. In consequence, speech began to be viewed as an activity following bodily movements (Żywiczyński & Wacewicz, 2015).

After several decades of silence interest in the origins of speech revived due to developments in cognitive sciences, neurolinguistics and primatology. Today speech as involving articulatory movement is treated by many researchers as part of gestural modality. Even more often gesture and voice are considered realizations of one common system rather than as two different ones. At the same time scientists decided to concentrate on constraints as well as on converging evidence in this field. In 1973 Gordon W. Hewes formulated his gestural primacy hypothesis. Its plausibility was based on mimesis, a new research focus of cognitive scientists, who demonstrated that humans can store motor sequences *in abstracto*, as a result of which movements do not need contextualized, external stimuli. They become autonomous; therefore past movements can be recalled and analyzed, future movements can be planned, transferable motor skills can develop through autocuing, and triadic gestural communication is enabled (Donald, 2001; Zlatev, 2014). Gestural primacy hypothesis is supported by research on gestural transla-tions of stories which inadvertently show the SOV (Subject-Object+Verb) order in gesture sequences, thus helping to identify primary mental representation under-lying communication (Goldin-Meadow, 2011). Research on neuronal circuits responsible for bodily movement suggests that the human brain developed in response to the need of one-handed-throwing in the early stages of tribal life (Calvin & Bickerton, 2000), thus supporting the gestural primacy hypothesis.

Followers of the gestural primacy hypothesis point to the dominance of gesture with accompanying vocalization, while asking questions about the type of early gestural protolanguage which could be *synthetic* (with one gesture linked to one object) or *holistic* (with one gesture functioning as a whole utterance). They are also interested in modality changes and especially in trying to identify bridges between the earlier gestural and the later verbal or integrated communication. They argue that in the initial stage of communication gestures coexisted with sound due both to mirror neurons which are believed to be sensitive to sound and to orofacial neurons which control movements and affect sounds (Arbib, 2005). The development of mouth gestures, as Hewes (1973) calls, them is one possible explanation of how gestures led to verbal communication, a need to better differentiate between various kinds of gestures is another (Corballis, 2002), though some researchers, following in the steps of R. A. S. Paget, point to the bridging role of echophonological elements where lip movements echo hand movements as can be seen in sign languages (Woll, 2014). The question of the origins of language and the role of gesture in its development will forever remain in the realm of speculation, yet in an era of alternative facts, speculation is certainly a purer form of mental activity.

5 Approaches to the Relationship Between Speech and Gesture

Although controversy still continues over the developmental sequence of vocal and visual modality in the evolution of language, supporters of both the gesture first and the vocalization first hypotheses agree on interwoven coexistence of the two in the history of mankind; speech is believed to have been accompanied by gestures and other forms of *extra-oral visible bodily action* for a very long time (Kendon, 2014; Lewis, 2014). The present coexistence of gestural and vocal channels is now considered a valuable springboard for empirical study, especially that the integration of visual and sound modalities in human perception had been noticed much earlier and called for a convincing explanation, such as the Mc Gurk's effect when subjects are exposed to the recording of the syllable "ga" while watching lips producing the syllable "ba" and declare that they hear the syllable "da" (McGurk & MacDonald, 1976). Research on multimodality concentrated on extra-oral visible bodily action which consistently accompanies speech (Kendon, 2014); multi-modality in oral culture communities was also investigated. Also attracting attention was the function of each of the two modalities. Basing on Scheflen (1975), Rossano maintains that "a participant does not speak, gesture, smile and hold posture simultaneously to form a single message with redundant parts. Rather each modality is employed for a specific purpose, some of which can be purely communicational, others might be regulatory and others again might be used to induce or sustain specific relationship between the participants in the interaction" (Rossano, 2014, p. 311).

The interplay of the two modalities is particularly interesting in ways of expressing emotional stances and communicating information, as they vary across speech communities. Differences in the use of gesture have been noticed, for example, between Jewish and Italian communities. Efron's (1941/1972) research demonstrated that Jews tend to use gesture to mark logical patterns, while Italians more often use them to intensify or replace the verbal component. Significant differences in the frequency and variety of hand gestures have also been noticed between Scandinavian speakers and speakers from southern Europe (Ekman, 2001). This means that although gesture-speech combination is a product of evolution and multimodality characterises all the human beings, ways of using gesture and speech are culturally transmitted.

Having agreed that gesture is inherent in communication, researchers turned to the issue of motoricity. Today motoricity is considered to be responsible not only for the production, but also for the reception of speech as humans tend to identify sounds on the basis of articulatory movements they must perform in order to produce what they hear. This has led researchers to conclude that mental representations of phonemes are of a motor rather than of a sound format (Liberman & Whalen, 2000; Żywiczyński & Wacewicz, 2015). On the basis of research on motoricity, it has now been confirmed that SLI, that is, specific language impairment, caused by the FOXP2 gene called Developmental Verbal Dyspraxia (DVD) and mentioned before, correlates with facial movement disorders (Marcus & Fisher, 2003).

Questions, however, arise with respect to mutual relationships of gesture and speech. Inhibitory hypotheses/competitional hypotheses claim that gesture is inhibited by speech, but accessory to speech flow (Feyereisen & deLannoy, 1991), while excitatory ones see the two as being produced simultaneously due to their co-activation (McNeill, 2012). Today the excitatory hypothesis enjoys much more popularity as research on speech disturbances tends to confirm it (Mayberry & Jacques, 2000; Rauscher, Krauss, & Chen, 1996). For example, empirical research has corroborrated that in stutterers gestures are co-produced with fluent, but not with disfluent speech (Mayberry & Jacques, 2000) and that any attempt to inhibit gestures negatively affects fluency (Rauscher et al., 1996). What is more, inhibiting gestures—as in artificial immobilization of subjects—leads to reduced content, especially in utterances of the activity/movement category (Krauss, 1998; Rimé, Schiaratura, Hupet, & Ghysselinckx, 1984). On the other hand, allowing gestures facilitates lexical access and speeds up recall in tip of the tongue (TOT) states (Krauss, 1998). Speech co-occurs with manual gestures even when interlocutors cannot see each other. This can be clearly seen in how people behave during telephone conversations, their simultaneity of hand and mouth movement explained by the shared control system (Gentilucci & Corballis, 2006).

6 Gesture in Authentic and Manipulative Communication

From the beginnings of human interest in the origins of speech and the art of speaking, stress has been given to its persuasive functions geared at influencing others. According to Leith (2011), the earliest complete presentation of hand gestures for rhetorical use appeared in the 17th century and was authored by John Bulwer (1644), who concentrated on the description of 49 gestures in his *Chirologia* and moved on to the analysis of ways they can be used in rhetoric in another volume entitled *Chironomia*. He also worked on gestures of the head as well as on facework (*Cephalologia* and *Celphalonomia*), those masterpieces left unfinished at his premature death (Leith, 2011). Yet clarity and persuasive functions were—at least in the educational field—far removed from intentional manipulation which had never been considered part of rhetorical training.

Today, in the times of political propaganda and market economy, the role of persuasion explicitly taught grows exponentially, but at the same time research brings more and more information which helps to detect manipulation: "There is adequate reason to conclude that their use benefits speakers as much as or more than it does their addressees" (Rauscher et al., 1996, p. 230). This is confirmed by research on verbal and non-verbal behaviour of liars, which demonstrated that, although it is difficult to identify a lie on the basis of non-verbal behavior only, different gestures constantly accompanying speech offer clues useful for the listener in making decisions about the truth-value of the interlocutor's statements. Emblems, that is, gestures used intentionally and carrying meanings (e.g., *OK*) shared by the speech community, are less helpful here than the so-called leaks, that is, unconsciously used emblems, characterized by partial performance and a location outside their usual occurrence. Illustrative gestures as well as manipulations such as, for example, gestures oriented towards one's own body, subconsciously express emotions, especially those of anger and irritation, as do heightened pitch and facework, the evolutionary product of the autonomic nervous system, while reduction of illustrative gestures and diminished speech rate usually signify caution (Ekman, 2001).

Gestures, therefore, play an important role in the interlocutor's system of attributions which regulate the listener's differentiation between the speaker's emotions and intentions. It has been demonstrated, for instance, that true emotions typically involve symmetrical facework, while artificial ones tend to co-occur with asymmetrical movements, lack of muscle movement around the eyes, and sudden disappearance or prolonged appearance of changed facework. Negative emotions are also accompanied by facial microexpressions producing smiles of fear, contempt, and the so-called damped or miserable smiles when the speaker wants to reduce or hide positive emotions (Ekman, 2001). To hide true emotions and to intensify persuasion, non-verbal communication and especially hand gestures are often explicitly taught in courses on marketing, negotiation and public speaking where manipulation is the main aim. In communication devoid of manipulative purposes affiliation is often expressed by gesture and speech when the affective stance of the speaker is being supported by the interlocutor. Sometimes this is done by adding an intensifier in the same syntactic format as the evaluative term used by the conversation partner, as in the following dialogue (Lindström & Sorjonen, 2014, p. 354):

A: "It was fun"

B: "It was great fun".

Sometimes support is demonstrated in the format of a repetition as in:

A. "She said because I had had too much to drink. I said - no"

B: "Noooo"

Verbal support and conspicuous gestures appear in these types of conversations more often when relatively typical experiences are shared. More specific experiences are shared less readily and have been found to be less often responded to with expressive verbal and non-verbal affiliation signals (Heritage, 2011).

Disaffiliation leading to conflict is also expressed by powerful combinations of gesture and speech. Non-verbal signals in situations of conflict are stronger than words, but what forms a powerful cluster with a strong index of performativity is the combination of the so-called facework-hand gesture-design (FGD) with speech. According to Puppel (2013, 2014), the performative powers of the topographies accompanying speech are distributed as follows: the weakest performative power is demonstrated by hand gesture (G), the medium-ranged power belongs to facework (F) and the greatest performative power – to blended FGD, that is, the combination of the two. In her research, the human facial domain (F) was considered the most effective by 29.03% of the respondents, the hand-gesture domain without speech by 9.68%, and the combined human facial-gestural design (FGD) by 64.52% (Puppel, 2014). These results show that "particular performative topographies display different communicative power, or, that they demonstrate different potentials for expressing different degrees of affect in human communicative practice" (Puppel, 2013, p. 86).

7 Conclusions. Implications for the Language Classroom

To date teachers have been interested in gesture for two different reasons. Firstly, in many pre- and in-service courses where the issue of classroom management is crucial, the role of gesture in signaling the teacher's approval and disapproval is emphasized. Similar gestural signaling devices are recommended to raise the efficiency of error correction (Puppel, 2015). Secondly, teachers who give presentations at conferences are encouraged to consciously use gesture for rhetorical purposes: "most of us take little notice of our hands, until, that is, we have to speak in public, and then they appear uncommonly large and obtrusive" (Brandreth, 1983, p. 49). The gestural behavior of learners has not attracted educators' attention with the exception of teachers using drama techniques in their schools. It is only quite recently that a major work on optimizing learners' non-verbal behaviour has been published (Gregersen & MacIntyre, 2017). The question arises whether in general courses of English as a foreign language and especially in school language teaching it is indeed commendable to explicitly teach non-verbal behavior with a view to developing manipulative or even persuasive skills. Although persuasion is a useful part of communication, development of manipulative skills is not worth recommending in any context, let alone the educational one. Persuasive rather than manipulative skills may find their rightful place in the teaching of English for Specific Purposes, such as Business English or English for Public Speaking. In school language education, however, awareness of one's own non-verbal behavior seems to be a sufficient expectation as is awareness of other people's attributions connected with it. For that reason, activities in pairs and groups should be conducted in the drama rather than in the desk-to-desk format, as the latter, although still popular in many language classrooms, seriously reduces non-verbal behaviour. Interactive activities in the drama format should be followed by feedback from the observers and the reaction of the observed. Practical tips on the types of non-verbal signals of attentive and respectful listening would be needed, such as eye-contact and relaxed body-posture in combination with verbal signs, such as repetitive comments, e.g., "So you think it is...", or emotion-directed comments, e.g., "Why do you feel...".

Encouraging gesture in the classroom is not likely to reduce student speaking time. Research shows that no more than 7% of responses consist of visible response only, while the majority (93%) include a vocal component, with approximately 35% combining the two (Lee, 2014). The added value of gesture-rich activities lies in the fact that orofacial and manual gestures attract the attention of the conversation partner and thus facilitate interaction, while bodily engagement enhances motivation on task. An especially strong combination of gesture and speech motivating both interlocutors and observers can be seen in situations of both affiliation and disaffiliation, typical of pair work and group work. With more emphasis on gesture and the creation of authentic conditions for speaking in the language classroom, somewhat less attention needs to be given to the smoothness of speech, now stressed in most of the assessment criteria used in second and foreign language education. The reason for such refocusing lies in the fact that natural conversations of native speakers are full of simple, repetitive vocabulary and abound in hesitations and repairs, while learners are required to demonstrate smoothness and effortlessness of speech (Riggenbach, 1998; Sidnell & Stivers, 2014). If multimodal communication based on the combination of gesture and speech is our natural biological functioning, education should not ignore or counteract it.

References

Ades, D., & Baker, S. (Eds.). (2006). *Undercover surrealism: Georges Bataille and documents.* London: Hayward Gallery.

Arbib, M. A. (2005). The mirror system hypothesis: How did protolanguage evolve? In M. Tallerman (Ed.), *Language origins. Perspectives on evolution* (pp. 21–47). Oxford: Oxford University Press.

Argyle, M. (1988). *Bodily communication.* New York: Methuen.

Argyle, M., & Cook, M. (1976). *Gaze and mutual gaze.* Cambridge: Cambridge University Press.

Barthes, R. (1980). *Critical essays.* Evanston: Northwestern University Press.

Bataille, G., & Barthes, R. (2006). *Le gros orteil. Les sorties du text.* Paris: Farrago.

Beaumont, M. (2015). In the beginning was the big toe. Bataille, base materialism, bipedalism. *Textual Practice, 29*(5), 869–883.

Bertrand, C. (2012). Jean Jacques Rousseau. In E. N. Zalta (Ed.), *The Stanford encyclopedia of philosophy.* Retrieved from https://plato.stanford.edu/archives/sum2017/entries/rousseau.

Boë, L. J., Berthommier, F., Legou, T., Captier, G., Kemp, C., & Sawallis, T. R. (2017). Evidence of a vocalic proto-system in the baboon (papio papio) suggests pre-hominin speech precursors. *PLoS, 12*(1), e0169321. doi:10.1371/journal.pone.0169321.

Bristow, W. (2011). Enlightenment. In E. N. Zalta (Ed.), *The Stanford encyclopedia of philosophy.* Retrieved from https://plato.stanford.edu/archives/sum2011/entries/enlightenment.

Brandreth, G. (1983). *The complete public speaker.* London: Robert Hale.

Brooks, R., & Meltzoff, A. (2005). The development of gaze following and its relation to language. *Developmental Science, 8*(6), 535–543.

Burgoon, J. K., Guerrero, L. K., & Floyd, K. (2016). *Nonverbal behaviour.* London: Routledge.

Calvin, W., & Bickerton, D. (2000). *Lingua ex machine. Reconciling Darwin and Chomsky with the human brain.* Cambridge: MIT Press.

Corballis, M. C. (2002). *From hand to mouth. The origins of language.* Princeton: Princeton University Press.

Deacon, T. (2004). The symbol concept. In K. R. Gibson & M. Tallerman, M. (Eds.), *The Oxford handbook of language evolution* (pp. 393–405). Oxford: Oxford University Press.

Donald, M. (2001). *A mind so rare. The evolution of human consciousness.* New York: W.W. Norton & Company.

Dor, D., Knight, C., & Lewis, J. (Eds.). (2014). *The social origins of language.* Oxford: Oxford University Press.

Efron, D. (1941/1972). *Gesture, race and culture.* The Hague: Mouton.

Ekman, P. (2001). *Telling lies. Clues to deceit in the marketplace, politics and marriage.* New York: Norton.

Ekman, P. (Ed.). (2006). *Darwin and facial expression: a century of research in review.* Cambridge, MA: Malor Books.

Fahey, T. (2009). *Vico's road to postmodernism.* Dublin: Choice Publishing.

Falkenstein, L. (2010). Étienne Bonnot de Condillac. In E. N. Zalta (Ed.), *The Stanford encyclopedia of philosophy.* Retrieved from https://plato.stanford.edu/archives/fall2010/entries/condillac.

Feldman, R. S., & Rimé, B. (1991). *Fundamentals of nonverbal behavior.* New York: Cambridge University Press.

Feyereisen, P., & deLannoy, J. D. (1991). *Gestures and speech. Psychological investigations.* New York: Cambridge University Press.

Fitch, T. (2000). The evolution of speech: A comparative review. *Trends in Cognitive Sciences, 4* (7), 258–267.

Fitch, T. (2010). *The evolution of language.* Cambridge: Cambridge University Press.

Foster, S. H. (2013). *The communicative competence of young children A modular approach.* London: Routledge.

Gentilucci, M., & Corballis, M. (2006). From manual gesture to speech. A gradual transition. *Neuroscience and Biobehavioral Reviews, 30,* 949–960.

Goldin-Meadow, S. (2003). *Hearing gesture: How our hands help us think.* Cambridge: Harvard University Press.

Goldin-Meadow, S. (2011). What modern-day gesture can tell us about language evolution. In K. R. Gibson & M. Tallerman (Eds.), *The Oxford handbook of language evolution* (pp. 545–557). Oxford: Oxford University Press.

Gopnik, M. (1990). Feature-blindness: A case of genetic dysphasia. *Language Acquisition, 1,* 139–164.

Gorzelańczyk, E. J. (2003). Genetyczne źródła języka [Genetic origins of language]. *Scripta Neophilologica Posnaniensia, 5,* 49–54.

Gregersen, T., & MacIntyre, P. (2017). *Optimizing language learners' nonverbal behavior.* Bristol: Multilingual Matters.

Gullberg, M. (2008). Gesture and second language acquisition. In P. Robinson & N. C. Ellis (Eds.), *Handbook of cognitive linguistics and second language acquisition* (pp. 276–305). London: Routledge.

Heritage, J. (2011). Territories of knowledge, territories of experience. Emphatic moments in interaction. In T. Stivers, L. Mondada, & J. Steensig (Eds.), *The morality of knowledge in conversation* (pp. 159–183). Cambridge: Cambridge University Press.

Hewes, G. W. (1973). Primate communication and the gestural origin of language. *Current Anthropology, 14*(1,2), 5–24.

Hrdy, S. B. (2009). *Mothers and others. The evolutionary origins of human understanding.* Cambridge: Harvard University Press.

Hurford, J. (2007). *The origins of meaning. Language in the light of evolution.* Oxford: Oxford University Press.

Jackendoff, R. (2002). *Foundations of language, brain, meaning, grammar, evolution.* Oxford: Oxford University Press.

Jaworski, A., & Sachdev, I. (2004). Teachers' beliefs about students' talk and silence. Constructing academic success and failure through metapragmatic comments. In A. Jaworski, N. Coupland, & D. Galasinski (Eds.), *Metalanguage. Social and ideological perspectives* (pp. 227–246). Berlin: Mouton de Gruyter.

Kendon, A. (2004). *Gesture. Visible action as utterance.* Cambridge: Cambridge University Press.

Kendon, A. (2014). The poly-modalic nature of utterances and its relevance for inquiring into language origins. In D. Dor, C. Knight, & J. Lewis (Eds.), *The social origins of language* (pp. 67–76). Oxford: Oxford University Press.

King, J. (2013). *Silence in the second language classroom.* London: Palgrave Macmillan.

Kita, S. (2000). How representational gestures help speaking. In D. McNeill (Ed.), *Language and gesture* (pp. 162–185). Cambridge: Cambridge University Press.

Kobayashi, H., & Koshima, S. (2001). Evolution of the human eye as a device for communication. In T. Matsuzawa (Ed.), *Primate origins of human cognition and behavior* (pp. 383–401). Tokyo: Springer Japan.

Komorowska, H. (2016). Pitfalls of attribution—conversational styles in language education. In D. Gałajda, P. Zakrajewski, & M. Pawlak (Eds.), *Researching second language learning and teaching from a psycholinguistic perspective* (pp. 129–147). Berlin: Springer.

Kraus, R. (1985). *L'amour fou. Photography and surrealism.* Washington: Corcoran Gallery of Art.

Krauss, R. M. (1998). Why do we gesture when we speak? *Current Directions in Psychological Science, 7,* 54–59.

Lee, S.-H. (2014). Response design in conversation. In J. Sidnell & T. Stivers (Eds.), *A handbook of conversation analysis* (pp. 415–432). London: Blackwell.

Leith, S. (2011). *You talkin' to me?.* London: Profile Books Ltd.

Lewis, J. (2014). BaYaka Pygmy multi-modal and mimetic communication traditions. In D. Dor, C. Knight, & J. Lewis (Eds.), *The social origins of language* (pp. 77–91). Oxford: Oxford University Press.

Liberman, A. M., & Whalen, D. H. (2000). On the relation of speech to language. *Trends in Cognitive Sciences, 4,* 87–96.

Lindström, A., & Sorjonen, M.-L. (2014). Affiliation in conversation. In J. Sidnell & T. Stivers (Eds.), *A handbook of conversation analysis* (pp. 350–369). London: Blackwell.

Marcus, G. E., & Fisher, S. E. (2003). FOXP2 in focus: What can genes tell us about speech and language? *Trends in Cognitive Sciences, 7*(6), 257–262.

Mayberry, R. I., & Jaques, J. (2000). Gesture production during stuttered speech. Insights into the nature of speech-gesture integration. In D. McNeill (Ed.), *Language and gesture* (pp. 199–214). Cambridge: Cambridge University Press.

McCafferty, S., & Stam, G. (Eds.). (2008). *Gesture. Second language acquisition and classroom research.* London: Routledge.

McMahon, A., & McMahon, R. (2013). *Evolutionary linguistics.* Cambridge: Cambridge University Press.

McGurk, H., & MacDonald, J. (1976). Hearing lips and seeing voices. *Nature, 264,* 746–748.

McNeill, D. (Ed.). (2000). *Language and gesture.* Cambridge: Cambridge University Press.

McNeill, D. (2012). *How language began. Gesture and speech in human evolution.* Cambridge: Cambridge University Press.

Mehrabian, A. (1972). *Nonverbal communication.* Chicago: Aldine – Atherton.

Mithen, S. (2005). *The singing Neanderthals. The origins of music, language, mind and body.* London: Weidenfeld and Nicholson.

Monaghan, L., Goodman, J., & Robinson, J. M. (Eds.). (2012). *A cultural approach to interpersonal communication.* Oxford: Wiley-Blackwell.

Néret, G. (2003). *Kazimir Malevich and Suprematism 1878–1935.* Cologne: Taschen.

Puppel, J. (2013). Facework and gestures: A preliminary analysis of the communicative power of human performative non-verbal practices. *Scripta Neophilologica Posnaniensia, 13,* 85–90.

Puppel, J. (2014). Układ twarzy i gestosfery w kontekście konfliktu komunikacyjnego w komunikacji bezpośredniej [The use of face and gesture in communicative conflicts in face-to-face communication]. *Scripta Neophilologica Posnaniensia, 14,* 127–137.

Puppel, J. (2015). Siła performatywna komunikacji niewerbalnej używana przez nauczyciela i ucznia w formalnych warunkach klasy [The performative force of non-verbal communication used by the teacher and the learner in the Classroom]. MOTEK. Motywy ekolingwistyczne: W stronę ekoglottodydaktyki [Ecolinguistic motives: Towards ecoglottodidactics]. *Scripta de Communicatione Posnaniensia, 7,* 133–141.

Rauscher, F., Krauss, R. M., & Chen, Y. (1996). Gesture, speech and lexical access. The role of lexical movements in speech production. *Psychological Science, 7*(4), 226–231.

Richardson, R. (2000). *Larrey. Surgeon to Napoleon's imperial guard.* London: Quiller Press.

Riggenbach, H. (1998). Evaluating learner interactional skills: Conversation at the micro level. In R. Young & A. W. He (Eds.), *Talking and testing. Discourse approaches to the assessment of oral proficiency* (pp. 53–67). Amsterdam: John Benjamins.

Rimé, B., Schiaratura, L., Hupet, M., & Ghysselinckx, A. (1984). Effects of relative immobilization on the speaker's nonverbal behaviour and on the dialogue imagery level. *Motivation and Emotion, 8,* 311–325.

Rossano, F. (2014). Gaze in conversation. In J. Sidnell & T. Stivers (Eds.), *A handbook of conversation analysis* (pp. 308–329). London: Blackwell.

Roth, G., & Dicke, U. (2005). Evolution of the brain and intelligence. *Trends in Cognitive Science, 9,* 250–257.

Scheflen, A. E. (1975). *How behavior means.* New York: Rowman & Littlefield Publishers.

Sidnell, J., & Stivers, T. (Eds.). (2014). *A handbook of conversation analysis.* London: Blackwell.

Sueyoshi, A., & Hardison, D. M. (2005). The role of gesture and facial cues in second language listening comprehension. *Language Learning, 55*(4), 661–699.

Tallerman, M. (Ed.). (2005). *Language origins. Perspectives on evolution.* Oxford: Oxford University Press.

Tomasello, M. (2008). *Origins of human communication.* Cambridge: MIT Press.

Tomasello, M. (2009). *Why we cooperate.* Cambridge: MIT Press.

Tomasello, M., Hare, B., Lehmann, H., & Call, J. (2007). Reliance on head versus eyes in the gaze following of great apes and human infants: The cooperative eye hypothesis. *Journal of Human Evolution, 52,* 314–320.

Tomasello, M., Melis, A. P., Tennie, C., Wyman, E., & Herrmann, E. (2012). Two key steps in the evolution of human cooperation: The interdependence hypothesis. *Current Anthropology, 53* (6), 673–692.

Vico, G. (1744/1968). *Scienza nuova [The new science].* Ithaca: Cornell University Press.

Woll, B. (2014). Moving from hand to mouth: Echo phonology and the origins of language. *Frontiers in Psychology, 5,* Article 662. doi:10.3389/fpsyg.2014.00662.

Zlatev, J. (2014). The co-evolution of human intersubjectivity, morality and language. In D. Dor, C. Knight, & J. Lewis (Eds.), *The social origins of language* (pp. 249–266). Oxford: Oxford University Press.

Żywiczyński, P., & Wacewicz, S. (2015). Ewolucja języka. W stronę hipotez gesturalnych [Evolution of language: Towards gestural hypotheses]. Toruń: Wydawnictwo Naukowe UMK.

Author Biography

Hanna Komorowska is Full Professor of Linguistics and Language Pedagogy at the University of Social Sciences and Humanities. Former Vice-President of Warsaw University, the Polish delegate for the Modern Languages Project Group of the Council of Europe, member of the EU High Level Group on Multilingualism in Brussels and consultant to the European Centre for Modern Languages in Graz, she is now Head of the Department of Applied Linguistics at the SWPS University and President of the European Language Label Competition Jury. Professor Komorowska is co-author of the *European portfolio for student teachers of languages* and publishes widely in the field of FLT methodology and teacher education.

Tinker, Tailor…: Creativity in Foreign Language Learning and Teaching

Liliana Piasecka

> Creativity is *"not a capacity of special people but a special capacity of all people"*.
>
> Carter (2004, p. 13)

Abstract The word *creativity* has recently won great popularity in numerous contexts, showing both positive ("creative writing") and negative ("creative accounting") connotations. The concept itself has many meanings as it may refer to the end product of one's activity, the cognitive processes involved in the creative act, the personality of a creative person, the development of creativity across the life span, and also the factors that either stimulate or inhibit the process of creation (Łukasik, 2015; Simonton, 2000). There is also a distinction between *exceptional* creativity, manifesting itself in important works that are significant for a given society, and *everyday* creativity, which can be observed in everyday life activities that involve a degree of originality. In addition, creativity is no longer perceived as an individual propensity only but as a characteristic that all humans share but may not be aware of its potential. The aim of this chapter is to discuss the role of creativity in learning and using foreign languages. It brings together three perspectives on creativity, that is the psychological, the linguistic, and the educational. These three domains are extremely important for facing present-day challenges and understanding the meaning of creativity in life. Therefore, first the definition of creativity proposed by cognitive psychologists is discussed along with a variety of approaches to the phenomenon. Second, the creative nature of language is touched upon and the place of creativity in education is highlighted. Finally, the foreign language classroom is focused on as a nest of creativity. Learning a new language requires learners to create utterances they may not be confident about, yet they take the risk of producing them. Moreover, teachers may introduce many creative tasks and activities that are motivating, involving and rewarding and give learners a sense of joy, excitement, and fulfilment.

L. Piasecka (✉)
University of Opole, Opole, Poland
e-mail: elpia@o2.pl

© Springer International Publishing AG 2018
M. Pawlak and A. Mystkowska-Wiertelak (eds.), *Challenges of Second and Foreign Language Education in a Globalized World*, Second Language Learning and Teaching, DOI 10.1007/978-3-319-66975-5_6

89

Keywords Creativity · Linguistic creativity · Foreign language learning · Creative classroom activities

1   Introduction

Creativity is perceived as "one of the key 21st-century skills" (Runco, 2014), because presently people face challenges, changes and novel situations such as, for example, learning to operate a new cell phone, and they have to respond creatively and flexibly to them (Runco, 2004). Creativity, "the greatest gift of human intelligence" (Robinson, 2011, p. i), has attracted the attention of scholars, researchers, and practitioners from many disciplines such as, for example, psychology, linguistics, literary studies, cultural studies, media studies, education, sociology, anthropology, arts, economy, management, industry, and so on. This implies that creativity is important in all the spheres of human life for everybody Boden (2004, p. 1):

> It's not a special "faculty", but an aspect of human intelligence in general. In other words, it's grounded in everyday abilities such as conceptual thinking, perception, memory, and reflective self-criticism. So it isn't confined to a tiny elite: every one of us is creative, to a degree.

Moreover, Csikszentmihalyi (1996, p. 7) claims that "creativity is a central source of meaning in our lives" because it is behind all the important, interesting human activities and when people are involved in creative acts, they "are living more fully than during the rest of life" (p. 7). Such an egalitarian approach to creativity also means that people differ in how they exercise their creativity.

The chapter brings together three perspectives on creativity, that is the psychological, linguistic and educational. These three domains are extremely important for "we cannot confront our life as a creative challenge, nor can we assume a creative orientation towards it, unless we understand the nature of creativity and what it means for this life to be creative" (Mitias, 1985, p. 1). Therefore, first, the definitions, degrees, types, and correlates of creativity are discussed from the psychological and linguistic perspectives, then connections between foreign language learning and creativity are highlighted and, finally, some suggestions for a creative foreign language classroom are proposed.

2   Towards a Psychological Definition of Creativity

A brief review of psychological literature on creativity reveals a number of definitions that capture this concept from the perspectives of product, process, person, and context. Many of them overlap. In what follows, selected definitions, mostly from cognitive psychologists, are presented and then the common elements are highlighted.

Runco and Jaeger (2012, p. 92) insist that creativity involves "both originality and effectiveness". The idea that creativity combines novelty and value is also shared by Nęcka (2001). For Boden (2004, p. 1), "creativity is the ability to come up with ideas or artefacts that are *new, surprising,* and *valuable*" while Csikszentmihalyi (1996, p. 56) perceives creativity as "any act, idea, or product that changes an existing domain, or that transforms an existing domain into a new one". Simonton and Damian (2013, p. 796) claim that a creative idea "must be original, novel, or surprising" as well as "adaptive, functional, or useful". They propose the equation according to which creativity (C) is the result of originality (O) and adaptiveness (A): $C = O \times A$. Kaufman and Sternberg (2015, p. 34), in turn, distinguish three characteristics of creative ideas:

- they "must represent something different, new, or innovative";
- they "must be of high quality";
- they "must be appropriate to the task at hand or to some redefinition of that task. Thus, a creative response is novel, good, and relevant".

As the above definitions imply, creativity involves novelty (originality, surprise) and functionality (appropriacy, relevance, effectiveness, value), and results in ideas and artefacts that change individuals and the world around them.

All people are creative in different ways. Not all of them create artefacts and ideas, or make inventions that change the course of civilization, for example. Therefore, scholars have proposed various dichotomies that represent different degrees of creativity. Simonton and Damian (2013, p. 800) distinguish between *little-C creativity* and *Big-C creativity* while Barsalou and Prinz (1997, p. 267) discuss *mundane* and *exceptional* creativity, and Boden (2004, p. 2) writes about *psychological* and *historical* creativity (*P-creativity* and *H-creativity*). In all the pairs, the first element refers to everyday creativity that assists people in coping with novel situations and challenges on a personal level. The second element, in turn, concerns ideas and artefacts that have influenced and changed the world, that are important on a universal level. However, one cannot operate without the other because "mundane creativity is the workhorse that accounts for the bulk of human accomplishment and that makes exceptional creativity possible" (Barsalou & Prinz, 1997, p. 268).

There are also different ways of being creative. The first one is observed when familiar ideas are combined in unusual, unfamiliar ways. The second and the third ones concern exploration and transformation of people's conceptual spaces, understood as "structured styles of thought" (Boden, 2004, p. 3). Csikszentmihalyi (1996, pp. 50–51), in turn, distinguishes three groups of creative people. The first group involves people who are very bright and "with unusual thoughts" and who, he suggests, should be called brilliant. The second group includes personally creative people experiencing "the world in novel and original ways", while in the third group there are such people as Leonardo da Vinci or Einstein—they are "creative without any reservation". Csikszentmihalyi's distinction is interesting as it captures both intensity and impact of creativity on human existence.

Creativity is associated with such factors as personality, intelligence, knowledge, motivation, environment, and learning styles (Sternberg & Lubart, 1995). Researchers looking for connections between personality and creativity have been using the five-factor personality model (McCrae & Costa, 1997), which is made of five personality traits, that is, openness to experience, conscientiousness, extraversion, agreeability, and nervousness. Empirical findings show a consistent relationship between openness to experience and creativity, as measured by different tests. Other personality traits do not reveal such consistent patterns and the relations may be more domain-specific. Intelligence, however, appears to play an important role in creativity (Kaufmann & Sternberg, 2015). As regards knowledge, expertise and practice are necessary to earn recognition and they are related to the creative domains.

Social context, or the environment in which people operate, is also related to creativity through affect, motivation, and social power (Simonton & Damian, 2013). With respect to affect, De Dreu, Baas and Nijstad's (2008) idea of a dual pathway to creativity deserves attention because it brings together contradictory empirical evidence that shows that positive and negative emotions both increase creativity. In their model, affect has two separate dimensions, that is *valence* (positive and negative) and *activation level* (activating and deactivating). Higher levels of creativity are connected with activating moods since they support the release of dopamine and noradrenalin which, in turn, positively affect working memory and a broad attention focus. Affective valence, on the other hand, is associated with cognitive flexibility, while negative valence supports cognitive persistence. In the model, affect is connected with motivation in such a way that when it is positive, it suggests a friendly environment supportive of cognitive flexibility and triggers the so-called approach motivation. According to the Regulation Focus Theory (Higgins, 1997, as cited in Simonton & Damian, 2013), approach motivation is associated with promotion focus and avoidance motivation with prevention focus. Promotion focus involves "broader attention deployment (…) [that] (…) allows for automatic screening of a larger pool of information, which then leads to an increased probability of remote associations and creativity" (Simonton & Damian, 2013, p. 804). Moreover, the type of motivation (intrinsic vs. extrinsic) is also relevant for creative processing. When people work for intrinsic motives, for the enjoyment they find in the activity, they are more focused on the task, more involved and, in consequence, more creative than people working for external rewards (Amabile, 1996; Csikszentmihalyi, 1978; Nęcka, 2001). Intrinsic, or autonomous, motivation is also a sign of independence from external control and an attribute of socially powerful individuals who rely more on their individual, internal values, tendencies and processes when involved in creative tasks.

From the psychological point of view, then, creativity is a complex phenomenon marked by novelty and functionality, it is not absolute but has different levels of intensity and is associated with a range of individual characteristics that make individuals more or less creative. Most important, however, is the universal agreement that creativity is not reserved for a chosen few but a universal and powerful human characteristic. Ockuly and Richards (2013) set out to find out how people interested in creativity define it. The researchers recruited the participants through social media because they wanted a group that is "modern and creatively aware" (p. 258). Their study showed that the majority of the participants (75%) view creativity very much as a personal matter, that they associate it with a process rather than a product (97%), and that they perceive themselves as creative and regard creativity part of daily life. The following section discusses linguistic creativity—equally important and omnipresent as general creativity.

3 Linguistic Creativity

Language and creativity distinguish *homo sapiens* from other species. Language itself is creative because operating a limited set of grammatical rules, people are able to interpret and produce an unlimited number of utterances. As Chomsky (1964, p. 7) put it,

> [t]he central fact to which any significant linguistic theory must address itself is this: a mature speaker can produce a new sentence of his language on the appropriate occasion, and other speakers can understand it immediately, though it is equally new to them (…) the class of sentences with which we can operate fluently and without difficulty or hesitation is so vast that for all practical purposes (…) we may regard it as infinite.

The above points to unlimited possibilities of understanding and creating language forms that language users have never been exposed to, despite a limited repertoire of language resources at their disposal. This means that language is essentially creative and used in creative ways on a daily basis.

Although language is creative, it is also characterized by a wide range of routine expressions. Children acquiring their first language as well as foreign or second language learners at the early stages of learning imitate a lot of language they are exposed to. However, children's imitation is selective and related to what they are learning at a given moment, but not exclusively to what the linguistic environment offers (Lightbown & Spada, 1999). They also learn the language in chunks which are later analyzed for form and function in communication. Therefore children's speech is referred to as prefabricated language because it contains a lot of memorized routines and prefabricated patterns. Analyzing how a Japanese child was learning English, Hakuta (1974) distinguished between *routines* ("unvarying chunks of language", p. 289) and *prefabricated patterns* ("segments of sentences which operate in conjunction with a movable component, such as the insertion of a noun phrase or a verb phrase", p. 289). Also Wong-Fillmore (1976) found that Spanish-speaking children learning English used a lot of prefabricated language. Both researchers believe that routines and patterns that are central to language acquisition "evolve directly into creative language" (p. 640).

Language behavior is ritualized and lexical phrases, defined as "chunks of language of varying in length" (Nattinger & DeCarrico, 1992, p. 1) and represented by routinized formulas and prefabricated language chunks, play an important role both in language learning and use. Using ready-made forms (lexical phrases) allows learners to organize spoken and written discourse on the macro- and the micro-levels. It also helps them with discourse comprehension. What people do with language is as predictable as the steps in a waltz. They use routines and patterns along with fixed phrases and idioms that have a variety of functions, such as, for example, informational, evaluative, situational, moralizing, or organiza-tional. Fixed expressions cover such multi-word lexical items as frozen colloca-tions, grammatically ill-formed collocations, proverbs, routine formulas, sayings, similes, and idioms (Moon, 1998). In addition, the use of one lexical form entails a limited choice of another form, as in collocations. Unfresh bread is *stale*, but unfresh butter is *rancid*. This phenomenon is known as the idiom principle (Sinclair, 1991) and might be regarded as a limit to creativity, which may be more strongly associated with the open choice principle (Moon, 1998). Although all these multi-word expressions make interpersonal communication more effective, they are used in conjunction with other, less routine forms and in a wide variety of contexts which demand novel, unconventional ways of expression. A well-known expres-sion may be used in a situation that makes it original, effective, and memorable.

Scholars concerned with language and creativity view everyday creativity as a prevalent feature of language (e.g., Carter, 2004; Maybin, 2016). Having analyzed a five-million corpus of spoken interaction (CANCODE: Cambridge and Nottingham Corpus of Discourse in English), Carter (2004) observes that people communicate meanings in many different ways, using means characteristic of literary texts such as repetition, metaphor, simile, word play, irony, hyperbole, and so on. These means are related both to the goals and contexts of communication. Carter (2004, p. 6), explains: "Creativity is a pervasive feature of spoken language exchanges as well as a key component in interpersonal communication, and (…) it is a property actively possessed by all speakers and listeners; it is not simply a domain of a few creatively gifted individuals". Linguistic creativity, then, is not an exclusive feature of literature. Linguists like Jakobson (1960) and Halliday (1975) emphasize the important role of poetic, or imaginative function in communication. Jakobson (1960) writes that language study requires also a study of its poetic function which focuses on the message in the process of communication. However, poetic function is not limited to poetry and "dealing with poetic function, linguists cannot limit itself to the field of poetry" (Jakobson, 1960, p. 356). Halliday (1975) distinguished seven functions that motivate early development of language in children and the imaginative function is one of them. It refers to playing with words, telling jokes and stories, making puns, or creating imaginary worlds. As Cook comments, "it might be that (…) the first function of language is the creation of imaginative worlds: whether lies, games, fictions or fantasies" (2000, p. 47).

As in psychology, there is also a concern about creative products and creative processes in linguistics. While literary and art critics analyze the creative product, psychologists are concerned with mental processes and cognitive models of cre-ativity and there are also scholars who study creative processes from socio-cultural or interpersonal perspectives. They realize the role of cognitive processes but they underscore the importance of interaction and socio-cultural contexts in creativity. Moreover, discourse analysis in its current forms, through analyzing the product (discourse) allows researchers to find evidence for cognitive and social processes (Jones, 2016). Types of discourse are related to how language is conceptualized. Jones (2016) distinguishes three conceptualizations of language that are matched by three types of discourse and, consequently, three different, though not mutually exclusive, approaches to creativity:

- Discourse as language beyond the sentence implies looking for patterns in texts, how these patterns interact to create a whole text and how the text works in the context to which it belongs.
- Discourse as language in use, "as a kind of social action" (p. 11), involves analyzing how people use language/discourse both to make sense of their life and how to change it and "(...) creativity is seen as residing not in language itself but in the actions people take with language" (p. 11).
- Discourse as language that is a part of a wider spectrum of social practices connected with power and the social construction of knowledge.

In fact, these are "capital D discourses", defined as "ways of being in the world, or forms of life which integrate words, acts, values, beliefs, attitudes, and social identities" (Gee, 1996, p. 127). Although discourses set limits to what can be said and done, they are not fixed but dynamic and thus various transformations are possible when discourses are combined and used in new ways to meet the demands of specific situations. The transformations refer not only to the impact of great works of art and important scientific discoveries but also to everyday actions that people engage in satisfy the changing needs of their lives. Jones (2016) claims that such understanding of discourse integrates "small c creativity" with "big C Creativity", thus subscribing to the idea that vernacular and literary creativity are connected.

As the above suggests, creativity is inseparable from language and manifests itself in many forms and contexts, embracing both great literature and everyday communication, also in the digital environment. Every individual is creative but they differ in degrees, means of expression, needs and identities. Perhaps it might be more justified to talk about multiple creativities (Pope & Swann, 2011) rather than consider creativity a monolith. This chapter focuses on creativity and foreign language learning. Therefore, the following section briefly reviews selected empirical studies concerning the relations between bi- and multilingualism and creativity as well as creativity and foreign language learning.

4   Selected Empirical Research on Foreign/Second Language Learning and Creativity

Quite ample research on bilingualism reveals that bilinguals are superior to monolinguals on different tests of creativity, which implies that bilingualism is positively correlated with creativity (Hommel, Colzato, Fischer, & Christoffels,

2011; Ricciardelli, 1992). Hommel et al. (2011) found that high proficient bilinguals (Dutch-English who lived in the Netherlands and attended a high school where English was the language of instruction) outperformed low proficient bilinguals (German students who lived in Germany and attended various language courses at school) on tests of convergent thinking, whereas low proficient bilinguals were more fluent on tests of divergent thinking. The authors explain that "bilingualism should not be related to 'creativity' as a unitary concept but, rather, to the specific processes and mechanisms that underlie creativity" (p. 1).

Using two or more languages improves both verbal skills and general cognitive abilities. Analyzing translanguaging spaces of three Chinese youths in Britain, Wei (2011) focused on their criticality and creativity in using various socio-cultural resources. Two students were British-born Chinese while one came to Britain at the age of 15 to attend a boarding school. His parents live in China. Wei (2011) argues that multilingualism itself is "a rich source of creativity and criticality, as it entails tension, conflict, competition, difference, change in a number of spheres, ranging from ideologies, policies and practices to historical and current contexts" (pp. 1223–1224). Also exposure to multicultural experience enhances creativity (Leung, Maddux, Galinsky, & Chiu, 2008). European American undergraduate students with limited knowledge of Chinese culture watched slide shows of Chinese culture in various configurations, got information about Turkey, and were then asked to write a creative version of Cinderella story for Turkish children. It turned out that the participants who were exposed to American and Chinese cultures simultaneously wrote most creative stories. Leiken and Tovli (2014) found that balanced bilinguals were more creative than monolinguals on such tasks as semantic fluency and mathematical manipulations (Creating Equal Number task) but no differences were found between the groups with respect to fluency as a measure of creativity. This suggests that bilingualism has different effects on different tasks.

Although empirical studies on the relations between creativity and foreign language learning are scarce, they yield interesting outcomes. Ottó (1998) found statistically significant correlations between creativity, measured by a creativity test consisting of such subtasks as consequences, unusual uses, common problems, categories, and associations, and foreign language learning success, represented by end-of-term grades in English. In his study, creativity was analyzed in terms of four factors, that is, originality, sensitivity to problems, ideational fluency, understood as "the ability to think of different verbal responses falling into a specified class" (Ottó, 1998, p. 765), and associational fluency, understood as "the ability to think of different verbal responses semantically associated with a given stimulus" (p. 765). The results show that all the factors are significantly related to language achievement and that learners who score high on creativity are more successful in learning a foreign language.

Albert and Kormos (2004) intended to find how creativity may affect oral narrative tasks. They focused on such aspects of creativity as originality, flexibility and fluency, and found that only fluency was positively correlated with the quantity of narratives while originality was negatively correlated with it. Moreover, a positive correlation was found between originality and complexity of narratives, but the correlations were moderate and the authors concluded that "creativity can account for certain differences in learners' performance on oral narrative tasks" (p. 303). Albert (2006) investigated the effect of creativity on language proficiency and the relation between creativity and foreign language aptitude. She found a negative correlation between creative fluency and flexibility, and phonetic coding ability (a component of language aptitude). Contrary to Ottó's (1998) findings, she found no relations between creativity and language proficiency. Ghonsooly (2012) was interested in finding a link between foreign language learning and divergent thinking abilities. Divergent thinking—an ability to provide various responses to one stimulus—and learning a foreign language are positively correlated. Ghonsooly's study showed that advanced foreign language learners significantly outperformed monolinguals on all the measures of divergent thinking, that is fluency, originality, elaboration, and flexibility. The researcher explains this superiority by the fact that learning a foreign language involves a range of cognitive practices such as, for example, operating two language systems or suppressing one system when the other is active. In addition, foreign language learning also involves becoming familiar with other cultures, beliefs, traditions and value systems, thus making learners perceive their own and the other culture from different viewpoints and this way divergent thinking and cognitive flexibility are strengthened. The playful and informal atmosphere in a foreign language institution may also foster creativity.

Although bilingualism and creativity seem to be related, the studies on creativity and foreign language learning show conflicting findings and are inconclusive. This suggests that both language learning and creativity involve processes that are very complex, interconnected and overlapping, and thus may require different research approaches. Moreover, the studies were carried out in formal educational institutions which do not necessarily support creativity though they may claim otherwise.

5 Creativity and Education

As one of key 21st century skills (Runco, 2014), creativity should permeate school curricula on all levels of education, from kindergarten to university. It should be a good thing in education (Craft, 2003). Empirical research shows that there is a significant relation between creativity and educational achievement (e.g., Karnes et al., 1961; McCabe, 1991). However, education and creativity are not good partners. Hennessey and Amabile (1987) identified a number of ways in which education can kill creativity, for example, when children expect a reward for their work, when they compete, when they are focused on evaluation, when they are strictly controlled by teachers, and when they have limited options of choice. Robinson (2011) observes that education systems are preoccupied with academic ability and standardized testing which impede creativity and waste many talents, not deliberately but systematically. The point is that traditional academic education cannot produce "thoughtful, creative, self-confident people" (p. 15) with new ideas and the abilities to implement them, people with good communication skills, and people who can work in teams. In the quickly changing landscape of the 21st century there is a need to transform old and safe ways of thinking and acting so that new services and new technologies are developed. This places high demands on education because schools not only have to improve reading, writing and arithmetic but they should also develop entrepreneurship, innovation and creativity (Friedman, 2009). Runco (2014) adds that a traditional classroom does not support such aspects of creativity as autonomy, intrinsic motivation, playfulness or generating ideas. Moreover, since creativity is connected with originality, it is risky and difficult to put it into the frames of a curriculum. Yet, it is included in the list of qualities for college readiness. Sullivan (2012) argues that students preparing for college should focus on such character traits as curiosity and openness, creativity (*sic*), accountability and humility, and not exclusively on test scores, school achievement and some academic skills.

Despite the unfavorable conditions for developing creativity in formal educational systems, teachers take steps to work on creativity with their students. Burke (2013), for example, suggests that students' creativity can be improved when they learn "new and different ways to solve problems, identify other options, alternatives, solutions, connect seemingly unrelated ideas, results, or events, think about issues, problems, events, experiences, and ideas, interpret art, literary works, or data, and communicate information, explanations, arguments, or stories" (p. 25). Focusing on university education, Łukasik (2015) claims that academic teachers should be guided by two principles. First, they should understand the world and themselves, second, they should prepare their students for life-long learning. Thus, their teaching should inspire students to be autonomous and creative in their enquiries. Such teaching is characterized by direct communication with students, by evoking and supporting their cognitive curiosity and motivation, by creating a playful atmosphere through using humor, for example, as well as by tolerance which involves respect for the ideas and opinions of other students and allows all to trust one another rather than put on masks and pretend to be somebody else. Reviewing research on education and creativity, Fasko (2000–2001) reports ways that stimulate the development of creativity. These are techniques that support divergent and convergent thinking, individual assignments that require learners both to solve and find problems, as well as group activities that not only support creativity but also teach learners to accept the opinions of others. Inquiry-discovery learning and affectivity (aesthetic concerns) also encourage creativity.

Educators who want to include creativity in everyday teaching should realize that creativity combines originality and appropriate tasks that do not compete with but complement school learning. As already mentioned, there are different levels of creativity and cultivating everyday creativity may result in exceptional creativity. In addition, learners are more creative when they work on issues that are motivating and meaningful for them. Creative ideas require learners to work hard, expend a lot of effort and take risks. Learners should be aware of the costs and decide whether they are ready to accept them. Also, they need to be aware of their strengths and weaknesses, they should develop "creative metacognition—a combination of creative self-knowledge (knowing one's own creative strengths and limitations, both within a domain and as a general trait) and contextual knowledge (knowing when, where, how, and why to be creative)" (Beghetto & Kaufman, 2013, p. 15).

All in all, there is a high demand for creative, imaginative and innovative people who would faces the challenges of the 21st century. Schools do not seem to cope very well with educating creative people but many teachers are deeply concerned about supporting and developing the creative potential of their students and use various situations to involve them in tasks and activities that stimulate creativity. A foreign language classroom is a good place for creative activities.

6   Foreign Language Classrooms: Nests of Creativity

Foreign language classrooms are appropriate places for creative activities and creative expression. First, language is creative. Second, learners themselves bring a degree of creativity as a character trait into the classroom, and so do teachers. Third, teaching materials and activities that may be designed around them are potentially creative. This unusual combination of creative threads may turn a foreign language classroom into a genuine nest of creativity. Since the creative nature of language has already been discussed, now the focus is shifted to teachers, materials and activities that enhance creativity.

Richards (2013) identified eight characteristics that creative teachers share. First of all, they have solid subject matter knowledge that allows them to be flexible and see a purpose in what they do. This also makes them confident about their teaching and they are more inclined to follow their intuitions. They care about their learners' success and support their self-confidence. They are non-conformists who run original lessons and are ready to modify them if their learners' needs demand it. They "create effective surprises" (p. 8) and avoid repetition. This is connected with a rich repertoire of teaching techniques and strategies that account for flexibility and the possibility of modifying the lesson if such a need arises. Creative teachers are not afraid of taking risks and experimenting and they make their lessons learner-centered. This entails listening to learners' opinions, including accounts of their experiences in lesson content as well as allowing them to monitor their learning. Eventually, creative teachers are critically reflective, they analyze and evaluate their teaching practices, share their experiences with other teachers, and look for new ideas that they could implement in their teaching. Richards further claims that lessons taught by creative teachers are marked by a variety of approaches, materials and activities since "creativity is promoted by a mixture and combination of styles" (p. 12). Teachers also choose activities that stimulate creative responses from learners. Such activities should be challenging, personally meaningful, and intriguing, involve learners in problem-solving, have interesting content along with elements of novelty and fantasy. They should encourage risk-taking and original thinking. Learners should also have a possibility of choice as this makes them more personally involved in the task. A friendly classroom atmosphere, motivation, the recognition of learners' strengths, as well as the use of technology (e.g., blogging), and working in groups on unusual assignments also support creativity.

In the overview of *Creativity in the English language classroom* (2015), Maley offers valuable comments and advice to teachers on how to teach creatively. His "generic principles for developing more creativity" (p. 10) are of particular significance and therefore they are briefly discussed here. Maley, then, suggests that teachers should use the following principles:

- heuristics (e.g., doing the opposite, reversing the usual order of things, reducing/expanding something);
- the constraints principle: imposing tight constraints on activities is recommended; for example, limiting the number of words to be written, the amount of time to complete the activity, or the amount of materials;
- the random principle involves putting together things that do not belong together, and trying to find connections;
- the association principle: students react to evocative stimuli; for example, they write a text from the point of view of a stone or a flower;
- the withholding information principle: students receive only part of the information necessary to do the task as, for example, in jigsaw reading and listening;
- the divergent thinking principle consists in finding as many solutions to the problem as possible; for example, finding as many uses for common objects (e.g., a bottle, a sock) as possible;
- feeder fields "are domains outside the limited field of ELT but which may offer insights of use in ELT" (p. 11) and teachers may use NLP, literature, music, art, technology, and many others.

Actually, the principles that Maley recommends implementing in creative teaching resemble very much teaching practices that good teachers follow to motivate, involve, and challenge their students. Interesting and varied activities, not necessarily based on sophisticated or expensive materials, are always appreciated by foreign language learners and learners in general. The book *Creativity in the English language classroom* (Maley, 2015) contains 18 chapters by different authors who write about creative writing, story-telling, use of coursebooks, communication, visual aids, and many others. It is an excellent example of how creative teaching works. In the overview the reader may find a list of resource books that contain tasks and activities supportive of creative teaching.

The decision what materials and activities to use depends on factors such as students' language proficiency, their interests, their age, and the time at the teacher's disposal. Using literary texts, specifically short stories and poems involves different levels of creativity. First, students are exposed to language that is used in its poetic/imaginative function. Second, they are exposed to a creative product. Third, their responses reflect everyday language creativity because they use the language to reflect on the task. Fourth, they also reflect on their understanding of life and themselves. And, fifth, they find internal reward and enjoyment in the activities.

My own research on using literary texts (creative products) shows that foreign language students value working with literature. Jigsaw reading of a short story by Roald Dahl revealed that the participants used many creative strategies to recreate the story, they monitored their comprehension thus showing autonomy, they were motivated to do the task and they enjoyed it. They also showed originality and invention when trying to translate an unusual English expression into Polish (Piasecka, 2013a). In another study (Piasecka, 2013c), the participants read two poems concerning the event that changed the course of history at the beginning of the 21st century—the terrorist attack of September 11th, 2001, and then they reflected on their reading. One poem was in their L1 (Polish), the other was in English. The analysis of their reflections reveals their concern with such funda-mental human issues as life and death as well as the importance of making decisions about how one's life is to end. The participants were sensitive to languages used in the poems. They appreciated the power of poetic language along with metaphoric expressions evoking "strong emotions and deep reflection". Reading poems from other languages and cultures allows learners to look at apparently obvious and accepted values and beliefs form (a) different perspective(s), to appreciate otherness and to critically approach their own language, culture, history, and society as well as their identities. In yet another study (Piasecka, 2016), participants were asked to read two poems in English and to reflect on three good things they experienced while reading and why these experiences happened. According to the results, the participants were able to look at their own life and life in general in a new way, thus showing creativity. They were genuinely interested in and excited about the activity, and thought about the issues the poems addressed in new ways. They had the courage to speak honestly about their experience, they showed emotional involvement and awareness of their own feelings and the feelings of the characters from the poems. Moreover, they appreciated the beauty of poetic expression by noticing the unusual use of vocabulary and form.

Having foreign language students read poems is a difficult but rewarding activity for it involves a whole person, which means that cognitive activity connected with making sense of the text is linked with emotions raised by the text and experienced in a specific situational context. It also develops their language proficiency, imagination—a fellow traveler with creativity (Pope & Swann, 2011), knowledge and sensitivity. Reading poetry, students show their creativity, courage, curiosity, open-mindedness along with appreciation of literature as a manifestation of art. Using poetry in an EFL classroom is beneficial both in linguistic and non-linguistic terms and poems can be used on any educational and proficiency level. Exploring nursery rhymes with younger learners is not only enjoyable but it also develops their phonological awareness and supports reading. Adolescents may wish to explore lyrics of songs they particularly value although they may also enjoy working with more traditional songs such as, for example, "Clementine". Learners' encounters with poetry may be more motivating and interesting when the teacher allows them to bring to class their own favorite poems and share these with the class. Older learners may be asked to compare such forms of expression as Christmas carols in their L1 and L2 (Piasecka, 2013b, 2016).

7 Conclusion

There is a high demand for creativity in all spheres of human life and people use this uniquely human characteristic in a variety of contexts, often without realizing they do so. Since it is so important, especially against the backdrop of the 21st century with its changes and challenges, stimulating creativity and creative thinking should become one of the most important goals of education. Despite the fact that systems of education stifle rather than encourage creativity in learners, there are teachers and classrooms where creativity is stimulated and welcome. Actually, all school subjects should encourage learners to look at the old or given information in new ways to find out how this knowledge may be applied to solve everyday problems effectively.

Fig. 1 A stimulus for fostering creativity

In this regard, a foreign language classroom is a special place. Learning a new language requires learners to create utterances they may not be confident about, yet they take a risk and produce them. When teaching is not exam-oriented, teachers may introduce many creative tasks and activities that are motivating, involving and rewarding. They also give the learners a sense of joy, excitement and fulfilment. The examples given in the last section of the article were based on using literary texts, especially poems, but there are ample opportunities to use other resources to develop creativity. And creativity is important both for individuals and societies. Teachers are supposed to enhance creativity in their learners so they also should be creative in their work and approach to it. Often, teacher modelling of creative actions is followed by learners. This implies that pre-service teacher trainees should be given training on creative foreign language classrooms while qualified teachers might be invited to participate in workshops targeting creative teaching. I am leaving the readers with a picture (Fig. 1). I invite them to think about the ways in which it may be used to stimulate creativity in foreign language learners. And users.

References

Albert, Á. (2006). Learner creativity as a potentially important variable: Examining the relationships between learner creativity, language aptitude and level of proficiency. In M. Nikolov & J. Horváth (Eds.), *UPRT 2006: Empirical studies in English applied linguistics* (pp. 77–98). Pécs: Lingua Franca Csoport.

Albert, Á., & Kormos, J. (2004). Creativity and narrative task performance: An exploratory study. *Language Learning, 54*, 277–310.

Amabile, T. M. (1996). *Creativity in context. Update to the social psychology of creativity.* Boulder, CO: Westview Press.

Barsalou, L. W., & Prinz, J. J. (1997). Mundane creativity in perceptual symbol systems. In T. B. Ward, S. M. Smith, & J. Vaid (Eds.), *Creative thought: An investigation of conceptual structures and processes* (pp. 267–307). Washington, DC: American Psychological Association.

Beghetto, R. A., & Kaufman, J. C. (2013). Fundamentals of creativity. *Educational Leadership, 70* (5), 10–15.

Boden, M. A. (2004). *The creative mind: Myths and mechanisms.* London: Routledge.

Burke, J. (2013). Generating minds. *English Journal, 102*(6), 25–30.

Carter, R. (2004). *Language and creativity: The art of common talk.* London: Routledge.

Chomsky, N. (1964). *Current issues in linguistic theory.* The Hague: Mouton.

Cook, G. (2000). *Language play, language learning.* Oxford: Oxford University Press.

Craft, A. (2003). The limits to creativity in education: Dilemmas for the educator. *British Journal of Educational Studies, 51*(2), 113–127.

Csikszentmihalyi, M. (1978). Attention and the holistic approach to behaviour. In K. S. Pope, & J. L. Singer (Eds.), *The stream of consciousness* (pp. 335–358). New York: Plenum Press.

Csikszentmihalyi, M. (1996). *Creativity: Flow and the psychology of discovery and invention.* New York: Harper/Collins.

De Dreu, C., Baas, M., & Nijstad, B. (2008). Hedonic tone and activation level in the mood-creativity link: Toward a dual pathway to creativity model. *Journal of Personality and Social Psychology, 94*, 739–756.

Fasko, D., Jr. (2000). -2001). Education and creativity. *Creativity Research Journal, 13*(3&4), 317–327.

Friedman, T. L. (2009, October 20). The new untouchables. *New York Times.* Retrieved from http://www.nytimes.com/2009/10/21/opinion/21friedman.html.

Gee, J. P. (1996). *Social linguistics and literacies: Ideology in discourses* (2nd ed.). London: Taylor & Francis.

Ghonsooly, B. (2012). The effects of foreign language learning on creativity. *English Language Teaching, 5*(4), 161–167. doi:10.5539/elt.v5n4p161.

Hakuta, K. (1974). Prefabricated patterns and the emergence of structure in second language acquisition. *Language Learning, 24*(2), 287–297.

Halliday, M. A. K. (1975). *Learning how to mean.* London: Edward Arnold.

Hennessey, B. A., & Amabile, T. M. (1987). *Creativity and learning.* Washington, DC: NEA Professional Library.

Higgins, E. T. (1997). Beyond pleasure and pain. *American Psychologist, 52,* 1280–1300.

Hommel, B., Colzato, L. S., Fischer, R., & Christoff, I. K. (2011). Bilingualism and creativity: Benefits in convergent thinking come with losses in divergent thinking. *Frontiers in Psychology, 2,* 1–5. doi:10.3389/fpsyg.2011.00273.

Jakobson, R. (1960). Closing statement: Linguistics and poetics. In T. Seboek (Ed.), *Style in language* (pp. 350–377). Cambridge, MA: MIT Press.

Jones, R. H. (2016). Introduction. In R. H. Jones (Ed.), *The Routledge handbook of language and creativity* (pp. 1–22). London: Roultledge.

Karnes, M. B., McCoy, G. F., Zehrbach, R. R., Wollersheim, J. P., Clarizio, H. F., Costin, L., & Stanley, L. S. (1961). *Factors associated with underachievement and overachievement of intellectually gifted children.* Champaign, IL: Champaign Community Unit Schools.

Kaufman, J. C., & Sternberg, R. J. (2015). The creative mind. In C. Jones, M. Lorenzen, & J. Sapsed (Eds.), *The Oxford handbook of creative industries* (pp. 34–49). Oxford: Oxford University Press.

Leiken, M., & Tovli, E. (2014). Bilingualism and creativity in early childhood. *Creativity Research Journal, 26*(4), 411–417. doi:10.1080/10400419.2014.961779.

Leung, A. K., Maddux, W. W., Galinsky, A. D., & Chiu, C. (2008). Multicultural experience enhances creativity: The when and how. *American Psychologist, 63,* 169–181. doi:10.3389/fpsyg.2011.00273.

Lightbown, P., & Spada, N. (1999). *How languages are learned* (2nd ed.). New York: Oxford University Press.

Łukasik, B. (2015). Twórczość w edukacji akademickiej – zasady, metody i techniki stymulowania twórczego myślenia studentów [Creation in academic education—rules, methods and techniques of stimulation of students' creative thinking]. *Prace Naukowe Akademii im Jana Długosza w Częstochowie, 17,* 203–212.

Maley, A. (2015). Overview: The what, the why and the how. In A. Maley & N. Peachey (Eds.), *Creativity in the English language classroom* (pp. 6–13). London: British Council.

Maybin, J. (2016). Everyday language creativity. In R. H. Jones (Ed.), *The Routledge handbook of language and creativity* (pp. 25–39). London: Roultledge.

McCabe, M. P. (1991). Influence of creativity and intelligence on academic performance. *Journal of Creative Behaviour, 25*(2), 116–122.

McCrae, R. R., & Costa, P. R. (1997). Personality trait structure as a human universal. *American Psychologist, 52,* 509–516.

Mitias, M. (1985). Preface. In M. Mitias (Ed.), *Creativity in art, religion, and culture* (pp. 1–2). Amsterdam: Rodopi.

Moon, R. (1998). *Fixed expressions and idioms in English. A corpus-based approach.* Oxford: Clarendon Press.

Nattinger, J., & DeCarrico, J. (1992). *Lexical phrases in language teaching.* Oxford: Oxford University Press.

Nęcka, E. (2001). *Psychologia twórczości [Psychology of creativity]*. Gdańsk: GWP.

Ockuly, M., & Richards, R. (2013). Loving or fearing creativity. *NeuroQuantology, 11*(2), 256–262.

Ottó, I. (1998). The relationship between individual differences in learner creativity and language learning success. *TESOL Quarterly, 32*(4), 763–773.

Piasecka, L. (2013a). Putting bits and pieces together: Awareness of text structure in jigsaw reading. In A. Łyda & K. Szczesniak (Eds.), *Awareness in action, second language learning and teaching* (183–193). Heidelberg: Springer. doi:10.1007/978-3-319-00461-7_12.

Piasecka, L. (2013b). "In time of daffodils who know"—reading poetry in a foreign language classroom. In E. Mańczak-Wohlfeld & M. Jodłowiec (Eds.), *Exploring the microcosm and macrocosm of language teaching and learning. A festschrift on the occasion of 70th birthday of Professor Anna Niżegorodcew* (pp. 93–104). Kraków: Jagiellonian University Press.

Piasecka, L. (2013c). Reading poems in foreign language learning contexts—an educational option. *Journal of the Worldwide Forum on Education and Culture, 4*(1), 61–72.

Piasecka, L. (2016). Activating character strengths through poetic encounters in a foreign language—a case study. In D. Gabryś-Barker & D. Gałajda (Eds.), *Positive psychology perspectives on foreign language learning and teaching* (pp. 75–92). Heidelberg: Springer.

Pope, R,. & Swann, J. (2011). Introduction: Creativity, language, literature. In J. Swann, R. Pope, & R. Carter (Eds.), *Creativity in language and literature. The state of the art* (pp. 1–22). Basingstoke: Palgrave.

Ricciardelli, L. A. (1992). Creativity and bilingualism. *Journal of Creative Behavior, 26*, 242–254.

Richards, J. (2013). Creativity in language teaching. Plenary address given at the Summer Institute for English Teacher of Creativity and Discovery in Teaching University Writing, City University of Hong Kong, 5th June 2013. http://www.professorjackrichards.com/wp-content/uploads/Creativity-in-Language-Teaching.pdf.

Robinson, K. (2011). *Out of our minds* (new ed.). Chichester: Capstone Publishing Ltd.

Runco, M. (2004). Creativity. *Annual Review of Psychology, 55*, 657–687. doi:10.1146/annurev.psych.55.090902.141502.

Runco, M. (2014, March 1). *Common questions and difficulty of creativity education [Web log message]*. Retrieved from https://www.creativitytestingservices.com/blog/common-questions-difficulty-of-creativity-education.

Runco, M., & Jaeger, G. J. (2012). The standard definition of creativity. *Creativity Research Journal, 24*(1), 92–96.

Sinclair, J. (1991). *Corpus, concordance, collocation*. Oxford: Oxford University Press.

Simonton, D. K. (2000). Creativity: Cognitive, personal, developmental, and social aspects. *American Psychologist, 55*(1), 151–158. doi:10.1037/0003-066X.55.1.151.

Simonton, D. K., & Damian, R. I. (2013). Creativity. In D. Reisberg (Ed.), *The Oxford handbook of cognitive psychology* (pp. 796–808). Oxford: Oxford University Press.

Sternberg, R. J., & Lubart, T. I. (1995). *Defying the crowd: Cultivating creativity in a culture of conformity*. New York: Free Press.

Sullivan, P. (2012). Essential habits of mind for college readiness. *College English, 74*(6), 547–553.

Wei, L. (2011). Moment Analysis and translanguaging space: Discursive construction of identities by multilingual Chinese youth in Britain. *Journal of Pragmatics, 43*, 1222–1235.

Wong-Fillmore, L. (1976). *The second time around: Cognitive and social strategies in second language acquisition*. Unpublished doctoral dissertation. Stanford University.

Author Biography

Liliana Piasecka is Professor of English at the Institute of English, Opole University, Poland, where she works as an applied linguist, researcher and teacher trainer. She teaches SLA and ELT courses, and supervises M.A. and Ph.D. thesis. Her research interests include second/foreign language acquisition issues, especially L2 lexical development, relations between L1 and L2 reading, gender, and identity. She has published three books, numerous articles, and co-edited three collections of articles.

Making the News: An ICC Simulation in the Erasmus + Context

Teresa Siek-Piskozub

Abstract In recent years international educational documents for foreign language teaching have tended to assign intercultural communicative competence (ICC) as its major goal. It is particularly true in the context of teaching English due to its *lingua franca* role. Yet research shows that foreign language teachers feel unprepared to assume the role of intercultural mediators and foreign language course books do not make this task any easier. There are, however, special intercultural sets which may be of use and teachers' willingness and creativity is all that is needed. The goal of this article is to show how language and intercultural teaching can be intertwined using the example of one class run with Erasmus+ students in one of the Polish universities.

Keywords Intercultural communicative competence · Foreign language teaching · Simulations

1 Introduction

Intercultural communicative competence (ICC), understood as knowledge, ability and the willingness to communicate in a non-native language with representatives coming from different linguistic and cultural backgrounds, has become the goal of modern languages education as specified in European documents (e.g., *Common European framework of reference for languages,* CEFR, 2001) and US documents (Standards for foreign language learning in the 21st century, 1999). Yet, research on the opinions and practices of foreign language (FL) teachers shows that although there is a growing awareness of the need to develop ICC among FL teachers, their practices do not confirm that and the blame is on the FL teacher education programs and teaching materials (e.g., Derenowski, 2015; Sobkowiak, 2015). There are many more reasons given by FL teachers; however, the fact that teachers feel unprepared

T. Siek-Piskozub (✉)
Adam Mickiewicz University, Poznań, Poland
e-mail: piskozub@amu.edu.pl

© Springer International Publishing AG 2018
M. Pawlak and A. Mystkowska-Wiertelak (eds.), *Challenges of Second and Foreign Language Education in a Globalized World,* Second Language Learning and Teaching, DOI 10.1007/978-3-319-66975-5_7

107

to do so is of utmost importance. In the chapter, after discussing briefly some underpinnings for introducing an intercultural approach to foreign language teaching, I will describe one of my ICC classes carried out with Erasmus+ students spending their "semester abroad" at Adam Mickiewicz University in Poznań, Poland. The activities implemented were two combined simulations. They are to exemplify how intercultural competence can be intertwined with language teaching.

2   ICC as a Goal for FL Teaching

One of the targets of education in the European Union is to develop intercultural competence among its members. Cooperation of members from different countries is our reality for which we need to prepare young generations of European citizens. The educational system should be helpful in this respect as intercultural competence is appointed an important general competence which should accompany communicative competence in the foreign language(s) (CEFR, 2001). Intercultural communication in languages other than English is also a goal set in standards for education in the United States (*Standards for foreign language learning in the 21st century*, 1999) where the recommendation of the integration of 5 domains (i.e., communication, culture, cooperation, comparison, and communities) is given.

Byram (1997) claims that ICC can be developed in the classroom as a result of direct instruction; it can also be developed as field work (e.g., while participating in educational exchanges) which may or may not be assisted with instruction; or as independent study. This means that there is no one way to ICC development and no one way to approach it in the foreign language class (Cobett, 2003). What is more, cross-cultural studies reveal that cultural competence develops throughout our life and is best developed as a result of direct experience.

Cultural competence is difficult to define as it is a complex phenomenon composed of knowledge, skills and attitudes, and there is no agreement among scholars concerning its definition. *Intercultural competence* is even more problematic. The first to use the term was Edward Hall (Sobkowiak, 2015, p. 62, following Leeds-Hurwitz, 1990) who sensitized American diplomats to implicit culture, that is, language- and culture-related problems in cross-cultural encounters (Hall, 1959, 1966). Since then researchers have designed alternative models of culture and interculture concentrating on different facets, be it different dimensions which can characterize people from different cultures when interacting in an international business situation (Hofstede, 1991; Hall & Hall, 1987), stages of development of intercultural sensitivity of those functioning in a foreign context (Bennett, 1993; Holmes & O'Neill, 2012), interplay between various cultural factors (Deardorff, 2006), or reasons for possible conflicts that emerge from intercultural misunderstandings. These can be pictured as a collision of two icebergs if culture is explained with the use of the iceberg metaphor where there are visible features (the tip of the iceberg) and hidden features (beliefs, thought patterns etc.), the latter causing miscomprehension (Hall, 1976; Weaver, 2001).

(Inter)cultural research within ethnography and culture studies leads to a growing awareness of the nature and the importance of intercultural communication in the globalized world in the times of mass migration and technology enhanced communication. As teachers we should engage in the process of developing ICC among our students as a natural need of our times, and there are many ways to implement intercultural teaching. Newton (2012, p. 30) explains that intercultural teaching is:

> using classroom activities to raise awareness of the cultural influence on our lives. It focuses on the awareness and skills necessary to navigate crosscultural encounters and experiences, and successfully participate in a world in which intercultural communication in English is becoming ever more widespread (…).
>
> [It] recognizes the intertwined and inseparable nature of language and culture and so treats culture learning as an integral part of all language learning. It is, however, (…) not just about transmitting information about culture. Instead, it focuses on raising awareness of culture and culture-in-language in the lived experience of students as well as in lives of people in the target language community.

The author further recommends three principles on which intercultural teaching should be based, namely, the learners need to be engaged in "genuine social interaction"; the teacher and the learners should "explore culture in language, communication, behavior, and ways of being"; and, finally, comparing and connecting languages and culture should follow, as well as reflection on differences and similarities (Newton, 2012, p. 31).

3   Using Simulations to Develop ICC

A technique which enables following Newton's principles is simulation. It is also considered to be effective for ICC development (Lubecka, 1998). Simulations are rooted in the socio-constructivist theory of human cognition and learning in which the importance of both formal knowledge and private knowledge are treated as important for the process of meaning making (see e.g., Bruner, 1973; Siek-Piskozub, 2006). Simulations belong to problem-solving activities and enhance learners' autonomy, which is one of the goals of modern education. Simulations can also help in developing ICC skills because they enhance communicating in the target language while seeking solutions to an intercultural problem; they challenge learners' attitudes towards the simulated problem, and, as a result, raise awareness of different points of view; they also develop negotiation skills (Siek-Piskozub, 2013). All of these belong to what is considered to be the realm of intercultural communicative competence (Byram, 1997).

In the following section, I would like to describe one of the classes with "Erasmus+" students studying at different faculties of Adam Mickiewicz University in Poznań. They participated in an ICC class offered by the Faculty of English which I ran. During the class, which lasted for 90 min per week, many ICC activities in the form of simulations were implemented. I would also like to present the outcomes of one of the activities devoted to the impact of the media on our individual views and discuss the possibilities of further work on culture and language issues as a follow-up.

4 Media Making Simulation in the ICC Class

4.1 *The Framework for the* Media Making *Simulation*

The ICC related goals of the activity were to develop negotiation skills in culturally challenging situations, to develop empathy to "other", and to learn how to seek solutions. Participants were also expected to reflect on the impact the mass media have on our worldviews. The language-related problems concerned accuracy of the written texts/articles to further develop students' writing skills, namely, structuring of the text, coherence and accuracy of language. The materials used during the class were props in the form of scenarios prepared by the teacher and articles/texts written by student-journalists after they had observed a simulated intercultural encounter.

The students (N = 15) participating in the class came from different countries (Armenia, China, Italy, Portugal, Spain, and Turkey). They had chosen the course to further develop their competence in English and increase their ICC. During some earlier classes they had a chance to speak about themselves and their countries (e.g., educational systems, dominating religions, festivals, etc.), as well as share their own experiences with Polish culture and encounters with people outside the university. This gave them an opportunity to get to know each other better and feel more confident while performing different activities with other students or in front of them. They were competent at EFL A2 to B1 level (CEFR, 2001). For the described class I divided them into two teams, each having a different task to perform (see props below).

The scenario for Team 1
Please, subdivide into two groups: natives of Pyraland and refugees. The refugees want their children to get a proper education. However, there is only one school in Pyraland and its natives do not want their children to learn with refugees' children. Each subgroup has to think of arguments for their case and then carry on a debate in front of Team 2. The opponents should try to reach a consensus. The debate should last for approximately 15 min.

The scenario for Team 2
Choose a journal you work for and think of its policy. You can choose between a left/right wing paper, an international or a female journal. Listen to and observe the debate between two groups in a conflict-situation and make notes. Prepare a short article for your journal about the event. It is not to be a

summary of it but information and your opinion on what you have observed. When it is ready, place your work on the whiteboard. You will read it out to the class.

The first team chose a problem situation where participants were to split up into two different social groups and needed to express their opinions on an issue and negotiate an acceptable solution. The problem may typically concern a recent intercultural conflict, social or political event but also suggestions for the situations can come from an intercultural education package (e.g., Brander, Cardens, Gomes, Taylor, & de Vincente Abada, 1995; Huber-Kriegler, Lázár, & Strange, 2003). In a better integrated class I would have expected students to propose a situation themselves. But with such mixed abilities and students with different backgrounds the problematic situation was presented in the form of scenarios for the two teams. The problem situation in the described class was a meeting of two distinct social/ethnic groups: immigrant-parents of children at school age who wanted their children to be educated and the country/town authorities who saw some problems in meeting the demand. The team split into the two social groups and in approximately 5 min each group thought over their stance, rehearsed the language they needed, and planned the event (e.g., arranged seats for the debate). Then the two groups got together and simulated the debate on the issue. All members of both groups expressed their opinions, suggested solutions, agreed or disagreed with the opinions of others. Finally, the two groups had to reach a compromise, that is, take a decision that would satisfy both sides. The simulation lasted for about 15 min.

The second team were journalists who observed the event. Before the debate they had to decide on the kind of medium they would work for, give it a title and think over the policy it had (e.g., being a left/right wing newspaper or a tabloid). Depending on the number of participants in a class, it could be individual, pair or group work for each journal. In the case of my students, there were 2 persons for each of 4 journals. The journalists observed the debate, made notes, and, after the simulation was over, they had to write a short article which was motivated by what they had observed. I allowed members of the debate (students from the first team) to join the chosen medium and serve as additional informants. The article was not to be a simple summary of the event but needed to tackle the issue(s) which had been discussed. After 15 min the articles were ready. They were displayed on the board and later read out to the class.

In the follow-up phase, which lasted till the end of the class, a discussion continued on the differences between the articles, what influenced the differences, the impact the mass media have on our worldviews, what we should do to get an objective or fuller picture of an event, and so on. We also concentrated on some language-related problems.

4.2   The Outcome

Four articles were written by the student-journalists, each for a different mass medium. They served as stimulation for further discussion on the issue of the impact of the mass media on societies and on problems stemming from this. The texts were read out and displayed so that we could later work on language issues. Two of the four articles written by the journalists during this activity are placed below as examples. They are presented in their original written form.

Female journal

The Female's voice
    It was told that refugees were discriminated in many countries but the article you will read is totally out of your expectations.
    It happened in Pyraland where the local authorities met the refugees representative mothers who demanded equal learning conditions for their children. they applied without any hope because they had tried so many times to protect their children's right for learning.
    For any mother the most important thing is the right of her children and those mothers didn't want their children to have the status of refugees when they grow up. As mothers they knew their women rights and with supportive document they finally got what they wanted.
    The local authorities examined all their documents and they promised that they will proceed with procedure. So mothers were finally satisfied.

Conservative journal

A suggestion to both sides!
    Every refugee has right of education, it is one of the point of Human Rights, because all people are equal. But who will pay for this and who will take responsibility. Of course we are not against their education but we need to care about all people (all citizens who live in that country).
    Why do state should pay for the refugees' education? We should think about their physical and mental improvement, also about their language ability. But they should do the same for all citizens. If they learn the language together (only refugees' children) the results will be more uneffective. They should go into different classes. So it will be helpful and integration for their language learning, adopting of the culture and integration.
    As a conclusion, this question is a very difficult. Of course there are some solutions for this. We will help them giving them possibility of education but they will also help us paying some low payment (30%). It is the best solution for both sides and all children will learn in harmony.

4.3 Discussion on the Outcomes

As can be observed from the articles, the "journalists" placed emphasis on different issues that emerged from the debate; however, these were issues which could be expected from the policies of different political orientations, or when treated from different social perspectives. These issues were later further discussed in the follow-up phase. As can be seen, the reports are not without language errors. The coherence of the texts is sometimes blurred, the rule for reported speech is not followed, there are problems with punctuation, and so on, but all this was discussed and practiced in the follow-up phase.

I concentrated first on the expressed opinions to appreciate the students' willingness to communicate and their effort to look at the issue from a certain stance, to discuss the importance of reaching compromises in society, to appreciate education for one's development and to see the detrimental effects of its deprivation, etc. But then focus on the form of the article followed, that is, the importance of an appealing title for the article, the text's general structure, and clarity of the expressions. It was complemented with an analysis of some language-related problems which were motivated by the weaknesses of the written articles (e.g., how to build multi-word utterances using examples from the articles, suggestions for some more precise expressions of some intentions/concepts, correction of grammar and punctuation errors, etc.).

The class described above lasted 90 min, which is a typical arrangement for Polish tertiary education institutions. However, it can be easily split into two consecutive shorter lessons where the simulation of the debate is performed in one lesson and journal writing can be the task for the next class. Then the additional informants (members of the debate) may be even more useful. The articles could also be a task for a homework assignment or, alternatively, the homework can be an essay where students will express their opinions on the issue. After having heard different opinions and discussed the matter over, students may be more willing to share their opinions in writing, giving us as FL teachers some input for further language instruction.

5 Conclusion

The simulation described above shows that ICC issues can be brought to the attention of foreign language learners without the loss of the focus on language, which often is feared by foreign language teachers. As researchers have pointed out (e.g., Derenowski, 2015) young people are interested in cultural issues, they seek information on the Internet and would like their teachers to discuss cultural issues or make comparisons between their own and the target culture more often than is in fact done in the FL class. In both activities (debate and article writing) run with my students, there were plenty of opportunities for developing their communicative competence in the target language both in its oral form (e.g., practicing during the discussions different language functions, such as expressing opinions, agreeing and disagreeing, doubting, negotiating, evaluating, etc.) and in its written form (text/article writing skills, accuracy). Accuracy does not need to be compromised in simulations as FL teachers often fear; however, it can be tackled after the students have produced the utterances/text. It is then more interesting and appealing to them.

References

Bennett, M. (1993). Towards ethnorelativism: A developmental model of intercultural sensitivity. In M. R. Paige (Ed.), *Education for the intercultural experience* (pp. 21–71). Yarmouth: Intercultural Press.

Brander, P., Cardens, C., Gomes, R., Taylor, M., & de Vincente Abada, J. (1995). *All different all equal: Education pack. Ideas, resources, methods and activities for informal intercultural education with young people and adults*. Strasbourg: Council of Europe.

Bruner, J. S. (1973). *Beyond the information given: Studies in the psychology of knowing*. New York: Norton.

Byram, M. (1997). *Teaching and assessing intercultural competence*. Clevedon: Multilingual Matters.

Corbett, J. (2003). *An intercultural approach to English language teaching*. Clevedon: Multilingual Matters.

Deardorff, K. D. (2006). Identification and assessment of intercultural competence as a student outcome of internationalization. *Journal of Studies in International Education, 10*, 241–266.

Derenowski, M. (2015). *Teaching culture in the FL senior high school classroom. Coursebook evaluation and teachers' and learners' views*. Poznań: Adam Mickiewicz University Press.

Hall, E. T. (1959). *The silent language*. New York: Doubleday.

Hall, E. T. (1966). *The hidden dimension*. New York: Doubleday.

Hall, E. T. (1976). *Beyond culture*. Garden City, NY: Anchor Press.

Hall, E. T., & Hall, M. R. (1987). *Hidden dimensions: Doing business with the Japanese*. New York: Doubleday/Anchor Books.

Hofstede, G. (1991). *Cultures and organizations: A software of mind*. London: McGraw-Hill.

Holmes, P., & O'Neill, G. (2012). Developing and evaluating intercultural competence: Ethnographies of intercultural encounters. *International Journal of Intercultural Relations, 36*, 707–717.

Huber-Kriegler, M., Lázár, I., & Strange, J. (2003). *Mirrors and windows. An intercultural communication textbook*. Graz: European Centre for Modern Languages.

Leeds-Hurwitz, W. (1990). Notes in the history of intercultural communication: The Foreign Service Institute and the mandate for intercultural training. *Quarterly Journal of Speech, 76*, 262–281.

Lubecka, A. (1998). Interkulturowa kompetencja komunikacyjna – jak wykorzystać gry symulacyjne do jej osiągnięcia [Intercultural communicative competence—how to use simulation games to develop it]. *Biuletyn Glottodydaktyczny UJ Kraków, 4*, 59–74.

Newton, J. (2012). Teaching English for intercultural spoken communication: From CLT to iCLT. In H. P. Widodo & A. Cirocki (Eds.), *Innovation and creativity in ELT methodology* (pp. 29–42). New York: Nova Science Publishers Inc.

Siek-Piskozub, T. (2006). Constructivism in language pedagogy. In E. Jezińska-Lorek, T. Siek-Piskozub, & K. Więckowska (Eds.), *Worlds in the making. Constructivism and postmodern knowledge* (pp. 159–172). Toruń: Nicolaus Copernicus University Press.

Siek-Piskozub, T. (2013). Simulations as communication, culture and creativity (3 in 1). In E. Wąsikiewicz-Firlej & H. Lankiewicz (Eds.), *From classroom to workplace: Advances in applied linguistics* (pp. 16–30). Piła: Państwowa Wyższa Szkoła Zawodowa im. Stanisława Staszica.

Sobkowiak, P. (2015). *Interkulturowość w edukacji językowej [Interculturality in language education]*. Poznań: Wydawnictwo Naukowe UAM.

Standards for foreign language learning in the 21st century. (1999). Retrieved from http://global teachinglearning.com/standards/5cs.shtml; file:///C:/Users/tpisk/Documents/World-Readiness StandardsforLearningLanguages.pdf.

Weaver, G. (2001). *American cultural values.* Retrieved from www.gmfus.org/doc/mmf/American %20Cultural%20Values.pdf.

Author Biography

Teresa Siek-Piskozub is Full Professor in the unit of English Applied Linguistics and English Didactics of the Faculty of English, Adam Mickiewicz University in Poznań, Poland and was its head till 2012. In the years 2000–2006 she was the Chair of the English Department of Nicholas Copernicus University. She is an author of many articles and five books on foreign language teaching and learning, one of which, devoted to the use of games, was translated into Romanian. She (co)edited collections on applied linguistics and EFL pedagogy. For many years she was Editor of the Modern Language Association of Poland's journal Neofilolog and of the newsletter of the Fédération Internationale des Professeurs de Langues Vivantes FIPLV World News. She has lectured in many countries and has taken part in a great number of national and international conferences.

Toward an Integrated Model of Teaching Business English in Tertiary Education

Paweł Sobkowiak

Abstract Effective use of English in the international business context requires not only knowledge of business domains, such as micro- and macro-economics, marketing, finance and fundamentals of business law, but also professional, intercultural and interpersonal skills. All these components should be taken into consideration while designing Business English (BE) syllabi. The article discusses some of the important issues connected with designing BE courses for the tertiary education level and analyzes Bhatia's (2002) tripartite model for teaching English for business purposes, which, drawing to the concept of professional expertise, aims to combine teaching subject knowledge and business practices with developing students' discursive competence. The framework cultivates facilitating their business expertise and skills, rather than merely teaching discrete knowledge of the subject and a special language register. On the practical front, the author recommends adopting the case study approach in BE classes, because cases allow for working on the three modules of the model discussed in the theoretical part of the paper.

1 Introduction

The purpose of a Business English (BE) course, like any other English for Specific Purposes (ESP) courses, is to fulfill students' profession-related needs and develop expertise in a given profession they represent. To achieve this, the syllabus and materials used in the classroom try to imitate students' communication needs in workplace settings, which were determined by prior needs analysis. However, in the case of BE courses taught at tertiary level, where the participants are pre-experienced learners; i.e., apprentices in business contexts, those needs are often difficult to identify since it is impossible to foresee in which business sectors or at what positions the students will be employed and, thus, for what purposes they

P. Sobkowiak (✉)
Adam Mickiewicz University, Poznań, Poland
e-mail: pawelsob@amu.edu.pl

© Springer International Publishing AG 2018   117
M. Pawlak and A. Mystkowska-Wiertelak (eds.), *Challenges of Second and Foreign Language Education in a Globalized World*, Second Language Learning and Teaching, DOI 10.1007/978-3-319-66975-5_8

will be using English in the would-be workplaces, if they use it at all. Traditionally, in such courses, referred to in the literature as English for General Business Purposes (EGBP), students usually use materials set in business contexts, formed on the basis of language rather than job criteria. They work on the traditional four skills and develop specific grammar and vocabulary (Dudley-Evans & St John, 1998, p. 55).

This paper, which is of a descriptive and exploratory nature, analyzes BE, addresses some of the important issues associated with designing BE courses at the level of tertiary education and tries to answer the question regarding what contents such courses should include so that students can acquire both language proficiency and professional expertise enabling them to function successfully in the world of business. The author discusses Bhatia's (2002) tripartite, participant-focused and process-oriented model for teaching BE. It aims to integrate teaching subject knowledge and business practices with discursive competence,[1] hoping to prepare students to work in a multilingual and multicultural environment across a range of business sectors, and at diverse positions.

2   Business English, Business Communication and BE Course Design

BE register contains specialized language in terms of grammar and business terminology, and is used to relate language forms to the context in which they are used. Zhang (2007, p. 403) categorized BE lexis into three groups according to their functions, namely "participant, process and circumstance". He revealed that whereas in the business world the participants act in the capacity of customers, contractors, managers, sellers or buyers (i.e., are rather institutionalized and public), in everyday life they take roles of wife, mother or child (i.e., are personal and private). Along the same line, processes in the business world are more action-oriented (i.e., business people sell, manage, manufacture, deliver or confirm) than in ordinary life, where people see, feel, lie, love, marry or die. The circumstances of the two worlds also differ, which is illustrated, for example, by location (office, department, boardroom versus living room, kitchen, fitness club, forest, etc.).

---

[1]Discursive competence comprises: (a) textual competence—the ability to use language, i.e. sounds, words and grammar, appropriately to suit the context and use textual, contextual and pragmatic knowledge to construct and interpret texts; (b) generic competence—the ability to respond to recurrent and new communicative situations by producing, interpreting and using generic conventions to achieve professional goals; (c) professional competence—the capacity to use genres to become a competent member of a professional culture; and (d) social competence— the ability to use language more widely to participate effectively in a wide variety of social and institutional contexts to give expressions to their social identity (Bhatia, 2002).

Currently, thanks to advanced technology, an in-depth study of the language used in business communication is feasible, which has made determining the content of BE courses much easier: at the micro-level of grammar and lexis, BE is not any more as experience-, intuition- and materials-led as it used to be. For example, the Cambridge and Nottingham Business English Corpus (CANBEC), which contains one million spoken data from a range of purely spoken business contexts, allows for gaining access to frequency lists of the most important key-words and clusters used by business people at meetings and, thus, including them in a BE course (Handford, 2010). In a similar vein, access to more data has revealed practices showing that, in many situations, much shorter and more informal phrases than the ones taught in the past are used at business meetings, and that gambits employed on such occasions do not have to be verbal: topic closure can be signaled by shifting papers or taking out car keys, while topic introduction by opening a new file (Linde, 1991). Handford (2010, p. 251) reported that, in business meetings, the modal verb *must*, while formally possible, is highly unusual and potentially haz-ardous; *need to* and *have to* are more frequent. Similarly, expressions such as *I disagree with you* are not common even though they are still used in BE textbooks. Data bases such as CANBEC can contribute to offering students input more compatible with the language they will meet in their future workplaces.

However, BE is much more than a "the special nomenclature that reflects content knowledge" (Handford, 2010, p. 248) with specialized lexical, syntactic and dis-course features. Language used in business is a complex phenomenon subject to a range of variables and has its own subject matter, interpersonal relations, channels of communication, and patterns of organizing messages. All those factors contribute to significant variations and dynamic patterns of business communication of which students have to be made aware.

Researchers argue that in business communication language is often used to create messages in conventionalized forms, appropriate to the communicative goals of interaction participants. Studies of business genres[2] reveal that business inter-actions are staged and goal-oriented. This is illustrated by meetings which have typical structural features repeated in different contexts and companies. Holmes and Stubbe (2003) identified three stages into which corporate meetings are structured: opening, discussion and closing. Each phase is made up of a number of linguistic conventions, exchanges and moves, and the boundaries between the consecutive stages are marked by transitional moves. The participants also automatically employ relatively well-ingrained professional and discursive practices to achieve their objectives.

Recent research indicates that genres are standardized communicative events, and in the literature, researchers identify seven core communicative events in the business world (Bhatia, 2002; Holden, 1993; Yin & Wong, 1990). Five of them, namely telephoning, socializing, delivering presentations, taking part in meetings

---

[2]Genre comprises a class of communicative events, the members of which share the same set of communicative purposes (Swales, 1990, p. 58).

and negotiations, require oral language, while two are in written form: corresponding and reporting. Dudley-Evans and St John (1998, p. 64) noted how misleading the term "socializing" is by suggesting that the focus of interaction is social when, in fact, it remains business. The "social" aspect of interactions is primarily aimed at establishing a good relationship in order to enhance the conduct of business. All those communicative events have to be taken into consideration while designing a BE syllabus.

Currently, content offered in BE classes tries to incorporate the research findings discussed above and imitate how the language works and functions, and how people use it in business contexts. Consequently, this means that designing the course is preceded by a thorough analysis of discourse (exploring texts at a level beyond the sentence), genres and communicative events typical of a business community students hope to enter in the future (McCarthy & Carter, 2004, p. 3). Exposing students to various business genres stems from the premise that as novices they should be ushered into professions through engagement in its characteristic language and a set of practices mutually understandable within this community, along the way learning to replicate the values of the profession, if possible, by interacting with experts.

In addition, students should be exposed to and study the context in which communication takes place. As Bhatia (2008, p. 171) argues, contextualization is responsible for "the eventual success of professional activities usually undertaken by professionals to achieve their professional objectives". In practice, this means allowing students to go beyond textual studies (e.g., distinguishing features of promotional letters) and analyze text-external factors. If texts are to be sources of an in-depth analysis of a given professional community and their linguistic practices, they should not be treated as isolated artifacts, but, instead, their users and the uses to which the text is put and how the discourse is affected by the relationship between participants should be explored in detail. The knowledge about "who gets to say or write to whom with what effect using what channels and modes, how different genres are used, abused or subverted, and what the patterns of communication reveal about organizational structure, culture and decision-making processes" is necessary in understanding an organization's systems of communication (Hall, 2013, p. 5).

However, according to Bazerman and Russel (2003, p. 1), the study of texts and how they are produced and understood is meaningless, unless we can look at what the text actually causes to be done in the real world:

> It is in the context of their activities that people consider texts and give meaning to texts. And it is in the organization of activities that people find the needs, stances, interactions, and tasks that orient their attention toward texts they write and read. So to study text production, text reception, text meaning, and text value apart from their animating activities is to miss the core of text's being.

Thus, students' attention in BE class should be directed not only at the language and context, but also at what influences BE discourse significantly, namely the relationship between interlocutors (business partners), the issues of power between them, and their attitudes, identity and cultural values. All those variables shape and constrain the use of the language and have a significant impact on the utilized style in interaction, which can be either formal or informal, and direct and indirect. Research findings have revealed that the institutional relationship and status of the speakers, along with the goals of the encounter, seem to exert the foremost effect on business communication. For instance, status allows or restricts opportunities to take the floor or open or close topics in meetings, whereas both L1 and L2 clients and managers have more power and discursive opportunities than subcontractors or subordinates in business encounters (Dudley-Evans & St John, 1998, p. 61).

Another example of this kind is provided by Charles (1996), who showed that a dichotomy of "new/old" in a business relationship has a differentiating power in sales negotiation discourse. If the relationship is new, the Buyers and Sellers are likely to take the roles imposed on them by the business community: they will follow established business patterns and, during the negotiation, they will use a range of politeness strategies to save the professional face of the negotiating partner. However, if the relationship is established, those roles may well be relaxed and the established patterns set aside so that the politeness strategies both sides use might serve to save the personal face of the other party. Another distinguishing factor is the situation of the buyer's market, which gives the Buyer more power over the Seller in interactions.

In the light of what has been said above, BE students have to be aware that networks of interpersonal relations in the world of business are intricate and need to be considered if the message is to be communicated clearly and the relationship dealt with appropriately, e.g., the issue of social distance between the participants shapes discussion. The participants within those circles (i.e., business-customer, business-business, and members of different departments within the same company) differ in many respects, namely in access to knowledge of professional practice, market position, status and frames of reference,[3] and, thus, communicate in a different way. Those differences exert a considerable role in interpersonal interactions as they help shape the structure of the interaction and induce a strategic use of the language (Zhang, 2007, p. 404).

Since enterprises have globalized, intercultural aspect of communication has been contributing a lot to the interpersonal dimension of doing business and thus, students have to become familiar with the cultural context of language use, that is, national or local cultures, industrial cultures and corporate cultures. The participants of cross-cultural interactions may face a dilemma over whose frame of reference and code of conduct to adopt. Traditionally, it was assumed that in international encounters where English is used, Anglo-American norms dominate. This, however, is not valid anymore, according to researchers reporting various deviances from such standards.

---

[3]Frames of reference are concepts, values, views, etc. by means of which an individual perceives or evaluates data.

For example, Marriott (1995) investigating business negotiations in English between an Australian and a Japanese, noted the Australian's considerable disagreement with the Japanese's refusal to respond to his proposals in the forms and manners he had expected. The Japanese deviated from the Anglo-American norms because of his status, that is, he was an overseas representative of his home company and wanted to emphasize the differences in cultural norms to pay attention to his diverse cultural identity. Bilbow (1997), in turn, revealed that at corporate meetings in Hong Kong, Western staff used more directive forms than local Chinese staff members, who were more circuitous. Bilbow attributed these differences to the cultural norms of the two groups—for the Chinese indirectness is a strategy used to save face, which is a social value highly recognized in their culture. Other studies, however, reported that the participants of international business interactions are not bound by their cultural norms and, driven by their business objectives, tend to accommodate to each other. For example, Marriott (1995) demonstrated that convergence is common in business negotiations between the Japanese and the Australian, and that both parties treat their cultural norms like interpretative resources rather than rules to be followed blindly. Zhu (2005) studied sales letters from a cross-cultural perspective (English vs. Chinese) and found that in order to achieve a persuasive effect, they share a range of communicative purposes, such as attracting the reader's attention, giving positive assessment of the product, persuading the reader to purchase the product and eliciting a positive response. Interestingly, the Chinese sales letters contained one communicative purpose, that is, the goal of setting a long-term agent-client relationship with the reader, which was absent in the English letters. Since, on graduation our students may find themselves working for international companies, a grounding in intercultural communication seems to be of paramount importance and should be present in BE class.

A lot of changes in business communication which have taken place at the turn of the 20th century regard the mode of doing business and BE courses have to adapt to them accordingly. For example, Firth (1995, p. 6) pointed out that a negotiation activity takes place in many contexts, such as "offices, committee rooms, marketplaces, consultancy rooms, shops, used car lots". The actual bargaining may be done by telephone, fax or e-mail after the meeting. The electronic revolution has also changed the media used in business to transmit messages. Powell (2005) portrayed the way business is conducted in the electronic age in the following way:

> These days the telephone is a more automatic choice for problem-solving and negotiation than the boardroom. A lot of meetings are as likely to take place in pavement cafes, office corridors, hotel foyers or in front of a webcam as they are seated around a table with a formal agenda and a flipchart. In fact, 21st century Business English might be better defined as a series of ongoing conversations – electronic, telephonic and face-to-face – whether they are the cut-and-paste conversations of e-mail, the interest-seeking conversations of negotiation or the public conversations of PowerPoint presentations (Powell in Zhang 2007, p. 405).

IT technology is changing the format of communication. For example, in the domain of written correspondence, it has accelerated the move away from formal and impersonal written communication to more informal and personal. However, BE students should be made aware that it still needs the hallmarks of good written communication, that is, a clear purpose and well organized ideas, which lead to a coherent and cohesive text.

Thus, if a BE classroom aims to equip students well with necessary competencies and skills to deal with real business people in the workplace environment, it has to go far beyond the purely semantic approach and the teaching of discipline-specific linguistic forms and features. Instead, it has to recognize the importance of discipline-based genres and introduce their analyses into class. If students are to be prepared to convey and receive messages for professional purposes appropriately, it is requisite to analyze with them a range of text types, both written and spoken, so that they become aware of how workplace genres are constructed, and allow them to identify which genres are most common and what their characteristics are. Such knowledge constituting discursive competence, that is, knowledge and skills that expert professionals use in specific discourse situations of their everyday professional activities (Bhatia, 2004), is one of the markers of professional expertise and will help students understand specific communicative purposes of business texts they will encounter in their professional lives. As important is examining the business relationships between interlocutors. Only once students learn all the intricacies and conventions of how the members of a BE discourse community they aspire to enter negotiate meaning in professional contexts, will they be able to exert a desired impact on their colleagues in the future work environments.

3   An Integrated Model of Teaching BE at the University

Traditionally, it was assumed that BE taught at the tertiary level should help students acquire helpful details of language that are in harmony with those used in business circles. However, recent research in genre analysis proved that language should not be perceived as a unified single literacy. It was revealed that students require, among a number of other inputs, the discipline specific knowledge of how professionals conceptualize various issues and talk about them in order to achieve their disciplinary and professional goals (Bhatia, 2004).

Currently, there is an increasing awareness that teaching BE is an interdisciplinary endeavor and should focus on a combination of three essential competencies: disciplinary knowledge (the development of deep conceptual understanding in a domain is a necessary condition for the development of expertise), discursive competence (language, business and study skills), and professional practice (Bhatia, 2002). Those components should be integrated since successful business communication requires knowledge of the discipline, language proficiency along with procedures, strategies and tactics for conveying messages, and a range of professional contexts in which linguistic choices can be made (frameworks of business activities). A tripartite model of teaching BE presented in Fig. 1 refers to the

Fig. 1 Bhatia's tripartite
model of teaching business
english

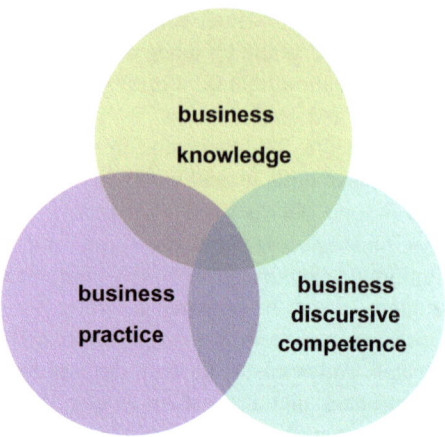

aforementioned Bhatia's professional expertise framework. It incorporates three interdependent modules, namely business knowledge, business discursive competence and business practice.

The first area, business knowledge, comprises studies of various business topics and concepts from micro- and macro-economics, marketing, company finance, human resource management and fundamentals of business law. It can be transmitted to students in the form of small lectures, presentations or a range of texts (oral and written) (Zhang 2007, pp. 406–407). Those texts are simultaneously aimed at developing students' four language skills.

The business discursive competence module is designed to develop students' language proficiency, study skills and business skills. It plays a pivotal role, since language and business interact here—successful and appropriate discourse requires a combination of subject knowledge and insights into business practices. Students work on various sets of genres and activities, namely academic writing, discussion and presentations (study skills), meetings, negotiations, talking over the phone, socializing and correspondence (business skills). They also analyze a range of genres in terms of their accuracy and appropriateness to enhance their abilities to reflect on the use of language in business contexts.

Contents in the business practice component show students how business professionals perform business in a professionally appropriate manner. When communicating about professional goals, business people automatically employ relatively ingrained professional practices to achieve them. For example, a logistics manager, when setting up a supply chain process, deploys a range of professional practices, among which are: brainstorming, decision-making, bargaining, hypothesizing, transforming information, making a client feel valued or delegating responsibility (Handford, 2010, p. 32). All of those professional practices can be implemented by various discursive practices, such as, for example, starting the decision-making process, bringing the discussion back on track, clarifying one's position or checking shared knowledge. Thus, students have to become familiar with a set of tools which imply an intentional choice of how to proceed in a given situation, namely they acquire the procedures, conventions, strategies and tactics necessary for attaining various goals and objectives in a professional community. Drawing from Levinson's (1992, p. 100) understanding of strategies, this entails searching for "optimal or self-maximizing patterns of behavior available to participants in particular roles, under the specific constraints of the relevant activity". Business practice also involves introducing students to politeness systems used in the business world. Since doing business is marked by high potential for conflict and confrontation, access to a system of interpersonal strategies used to minimize threats seems to be indispensable. Students acquire procedural and declarative knowledge in such domains as professional etiquette and business ethics, fostering critical awareness of business practices. In addition, the business practice module comprises language use in intercultural communication, namely knowledge of effective collaboration and building relationships between people across cultures, with particular attention to each other's needs. This domain also covers a set of skills which will enable students to navigate successfully through communicative intercultural situations. Awareness and experience in intercultural issues and contexts are profoundly important for BE students since they can bring long-lasting professional, personal and relational benefits. On a practical front, it means that in a BE classroom students should be encouraged to engage in critical exploration of authentic professional and institutional intercultural contexts, roles and dilemmas which have a great impact on the unfolding discourse and the assumptions of the interaction participants. With lower-level students, their native language can be the medium of instruction, although English as a working language is preferred whenever possible.

The business knowledge and the business practice domains cover the semantic content of BE. They are supported by the module of business discursive competence, which allows for acquiring language and skills enabling experts "to identify, construct, interpret and use professional genres, and thus, participate in everyday professional activities" (Bhatia, 2004, p. 146). Business discursive competence, in turn, responsible for students' accommodating sets of genres, draws on the information obtained from the two other components, namely business knowledge and business practice.

The rationale behind integrating the three modules of business expertise within Bhatia's tripartite framework is that it will help students develop language awareness, that is, go beyond the lexical, syntactic and discursive features of BE, see how they are contextualized for communicative purposes, and simultaneously focus on the way these features relate to interpersonal relations. Students will become familiar with business practices and acquire prerequisite business knowledge enabling them to act as well-educated professionals. The model seems to comprise all the necessary elements students have to learn to be prepared to function appropriately in English in the world of business. As we know, language ability is not the most important issue in business, what often contributes to success is the experience and ability to maneuver dynamically within a particular context. Nevertheless, a working knowledge of specific clusters or key words may allow an individual who lacks either an extensive grammar or considerable experience to short-wire the system and be a more effective communicator. The discussed model takes all this into consideration.

4 Case Studies—A Practical Application of Bhatia's Model

The presented model can be applied in a BE classroom by using the case study approach, which, according to Handford (2010, p. 250), has considerable potential to offer students "an effective way of shortcutting the apprenticeship stage to become an accepted member of the business community". If students are to perform business by means of English, it is not enough for them to acquire knowledge about business—as important for them are the language and skills with which to conduct business. The best way to achieve this would be to design BE classes in such a way that students would be encouraged to simulate doing business in class themselves. Bhatia (2004, p. 49) argues that business cases are "used for the development of professional business skills in somewhat realistic, though largely simulated contexts". Although we realize that workplace discourses and practices can never be exactly replicable in a classroom situation because of a range of constraints, such as the inability to explicitly duplicate many of the pressures business people experience in the workplace environment, for instance, time and financial constraints in negotiating a contract, these practice cases do provide students with ample opportunities to mirror the activities and practices of real-life business situations.

The aim of case studies is to engage students in business problem-solving processes and prompt them to apply conceptual business categories to concrete situations. Students first analyze the available input and then recommend a course of action. In order to do this effectively, they must adopt the methods of argumentation and reasoning appropriate to business culture standards. Since success with a business case relies on creative and pragmatic application of various business theories, students turn to reflection using a synthesis of their prior background knowledge, drawing inferences from the provided texts and the ideas discussed in the class. Simultaneously they get immediate, formative feedback through follow-up discussion with classmates and/or the instructor.

Business case responses generally can be classified into three categories: an assessment of a situation, an evaluation of an action, and a solution to a problem or situation, all of which are defined by the actions business students have to take, that is, assessing, evaluating and solving (Uhrig, 2012, p. 130). Multi-faceted problems which students are expected to analyze require them to integrate multiple business concepts to construct a solution. On the one hand, by analyzing various texts and documents, students can develop a feel for the types of business discourse through practice. On the other hand, acting out a range of simulations, they are provided with a stimulus to develop their abilities in handling business genres in English. If students want to complete the assigned task, they simultaneously have to resort to their professional knowledge of business, activate the business practice domain and deploy their business discursive competence.

The business case study technique demonstrates a range of genre networks typical of the business world. Doing business involves multimodality, as well as doing a case does, namely reading texts, listening to audio materials, writing responses, delivery of presentations and responding to follow-up questions, negotiating and participating in meetings, telephoning, engaging in classroom discussions and writing recommendations in forms of various letter types, e-mails, memos or reports (see Fig. 2). In this way, working on a particular case, students get a lot of stimuli to develop not only the four language skills, but also business and study skills. They also develop interpersonal and interactional skills that are of greatest concern in workplace settings, that is, they learn and practice how to take turns, clarify meanings, block interruptions, politely contain a troublesome interlocutor and direct the other company to follow the desired procedure (Handford, 2010, pp. 252–253).

Case studies have the potential to introduce students successfully into the intertextual nature of business communication by revealing how participants build on and draw from previous meetings, how they discuss and relate preceding communication to the ongoing encounter, and how BE often references written texts, such as e-mails, reports and agendas. Handford (2010, p. 252) argues that "making learners aware of this intertextuality is an important pedagogical aim" of a BE classroom.

Cases as examples of an integrative engagement approach are, by and large, a primary tool by which a BE course can socialize students into the business

Fig. 2 Genre networks in the case study approach (own source)

profession. They align with the values of the business profession; that is, interaction and persuasion are at the heart of the process. Progress of an individual student is measured by the extent to which his or her responses to a business case match an expert's opinion or solution. Thus, the use of case studies seems to be a well-established method of inducing future professionals into the job demands of business. All language, business and study skills are potentially involved and students' cognitive skills, such as reasoning, decision-making and problem-solving are activated. Finally, another advantage of cases is their compatibility with how adults learn foreign languages, that is, not sequentially in isolated parts, but in a nonlinear fashion.

It is significant to note that success of the case study approach depends to a large degree on students' willingness to co-operate with each other in maintaining the illusion of reality created in the classroom. Given some students' reluctance to get involved in learning the language by doing something actively in class, implementing the technique will demand a lot of skills and determination on the part of the teacher.

5   Concluding Remarks

Bhatia's (2002) model discussed in the paper approaches BE from a discursive perspective by recommending analyzing the contextual, organizational and cultural factors of texts. It demonstrates that BE teaching has to acquaint students not only with the knowledge of the discipline and the discourses they will encounter, thus raising their consciousness in this respect, but also has to become a springboard for sensitizing them to real-world business practices typical of the community they will be entering. Moving through the stages of apprenticeship to become an expert in any discipline and an accepted member of the business community requires learning appropriate ways of communicating. The recommended model, where the integrated three modules form the basis for the syllabus design, seems to provide students with the necessary knowledge, language and skills, and will navigate them through those stages and equip them with the English relevant to cater to their professional needs. Thus, on graduation, they will be able to use it effectively in the world of business. BE classes centering around cases which require students to interact in the way that might mirror professional practices seem to give students an opportunity to develop all the three modules of the model discussed. Characterized by authenticity of purpose and task, business cases introduce students to the business genres and prompt them to practice them, along with business knowledge and practice.

Some limitations of the proposed solutions should be addressed because they can set an agenda for future empirical inquiry. Firstly, more research is needed to bridge the gap between frameworks and models of BE teaching, the one discussed in the paper included, and the professional practices common for the corporate world. Since the world of business is changing rapidly, researching how and why business people communicate the way they do seems to be a never-ending endeavor. Secondly, the model should be tested in the classroom. Only then can a more reliable assessment be carried out.

References

Bazerman, C., & Russel, D. (2003). *Writing selves/writing societies: Research from activity perspectives*. Fort Collins, CO: The WAC Clearinghouse and Mind, Culture, and Activity.

Bhatia, V. K. (2002). Professional discourse: Towards a multi-dimensional approach and shared practice. In C. Candlin (Ed.), *Research and practice in professional discourse* (pp. 39–59). Hong Kong: City University of Hong Kong Press.

Bhatia, V. K. (2004). *Words of written discourse: A genre-based view*. London: Continuum.

Bhatia, V. K. (2008). Genre analysis, ESP and professional practice. *English for Specific Purposes, 27*, 161–174.

Bhatia, V. K., Anthony, L., & Noguchi, J. (2011). ESP in the 21st century: ESP theory and application today. In *Proceedings of the JACET 50th Commemorative International Convention*, Vol. 143.

Bilbow, B. T. (1997). Spoken discourse in the multicultural workplace in Hong Kong: Applying a model of discourse as "impression management". In F. Bargiela-Chiappini & S. J. Harris (Eds.), *The language of business: An international perspective* (pp. 21–48). Edinburgh: Edinburgh University Press.

Charles, M. (1996). Business negotiations: interdependence between discourse and the business relationship. *English for Specific Purposes, 15*, 19–36.

Dudley-Evans, T., & St John, M. J. (1998). *Developments in English for specific purposes*. Cambridge: CUP.

Firth, A. (1995). *The discourse of negotiation: Studies of language in the workplace*. Oxford: Pergamon Press.

Hall, D. (2013). Introduction. In M. Huhta, K. Vogt, E. Johnson, & H. Tulkki. (Ed.), *Needs analysis for language course design. A holistic approach to ESP* (pp. 1–8). Cambridge: CUP.

Handford, M. (2010). *The language of business meetings*. Cambridge: Cambridge University Press.

Holden, B. (1993). Analyzing corporate training needs—a three way approach. *Language and Intercultural Training, 14*, 4–6.

Holmes, J., & Stubbe, M. (2003). *Power and politeness in the workplace: A sociolinguistic analysis of talk at work*. London: Longman.

Levinson, S. (1992). Activity types and language. In P. Drew & J. Heritage (Eds.), *Talk at work* (pp. 66–100). Cambridge: Cambridge University Press.

Linde, C. (1991). What's next: the social and technological management of meetings. *Pragmatics, 1*, 297–317.

Marriott, H. E. (1995). "Deviations" in an intercultural business negotiation. In A. Firth (Ed.), *The discourse of negotiation: Studies of language in the workplace* (pp. 247–268). Oxford: Pergamon Press.

McCarthy, M., & Carter, R. (2004). *Language as discourse: Perspectives for language teaching*. Beijing: Peking University Press.

Powell, M. (2005). Blur: 21st century Business English. *Keynote Speech at the IATEFL BESIG STETS Conference*.

Swales, J. (1990). *Genre analysis: English in academic and research settings*. Cambridge: CUP.

Uhrig, K. (2012). Business and legal case genre networks: Two case studies. *English for Specific Purposes, 31*, 127–136.

Yin, K. M., & Wong, I. (1990). A course in business communication for accountants. *English for Specific Purposes, 9,* 253–264.

Zhang, Z. (2007). Towards an integrated approach to teaching business English: A Chinese experience. *English for Specific Purposes, 26,* 399–410.

Zhu, Y. (2005). *Written communication across cultures. A socio-cognitive perspective on business genres.* Amsterdam: John Benjamins.

Author Biography

Paweł Sobkowiak, Ph.D., is Senior Lecturer at the School of Law and Administration, Adam Mickiewicz University, Poznań, where he teaches courses in Business English and Business Communication to students of Management. His main research interests include different aspects of teaching ESP, mainly Business English, professional development of language teachers as well as the development of learners' intercultural competence and intercultural teaching and learning. His recent publications include *Intercultural language education* (Adam Mickiewicz University Press, 2015). He is a member of the editorial board and a reviewer of two academic journals *US-China Foreign Language* (ISSN 1539-8080) and *Sino-US English Teaching* (ISSN 1539-8072), both published in the USA.

English Instruction in Polish and Norwegian Secondary Schools: Convergent Goals, Divergent Means

Paweł Scheffler, May Olaug Horverak and Anna Domińska

Abstract This article examines selected aspects of English instruction in Poland and Norway. We begin with a general discussion of the stages in which English instruction is provided in the Polish and Norwegian education systems. This is followed by a presentation of the main curriculum goals in the two countries, which demonstrates that in many respects the educational authorities in Poland and Norway share the views on the knowledge and skills that learners should achieve in the English subject. Next, we look at how curriculum goals are translated into teaching practice in coursebooks. We show some major differences in how the teaching material is organized and taught in popular Polish and Norwegian secondary school coursebooks. After that, we address the way in which learners' achievements are verified in secondary school examinations and we again identify crucial differences between the two contexts. In the discussion, we offer possible explanations for these differences, which involve the status of English in Poland and Norway and linguistic distance between English, Norwegian and Polish.

Keywords English curriculum in Poland and Norway · English coursebooks in Poland and Norway · English examinations in Poland and Norway

P. Scheffler (✉) · A. Domińska
Adam Mickiewicz University, Poznań, Poland
e-mail: spawel@wa.amu.edu.pl

A. Domińska
e-mail: dominska@amu.edu.pl

M.O. Horverak
Agder University, Kristiansand, Norway
e-mail: may.o.horverak@uia.no

© Springer International Publishing AG 2018
M. Pawlak and A. Mystkowska-Wiertelak (eds.), *Challenges of Second and Foreign Language Education in a Globalized World*, Second Language Learning and Teaching, DOI 10.1007/978-3-319-66975-5_9

1 Introduction

Given the present status of English as a global language and its position in areas like science, education, communications and many others, it is hardly surprising that English is the most widely taught foreign language (FL) in the world. As Crystal (2003, pp. 4–5) says, English is the chief foreign language in over 100 countries, for example, China, Russia, Germany, Spain, Egypt, Brazil, and Algeria. According to the estimates of the British Council (Graddol, 1997, p. 2), by the end of the 1990s around a billion, that is thousand million, people all over the world were engaged in learning English as a foreign language.

Educational authorities in many countries obviously recognize the position of English in international communication. Hence, in many modern language curricula the English language is prioritized. For example, in Norway, there is a separate English language curriculum, in which English is described as a "universal language" needed to succeed in the modern world (Norwegian Directorate for Education and Training, 2013, p. 2). English is also said there to be a tool which will "enable the pupils to communicate with others on personal, social, literary and interdisciplinary topics". In Poland, there is no specific national curriculum for English. However, there is a detailed modern language curriculum which states that one of the modern languages that are taught in Polish schools should be English. The data provided by the Central Statistical Office (2014) show that the vast majority of students in the Polish school system do indeed receive English instruction: in the school year 2013/2014, 94.3% of the students had English classes. For these pupils, according to the curriculum, the main goal of instruction should be effective communication in speech and in writing (Journal of Laws, item 356 of 24 February 2017). Both the Polish and the Norwegian curricula present the linguistic components of communicative competence that students need to master. The Polish curriculum refers to lexical, grammatical, orthographic and phonetic means which are supposed to enable pupils to reach the required communicative goals. According to the Norwegian document, students need to develop "a vocabulary and skills in using the systems of the English language", (2013, p. 2) for example grammar.

It seems, then, that in terms of both general aims and general guidelines for achieving them, the Polish and the Norwegian curricula for English instruction have much in common. The purpose of this article is to examine how these guidelines are implemented in coursebooks that are used in secondary schools and how the achievement of the aims is verified in the final secondary examination. The focus in the analysis will be on content organization in coursebooks and the types of tasks used in the examinations.

2 English Instruction in the Polish and Norwegian School Systems

2.1 Poland

Polish children start learning modern foreign languages in preschool (Journal of Laws, item 356 of 24 February 2017). The general aims of these lessons are to raise children's language and cultural awareness and to motivate them to learn foreign languages in the future. Children do not have to continue learning the same foreign language once they start their primary school education.

Excluding pre-school education, the Polish educational system enables students to learn from two to three modern foreign languages. The first modern foreign language is introduced as a compulsory subject in year one of primary school, and becomes an obligatory subject for 12/13 years, which means that the very same foreign language is taught throughout the whole course of formal education. During the first three years of primary school (1st educational stage) pupils are provided with 180 h of FL lessons, which amounts to two lessons a week. They are expected to reach the A1 level on a *Common European framework of reference for languages* (CEFR) scale, taking into account children's age. During the 2nd educational stage (4th–8th form), students are guaranteed three lessons of the first modern foreign language a week (450 h) and they are expected to reach the A2+/B1 level on a CEFR scale. Additionally, beginning with the 7th form until the end of the 2nd educational stage (8th form), students start learning another, obligatory, modern foreign language. Altogether, they are provided with 120 h of lessons in the next foreign language and on completion of the 2nd stage of education, learners are expected to reach the A1 level on a CEFR scale. In the 7th and 8th form, primary schools are allowed to increase the number of hours devoted to teaching one of the two modern foreign languages by 120 h if they create bilingual groups.

Education in the 3rd stage lasts four years if students go to a general secondary school, and five years if they choose to study in a technical secondary school, and three years if they decide to continue their education in a vocational school, which prepares them for a specific job. At this stage of education, a student can choose to continue learning the second modern foreign language started in the 7th form of primary school or can choose to begin studying the third modern foreign language as a compulsory subject. Students are expected to master the third modern foreign language at the A2 level on a CEFR scale. Both in general and technical secondary schools, there are 360 h allocated to lessons in the first modern foreign language and 240 h in another modern foreign language. The number of hours devoted to teaching the first modern foreign language can be increased by additional 180 h if the school sets up classes with extended FL instruction. Depending on students' initial command of a foreign language at the beginning of secondary school, they are expected to reach the B1+/B2 level and C1+/C2 level on a CEFR scale, in the case of students who have attended both bilingual and extended FL groups. Students who continue learning the second modern foreign language should master it at the B1 level. To sum up, a Polish learner is guaranteed a minimum of 990 teaching hours of the first modern foreign language.

2.2   Norway

In Norway, children start learning English in school from the age of 6, or from their first year in school. It is a compulsory subject from the first year in primary school to the second or third year in upper secondary school, meaning eleven or twelve years in total (Norwegian Directorate for Education and Training, 2013). The first ten years, that is, primary and lower secondary school, are obligatory for all and most children also move on to upper secondary school for three more years. There are no grades until the eighth year, the first year of lower secondary school. In elementary school, from years 1 to 4, there are 138 teaching hours. In middle school, from years 5 to 7, the number of teaching hours increases to 228. In lower secondary school, from years 8 to 10, there are 222 teaching hours.

After lower secondary school, the pupils can choose between general studies, to prepare for higher education, or vocational studies, to prepare for a specific job. These studies are often located in the same schools and English teachers often teach both general studies groups and vocational studies groups. The English courses given to these different groups of students are quite similar, as they have the same curriculum. English is obligatory for one year for general studies students, and for two years for vocational studies students, and there are 140 teaching hours. The former have five lessons a week for a year, whereas the latter have three lessons a week during the first year and two lessons a week during the second year. Altogether, from their first year at school, Norwegian students are provided with 728 h of English instruction.

The general studies students can choose to continue learning English for the second year, and attend a course called *International English*. It is also possible to continue a third year, and they can then choose between *Social studies English* and *English literature and culture*. In practice, most schools only offer one of these two courses in the third year due to low numbers of students.

3   L2 Curriculum Goals in Poland in Norway

3.1   The Modern Language Curriculum in Poland

The main aim of teaching modern foreign languages in Polish schools (Journal of Laws, item 356 of 24 February 2017) is for the students to be able to communicate effectively, both in speaking and writing, assuming that accuracy focus becomes more important at higher levels of advancement. At an initial stage, it is essential to help learners develop a positive attitude towards learning foreign languages and focus on developing fluency.

General aims for teaching modern foreign languages are formulated in the same way for every educational stage and concern the following areas: (a) the range of vocabulary and structures which should enable students to meet other general as well as specific aims with reference to selected topics (e.g., people, work, health, travelling and tourism, sport, culture, etc.) to be covered at each educational stage, (b) comprehension of oral and written information, (c) oral and written production which refers to students' ability to make cohesive and coherent utterances as well as express similar ideas in writing, (d) communicative competence in speaking and writing which refers to students' efficiency in responding to oral or written information, and (e) transfer and interpretative competence, which refers to students' ability to comment on pictorial, audiovisual or written materials.

Additionally, courses in modern foreign languages, at each educational stage, should emphasize the following: developing students' knowledge about lives and cultures of people in English speaking countries, raising intercultural awareness, especially by encouraging students to make comparisons with their own culture, and developing students' independence by teaching them how to learn on their own and promoting cooperation.

3.2 The English Subject Curriculum in Norway

In the English subject curriculum for Norwegian schools, the curriculum goals are aligned from the first year in primary school to the final year of obligatory English in upper secondary school. The four main areas outlined in the current curriculum are (Norwegian Directorate for Education and Training, 2013): (a) language learning, (b) oral communication, (c) written communication, and (d) culture, society and literature. There are competence aims that pupils are expected to reach after year two, year four, year seven, year ten and year one or two in upper secondary school. In addition, there is an emphasis on developing five basic skills in all subject curricula, and these are: (a) oral skills, (b) being able to express oneself in writing, (c) being able to read, (d) numeracy and (e) digital skills. There is generally a focus on the communicative aspect of language learning as well as a focus on learning to use English in different contexts for different purposes.

The first main area in the curriculum, language learning, includes curriculum aims concerning using different situations and learning strategies to develop English skills, identifying similarities and differences between English and Norwegian, and using digital resources when learning English. The focus moves on to evaluating learning strategies, digital resources and own progress on the higher levels, and in upper secondary school, there is no aim dealing with linguistic features.

The second main area in the curriculum, oral communication, concerns using listening and speaking strategies, developing vocabulary and understanding different types of oral texts. There is an increased focus on fluency and accuracy on the higher levels, as well as understanding different varieties of English. The pupils are to understand more challenging oral texts on higher levels, and they are to express their opinions from after year seven.

The third main area in the curriculum, written communication, includes both reading and writing. This part is focused on understanding the meaning of what is read and learning to write coherent texts suited to the purpose and situation of writing. Pupils are to be able to write short texts where they narrate, describe and express their opinions in writing, as well as use digital tools to find information and create texts, already from after year four. In upper secondary school, they are also to evaluate sources critically.

The fourth main area in the curriculum, culture, society and literature, involves developing knowledge about the lives and cultures of people in English-speaking countries, and also about English as a world language. There is a development from learning about children's culture in the early years to discussing more complex social issues and English literature, films and other cultural expressions in lower and upper secondary school. After year ten, and year one or two in upper secondary school, pupils are also to be able to discuss contemporary topics or news items and reflect on and discuss texts about indigenous people. It is not specified what texts are to be included in the teaching.

The curriculum is the same for vocational and general studies in upper secondary school, but it is specified throughout the competence aims that students should develop their English competence in relation to their education program. They are to learn vocabulary, discuss topics, read and write texts and select an in-depth study topic related to their education program. This means that both general and vocational studies students are to work with the topics indicated in the competence aims under "culture, society, and literature", but in addition, vocational study students have to work with topics relevant for the vocation they have chosen.

4 Implementing English Instruction in Secondary School: Coursebooks

4.1 Coursebooks for Polish Upper Secondary School Students

Since English instruction in Norwegian upper secondary schools is obligatory only for year one students, our discussion of coursebooks will deal only with those used in the first year of Polish secondary school. Through informal interviews with booksellers in Poznań specializing in foreign language materials, we identified two coursebooks commonly selected by teachers teaching first year secondary students: *Oxford Solutions*, published by Oxford University Press, and *Matura focus 2*, published by Pearson. We will first describe general content organization in both of the books and then focus on how vocabulary, grammar and skills are taught in a selected unit of *Oxford solutions*.

In both books, the units are topic-based and they comply with the requirements of the core curriculum for the third educational stage (i.e., secondary school). Table 1 shows the themes that are included in both books and the corresponding themes from the core curriculum. Each unit in the coursebooks is usually equally devoted to grammar, vocabulary, listening, reading, speaking and writing, allowing students to exploit a particular theme comprehensively. For example, Unit 9 of *Oxford solutions* concerns the topic of science. The unit has two vocabulary sections. In the first, learners are engaged in activities like looking up technology-related words in a dictionary, describing gadgets and talking about materials used to produce various objects. In the second, a short text about colonizing the planet Mars is a springboard for presentation and practice of combinations of verbs and prepositions. Sections devoted to the development of reading and listening comprehension focus on top-down processing of information. They usually contain short discussion tasks aimed at activating students' schemata and/or brainstorming key vocabulary and/or making predictions. There are also examples of while reading/listening tasks which focus on checking students' comprehension as well as encouraging students to practice reading strategies (skimming, scanning) and listening strategies (listening for gist, listening for specific information). The reading sections can also include an exercise which requires students to identify the meaning of new words from context (contextual guessing). The listening sections, on the other hand, can include an exercise which focuses explicitly on pronunciation. Tasks which require intensive reading (e.g., reading between the lines) and in-depth analysis of the written or spoken discourse are very rare. Grammar sections usually contain short texts seeded with examples of the target structure. There are brief rules of form and/or use provided, followed by writing and speaking exercises. A section devoted to speaking usually contains exercises which require students to express opinions, justify their decisions and role-play semi-structured dialogues using appropriate language functions. Writing sections usually include an example of a model text, an exercise which focuses on helping students identify the functions of discourse patterns and a communicative writing task.

Table 1 Themes in Oxford Solutions and Matura Focus 2

Core curriculum theme	*Oxford solutions*	*Matura focus 2*
People	Feelings	Personality
Natural science	Our planet	
Culture	On screen	The art
Work	Ambition	Working life
Travelling/Tourism	Adventure, Tourism	Living
Shopping and Service	Money	Shopping
Country and society	Crime	Society
Science and Technology	Science	Invention
School		School

4.2   Coursebooks for Norwegian Upper Secondary School Students

English teaching in Norwegian schools is generally focused on communication and content rather than form or grammar, just as the curriculum. On lower levels, pupils are taught how to communicate about familiar issues, and this is also what is focused on in textbooks. Texts typically deal with topics like family, friends, food and animals, and there are children's songs and excerpts from children's literature. Some grammar explanations and grammar exercises are generally included throughout the textbooks, but whether this is included or not in the teaching is up to the individual teachers.

In lower and upper secondary school, pupils have to learn to communicate about more complex issues, such as social issues in English-speaking countries, the situation of indigenous people, and relevant news, and this is what we also find in textbooks. There are both factual texts and literary texts in the textbooks, and often pupils are also asked to read a complete English novel, at least in upper secondary school. There are some grammar exercises following the texts in the textbooks, but the majority of the exercises concern content. Whether or not grammar is taught depends on the choices of the individual teachers. Teachers also choose what texts and topics to include, as there is no guideline, neither on a national nor on local levels, as to what texts to teach.

In general, teachers look to exams and exam requirements when planning their teaching in addition to the curriculum. As students are to give a presentation in the oral exam, presentation work is often included in the teaching. When it comes to writing, the focus is on writing coherent texts, and many teachers in upper secondary school seem to focus on teaching argumentative writing or how to write five-paragraph essays, as well as how to write in formal style (Horverak, 2015). There are no central guidelines as to how writing should be taught to prepare for a possible written exam, so this is up to the individual teachers, and practices seem to vary. Even though the English curriculum and exam are the same for vocational and general studies, teaching and textbooks may be somewhat different. We will describe one English coursebook for vocational studies students and one for general studies students in the following with a specific focus on how grammar is dealt with in the two books.

Tracks is a popular coursebook for vocational studies students in general, and not specifically for one vocational program. This book combines job-related issues and issues related to English-speaking countries. The topics covered are: (a) *A world of English*, (b) *Life & society: North America*, (c) *Work matters*, (d) *Life & society: The British Isles*, (e) *Life & society: The English-speaking world*, which includes India, New Zealand, Australia and South Africa, (f) *Work values*, and (g) *We were here first*, which includes texts by and about native people in English-speaking countries. After each text, there are exercises focused on the basic skills in the English curriculum, reading and understanding, listening, talking and writing. There are some short exercises focused on grammar after some of the texts, but there is no proper grammar overview in the book. There is a writing course on informal and formal English covering almost three pages, followed up by exercises on this topic. About half of the grammar exercises in the book, 15 in total, deal with the formality level of language. Otherwise, there are some exercises on adjectives, pronouns, verbs and some other grammar topics, but very few.

Targets is a much used book for general studies students, and is quite different from *Tracks* concerning how grammar is dealt with. Much of the content otherwise is the same, except for the work-related topics in *Tracks*, which are not included in *Targets*. The following chapters are included: (1) *Let's communicate*, (2) *The English language*, (3) *The UK and Ireland*, (4) *The USA and Canada*, (5) *Around the world* and (6) *Words, sentences and rules of English*. The last chapter here is like a grammar book the students can look up into find explanations. The issues included are word formation, sentence structure, adverbials, different types of clauses, verbs, pronouns, nouns, determiners, adjectives, adverbs and negation. This chapter covers about 30 pages, and includes explanations for all topics dealt with in grammar exercises throughout the different chapters. There is also a section on formal and informal language covering half a page in the book, and a section on cohesion and linking words covering a page. Also this book includes exercises focused on the basic skills as outlined in the curriculum: reading, listening, speaking and writing. In addition, there are quite a few grammar exercises in this book covering the topics presented in the last chapter of the book, as well as exercises on formality level of language. In addition to grammar exercises included in the exercises following texts, there are five separate sections with language work with between 10 and 17 grammar exercises. Even though this textbook allows for more teaching of grammar than *Tracks*, it is still up to the teacher whether or not to use grammar exercises in the classroom.

In the different units in the coursebooks, the text and exercises related to the content of the text often dominate. For example in *Targets*, in Chap. 3, *The UK and Ireland*, there is a unit called *British Government*. This unit starts with a text covering 3 pages, and this is followed up by one page with exercises. Within the text, there are some comprehension questions concerning the content of the text. The exercises following the text start with a speaking exercise where the students are asked to sum up, or explain, important terms in the text, and in the next exercise, they are to make questions about how Britain is governed and ask a partner. This is followed up by a writing exercise where students are to sum up the main points of the text with words from a word bank. Finally, there are two exercises dealing with language work, focusing on the grammatical topic of passive and active forms. Students are asked to rewrite passive sentences into active form in one exercise, and to rewrite active sentences into passive in the last exercise. In general, there are more exercises related to speaking and writing about the content of texts than to language work in the different units in coursebooks in Norway.

5   Learner Assessment: Secondary School Examinations

5.1   *The Polish Examination*

Once the secondary educational stage is completed, students of general and technical schools in Poland may take the final examinations which, if passed, entitle them for admission to higher education. A modern foreign language is one of the obligatory exam subjects. The exam is based on the requirements defined in the core curriculum and consists of an external written part, which is prepared centrally and assessed by regional examination commissions, and an internal, oral part, which is prepared centrally but assessed by school examination committees. Students must take an exam in a selected foreign language at a basic level, but can choose to take an additional exam in the same or other foreign language at an advanced level.

At the basic level, the written part is made up of closed tasks of various kinds, for example, multiple choice, true false, choosing the correct statement, and one open task which assesses written production and requires students to respond to a short communicative task using 80–130 words. All the tasks aim at the assessment of students' declarative and procedural knowledge in four main areas: listening comprehension, reading comprehension, range of lexis and grammar and written production. This part of the exam lasts 120 min. Below we first provide examples of tasks assessing the range of lexis and grammar during the written part of the basic level exam and then an example task assessing written production (instructions for all the tasks are our translations from Polish).

Choose the word in A, B or C which fits the gaps in both sentences.

My brother will have to look _____ my dog when I go on holiday.

Finally, _____ an hour I decided to walk back home.

A. after

B. for

C. at

Circle the phrase (A, B or C) which means the same as the word on bold type.

I spent a few weeks thinking which university to go to and I have finally **decided** this weekend.

A. made my choice

B. taken my chance

C. found my way

Circle the appropriate translation (A, B or C) for the word in brackets.

Where on earth is this bus? We (czekamy) _____ here for over an hour!

A. are waiting

B. wait

C. have been waiting

Complete the mini-dialogue below by circling A, B or C.

10.1. X: Did you enjoy the film?

Y: _____

X: That's a pity.

A. Not really, to tell the truth.

B. In fact, I did. More than I expected.

C. Of course. It was terrific!

You have taken part in an international exchange in London. Write a letter to a friend from England in which you:

- Describe the family you were staying with.
- Report an event which you liked/did not like.
- Present advantages and disadvantages of the exchange.
- Suggest spending holiday together in a place of your choice. Justify your choice.

(Adapted from *Informator o egzaminie maturalnym z języka angielskiego od roku szkolnego 2014/2015*, pp. 55–57).

At the advanced level, the written part lasts 150 min and contains 29 closed tasks, which in their form resemble the types of exercises present in the exam paper for students taking their exam the basic level. The exam paper also includes nine open tasks, eight requiring short written answers and one assessing written production. This task requires students to respond to a communicative task using 200–250 words. Similarly to the exam at the basic level, all the tasks at an advanced level focus on the assessment of both declarative and procedural knowledge in the four language areas: listening comprehension, reading comprehension, range of lexis and grammar and written production. The following is an example task assessing the range of lexis and grammar during the written part at an advanced level.

Complete sentences 6.1.–6.2. using the correct form of the words in brackets. Do not change the order of the words. If necessary, add other words in order to make logical and grammatically correct sentences. The sentences must also be spelt correctly. Each gap can be maximally filled with six words, including the words already provided in brackets.

6.1. Why didn't you say anything? You (*should/warn/students*) _____ swimming in this place!

6.2. While (*President/have/argument*) _____ with his advisors, a group of journalists burst into the room.

Finally, an example task which assesses written production at an advanced level:

Choose one of the topics below. Write a 200–250 word long text which meets the requirements typical for the genre mentioned in the task chosen.

1. Your school has banned the use of mobile phones at its premises. Students have staged a protest. Write an article for the school website in which you give a report on what happened, express your own opinion and present arguments illustrating your stance on this matter.

2. You have come back dissatisfied with an international camp which was organized by your school. Write a letter to a school newspaper explaining why you think the camp was a failure and suggest ways to improve the quality of such events in the future.

3. More and more young people no longer take into account their interests but job market requirements, when making decisions about what to study. Write an essay presenting advantages and disadvantages of such a decision.

(Adapted from *Informator o egzaminie maturalnym z języka angielskiego od roku szkolnego 2014/2015*, pp. 70–71).

The aim of the oral part of the English exam is to assess communicative competence, the range of lexis and grammar as well as accuracy in lexis and grammar used, pronunciation and fluency. The exam lasts 15 min and the tasks are the same for all students, irrespective of whether they have taken an exam at the basic and advanced level or only at an advanced level. It consists of four components: an initial chat/conversation with an examiner on a general, life-related topic, for example, eating habits, neighborhood, free time, and so on, role-playing a structured dialogue, description of a picture, which also requires a student to answer three open questions, and a task which requires a student to solve a problem. An example of a problem solving task is as follows:

Your boyfriend/girlfriend comes from Great Britain. His/her parents are coming to Poland and you would like to invite them to a restaurant. Look at the photos of three restaurants.

- *Choose the one which in your opinion is the most appropriate and justify your choice.*
- *Explain why other restaurants do not seem to be appropriate for the occasion.*

(Adapted from *Informator o egzaminie maturalnym z języka angielskiego od roku szkolnego 2014/2015*, p. 41).

5.2   The Norwegian Examination

In Norway, not all students have to take an English exam, but they may all be selected for an oral or written exam after year ten, at the end of lower secondary school, and after the final year of obligatory English in upper secondary school (Norwegian Directorate for Education and Training, 2013). For general studies students, this would be after the first year, and for vocational studies students, this would be after the second year. The written exam is prepared and graded centrally on all levels, and the exam after the obligatory English in upper secondary school is the same for both general studies and vocational studies. If students choose to continue with English in upper secondary school, they may be selected for an oral or written exam after both the second and the third year.

In all written exams, students are generally supposed to answer two parts. In the first part, they get questions where they are expected to write rather short answers. After K06, there has often been at least one task dealing with the topic of formal and informal language. Either students have been asked to rewrite an informal text in more formal style, or/and they have been asked to identify informal features in a text. In the second part of the written exam, students write a longer coherent and well-structured text on a given topic, as well as use and refer to reliable sources in the text. No indication is given about the length of the text. There are often attachments including texts students are to use in the exam. To prepare for the exam after year ten and the obligatory English in upper secondary school, students are given a folder with relevant texts on the topic for the exam the day before the actual exam. In addition to working with the folder they have been given, they can use the preparation time to find additional material on the topic, and on the exam day, they can bring what they think they will need of books, print-outs from websites and notes.

As general studies students and vocational studies students take the same exam in upper secondary school, there are often both exercises including general topics such as social and cultural issues and exercises including a focus on work-related issues. Some examples of exam tasks are:

Example 1:

Literary characters often choose to violate social norms or break laws, often for very good reasons. Create a text in which you compare two such characters and discuss the choices they make. The characters must be from English-language novels, films, plays or short stories you have studied (Norwegian Directorate for Church Education and Research, 2016b, p. 5).

Example 2:

Create an informative text in which you present some of the standards of behaviour in your future trade or profession and discuss why they are important and how they are enforced (Norwegian Directorate for Church Education and Research, 2016b, p. 5).

As can be seen, students are to discuss issues, which is typical of exam exercises on this level. In lower secondary school, students are more often asked to reflect on various issues, as we see in the following example:

Example 3:

You have explored traditions and lifestyles in India, Jamaica and Nigeria during your preparation day. Create a text in which you reflect on the differences and similarities between one of these countries and another English-speaking country you have studied in your English class (Norwegian Directorate for Church Education and Research, 2016a, p. 4).

Whereas the written exam is centralized, the oral exam is locally prepared and graded. In lower secondary school, this means that the exam is prepared on the municipality level, and in upper secondary school, on the county level. The topics are generally not very different from written exams, but in practice, teachers may choose to emphasize vocational topics more for vocational students in upper secondary school. Also in the case of the oral exam, students get a topic a day before the exam and they are to prepare a presentation, but there is no specific preparation material. In addition to the presentation they give in the exam situation, they are questioned about other topics as well, and it is tested whether they can participate in a conversation about various issues.

6 Discussion

As we have shown, when Polish and Norwegian pupils reach (upper) secondary school, they will normally have studied English for eight or more years. Yet, in Poland, judging by the textbooks we have examined, the instruction they receive is still very much language focused: pupils are provided with a great deal of explicit vocabulary and grammar training which follows the traditional presentation-practice-production (PPP) model. Sections which focus on developing students' reading or listening comprehension include tasks which aim at activating students schemata, testing their general and specific comprehension of written or oral texts (predicting, skimming/scanning and listening for gist/specific information). They can also include an exercise on developing the skill of contextual guessing, that is, helping students identify the meaning of new words from the context. It must be pointed out that teachers often use such texts as a context for grammar introduction. Thus, the last stage of a pre-reading/listening-while reading/listening-post reading/listening model of a lesson usually becomes the first stage of the PPP.

It seems that the model of teaching we have identified in the Polish context can be described as weak communicative instruction, that is a combination of explicit language focus and communicative language use (Howatt, 1984, p. 279). By contrast, the dominant approach in Norwegian upper secondary schools seems to be a strong version of communicative teaching: Learners are made to use English by discussing content in authentic language materials, which very often consist of samples or even whole pieces of literature. Unlike in Polish coursebooks, tasks which accompany such materials do not aim at developing students` general and specific comprehension (skimming/scanning, listening for gist/for specific information) but already focus on intensive reading, in-depth interpretation and analysis of discourse pattern. From the Polish perspective, such tasks are very common during a literature class, but not a lesson in a foreign language. Grammar work in particular seems to be an add-on which teachers may or may not choose to focus on.

English classroom instruction obviously reflects the format and requirements of the examination. Poland and Norway differ here as well. In Poland, the secondary school written examination includes numerous items targeting specific vocabulary, grammar issues and general comprehension. By contrast, the only task in the Norwegian written exam is a writing task in which students are allowed to make use of sources compiled beforehand.

In trying to explain the reasons for the differences that we have identified between the two contexts, we will discuss two areas: the status of the English language in Norway and Poland and the linguistic distance between Polish, Norwegian and English. In our view, a combination of these two factors is significant in making it possible to implement content-focused instruction and examinations in Norwegian upper secondary schools.

6.1 The Status of English in Poland and Norway

In the past, English was considered a foreign language in Norway, but this is now changing. With an increased use of English in education, business and governance (Hellekjær, 2007), it is now considered to have a status in between a foreign and a second language (Graddol, 1997; Rindal, 2012, p. 23; Rindal & Piercy, 2013). Also in the English curriculum in school, we see that English has changed its status in Norway, as it has been considered a second language since the Knowledge Promotion of 2006 (Norwegian Directorate for Education and Training, 2006).

Another change concerning English in Norway is the increased access to it through international media sources (Rindal, 2012). Young Norwegians have had access to English through television for many years, as programs are not dubbed, but in the last decades, the development of the Internet has led to young people being even more exposed to the English language. Not only do they listen to and read English, but they also produce English by, for example, writing on blogs and communicating on Skype when playing computer games. Hence, English is perhaps like a second language for many young people.

In Poland, English is a foreign language, that is, it is not an official language used as a means of communication in certain domains of life. In sharp contrast with Norway, English is conspicuously absent from television in Poland, where a voice-over commentary is the primary means of translating foreign movies. Further, voice-over is favored by the vast majority of TV viewers in Poland (Kutyłowska, 2013).

The beneficial effect of watching subtitled television programs and movies is well-documented. As an illustration, we would like to present some of the findings from two large-scale survey studies: *First European survey on language competences*, (2012) and the *Early language learning in Europe* project from 2011. The following conclusion was reached by the authors of the former (*First European survey on language competences*, 2012, p. 78)

> In general, a very large positive effect appears of students' target language exposure and use through traditional and new media on language test scores; this means that more exposure and use goes together with higher test scores. This holds for all skills and almost every educational system and language.

The survey involved approximately 53,000 students, aged around 15, from 16 educational systems in Europe, including the Polish system. Since Norway is not an EU member, its system was not covered by the survey. However, it may be interesting and relevant to compare some of the results achieved by Polish and Swedish learners, since Swedish, like Norwegian, is a Scandinavian language and since Swedish television also uses subtitles for English translation. Table 2 shows the percentages of students achieving CEFR levels for English as the first target language in reading, listening and writing. Sweden was also one of the countries with the highest exposure to English through traditional and new media, with a

Table 2 CEFR levels achieved by Polish and Swedish learners

Country	Reading			Listening			Writing		
	Pre-A1	A2	B	Pre-A1	A2	B	Pre-A1	A2	B
Poland	27	49	24	27	45	28	19	59	23
Sweden	1	18	81	1	9	91	0	24	75

mean exposure of over 2.5 on a scale from 0 to 4, while the mean for the Polish students was over 1.5.

The participants of the *Early language learning in Europe* project were primary school children, but the conclusions concerning the relation between out-of-school exposure and foreign language skills were similar to those from the previous study: "Out-of-school exposure, particularly subtitled television and films, has a significant impact on children's FL achievement" (Muñoz & Lindgren, 2011, p. 119). The leads to the following recommendation: "European countries should offer children possibilities for contact with the FL through the media by, for example, increasing the availability of undubbed TV programs (Muñoz & Lindgren, 2011, p. 119). This recommendation is particularly applicable to the Polish context for reasons already discussed. The findings of the *Early language learning in Europe* also demonstrate that Polish children do not make the best possible use of foreign language media: their exposure to foreign languages is about five hours a week, most of which consists in listening to songs. This contrasts sharply with Swedish children, who on average spend eight hours a week watching FL television programs and films (Norway, again, was not part of the project t).

6.2   Language Distance: Polish and Norwegian Versus English

Making use of English input through the media is certainly beneficial for any learners. However, it may be the case that Norwegian students are particularly likely to benefit as English and Norwegian are closely related and share numerous lexical and grammatical features. In general, the influences between learners' L1s and L2s are certainly complex, as for example Odlin's (1989) book shows. Still, some tendencies can be identified. For Odlin (1989), a general rule is that similarity between languages "often confers important advantages" (for example in lexical semantics) and "language distance is most probably a major determinant of the amount of time students will need in order to become highly proficient in a language" (p. 153). Let us now demonstrate some of the lexical and grammatical features which set Norwegian and English apart from Polish.

First, many lexical similarities between Norwegian and English are due to historical links between the two languages. For example, English adopted numerous

Table 3 Words of Scandinavian origin in modern English (from Scheffler, Horverak, Krzebietke, & Askland, 2017, p. 199)

English	Norwegian	Polish
die	dø	umrzeć
egg	egg	jajko
rotten	råtten	zgniły
take	ta	wziąć
they	de/dei	oni

Table 4 Selected forms of the verb *like* (from Scheffler et al., 2017, p. 200)

Infinitive	Present	Past	Present perfect	Past perfect
like (E)	like (s)	liked	have/has liked	had liked
like (N)	liker	likte	har likt	hadde likt
lubić (P)	lubię (-isz, -i, -imy, -icie, -ią)	lubiłem/am (eś/aś, -/a/o, liśmy/yśmy, liście/yście, li/y)	–	–

Table 5 English and Norwegian case forms (from Scheffler et al., 2017, p. 200)

English	Nominative Accusative	Genitive	Norwegian	Nominative Accusative	Genitive
	horse daughter	horse's daughter's		hest datter	hestens datterens

Table 6 Polish case forms (from Scheffler et al., 2017, p. 200)

Polish	Nominative	Genitive	Dative	Accusative	Locative	Instrmental	Vocative
	koń córka	konia córki	koniowi córce	konia córkę	koniu córce	koniem córką	koniu córko

Old Norse words in the Old and Middle English periods. As Table 3 shows, the corresponding Polish lexical items do not bear any resemblance to the English and Norwegian forms.

Second, as far as grammar is concerned, there are a number of features which separate Norwegian and English from Polish. As can be seen in Table 4, there are striking similarities between English and Norwegian in the verbal system. The Norwegian and English case systems are also much simpler than the Polish system: the former can be described as having two/three cases whereas Polish has seven, as shown in Tables 5 and 6.

7 Conclusion

The presence of English in the lives of young Norwegian people and the similarities between Norwegian and English may be two important factors which make Norwegian students ready for largely content-oriented instruction in upper secondary school. The fact that the English language is something tangible in many Norwegian families may also increase young Norwegians' motivation to seek exposure to English and to become proficient users of that language. It would be interesting to investigate the relation between these variables in the Norwegian and Polish contexts. Polish will not acquire a verbal or a nominal system which is more akin to English: In some sense, Polish pupils will always be at a disadvantage against their Norwegian peers. However, perhaps more could be done to turn Poland into a more (foreign) language-friendly environment, as recommended by the European Commission. This would entail, among other things, fully exploiting the potential of exposure to English through both traditional and new media. This is perhaps one of the most important challenges that educational authorities in Poland face in the field of foreign language instruction at the moment.

References

Central Statistical Office (2014). *Statistical Yearbook of the Republic of Poland 2014*.
Crystal, D. (2003). *English as a global language*. Cambridge: Cambridge University Press.
European Commission. (2012). *First European survey on language competences*. Retrieved from http://ec.europa.eu/dgs/education_culture/repository/languages/policy/strategic-framework/documents/language-survey-final-report_en.pdf.
Graddol, D. (1997). *The future of English*. London: The British Council.
Hellekjær, G. O. (2007). The implementation of undergraduate level English medium programs in Norway: An explorative case study. In R. Wilkinson & V. Zegers (Eds.), *Researching content and language integration in higher education* (pp. 68–81). Maastricht University Language Centre.
Horverak, M. O. (2015). English writing instruction in Norwegian upper secondary schools. *Acta Didactica Norge, 9*(1), Art. 11, 20 pages.
Howatt, A. P. R. (1984). *A history of the English language teaching*. Oxford: Oxford University Press.
Kutyłowska, K. (2013). *Polityka językowa w Europie*. Warszawa: Instytut Badań Edukacyjnych. Retrieved from http://www.ibe.edu.pl/pl/component/content/article/36-wazne-tematy/398-jezyki-obce.
Muñoz, C., & Lindgren, E. (2011). Out-of-school factors: the home. In Enever, J. (Ed.), *Early language learning in Europe*. British Council. Retrieved from https://www.teachingenglish.org.uk/sites/teacheng/files/B309%20ELLiE%20Book%202011%20FINAL.pdf.
Norwegian Directorate for Church Education and Research. (2016a). ENG0012 Engelsk: Sentralt gitt skriftlig eksamen etter 10. trinn - for elever og for voksne deltakere og privatister. Retrieved from http://filgrms1/u01$/mayoh/Downloads/ENG0012_Engelsk_10_trinn_eksamen_V16.pdf.
Norwegian Directorate for Church Education and Research. (2016b). ENG1002/ENG1003 Engelsk fellesfag: Elever og privatister. Retrieved from http://filgrms1/u01$/mayoh/Downloads/ENG1002_ENG1003_Engelsk_fellesfag_E_V16.pdf.

Norwegian Directorate for Education and Training. (2006). Læreplanverket for Kunnskapsløftet midlertidig utgave. Retrieved from http://www.udir.no/upload/larerplaner/Fastsatte_lareplaner_for_Kunnskapsloeftet/Kunnskapsloftet_midlertidig_utgave_2006_tekstdel.pdf.

Norwegian Directorate for Education and Training. (2013). English subject curriculum. Retrieved from http://www.udir.no/kl06/ENG1-03/Hele/?lplang=eng.

Odlin, T. (1989). *Language transfer: Cross-linguistic influence in language learning*. Cambridge: CUP.

Rindal, U. (2012). *Meaning in English, L2 attitudes, choices and pronunciation in Norway*. (Ph.D. Thesis), Oslo.

Rindal, U., & Piercy, C. (2013). Being "neutral"? English pronunciation among Norwegian learners. *World Englishes, 32*(2), 211–229.

Scheffler, P., Horverak, M. O., Krzebietke, W., & Askland, S. (2017). Language background and learners' attitudes to own language use. *ELT Journal, 71*(2), 197–217.

Author Biographies

Paweł Scheffler is an Associate Professor and researcher in the Faculty of English at Adam Mickiewicz University in Poznań. His research interests are second language acquisition, classroom foreign language instruction, and modern English grammar. He has published in a variety of journals both in Poland and abroad. He also writes language materials for Polish learners of English.

May Olaug Horverak is Associate Professor at the University of Agder, Kristiansand, Norway, in the Department of Foreign Languages and Translation. Her research area is English didactics, and the main focus of her research is on how linguistic theory may contribute in the context of writing instruction. She also has a background as a teacher in secondary school.

Anna Domińska is a lecturer at the Faculty of English at Adam Mickiewicz University, Poznań, Poland. She is interested in the didactics of teaching English as a foreign language and mentoring. She is also the author of EFL materials for teachers of English.

Part II
Challenges of Researching Language Classrooms

Individualized Categories of Verbal Reports in Classroom Think-Aloud Translation Tasks

Anna Michońska-Stadnik

Abstract Introspection is one of the most popular qualitative research methods in psychology and it consists of asking participants to report verbally on their cognitive and/or emotional states while performing a specific task or activity (Brown & Rodgers, 2002, p. 53). In second language acquisition studies, introspection is frequently used to observe and analyze learners' mental processes while they are engaged in a language task. This type of research has an interdisciplinary character as it employs data gathering techniques used primarily in social sciences. Such verbal reports, either audio- or video-recorded, are often referred to as think-alouds or talk-alouds (Ericsson & Simon, 1993). The collected data, often quite extensive, must be then analyzed and categorized in order to define learners' mental and emotional states. Different sets of categories for coding think-alouds have been proposed, for example, monitoring, signaling, elaborating, and reasoning (Brown & Lytle, 1988). This chapter presents an analysis of the recorded set of think-alouds done by secondary-school students during a written translation task from L2 (English) to L1 (Polish). Apart from categories suggested in different coding schemes for verbal protocols, some new categories emerged, for example, abandoning the message, commenting on other students' work, asking for help, planning for the task, and many others. They reveal a wide spectrum of learners' emotional states, which may contribute to a better understanding of task demands, classroom interaction patterns, and may allow the broadening of the repertoire of coding categories in the analysis of think-alouds.

Keywords Introspection · Think-aloud protocols · Written verbal reports · Translation tasks · Coding categories

A. Michońska-Stadnik (✉)
University of Wrocław, Wrocław, Poland
e-mail: anna.michonska-stadnik@uwr.edu.pl

© Springer International Publishing AG 2018
M. Pawlak and A. Mystkowska-Wiertelak (eds.), *Challenges of Second and Foreign Language Education in a Globalized World*, Second Language Learning and Teaching, DOI 10.1007/978-3-319-66975-5_10

1   Introduction

At the present time, increasing attention is being given to qualitative research methods in applied linguistics. They make use of several data collection techniques which allow a certain degree of in-depth analysis of participants' opinions, attitudes, values, and other phenomena which are difficult to measure with the use of quantitative methodology. Translation involves complex mental processing and verbal reports allow gaining insight into the nature of this procedure.

The current article reports a study analyzing the think-alouds of intermediate secondary-school students working on a written translation task in the classroom. The aim of the study was to prove that written verbal reports, similarly to oral ones, show an extensive repertoire of mental processes during a translation procedure. The study revealed the existence of a number of categories of verbal protocols, including those showing students' emotional states and personal attitudes. It is then suggested that the list of think-aloud categories may be broadened to include more affective and social aspects of mental processing, related to the characteristic features of the learning environment.

2   Introspection as a Research Method: Its Nature and Principles

Introspection is one of the oldest methods employed in psychological research. It consists in asking the participants to report verbally on their mental and emotional states while performing a specific task or activity (Brown & Rodgers, 2002, p. 53). At the beginning of the 20th century, introspection was so popular that it had an impact on literature, which is reflected in, for example, the stream-of-consciousness writing style of Marcel Proust, James Joyce, and Virginia Woolf (Brown & Rodgers, 2002, p. 54). Later, introspection was strongly criticized by the representatives of behaviorist schools in mainstream psychology, primarily for its lack of objectivity. This, in their opinion, rendered the method invalid and unreliable to be used in scientific research. Since that period of criticism and rejection, introspection and other qualitative data collection techniques have once again emerged in psychological research as relatively valid and reliable in some restricted contexts. For example, as Larsen-Freeman and Long (1991, p. 15) report, introspection allowed researchers in applied linguistics to reveal the existence of numerous language learning strategies that learners used, and which were not directly observable. It has also been observed that introspection, similarly to other qualitative methods, treats reality as holistic, dynamic, and theory-grounded (Larsen-Freeman & Long, 1991, p. 12), which seems to be more truthful than a quantitative, objective, and stable interpretation of life. Nowadays, both types of research, qualitative and quantitative, are widely used in the humanities, and one method seems to complement the other.

The reacceptance of introspection in modern psychological studies allowed Ericsson and Simon ([1984]1993) to formulate several principles to be followed by researchers employing this method. First of all, the time between mental operations and reporting should be as short as possible. The longer the time, the more fabricated elements appear in the report, making it unreliable. Next, care must be given not to let verbalization overwhelm mental processing. Verbalization itself requires concentration, and, therefore, the subjects should keep their language as simple as possible and remember that verbal reports are different from social talk. Verbal reports do not contain paralinguistic information, which may otherwise be essential for the interpretation of mental processes. The analysts must be aware of that fact. Last but not least, researchers must know that it is not possible to report on automatic reactions, for example, on using routine expressions in social talks.

An exhaustive summary on how introspective research can be employed in second language acquisition (SLA) studies was presented by Faerch and Kasper in their book *Introspection in second language research* (1987). Thus, introspection can be used in reading comprehension activities, problem-solving tasks, self-correction, translation, test-taking, and many other mental operations. In consequence of analyzing collected verbal report data, different categories of think-aloud protocols and ways of coding them were established (Brown & Lytle, 1988). According to Ericsson and Simon (1993), three levels of verbal reports exist, which are the essence of introspection: talk-alouds, think-alouds, and retrospection. These are discussed in the next section.

3   The Levels of Verbal Reports: Think-Alouds

The authors mentioned above, Ericsson and Simon (1993), presented characteristics of their three levels of verbal reports. The first level includes talk-alouds, where the task to be done involves some kind of language-related procedures, for example, solving an anagram, translation, or crossword puzzle. The second level involves think-alouds, where the task has to be somehow transferred into a language code before an attempt is made to carry it out. A good example here would be to describe a bicycle or to say what a screw-driver is used for and in what way. The third and last level of verbal reports involves retrospection in which verbalization takes place after the event or activity, not simultaneously. This allows for descriptions, interpretations, and explanations, which may be also of interest to the researcher. A good example here would be the talking about a meal prepared the previous day.

There is no agreement, however, on whether think-aloud and talk-aloud procedures are different or the same phenomena. The think-aloud method of data collection was, in fact, introduced by Lewis (1982) for the IBM Company, and that author did not emphasize the difference between think- and talk-aloud protocols. In spite of what Ericsson and Simon (1993) claimed, their definitions and explanations provide little clarity in this respect, because, as will be seen below, other descriptions of both processes have been offered by the same authors, which makes the issue even more confusing. According to Ericsson and Simon's classification (1993), the study that is presented in this chapter will, in fact, make use of talk-aloud protocols in a translation task because it involves language-related procedures. Still, for a better understanding of the observed processes, a more thorough explanation of terminology needs to be made. Talk-alouds are generally used to confirm to what extent a person understands a text, spoken or written. Ericsson and Simon (1993) refer to talk-aloud protocols as a specific method of data gathering, where the researcher concentrates only on describing actions to complete the task, and other types of comments are not allowed. It is thus claimed that talk-alouds are more objective than think-alouds because they do not offer any self-interpretations or evaluations. On the other hand, in think-alouds, participants are asked to report not only on their final product but on all their thoughts, actions, opinions, and emotions while performing the task. To researchers, think-alouds show not only comprehension processes, but also how respondents link information in the text with their background knowledge. In language teaching, think-alouds may enable teachers to diagnose learners' strengths and weaknesses. In formal research think-alouds are usually audio- or video-recorded and analyzed later. Thus, for the purpose of this chapter, the tasks given to students and subsequent analysis of their written translations and comments will be referred to as think-aloud protocols.

Ericsson and Simon (1993) proposed some procedures for analyzing think-aloud protocols. Initially, the three levels of analysis mentioned at the beginning of this section, that is, think-alouds, talk-alouds, and retrospections, were associated with different memory types. The first two included information processing performed in the short-term memory (STM), that is, together or immediately after the task had been done. The third level, retrospection, referred to information processing done using the long-term memory (LTM), that is, some time after the activity had been completed. Ericsson and Simon (1993) observed as well that the levels that focused on STM involvement were more reliable than the level of retrospection. Comments like "keep talking", "keep writing", or "uhm" did not seem to disturb the partici- pants' process of thinking aloud, whereas comments that required retrospection, for example, "how did you do that?", hindered the thinking-aloud process consider- ably. In other words, LTM involvement seems to disturb the natural flow of thinking because the participants lose concentration. Thus, Ericsson and Simon claimed that only STM-related verbalizations, that is think-alouds (or talk-alouds), which are performed without external intervention, create a reliable source of data for analyzing mental processes.

A similar opinion on the limitations and usefulness of think-alouds was expressed by Silvia Bernardini (n.d.) in her article "Using think-aloud protocols to investigate the translation process: Methodological aspects". She claims that think-alouds provide useful data on the individual's mental states while performing a task. On the basis of mental states, mental processes can be observed and cate- gorized. However, the right conditions need to be secured in order to view the data obtained as reliable, for example, prompting and interruptions should be avoided at all cost. Here Bernardini agrees with Ericsson and Simon that only STM-operated processes can provide rich data for analysis. Let us now look at the process of think-aloud protocols in translation tasks in more detail.

4 Identifying Problems and Strategies in Think-Aloud Translation Tasks

Some specialists have observed that the translation process requires a selection of specific strategies. For example, Krings (1986, p. 267, as cited in Bernardini, 2001, p. 246) reported that in their written think-aloud translations, students used explicit statements of problems, made use of reference materials, and also employed a mechanical strategy of underlining problematic passages. In oral translation tasks they made use of different kinds of hesitation phenomena and paid attention to paralinguistic and non-linguistic features of discourse. Further, Bernardini (2001, p. 246) proposes a subdivision of translation strategies. She makes a distinction between *production* and *evaluation* tactics. Production strategies are directly related to the task itself and they can be either *achievement* or *reduction* strategies. An example of achievement strategy is reformulation or association, whereas avoidance is a type of reduction strategy. Evaluation strategies appear as reflections on the acceptability or adequacy of translation.

Another researcher, Tirkkonen-Condit (1997) drew attention to the role of affective factors in think-aloud translation tasks, which will also be dealt with in the study presented in this chapter. In her view, involvement in the task has a positive influence on the quality of translation. The same can be said about having a relaxed atmosphere while performing the task. Difficulties, on the other hand, may result in frustration and unwillingness to continue the task, which may lead to the use of reduction strategies and even to task abandonment. Tirkkonen-Condit (1997) also observes some differences in the use of verbalizations between student and professional translators. The latter verbalize less in routine tasks but more in challenging ones, whereas the former use verbalizations excessively in all types of tasks. This phenomenon was also observed in students' written verbalizations reported on later in this chapter.

5 Coding Schemes for Categorizing Verbal Think-Aloud Protocols

In order to analyze the structure of think-alouds as an example of discourse, several categorization schemes were proposed. The first to be discussed here was suggested by Brown and Lytle (1988) and it contains the following categories of think-alouds:

1. *Monitoring*, e.g., "I don't understand," "This doesn't make sense"; here the participants doubt their understanding of the passage.
2. *Signalling*, e.g., the translators signal their present interpretation of the text ("What I do understand is…").
3. *Analysing*, when the readers notice, describe, or comment on the features of the text itself, e.g., "How does this text work?".
4. *Elaborating*, where the translators try to respond to the text by using background knowledge, e.g., "What does this make me think of?".
5. *Judging*, when the readers evaluate their ideas or examples, e.g., "How good is this?".
6. *Reasoning*, that is, comments and statements regarding how the participant is trying to resolve doubts, e.g., "What might that mean?".

This coding scheme was later supplemented by van Someren, Barnard, and Barnard (1994, p. 122), who added categories with a more emotional character:

1. *Talking about issues not related to the task* (e.g., "I must remember to call my friend").
2. *Evaluating the task at the more general (meta) level* (e.g., "It's boring to talk so much").
3. *Making personal comments* (e.g., "I don't like it here").
4. *Silence*—sometimes the researcher needs to remind participants that they should talk, not only perform the task in silence.
5. *Actions*, that is, doing something different from the task itself (e.g., drinking water).

A more contemporary categorization proposal comes from the article based on a conference presentation by Zhao and McDonald (2010, p. 584). The authors distinguish the following utterance categories and provide their explanations:

1. *Reading*—reading out text giving yourself time to think about possible translation or action.
2. *Action description*—describing what the participant just did or is planning to do.
3. *Action explanation*—explaining the reasons for executing some action in the past or in the future.
4. *Result evaluation*—commenting on understanding or evaluating the content of the final product.
5. *User experience*—expressing positive or negative feelings about similar actions performed before.
6. *Problem formulation*—verbalizing difficulties, uncertainty, expressing disapproval of own actions.
7. *Causal explanations*—saying why problems occurred.
8. *Impact*—describing the possible impact of difficulties, possibly restarting the task.

9. *Recommendation*—commenting on improving the task in order to avoid difficulties in the future and offer solutions.
10. *Task confusion*—indicating misunderstandings within the task itself.
11. *Other*—"utterances that do not fit into one of the categories".

For the purpose of the research described in this paper different categorizations were employed to reveal a variety of mental and emotional states present during the translation task under study.

6   The Study

6.1   Research Questions

Since most research studies of think-aloud protocols made use of audio-recorded transcripts and not of reports written by students themselves, this research aims to answer the following three research questions:

1. Which translation strategies and/or categories of verbal reports can be observed in written think-aloud protocols during a translation task in the secondary classroom?
2. Do affective strategies appear in written reports and how can they be categorized?
3. Is it possible to encounter any other think-aloud categories that are not mentioned in previous research studies?

As mentioned before, this research used a qualitative methodology which relied on the analysis of verbal reports.

6.2   Participants and Procedure

The participants of the study were 45 high-school students, aged 17–18. Their language level approximated B1, as described in *Common European framework of reference for languages* (2001). The secondary school they attended is situated in the city of Wrocław in south-east Poland.

The task they were asked to complete consisted of preparing a written translation and simultaneously verbalizing their thinking-aloud process. A text to be translated from English into Polish was a short article from *The Guardian* (Borger, 1993), which was devoted to political changes that took place in Poland at the beginning of the 1990s. The article contains a joke about police officers and another one about Lech Wałęsa, the President of Poland at that time. The text is provided as Appendix 1.

It is important to mention that students' verbalizations were recorded in writing and not orally, that is, they were not audio-recorded. As the task was a translation from English into Polish, the verbalizations were written in the students' first language. The students were asked to use a stream-of-consciousness technique while preparing a written translation of the text. As their regular English teacher, I wanted to avoid transcript preparation, as that would probably involve an increase in subjective evaluation of recorded data. Thus I was left with what I had on paper.

The translation task, including the think-alouds, was supposed to last one lesson unit, that is, 45 min. Therefore, as it turned out later, most translations were left unfinished, since the task proved to be quite challenging. The students were not allowed to use English-Polish dictionaries in any form, which later proved to be a good decision because many interesting think-alouds in relation to having to struggle with unknown vocabulary and ambiguous sentence structures of the article were reported in writing. The students were asked to hand in their translations to the teacher on separate sheets of paper, and the teacher explained that the results of their work would not affect their course grades in any way. As it turned out, students liked the article from *The Guardian*, found it amusing and, consequently, were very involved in the task. All students consented to take part in the research and they were assured that their names would remain unknown should the results be published. One completed translation together with its think-aloud reports is provided in Appendix 2, and the list of 30 examples of written think-alouds is presented in Appendix 3.

6.3 Results of the Study and Discussion—Observed Categories of Think-Aloud Protocols

As was already mentioned, students enjoyed the task of translating and even more so enjoyed writing their think-alouds in the form of the stream-of-consciousness technique. Practically all of the verbal report categories enumerated by Brown and Lytle (1988) and van Someren et al. (1994), appeared in students' reports. It was possible to distinguish the following examples:

1. Monitoring, e.g., "The next sentence appears to be too long and I can't find any sense in it. Words do not seem to logically follow one another. Perhaps somebody else has translated it—I'll ask around. Got it!"; "This fragment looks silly".
2. Signalling, e.g., "Fertile can be associated with fertilizers"; "Climax—perhaps a culmination point; it can be associated with climate plus maximum".
3. Analysing, e.g., "Flamboyant—I can associate this word with flame, perhaps with something hot and fresh like fresh bread; perhaps popular; on the other hand it may refer to tabloid newspapers, sensational, but this doesn't fit *Rzeczpospolita*—it is a serious newspaper".

4. Elaborating, e.g., "Up the pole can be associated with above the pole or a Pole, with Polish jokes, but most probably this is some idiom I don't know at all".
5. Judging, e.g., "I just invented that translation!"; "I believe it is a good translation".
6. Reasoning, e.g., "Hardships I understand as hard relationships but it sounds strange".
7. Talking about other issues, e.g., "Now I need a break to do my Spanish homework".
8. Personal comments, e.g., "Shall I go out? It's recess time. Perhaps I'll stay and finish this translation".
9. Evaluating at meta-level, e.g., "I am reading the whole text without concentrating on single words I don't understand".
10. Abandoning the task (Bernardini, 2001), e.g., "Perhaps I should leave this word? It doesn't seem to be important...".

Other categories of think-aloud protocols that are mentioned in any of the cited classifications also appeared. The names given to these new categories are coined by the author of this paper:

1. Suspending the task, e.g., "Flamboyant—I'll translate this word later"; "Now I am checking those fragments I have been leaving for later".
2. Cooperating with others, e.g., "I don't know—Figa (another boy's nickname) doesn't know either".
3. Misunderstanding the text without correction, e.g., "Why does the policeman go around trees?" (in fact: policemen go around in threes).
4. Preparing for translation task, e.g., "At the beginning I am going to read the whole text; when I know what the text is about, translating will be easier".
5. Irritation caused by other students' behavior, for example, "They are writing some silly things about me and it's disturbing".

Apart from a number of cognitive-type categories enumerated in other studies, such as, for example, monitoring, signaling, analyzing, elaborating, reasoning or judging (cf. Research Question 1), affective processes could be observed as well. These include: talking about other things, not connected with the task, comments about immediate class reality, abandoning the task because of its difficulty and length, annoyance and irritation (cf. Research Question 2). All were freely expressed in writing. A few other think-aloud categories, not observed previously, appeared as well (cf. Research Question 3): preparing for the task, explaining own procedures, cooperating with others and suspending the task. They expose learners' engagement in the translation activity, their willingness to do the task correctly, and their use of metalinguistic strategies to organize the translation process, and they uncover the positive group atmosphere.

7   Conclusions

On the basis of data analysis, it could be observed that the written form of think-alouds made students quite confident. They verbalized freely and excessively, without restraint. The atmosphere during the translation task was relaxed and generally positive and it was evident that students trusted their teacher fully. The analysis of the data collected by means of verbal protocols revealed the existence of a number of utterance categories, including those of more individualized emotional character. It was possible to observe all categories referred to by Brown and Lytle (1988), van Someren, Barnard, and Barnard (1994), and Bernardini (2001). Still, other utterance types could be discerned as well. Students seemed to be more personal in their comments and expressed such feelings as, for example, irritation at the behavior of others and annoyance. Other interesting categories also appeared such as, for example, strategies showing how students prepared for the task of translation, suspended the task, and cooperated with others. It seems that the written form of verbal reports made students quite confident and expressive in their streams-of-consciousness and the lack of audio-recording did not appear to restrain the genuine character of thinking-aloud. The study has, to some extent, contributed to the understanding that written verbal reports could supplement the audio-recorded think-aloud protocols and reveal additional interesting details about mental processing. It may be concluded that categorizations of verbal reports are hardly ever final and still more utterance types can be observed and added to existing classifications.

Appendix 1

The Article to be translated by students

Sense of humour up the pole (The Guardian, 17.03.1993)

Whatever happened to the Polish political joke, asks "Rzeczpospolita", not normally one of Warsaw's most flamboyant newspapers. Under communism, the streets were alive with satirical jibes against the system. When the American humourist P.J. O'Rourke came to Warsaw for his book *Holidays in Hell*, he ended up devoting pages to policeman jokes. For example: Why do policemen go around in threes? Answer: One reads, one writes, and one keeps eye on those two bloody intellectuals.

Why is the free market not such fertile ground, asks "Rzeczpospolita" reporter Kazimierz Groblewski. He turns to Parliament, which in Poland features the Beer Lover's Party and the Women's Alliance Against the Hardships of Life. Jokes, says the Christian National Union spokesman, Ryszard Czarnecki, were a "natural self-defence mechanism against the tedium of communism". Despite looking high and extremely low for contemporary jokes, Groblewski admits he can find little

more than reprocessed old gags, with President Lech Walesa as butt: Walesa and his sidekick Mieczysław Wachowski go to see a war film. As the climax approaches, Wachowski asks Walesa: "What do you think, Lech, are they going to make it across the bridge?" "No way," says Walesa. So they bet. The soldiers make it to the other side, and Lech pulls out his wallet. Says Wachowski: "I have to admit I saw this film yesterday, and I knew they'd get across". "I saw it too," replies the President, "but I thought this time they wouldn't manage".
(Author: Julian Borger)

Appendix 2

An example of the translated passage. Thinking-aloud protocols appear in square brackets, in English.

Poczucie humoru

["up the pole" can be associated with a geographical pole, "over the pole"; "pole" is also a Pole, Polish jokes, but most probably it is an idiom which I don't know].

Co się stało z polskim dowcipem politycznym, pyta *Rzeczpospolita*, na ogół nie jedna z najbardziej [this word seems to be associated with "flame", perhaps with fresh hot bread rolls, perhaps sold quickly, on the other hand—a tabloid, sensational paper, "hot issues"—this doesn't fit *Rzeczpospolita*—it's a serious newspaper] gazet Warszawy. Za panowania komunizmu ulice żyły satyrycznymi [I don't know this word, but it must mean "a joke" in this context] antysystemowymi. Kiedy amerykański humorysta PJ O'Rourke przybył do Warszawy dla swojej książki [I think—to write the book, to collect data] "Wakacje w piekle", zakończył poświęcając jej ostatnie strony kawałem o policjantach. Na przykład: dlaczego policjanci chodzą trójkami? Odpowiedź: jeden czyta, drugi pisze [perhaps it would be better to say "can read", "can write"], a trzeci pilnuje tych dwóch strasznych [perhaps "bloody" would have been better, as it is a stronger word] intellectuals.

Dlaczego wolny rynek nie jest tak [this can be associated with "fragile", but on the basis of the context it looks better to use "good", "appropriate"—reason, attitude, and here perhaps "appropriate conditions"—for political jokes] pyta reporter *Rzeczpospolitej*, K. Groblewski. Zwraca się [perhaps with this question] do Parlamentu w Polsce ["feature" – cecha, so the verb "appear" could be used? From the context it could be inferred that we rather need "means"] Polską Partię Przjaciół Piwa i Ruch Kobiet przeciw Trudnościom Życia. 'Dowcipy – mówi rzecznik ZChN-u R. Czarnecki – były naturalnym mechanizmem samoobronnym przeciwko komunizmowi'. Pomimo [hunt high and low—to look everywhere—there is no such expression in Polish—looking high and low for—looks the same, "extremely low"—perhaps—perhaps it is only to strengthen the power of the word, perhaps it refers to low jokes of blue collar workers] gruntownych poszukiwań współczesnych dowcipów, Groblewski [this must mean "claims", "notices"], że jest w stanie znaleźć niewiele oprócz "odgrzewanych" [reprocessed—processed once again, but

context forces me to use a different expression] kawałów z prezydentem Wałęsą
jako [I have no idea, perhaps just "a simpleton"]: Wałęsa i jego [surely it's not
"pagekick", more likely "a helper"—there is a computer IBM software called
"sidekick"—helper, associate, somebody who remains at the side, close at hand,
perhaps "zausznik"] poszli na film wojenny. W punkcie kulminacyjnym ["climax
approaches"—I don't understand but it fits the joke] Wachowski pyta: Jak myślisz,
Lechu, przejdą przez most? Nie – odpowiada Wałęsa. Zakładają się. Żołnierze
przechodzą i Lech wyjmuje portfel. Wachowski mówi: "Muszę przyznać, że
widziałem ten film wcześniej i wiedziałem, że przejdą". "Ja też widziałem" – odparł
prezydent – "ale myślałem, że tym razem im się nie uda" [the joke is not really
translated—I know it in Polish].

Appendix 3

Examples of students' think-alouds (translated from Polish):

1. "Flamboyant"—I can associate this word with "flame", perhaps with something
   hot and fresh like fresh bread; perhaps popular; on the other hand it may refer to
   tabloid papers, sensational, but this doesn't fit "Rzeczpospolita"—it is a serious
   newspaper.
2. "Fertile"—looks a bit like "fragile"? From the context it can be inferred that it
   may be associated with good, appropriate attitude; here perhaps it may mean
   "appropriate conditions" for political jokes.
3. "Flamboyant"—I'll translate this word later.
4. "Fertile" can be associated with fertilizers.
5. "Alliance"—I want to ask a friend if she has ever heard such word; before I
   even started to ask this question she also asked me about "Alliance"; she
   doesn't know the word.
6. "High and low"—it probably refers to the society.
7. "Climax"—perhaps a culmination point; it can be associated with climate plus
   maximum.
8. I am checking now those fragments I have been leaving for later.
9. "Flamboyant"—one of Warsaw's best-selling newspapers.
10. "Why does the policeman go around trees?" (A misunderstanding: policemen
    go around in threes),
11. "Fertile"—perhaps it means ripe? It would have been then "ripe ground"; but I
    would also add a comment—for creating new political jokes; perhaps I should
    leave this word? It doesn't seem to be important…
12. The next sentence appears to be too long and I can't find any sense in it. Words
    do not seem to logically follow one another; Perhaps somebody else translated
    it—I'll ask around. Got it!
13. Now I need a break to do my Spanish homework.

14. I am reading the whole text without concentrating on single words I don't understand.
15. Shall I go out? It's recess time. Perhaps I'll stay and finish this translation.
16. They are writing some silly things about me and it's disturbing.
17. Devoted—can be associated with devotion.
18. Jesus, they are all shouting so loudly!!
19. Sense of humour... I don't know if "up the pole" means in Poles or about Poles.
20. "Flamboyant"—I don't know what it means but it can be somehow associated with flames??
21. I don't know what "devoting" means; I associate it with filling something in but also with voting, in this context, however, it seems to be inappropriate
22. "Hardships" I understand as hard relationships, but it sounds strange.
23. "Reprocessed"—done once again?
24. I just invented that translation!
25. I don't know—Figa doesn't know either.
26. At the beginning I am going to read the whole text; when I know what the text is about, translating will be easier.
27. I believe it is a good translation.
28. I'm not giving up!
29. This fragment looks stupid.
30. "Up the pole" can be associated with above the pole or a Pole, with Polish jokes, but most probably this is some idiom I don't know at all.

References

Bernardini, S. (n.d.). Using think-aloud protocols to investigate the translation process: methodological aspects. Retrieved from https://www.researchgate.net/publication/267956423.

Bernardini, S. (2001). Think-aloud protocols in translation research: Achievements, limits, future prospects. *Target*, *13*(2), 241–263. doi:10.1075/target.12.2.03ber.

Borger, J. (1993, March 17). Sense of humour up the pole. *The Guardian*, p. 4.

Brown, C. S., & Lytle, S. L. (1988). Merging assessment and instruction: Protocols in the classroom. In S. M. Glazer, L. W. Seafross, & L. M. Gentile (Eds.), *Re-examining reading diagnosis: New trends and procedures* (pp. 94–102). Newark, Del.: International Reading Association.

Brown, J. D., & Rodgers, T. S. (2002). *Doing second language research*. Oxford and New York: Oxford University Press.

Common European framework of reference for languages. (2001). Strasbourg: Council of Europe.

Ericsson, K. A., & Simon, H. A. ([1984]1993). *Protocol analysis*. Cambridge, Mass.: Bradford/MIT Press.

Faerch, C., & Kasper, G. (Eds.). (1987). *Introspection in second language research*. Clevendon: Multilingual Matters.

Krings, H. (1986). Translation problems and translation strategies of advanced German learners of French (L2). In J. House & S. Blum-Kulka (Eds.), *Interlingual and intercultural communication: Discourse and cognition in translation and second language acquisition studies* (pp. 263–275). Tübingen: G.Narr.

Larsen-Freeman, D., & Long, M. H. (1991). *An introduction to second language acquisition research*. London and New York: Longman.

Lewis, C. H. (1982). *Using the 'thinking aloud' method in cognitive interface design*. Yorktown Heights, NY: IBM T. J. Watson Research Center.

Tirkkonen-Condit, S. (1997). Who verbalizes what: A linguistic analysis of TAP texts. *Target, 9* (1), 69–84. doi:10.75/target.9.1.05tir.

van Someren, M. W., Barnard, Y. F., & Barnard, J. A. C. (1994). *The think-aloud method: A practical guide to modelling cognitive processes*. London: Academic Press.

Zhao, T., & McDonald, S. (2010). Keep talking: An analysis of participant utterances gathered using two different think-aloud methods. *Proceedings of the 6th Nordic Conference on Human-Computer Interaction Extending Boundaries—NordiCHI* (pp. 581–590). New York: ACM Press. doi:10.1145/1868914.1868979.

Author Biography

Anna Michońska-Stadnik, Ph.D. is Professor of English at the Institute of English Studies, University of Wrocław, Poland. She is a graduate of the University of Wrocław (1977) and Victoria University of Manchester, UK (MEd TESOL in 1985). Professor Stadnik teaches mostly diploma courses, M.A. and B.A., and ELT methodology. She is a member of IATEFL, the Modern Language Association of Poland, and the Wrocław Scientific Society. Her scholarly interests include psycholinguistics, SLA studies, foreign language teacher training, and SLA research methodology. She has published five books and more than seventy research articles in Poland and abroad.

The Influence of Ambiguity Tolerance on Willingness to Communicate in L2

Ewa Piechurska-Kuciel

Abstract The main purpose of this chapter is to find empirical evidence for the role of ambiguity tolerance (AT) in shaping one's L2 willingness to communicate levels in the context of the English-as-a-foreign-language (EFL) classroom, in the Polish educational context. As the pyramid model of L2 WTC proposes (MacIntyre et al., 1998), AT's basis is constituted by the most distal and enduring influences of personality. For this reason, ambiguity tolerance, conceived of as a personality variable (Furnham and Marks, 2013), can have a significant impact on L2 WTC. The complexity of interrelated mechanisms embedded in the foreign language learning context induce ambivalent feelings of being simultaneously willing and unwilling to communicate (MacIntyre et al., 2011). On the one hand, learners are conscious of the importance of practising communication skills, but, on the other they, are afraid of losing face in front of the teacher and peers. For this reason, it can be expected that higher AT levels are likely to induce greater L2 WTC. As this research demonstrates, L2 WTC can mostly be predicted by language anxiety and self-perceived FL skills, while one's AT levels, though statistically significant, constitute a minor predictor of L2 WTC. These results can mostly be attributed to the nature of the key variables, as well as the specificity of the foreign language learning process.

Keywords Ambiguity tolerance · Willingness to communicate · Personality · English as a foreign language · Language anxiety · Self-perceived competence

E. Piechurska-Kuciel (✉)
University of Opole, Opole, Poland
e-mail: epiech@uni.opole.pl

© Springer International Publishing AG 2018 167
M. Pawlak and A. Mystkowska-Wiertelak (eds.), *Challenges of Second and Foreign Language Education in a Globalized World*, Second Language Learning and Teaching, DOI 10.1007/978-3-319-66975-5_11

1   Introduction

The ability to communicate and interact with other people is connected with a number of positive psychological and social consequences. Additionally, ability to communicate has a strong relationship with mental health, self-esteem, satisfaction with social interactions, and levels of perceived stress (Schachner, Shaver, & Mikulincer, 2005). This may be the reason why the ability to communicate and interact successfully with others has become one of the main objectives of the curriculum. For this reason, the goal of learning a foreign language (FL) should also be seen as the need to be able to communicate with people of different languages and cultures. Yet, the process of language learning is full of obstacles, some of which can be difficult to overcome. First of all, the student is forced to use a language with which he or she is not fully proficient. This fact may create a particular threat directly connected with the specific situation of foreign language use (Horwitz, Horwitz, & Cope, 1986). As well, classroom communication, although modeled on real-life processes, is ultimately artificial and shaped by classroom demands, such as teacher dominance and language learning requirements. The conversation is mostly directed by the teacher, who chooses topics, evaluates the students, and generally wields power in the classroom. Students, then, may have no control over their classroom roles or learning patterns. In effect, due to the ambiguity embedded in the specificity of the language learning process (e.g., unclear meaning of new vocabulary items, different uses of a grammatical tense, or doubts about pronunciation), as well as classroom procedures, learners are rarely able to effectively step out of their comfort zone and risk behaviors that could lead to their losing face or to threatening their language ego. Consequently, the aim of this chapter is to present empirical research carried out in order to investigate the influence of the personality factor of ambiguity tolerance on students' willingness to communicate in a foreign language in the context of Polish secondary grammar schools.

2   Willingness to Communicate in a Foreign Language

The studies on willingness to communicate in a foreign language (L2 WTC) originate from research on universal willingness to communicate, related to L1 use. They have focused on examining an individual's general propensity towards initiating communication with other people, defining it as "a personality-based, trait-like predisposition which is relatively consistent across a variety of communication contexts and types of receivers" (McCroskey & Richmond, 1987, p. 129). Its basis is constituted by personality, among other things, which assigns WTC a stable character (McCroskey & Richmond, 1990). It can be inferred that one's cognitive choices about communication and one's volitional character are ingrained in the personality profile, though it appears that only the roles of extroversion and neuroticism have been sufficiently explained (McCroskey & Richmond, 1987).

Nevertheless, one needs to bear in mind that, generally, a higher level of WTC is connected with a smaller number of receivers/interlocutors, and a closer relationship with them (Zakahi & McCroskey, 1989). Hence, aside from the trait-like conceptualization, the WTC phenomenon is also proposed to be situation-dependent (Barraclough, Christophel, & McCroskey, 1988). There are numerous situational variables that may affect an individual's willingness to communicate at a certain point of time in a given context (e.g., one's mood, frame of mind, previous experiences connected with communicating with a specific person, or a probable gain or loss signaled by the specific communication act). These fluctuate depending on the altered constraints brought by other people or groups (McCroskey, 1984).

Among the trait communication constructs shaping one's WTC, there are communication apprehension and self-perceived communication competence (Burroughs, Marie, & McCroskey, 2003). The first concept designates anxiety connected with real or anticipated communication with another person or persons. Its effects on one's WTC are particularly destructive, forcing anxious individuals to avoid and withdraw from communication (McCroskey, Burroughs, Daun, & Richmond, 1990). On the other hand, self-perceived communication competence is connected with one's perception of their communication abilities. It appears that, irrespective of external evaluation of one's communicative competence, when individuals are convinced that they possess good communication skills, their level of communication apprehension is low, and that of WTC—high (McCroskey & Richmond,1990). For this reason, perceived competence is more critical for predicting WTC than actual competence (MacIntyre, MacMaster, & Baker 2001). Unsurprisingly, research demonstrates that the use of a language other than L1 is connected with a higher level of communication anxiety (Burroughs et al., 2003).

The above conceptualization of WTC in L1 (or universal WTC) has been adopted as a basis for the analysis of communication carried out in foreign and second languages. In this specific situation, WTC is understood as "a readiness to enter into discourse at a particular time with a specific person or persons, using a L2" (MacIntyre, Dörnyei, Clément, & Noels, 1998, p. 547). Similarly to the studies on universal WTC, the L2 concept covers not only a volitional, trait-like tendency to engage in communication, but also stresses the role of situational factors that may shape one's inclination, such as interlocutor(s), topic, and conversational context (Kang, 2005). However, most importantly, it is postulated that in the specific situation of learning and using an L2, it is the language of communication that holds the key to the structure of the individual's willingness. The change of language brings about a substantial modification of the communication act (MacIntyre et al. 1998), playing havoc with one's willingness to communicate. Contrary to the stable and predictable conditions of L1 use, one's WTC, limited by L2 proficiency, tends to be extremely sensitive to both external and internal influences beyond the learner's control. First of all, the situation of formal instruction may drastically limit the spontaneity driven by the volitional character of interpersonal communication. Secondly, a string of negative experiences is bound to develop in the foreign language learning context, where obligatory, formal language instruction takes place and creates adequate conditions for developing aversive approaches to FL communication, thus limiting one's L2 WTC. It seems clear that, aside from the trait-like nature of WTC, state-like WTC, transforming into situational L2 WTC, shapes verbal behavior. Here, a learner assesses an opportunity to communicate as suitable and enters the communication act (Cao & Philp, 2006). The state-dependent and dynamic fluctuations of WTC, influenced by situational variables, are thus complementary to the stable trait-like nature of WTC (MacIntyre & Doucette, 2010), laying the foundations for situational WTC, that is, L2 WTC. Obviously, the cultural context of FL learning and use plays a major role. In a country like Poland (especially the Silesian region), where chances for authentic communication in English outside the classroom are scarce, students' inclinations to use the foreign language in a voluntary manner will likely be shaped by their classroom experiences. These specific challenges embedded in L2 willingness to communicate make it uniquely distinct from L1 willingness to communicate. Consequently, L2 WTC cannot be regarded a simple transfer from the L1 model, because of the individually varying L2 communicative competence, which plays a crucial role in shaping L2 WTC (Dörnyei, 2003).

The early model of WTC (MacIntyre, 1994), which accommodated the trait-like factors of perceived communication competence and communication anxiety, failed to explain the role of situational variables, as well as the more constant (stable) factors influencing communication initiation. Therefore, a multi-layered pyramid model of WTC has been recommended (MacIntyre et al., 1998). This heuristic model comprises L2 WTC shapers (antecedents) arranged in a proximal–distal continuum in six layers (MacIntyre, 2004). The model demonstrates the immediate and more distant influences on the individual's WTC. The three bottom layers contain enduring influences, while the three upper ones accommodate situational stimuli. The lowest level (Layer VI) comprises the social and individual context (intergroup climate and stable personality characteristics, the focal point of this study). Above it, in Layer V, the affective-cognitive context is found, catering for more individually-based variables (intergroup attitudes, social situation, and communicative competence). Layer IV includes motivational propensities (interpersonal motivation, intergroup motivation, and L2 self-confidence). Situated antecedents, the most proximal determinants of WTC, are placed in Layer III, where the desire to communicate with a specific person and state communicative self-confidence can be found. Layer II is the level where behavioral intention, that is, the actual construct of willingness to communicate, is located. It represents the final psychological stage of one's preparation for L2 communication. At the top of the pyramid there is Layer I, accommodating actual communication behavior, the direct L2 use. All these factors represented in the model, personality among them, have the potential to influence the individual's L2 WTC. Placing personality at the lowest and broadest layer of the pyramid appears to indicate its permanent and unwavering effect on L2 WTC. However, one needs to bear in mind that, aside from its direct influence on one's readiness, it also sets "the stage for L2 communication" (MacIntyre et al., 1998, p. 558). It follows that personality may affect the relationship between WTC and other factors whose role in shaping WTC is paramount, such as language anxiety or communicative self-confidence.

The importance of L2 WTC as an extremely influential variable underlying the second and foreign language learning processes, and as a fundamental goal of second language education, has been recognized in SLA research (Clément, Baker, & Macintyre, 2003). Its higher levels induce "increased opportunity of L2 practice and authentic L2 usage" (MacIntyre et al., 2001, p. 382). A student with high WTC levels has a chance to develop their FL proficiency, constantly building their L2 communicative competence, especially when students communicate with familiar receivers in small groups or pairs on topics related to personal experiences (Pawlak, Mystkowska-Wiertelak, & Bielak, 2016). Aside from that, recent research proves that personality (i.e., extroversion) is both directly (Mahdi, 2014) and indirectly related to L2 WTC (through linguistic self-confidence and language anxiety) (Xie, 2011). Moreover, personality also shapes students' attitudes toward the international community (Cetinkaya, 2005). There are, however, studies where no direct effect of personality (i.e., extroversion) on L2 WTC can consistently be confirmed (Alemi, Tajeddin, & Mesbah, 2013; Kamprasertwong, 2010).

3 Ambiguity Tolerance (AT)

Personality constitutes the most extensive foundation for L2 WTC; hence, its apparently distant though sound influence may have a lasting effect on one's readiness to communicate in a foreign language. Belonging to the realm of personality variables (Budner, 1962, as cited in Furnham & Marks, 2013), ambiguity tolerance (AT) can be considered a significant source of communicative behavior. Its cognitive nature is reflected in the individual's cognitive style, beliefs and attitudes, problem-solving behavior, as well as interpersonal and social functioning (Budner, 1962, as cited in Furnham & Marks, 2013).

The use of the term *ambiguity* itself has been unclear in psychology studies. Ambiguity has been connected with numerous meanings, incompleteness or vagueness, contingency, lack of structure or information, unpredictability, or a lack of clarity (Norton, as cited in Liisberg, 2015). The first conceptualizations of *tolerance of ambiguity* began with the work of Frenkel-Brunswik (1949), who generalized AT to diverse aspects of both the emotional and mental functioning of the individual. In her view, AT was conceptualized as "a general personality variable relevant to basic social orientation" (p. 268). AT is crucial for one's cognitive potential, problem-solving abilities, and the organization of one's belief system. According to Budner (1962), tolerance of ambiguity is the "tendency to perceive ambiguous situations as desirable" (p. 29), while intolerance is connected with perceiving ambiguous situations as a treat. In a similar vein, the role of contextual information is stressed when defining AT as "a range, from rejection to attraction, of reactions to stimuli perceived as unfamiliar, complex, dynamically uncertain or subject to multiple conflicting interpretations" (Mclain, 1993, p. 184). A more contemporary AT definition proposes that it can be viewed as (Furnham & Ribchester, 1995, p. 179):

> The way an individual (or group) perceives and processes information about ambiguous situations or stimuli when confronted by an array of unfamiliar, complex, or incongruent clues (…). The person with low tolerance of ambiguity experiences stress, reacts prematurely, and avoids ambiguous stimuli. At the other extreme of the scale, however, a person with high tolerance for ambiguity perceives ambiguous situations/stimuli as desirable, challenging, and interesting and neither denies nor distorts their complexity of incongruity.

There is supporting evidence of AT as a personality trait and as a cognitive style (Valutis, 2015). For this reason, the individual's response to ambiguity varies and can be more or less difficult, conditioned by their personality and cognitive style.

Situations that can be considered ambiguous are characterized by: novelty, when there are no familiar clues provided, complexity, when there are too many clues, and contradictoriness, when the clues are conflicting. An ambiguous situation can be described as one that is new, complex, or insoluble. In general, people who do not tolerate ambiguity tend to rely on their previous experience when interpreting situations. Unable to analyze conflicting evidence, they tend to choose the most familiar solution, although its effect may be negative. Moreover, as Lazarus and Folkman (1984) propose, "ambiguity can intensify threat by limiting the individual's sense of control and/or increase a sense of helplessness over the [perceived] danger" (p. 106). Therefore, new and complex elements are perceived as a disturbing and threatening cognitive challenge. For this reason, an individual with a low level of ambiguity tolerance experiences stress, reacts prematurely, and—above all—avoids ambiguous stimuli. The lack of sufficient information prevents optimal risk assessment and decision-making due to rising threats and discomfort. In effect, stress, avoidance, delay, suppression, or denial result (Furnham & Marks, 2013), leading to a rigid, black-and-white style of thinking, a negative perception of life events, and stereotyped thinking (Friedland, Keinan, & Tytiun, 1999). Understandably, low AT is now "considered a 'cognitive vulnerability' factor" (Bayer, Lev-Wiesel, & Amir, 2007, p. 7), predisposing an individual to protect themselves from the dangers of the unknown. Meanwhile, an individual with a high AT level is not fazed by ambiguous situations, because they produce consequences that are desirable, challenging, and interesting. A high degree of tolerance allows for risk-taking, assisted by persistent processing (Jonassen & Grabowski, 1993). They use more complex structures but their error tolerance leads to lower accuracy levels. This is particularly relevant for adolescents, whose increased risky behavior may not be driven by risk itself but a higher tolerance for ambiguity (Tymula et al., 2012). For those with high AT, new situations that have unfamiliar rules or procedures are a challenge, allowing for numerous ingenious and creative opportunities. However, the impact of AT on creativity is still unclear (Merrotsy, 2013).

The investigation into the role of tolerance of ambiguity in the learning situation has brought conclusive results. It has been found that tolerant individuals perform better than intolerants in new and complex learning situations (Jonassen & Grabowski, 1993). They brainstorm more ideas, and excel at divergent learning tasks whose consequences are not clear. They effectively select information sources, generate metaphors, and evaluate implications (Jonassen & Grabowski, 1993). They are not shy, anxious or resistant to a premature closure of a communicative event (Liu, 2015). Intolerant learners, however, may tend to avoid or give up when encountering ambiguous situations. They prefer explicit instructions, and want to know the correct answers, valuing clear structures and rules (Huang, 2010). Furthermore, ambiguity intolerant individuals manifest behavioral dispositions that negatively affect essential problem-solving and decision-making skills (Parker, Rubin, Erath, Wojslawowicz, & Buskirk, 2015).

In the field of learning foreign languages, the interest in tolerance of ambiguity has widened, producing much research prompted by the complexity and ambiguity of this specific language learning situation. L2 students are surrounded by numerous unfamiliar grammatical, lexical, phonological and cultural cues that cannot be easily interpreted (Chapelle & Roberts, 1986). With their specific nature of novelty, complexity and insolubility, these situations easily meet the requirements of ambiguity, creating threats and tension. The learner who has not mastered the foreign language does not understand what is happening around them: the teacher's instructions and explanations are meaningless, and the behavior of classmates may be undecipherable and unpredictable, while the learning material is unclear. Overburdened by multiple complex stimuli, such a learner cannot make decisions with predictable results, and cannot harbor solid expectations about any new clue, because of their inability to organize the information in a coherent way. Tolerance of ambiguity, with its unpredictability and considerable uncertainty, is inherently connected with the interpersonal nature of the language learning process (Ehrman, 1999), and as such may be crucial for effective language learning.

In the SLA field, ambiguity tolerance has been conceptualized on three functional levels: intake, tolerance of ambiguity proper, and accommodation (Ehrman, 1999). The *intake* level is related to one's ability to notice information so that it can later become part of the existing knowledge structure. At the *tolerance of ambiguity proper* level, when the information has been taken in, the learner deals with the contradictions or incompleteness of the new data. Tolerant students accept incongruities, and make a proper selection of items for intake, while intolerant ones may experience problems choosing items for intake or even accepting them. As a result, they may store information that is incomplete or inconsistent because they have been unable to reject a contradictory element, or have prematurely subsumed an incomplete schema. The last level, *accommodation*, focuses on integrating the new data with existing schemata. In individuals low in tolerance for the new, incomplete or contradictory information cannot be easily related to the already existing schemata, causing problems with data subsumption and manipulation. In effect, they have trouble adapting their existing cognitive, affective, and social representations from the perspective of the new material (Ehrman, 1996).

Not surprisingly, the ability to tolerate ambiguity as a personality characteristic has been accepted a crucial condition for successful language acquisition (Ehrman, 1999). Intolerant learners particularly suffer from uncertainty embedded in interpersonal and intercultural uncertainties, as well as the linguistic ambiguity inherent in L2 situations (Kimura, 2016). It is postulated that the particular merit of tolerance is connected with risk-taking (Ehrman & Oxford, 1995), the ability to refrain from using the native language when appealing to authority, for example, the teacher

(Ellis, 1994), and the ability to refrain from frustration and resulting diminished performance (Larsen-Freeman & Long, 2014). Adolescents are more ambiguity-seeking than adults (Blankenstein, Crone, van den Bos, & van Duijvenvoorde, 2016) (also confirmed in EFL studies on Finnish upper secondary school students), and likely to tolerate ambiguity rather well when learning English (Mäntysaari, 2013). Additionally, EFL learners with higher tolerance of ambiguity seem to be more willing to initiate and/or participate in communication (Vahedi & Fatemi, 2015). In a similar vein, more ambiguity tolerant Chinese learners of English are less anxious in their EFL classes, and, by the same token, they also feel more proficient (Dewaele & Ip, 2013). The negative relationship between tolerance and anxiety has been confirmed by Erten and Topkaya (2009) in their study of tertiary Turkish learners, and by Lee (1999) in reference to Chinese students learning EFL writing. In Polish learners, this relationship has also been acknowledged. Więckowska (2012) has stressed the importance of an optimal level of ambiguity tolerance, allowing learners to experience moderate language anxiety and its motivating role.

The aim of this study is to investigate the influence of ambiguity tolerance as a personality factor on willingness to communicate in the foreign language. It can be speculated that tolerant students will be more willing to risk initiating communication in a language in which they may not be fully proficient. They will experience less language anxiety, allowing them to experience more rewards and less stress in the situation of learning and using the language. In effect, they can be expected to be more proficient learners, taking every opportunity for practicing their language skills and skillfully organizing their FL knowledge. Intolerant learners, in contrast, are bombarded by ambiguity and uncertainty. They will not be willing to commence an exchange because it is likely to produce even more ambiguity and fear. Obviously, they will try to avoid more stress, and stay away from danger at the expense of their L2 proficiency. Hence, for the purpose of this study, it is stipulated that the personality factor of ambiguity tolerance plays a significant role in predicting the students L2 WTC levels.

4   Method

4.1   Participants

The participants in this study were 537 students who came from 20 randomly selected classes of the six secondary grammar schools in Opole, southwestern Poland (313 girls and 224 boys, mean age: 18.50, range: 18–21, SD = 0.53). They attended the third (last) grade/form of their schools, where they had three to six hours a week of compulsory English instruction. Their level of proficiency was intermediate to upper-intermediate, with almost eleven years as the average length of their English language experience, with a vast majority (above 90%) studying the language for seven to 17 years. They also attended another compulsory foreign language course: French or German (two to four lessons a week). The students came from different residential locations; 254 of them came from the city of Opole, 133 from neighboring towns), and 150 students from rural regions.

4.2 Instruments

The basic instrument adopted was a questionnaire. It included demographic variables: age, gender (1—*male*, 2—*female*), and place of residence (1—*village: up to 2500 inhabitants*, 2—*town: from 2500 to 50,000 inhabitants*, 3—*city: over 50,000 inhabitants*). Students also assessed the *length of their English instruction* by stating how long they had studied the language in a formal context (private classes, school education, etc.).

The *Willingness to Communicate in the Classroom Scale* (WTCI) (MacIntyre, Baker, Clément & Conrod, 2001), consisting of 27 items, assessed the students' willingness to engage in communication tasks during class time in the four skill areas (hereby called WTCI). Eight items measured WTC in speaking, six—reading, eight—writing, and five—comprehension (listening). Sample items in the scale were: *How often are you willing to speak to your teacher about your homework assignment?* or *How often are you willing to read reviews of popular movies?* The participants indicated their answers on a Likert scale, within a range from 1 to 5, assessing how willing they would be to communicate in given contexts. 1 indicated *almost never willing*, 2—*sometimes willing*, 3—*willing half of the time*, 4—*usually willing*, and 5—*almost always willing*. The minimum number of points on the scale was 27, while the maximum was 135. The scale's reliability was measured in terms of Cronbach's alpha, ranging the level of 0.94.

Another scale, *Willingness to Communicate Outside the Classroom* (WTCO) (MacIntyre et al., 2001), was applied to determine the students' willingness to engage in communication tasks outside the classroom in the four skill areas (hereby called WTCO). It included the same items as the previous scale, adapted to the out-of-school context. Since the Polish respondents had virtually no chances of participating in authentic communication outside school, the results obtained on the WTCI and WTCO scales were later aggregated to assess the global L2 WTC level.

The next scale was *The Second Language Tolerance of Ambiguity Scale* (Ely, 1995), designed to measure AT in the L2 learning environment, adapted to the EFL learning situation. It included such items as: *When I am reading something in English, I feel impatient when I don't totally understand the meaning* or *It bothers me that I don't get everything the teacher says in English*. The items were key-reversed so that a high score on this measure would indicate high ambiguity tolerance. The respondents noted their answers on a 7-point Likert scale (from 1—*I totally agree* to 7—*I totally disagree*). The minimum number of points was 12, the maximum was 84. The scale's reliability was assessed at the 0.90 level.

The *Foreign Language Classroom Anxiety Scale* (Horwitz et al., 1986) was used to estimate the degree to which students felt anxious during language classes. Sample items were as follows: *I can feel my heart pounding when I'm going to be called on in language class* and *I keep thinking that the other students are better at languages than I am*. A Likert scale was used (from 1—*I totally disagree* to 5—*I totally agree*). The minimum number of points was 33, the maximum was 165. The scale's reliability was $\alpha = 0.94$.

There were two additional types of assessment tools used: external (grades) and internal (self-assessment of the foreign language skills). As far as *grades* are concerned, the participants gave the final grades they had received in junior high school, and the first semester of secondary grammar school. They also included the grade they expected to receive at the end of the school year. All these grades were placed on the Likert scale ranging from 1 (*unsatisfactory*) to 6 (*excellent*). The scales reliability was $\alpha = 0.87$. The scale describing *self-perceived levels of FL skills* (speaking, listening, writing and reading) was an aggregated value of separate assessments of the FL skills, measured with a Likert scale ranging from 1 (*unsatisfactory*) to 6 (*excellent*). The minimum number of points on the scale was 4, while the maximum was 24. The scale's reliability was Cronbach's $\alpha = 0.88$.

4.3   Procedure

The data collection procedure consisted in asking the students to fill in the questionnaire, which took them about 15–45 min. The participants were requested to give sincere answers without taking excessive time to think. Each new set of items in the questionnaire was preceded with a short statement introducing them in an unobtrusive manner.

The data were later computed by means of the statistical program STATISTICA, with the main operations being descriptive statistics (means and *SD*), correlations, and an inferential statistics operation: step-wise hierarchical multiple regression, where in each step more significant variables are entered into the model. This included the indicator of the significance of variables, that is, the range of the explained variance R^2, as well as the value and significance of the β weights.

5   Results

First, means and SD were calculated for all the variables included in the study. The summary of the results can be found in Table 1.

Then, all the variables measured on interval scales were correlated with one another. The results showed that L2 WTC is significantly related to all the variables;

Table 1 Means and SD of the variables ($N = 537$)

Variable	Mean	SD
L2 WTC (WTCI + WTCO)	158.75	44.07
Tolerance of ambiguity	46.50	13.94
Language anxiety	84.04	23.30
Length of study	9.89	2.46
Final grades	3.82	0.76
Self-perceived FL skills	3.97	0.87

in a positive manner with AT, length of the English study, final grades and self-perceived levels of FL skills, and negatively related to language anxiety. Worth noting is a very strong, negative correlation of AT with language anxiety. A summary of the correlation procedures is presented in Table 2.

Then, step-wise multiple regression was performed in order to compute the predictive value of the selected variables for assessing L2 WTC levels. In Step 1 AT as the item weakly correlated with L2 WTC was entered. This computation showed weak, though statistically significant predictability of the WTC results with $\beta = 0.13$, $p = 0.00$. The variable was found to be responsible for about 2% of the WTC variability with $F(1535) = 9.10$, $p = 0.00$.

In Step 2 the length of FL study and final grades were introduced into the regression model. The results were: $\beta = 0.26$, $p = 0.00$, proving that the variable can explain 8% of the WTC variability, independently from the previous variable with $F(3533) = 15.63$, $p = 0.00$.

In Step 3, the most powerful variables were entered: language anxiety and self-perceived levels of FL skills. In the case of language anxiety, the result was $\beta = -0.21$, $p = 0.00$, while in the case of self-perceived levels of FL skills: $\beta = 0.31$, $p = 0.00$. The variables appeared to be responsible for 20% of WTC variability, independently from the other variables with $F(5531) = 27.03$, $p = 0.00$. All the variables in the model were responsible for explaining about 30% of L2 WTC variability. A summary of the multiple regression procedure can be found in Table 3.

Table 2 Correlation matrices for the variables ($N = 537$)

	2	3	4	5	6
1. L2 WTC	0.13^{**}	-0.35^{***}	0.16^{***}	0.25^{***}	0.41^{***}
2. Tolerance of ambiguity	–	-0.49^{***}	0.19^{***}	0.17^{***}	0.42^{***}
3. Language anxiety	–	–	-0.25^{***}	-0.38^{***}	-0.56^{***}
4. Length of study	–	–	–	0.20^{***}	0.34^{***}
5. Final grades	–	–	–	–	0.45^{***}
6. Self-perceived FL skills	–	–	–	–	–

*Denotes $p \leq 0.05$; **$p < 0.01$, ***$p < 0.001$

Table 3 Summary of multiple regression results for L2 WTC ($N = 537$)

Variable	Adjusted R^2 change	B	p
Step 1[*]		0.13	0.00
Tolerance of ambiguity			
Step 2	0.08	0.10	0.00
Length of FL study		0.22	0.00
Final grades			
Step 3	0.20	−0.21	0.00
Language anxiety		0.31	0.00
Self-perceived FL skills			

[*]Adjusted $R^2 = 0.02$
[*]Denotes $p \leq 0.05$; [**]$p < 0.01$, [***]$p < 0.001$

6 Discussion

This study has attempted to examine the impact of ambiguity tolerance as a personality factor on willingness to communicate in a foreign language. The results of the multiple regression procedure demonstrate that in the proposed model, ambiguity tolerance can be regarded a statistically significant, though weak predictor of L2 WTC.

The descriptive WTC scores show that the Polish cohort declares quite high willingness to communicate (the sample mean value falls within one standard deviation above the mean of the two aggregated scales), meaning that Polish secondary school students who encounter the English language mostly in the classroom setting still show readiness to initiate communication in a language in which they are not fully proficient. This is quite an optimistic finding that can be attributed to two main sources: the age of the participants (older adolescents), as well as to the high standing of English in the Polish and foreign labor markets. Obviously, a positive perception of a foreign language induces a greater desire to learn it. In the case of English, the reasons for this opinion can be traced back to the dominance of English as a *lingua franca* in Poland and worldwide (Piechurska-Kuciel, 2016). As far as ambiguity tolerance levels are concerned, a similar conclusion can be drawn. Polish teenagers appear to be quite tolerant of ambiguity (the mean value in the sample is slightly above the mean of the scale) when learning English. Again, this can be attributed to their age specificity (Blankenstein, Crone, van den Bos, & van Duijvenvoorde, 2016), but also to the motivational orientations embedded in EFL learning prospects.

The minor strength of ambiguity tolerance as a predictor of L2 WTC appears to be a consequence of several factors. First, one needs to bear in mind the fact that personality, though having an enduring influence on WTC, is its most distal shaper. One's personality simultaneously interacts with a multitude of other factors shaping WTC, as well as with WTC itself. Secondly, though its direct influence may be considered marginal, its unquestionable interrelationships with language anxiety and perceived communicative competence may be treated as the key to uncovering its real impact, because its correlations with both constructs are strongest of all. Thirdly, the cumulative power of both direct and indirect effects of AT on WTC may in effect lead to the speculation that ambiguity tolerance should be regarded a vital, though covert, antecedent of WTC, whose greatest explanatory power can be attributed to moderating language anxiety and perceived communicative competence. In consequence, a student who is willing to communicate in English perceives ambiguous situations created by the use and learning of English as desirable, challenging, and interesting. In this overall pleasant situation negative experiences, such as language anxiety, diminish, giving way to the production of an array of other positive effects, such as a high assessment of one's FL proficiency. The optimism and satisfaction induced by pleasant experiences allows learners to safely take risks and enjoy learning, producing risk-approach behaviors. In contrast, students intolerant of ambiguity cannot feel safe, and try to remain risk-averse by not initiating communication of their own accord. The complexity and incongruity of stimuli they encounter in the FL classroom produces great levels of stress, such as language anxiety, discouraging them from leaving their comfort zone. Convinced of their debility and unable to interpret ambiguous stimuli, they prefer to stay reticent, losing chances for optimal development of a linguistic, social or cultural nature. Indeed, they remain victims of their cognitive vulnerability, which condemns them to protective behaviors. Be that as it may, it would be too risky to conclude that high levels of AT are beneficial for L2 WTC. Very tolerant learners might show unrestricted acceptance and cognitive passivity (Dewaele & Wei, 2013), which may lead to their disorganized and misguided development. It appears that a moderate level of AT may be optimal for effective foreign language learning (Ehrman, 1999), ensuring self-regulation and complex decision-making.

The regression model of WTC uncovers the critical role of perceived communicative competence (operationalized as self-perceived assessment of FL skills). Indeed, it appears that self-perception (internal assessment of FL skills) is more influential than external assessment (final grades) in predicting L2 WTC. The decision to initiate communication is based on self-perceptions of skills, not on the actual skills. Therefore, self-perceived assessment plays a decisive role (Richmond & McCroskey, 1989). Another explanation is that self-perceptions are entwined with ambiguity tolerance. In tolerant individuals, complex and contradictory stimuli do not decrease the general positive self-assessment of FL skills, while intolerant learners have serious problems matching stimuli to their existing self-assessment. Obviously, under the influence of ambiguous clues their self-perceived FL skills are bound to suffer due to the student's inability to produce a well-informed evaluation, free from the constraints of anxiety and stress.

Language anxiety is the other variable whose predictive power for L2 WTC should be acknowledged. Its double impact on one's readiness to initiate communication in a foreign language is realized through its direct correlations with AT and WTC. A low level of tolerance of ambiguity creates stress and tension, culminating in high language anxiety levels. Its specific effects hamper the adequate assessment of the communicative situation and cognitive processes underlying effective decision-making, discouraging the student from speaking. At the same time, low tolerance produces low self-perceptions, making independent communication impossible. Altogether, under the impact of high language anxiety and low self-perceptions, the student has no chance to develop their communicative competence and performance. Self-protective behaviors then become routine in the classroom, so such learners remain reticent and evasive in order to survive.

The last factor included in the model is the length of one's FL instruction. Obviously, it is related to growing proficiency, allowing for greater freedom in the classroom. Experience connected with teaching and learning procedures, peer behaviors and instructional techniques allows even most intolerant students to internalize the basic strategies that reassure their basic performance in the classroom. However, it should not be expected that they will eventually risk initiating communication in a foreign language of their own accord. When not allowed to flee, they are more likely to freeze to survive, abstaining from the perils of communication.

7   Conclusions

Although the personality factor of ambiguity tolerance does not appear to play a strong role in predicting L2 WTC levels, the dangers it evokes may produce serious side-effects, impeding the language learning process. For this reason, it is worthwhile to address ambiguity tolerance in order to reduce its negative influences and improve learner performance. For this purpose, the teacher's actions should primarily aim at reducing ambiguity in the FL classroom.

In order to assist learners in their efforts to succeed in language learning, teachers can help students increase their awareness of classroom procedures, as well as the content to be learnt (Erten & Topkaya, 2009). In this way, students can feel more relaxed, self-assured and motivated in the language classroom, which may in return help raise their tolerance of ambiguity. Eliminating all ambiguity is not feasible; however, the establishing of teaching and learning routines, aided by the explicit introduction of lesson objectives and effects, can hopefully lead to a more balanced learner attitude to the FL class. Secondly, teachers may pay special attention to the effects of negative emotions and ways of combatting them by incorporating relaxation training, desk yoga or breathing techniques sessions into their teaching. Thirdly, the use of the mother tongue should be allowed, giving learners the impression of being always able to resort to well-known and familiar linguistic and cognitive patterns. In the long run, this permissive attitude may lead to a more reliable cognitive cohabitation of the languages in the learner's mind. Fourthly, the conscious development of willingness to communicate should primarily focus on creating more opportunities for learning and using the FL in and out of the classroom, gradually exposing students to greater degrees of ambiguity. Such intervention may include authentic communication (authentic videos, bringing native speakers to the classroom, or analyzing real-life facts and behaviors). Obviously, pursuing intercultural communication within the constraints of a non-native language classroom may be extremely difficult, yet it may offer students valuable experience that cannot be overrated.

This study is not free from limitations that need to be addressed. The proposed model does not appear to have a significant explanatory power, because it explains only 30% of L2 WTC variability. There are also other influential variables that need to be taken into consideration while predicting the WTC levels. Furthermore, the study is limited to only one research method, excluding triangulation, which could offer a greater degree of confidence in data validation. Moreover, the cross-sectional nature of the study does not allow drawing more complex cause-and-effect conclusions providing for a broader collection of variables. Hence, applying longitudinal studies or panel designs in culture-specific contexts may shed more light on the intricate relationship of L2 WTC and personality factors.

In spite of its weaknesses, it is hoped that this research sheds more light on the role of ambiguity tolerance in one's readiness to initiate communication in a foreign language. Obviously, investigating such relationships may offer valuable insights into how to bring people of different languages and cultures together. It may also allow for facilitating communication, and diminishing geographical and social distances.

References

Alemi, M., Tajeddin, Z., & Mesbah, Z. (2013). Willingness to communicate in L2 English: Impact of learner variables. *Research in Applied Linguistics, 4*(1), 42–61.

Barraclough, R. A., Christophel, D. M., & McCroskey, J. C. (1988). Willingness to communicate: A cross-cultural investigation. *Communication Research Reports, 5*(2), 187–192.

Bayer, S., Lev-Wiesel, R., & Amir, M. (2007). The relationship between basic assumptions, posttraumatic growth, and ambiguity tolerance in an Israeli sample of young adults: A mediation-moderation model. *Traumatology, 13*(1), 4–15. doi:10.1177/1534765607299908.

Blankenstein, N. E., Crone, E. A., van den Bos, W., & van Duijvenvoorde, A. C. K. (2016). Dealing with uncertainty: Testing risk- and ambiguity-attitude across adolescence. *Developmental Neuropsychology, 41*(1–2), 77–92. doi:10.1080/87565641.2016.1158265.

Budner, S. (1962). Intolerance of ambiguity as a personality variable. *Journal of Personality, 30* (1), 29–50. doi:10.1111/j.1467-6494.1962.tb02303.x.

Burroughs, N. F., Marie, V., & McCroskey, J. C. (2003). Relationships of self-perceived communication competence and communication apprehension with willingness to communicate: A comparison with first and second languages in Micronesia. *Communication Research Reports, 20*(3), 230–239. doi:10.1080/08824090309388821.

Cao, Y., & Philp, J. (2006). Interactional context and willingness to communicate: A comparison of behavior in whole class, group and dyadic interaction. *System, 34*(4), 480–493. doi:10.1016/j.system.2006.05.002.

Cetinkaya, Y. B. (2005). *Turkish college students willingness to communicate in English as a foreign language* (Ph.D. thesis). The Graduate School of The Ohio State University. Retrieved from https://www.researchgate.net/profile/Yesim_Bektas-Cetinkaya/publication/35442471_Turkish_college_students'_willingness_to_communicate_in_English_as_a_foreign_language_electronic_resource_/links/556c446f08aefcb861d63aa8.pdf.

Chapelle, C., & Roberts, C. (1986). Ambiguity tolerance and field independence as predictors of proficiency in English as a second language. *Language Learning, 36*(1), 27–45. doi:10.1111/j.1467-1770.1986.tb00367.x.

Clément, R., Baker, S. C., & Macintyre, P. D. (2003). Willingness to communicate in a second language: The effects of context, norms, and vitality. *Journal of Language and Social Psychology, 22*(2), 190–209. doi:10.1177/0261927X03022002003.

Dewaele, J.-M., & Ip, T. S. (2013). The link between foreign language classroom anxiety, second language tolerance of ambiguity and self-rated English proficiency among Chinese learners. *Studies in Second Language Learning and Teaching, 3*(1), 47–66. https://doi.org/10.14746/ssllt.2013.3.1.3.

Dewaele, J.-M., & Wei, L. (2013). Is multilingualism linked to a higher tolerance of ambiguity? *Bilingualism: Language and Cognition, 16*(01), 231–240. https://doi.org/10.1017/S1366728912000570.

Dörnyei, Z. (2003). Attitudes, orientations, and motivations in language learning: Advances in theory, research, and applications. *Language Learning, 55*(1), 3–32.

Ehrman, M. E. (1996). *Understanding second language learning difficulties*. Thousand Oakes, CA: SAGE Publications.

Ehrman, M. (1999). Ego boundaries and tolerance of ambiguity in second language learning. In J. Arnold (Ed.), *Affect in language learning* (pp. 68–86). Cambridge: Cambridge University Press.

Ehrman, M. E., & Oxford, R. L. (1995). Cognition plus: Correlates of language learning success. *The Modern Language Journal, 79*(1), 67–89. doi:10.1111/j.1540-4781.1995.tb05417.x.

Ellis, R. (1994). *The study of second language acquisition*. Oxford: Oxford University Press.

Ely, C. M. (1995). Tolerance of ambiguity and the teaching of ESL. In J. M. Reid (Ed.), *Learning styles in the ESL/EFL classroom* (pp. 87–95). Boston: Heinle & Heinle.

Erten, İ. H., & Topkaya, E. Z. (2009). Understanding tolerance of ambiguity of EFL learners in reading classes at tertiary level. *Novitas-Royal, 3*(1), 29–44.

Frenkel-Brunswik, E. (1949). Intolerance of ambiguity as an emotional and perceptual personality variable. *Journal of Personality, 18*(1), 108–143. doi:10.1111/j.1467-6494.1949.tb01236.x.

Friedland, N., Keinan, G., & Tytiun, T. (1999). The effect of psychological stress and tolerance of ambiguity on stereotypic attributions. *Anxiety Stress and Coping, 12*(4), 397–410. doi:10.1080/10615809908249318.

Furnham, A., & Marks, J. (2013). Tolerance of ambiguity: A review of the recent literature. *Psychology, 04*(09), 717–728. doi:10.4236/psych.2013.49102.

Furnham, A., & Ribchester, T. (1995). Tolerance of ambiguity: A review of the concept, its measurement and applications. *Current Psychology, 14*(3), 179–199. doi:10.1007/BF02686907.

Horwitz, E. K., Horwitz, M. B., & Cope, J. (1986). Foreign language classroom anxiety. *The Modern Language Journal, 70*(2), 125–132. doi:10.1111/j.1540-4781.1986.tb05256.x.

Huang, L.-S. (2010). *Academic communication skills: Conversation strategies for international graduate students*. Lanham, Maryland: University Press of America.

Jonassen, D. H., & Grabowski, B. L. H. (1993). *Handbook of individual differences, learning, and instruction*. New York; London: Routledge.

Kamprasertwong, M. (2010). Willingness to communicate in English speech as a second language: A study of Thai, Chinese, and Dutch samples (MA thesis). Faculty of Liberal Arts, University of Groningen. Retrieved from http://arts.studenttheses.ub.rug.nl/9753/1/MA_1700820_T_Kamprasertwong.pdf.

Kang, S.-J. (2005). Dynamic emergence of situational willingness to communicate in a second language. *System, 33*(2), 277–292. doi:10.1016/j.system.2004.10.004.

Kimura, H. (2016). L2 intolerance of ambiguity revisited: Toward a comprehensive understanding. *Konin Language Studies, 4*(2), 197–216.

Larsen-Freeman, D., & Long, M. H. (2014). *An introduction to second language acquisition research*. Abingdon, Oxon: Routledge.

Lazarus, R. S. L., & Folkman, S. (1984). *Stress, appraisal, and coping*. New York: Springer Publishing Company.

Lee, E.-K. (1999). The effects of tolerance of ambiguity on EFL task-based writing. Retrieved from http://s-space.snu.ac.kr/handle/10371/70570.

Liisberg, S. (2015). Trust as the life magic of self-deception: A philosophical-psychological investigation into tolerance of ambiguity. In S. Liisberg, E. O. Pedersen, & A. L. Dalsgård (Eds.), *Anthropology and philosophy: Dialogues on trust and hope* (pp. 158–175). New York: Berghahn Books.

Liu, C. (2015). Relevant researches on tolerance of ambiguity. *Theory and Practice in Language Studies, 5*(9), 1874–1882. https://doi.org/10.17507/tpls.0509.15.

MacIntyre, P. D. (1994). Variables underlying willingness to communicate: A causal analysis. *Communication Research Reports, 11*(2), 135–142. doi:10.1080/08824099409359951.

MacIntyre, P. D. (2004). Variables underlying willingness to communicate: A causal analysis. *Communication Research Reports, 11*(2), 135–142.

MacIntyre, P. D., Baker, S. C., Clément, R., & Conrod, S. (2001a). Willingness to communicate, social support, and language-learning orientations of immersion students. *Studies in Second Language Acquisition, 23*(3), 369–388.

MacIntyre, P. D., Burns, C., & Jessome, A. (2011). Ambivalence about communicating in a second language: A qualitative study of French immersion students' willingness to communicate. *The Modern Language Journal, 95*(1), 81–96. doi:10.1111/j.1540-4781.2010.01141.x.

MacIntyre, P. D., & Doucette, J. (2010). Willingness to communicate and action control. *System, 38*(2), 161–171. doi:10.1016/j.system.2009.12.013.

MacIntyre, P., Dörnyei, Z., Clément, R., & Noels, K. A. (1998). Conceptualizing Willingness to communicate in a L2: A situational model of L2 confidence and affiliation. *The Modern Language Journal, 82*(4), 545–562. doi:10.1111/j.1540-4781.1998.tb05543.x.

MacIntyre, P. C., MacMaster, K., & Baker, S. C. (2001b). The convergence of multiple models of motivation for second language learning: Gardner, Pintrich, Kuhl, and McCroskey. In Z. Dörnyei & R. Schmidt (Eds.), *Motivation and second language acquisition* (pp. 461–492). Honolulu, HI: University of Hawai'i, Second Language Teaching and Curriculum Center.

Mahdi, D. (2014). Willingness to communicate in English: A case study of EFL students at King Khalid University. *English Language Teaching, 7*(7). https://doi.org/10.5539/elt.v7n7p17.

Mäntysaari, M. (2013). *Ambiguity tolerance as an instrument of learner profiling: A Q Methodological study of how upper secondary school students' perceptions of EFL reading reconstruct a learner variable* (M.A. thesis). Department of Languages, University of Jyväskylä.

McCroskey, J. C. (1984). The communication apprehension perspective. In J. A. Daly & J. C. McCroskey (Eds.), *Avoiding communication: Shyness, reticence and communication apprehension* (pp. 13–38). Beverly Hills, CA: Sage.

McCroskey, J. C., Burroughs, N. F., Daun, A., & Richmond, V. P. (1990). Correlates of quietness: Swedish and American perspectives. *Communication Quarterly, 38*(2), 127–137.

McCroskey, J. C., & Richmond, V. P. (1987). Willingness to communicate. In J. C. McCroskey & J. A. Daly (Eds.), *Personality and interpersonal communication* (pp. 113–119). CA: Newbury Park.

McCroskey, J. C., & Richmond, V. P. (1990). Willingness to communicate: A cognitive view. *Journal of Social Behavior and Personality, 5*(2), 19.

Mclain, D. L. (1993). The Mstat-I: A new measure of an individual's tolerance for ambiguity. *Educational and Psychological Measurement, 53*(1), 183–189. doi:10.1177/0013164493053001020.

Merrotsy, P. (2013). Tolerance of ambiguity: A trait of the creative personality? *Creativity Research Journal, 25*(2), 232–237. doi:10.1080/10400419.2013.783762.

Parker, J. G., Rubin, K. H., Erath, S. A., Wojslawowicz, J. C., & Buskirk, A. A. (2015). Peer relationships, child development, and adjustment: A developmental psychopathology perspective. In D. Cicchetti & D. J. Cohen (Eds.), *Developmental psychopathology* (pp. 419–493). Hoboken, NJ: Wiley. https://doi.org/10.1002/9780470939383.ch12.

Pawlak, M., Mystkowska-Wiertelak, A., & Bielak, J. (2016). Investigating the nature of classroom willingness to communicate (WTC): A micro-perspective. *Language Teaching Research, 20* (5), 654–671. doi:10.1177/1362168815609615.

Piechurska-Kuciel, E. (2016). Polish adolescents' perceptions of English and their desire to learn it. In D. Gałajda, P. Zakrajewski, & M. Pawlak (Eds.), *Researching second language learning and teaching from a psycholinguistic perspective* (pp. 37–52). Berlin: Springer. https://doi.org/10.1007/978-3-319-31954-4_4.

Richmond, V. P., & McCroskey, J. C. (1989). *Communication: Apprehension, avoidance, and effectiveness*. Scottsdale, AZ: Gorsuch Scarisbrick.

Schachner, D. A., Shaver, P. R., & Mikulincer, M. (2005). Patterns of nonverbal behavior and sensitivity in the context of attachment relations. *Journal of Nonverbal Behavior, 29*(3), 141–169. doi:10.1007/s10919-005-4847-x.

Tymula, A., Rosenberg Belmaker, L. A., Roy, A. K., Ruderman, L., Manson, K., Glimcher, P. W., & Levy, I. (2012). Adolescents' risk-taking behavior is driven by tolerance to ambiguity. *Proceedings of the National Academy of Sciences of the United States of America, 109*(42), 17135–17140. doi:10.1073/pnas.1207144109.

Vahedi, V. S., & Fatemi, A. H. (2015). The role of emotional intelligence and tolerance of ambiguity in academic Iranian EFL Learners' willingness to communicate. *Journal of Language Teaching and Research, 7*(1), 178–184. https://doi.org/10.17507/jltr.0701.20.

Valutis, S. (2015). Tolerance of ambiguity: Individual differences and teaching. *Journal of Baccalaureate Social Work, 20*(1), 79–88.

Więckowska, A. (2012). *The influence of ego boundaries and ambiguity tolerance on foreign language oral communicative competence* (PhD thesis). Institute of English Studies, Faculty of Philology, Wrocław University.

Xie, Q. (Melody). (2011). *Willingness to communicate in english among secondary school students in the rural Chinese English as a Foreign Language (EFL) classroom* (M.A. thesis). Auckland University of Technology. Retrieved from http://aut.researchgateway.ac.nz/handle/10292/2548.

Zakahi, W. R., & McCroskey, J. C. (1989). Willingness to communicate: A potential confounding variable in communication research. *Communication Reports, 2*(2), 96–104.

Author Biography

Ewa Piechurska-Kuciel is Professor of Applied Linguistics at the Institute of English, Opole University (Poland), where she teaches EFL methodology and SLA courses. She specializes in the role of affect in the foreign language learning process (anxiety, motivation, willingness to communicate in L2 and personality). Her interests also include special educational needs (developmental dyslexia, autism, and AD/HD). She has published two books—*The importance of being aware: Advantages of explicit grammar study* and *Language anxiety in secondary grammar school students*—and numerous papers in Poland and abroad.

Tracing the Motivational Trajectories in Learning English as a Foreign Language. The Case of Two English Majors

Mirosław Pawlak and Anna Mystkowska-Wiertelak

Abstract There has been a major shift in research on second language motivation in the last fifteen years, with researchers becoming more and more interested in how this attribute changes over time rather than merely establishing the reasons for learning and seeking relationships between levels of motivation and attainment (cf. Dörnyei, 2005; Dörnyei & Ryan, 2015; Ushioda & Dörnyei, 2005; Dörnyei & Ryan, 2012). As a result, there are more and more studies which seek to determine how learners' motives and the intensity of their engagement change over longer periods of time but also such which are aimed to track fluctuations in motivation in the course of tasks, lessons or sequences of such lessons, also attempting to pinpoint contextual and individual factors responsible for such changes. The chapter reports the results of a study, which constitutes part of a larger-scale empirical investigation using retrodictive qualitative modeling (RQM) (Dörnyei, 2014a) and falls within the former category by tracing the motivational trajectories of two English majors. This is done with a view to gaining insights into the dynamic nature of their motivation, identifying the factors that affected their motivational processes at different educational levels, seeking explanations of their successes and failures, and trying to identify distinctive profiles of these students. The results show that RQM is indeed capable of providing insights into motivational dynamics, although the procedure also suffers from some limitations.

Keywords L2 motivation · Motivational dynamics · Retrodictive qualitative modeling · L2 motivational self system · Ideal L2 self

M. Pawlak (✉) · A. Mystkowska-Wiertelak
Adam Mickiewicz University, Kalisz, Poland
e-mail: pawlakmi@amu.edu.pl

A. Mystkowska-Wiertelak
e-mail: mystkows@amu.edu.pl

M. Pawlak · A. Mystkowska-Wiertelak
State University of Applied Sciences, Konin, Poland

© Springer International Publishing AG 2018
M. Pawlak and A. Mystkowska-Wiertelak (eds.), *Challenges of Second and Foreign Language Education in a Globalized World*, Second Language Learning and Teaching, DOI 10.1007/978-3-319-66975-5_12

1   Introduction

The last two decades or so have witnessed a major shift in research on second language (L2) motivation from studies approaching it as a relatively stable attribute of learners to empirical investigations of its dynamic nature, both in relation to the reasons for undertaking the challenge of learning a second or foreign language and the intensity of the motivated learning behavior (e.g., Dörnyei, 2005, 2014b; Dörnyei & Ryan, 2015; Dörnyei & Ushioda, 2011; Dörnyei, MacIntyre, & Henry, 2015). One manifestation of this shift is the *process-oriented period* in the study of L2 motivation, initiated, by theoretical models proposed, among others, by Williams and Burden (1997), and Dörnyei and Ottó (1998), which, while differing with respect to specific stages, make a clear-cut distinction between the emergence of motivation (i.e., choices, decisions or goals) and engagement in the process of learning as such (i.e., feelings, behaviors, reactions). This approach has been taken even further in studies representing the socio-dynamic period in the study of L2 motivation which, in the words of Ushioda and Dörnyei (2012, p. 398), is "(…) characterized by a focus on the situated complexity of the L2 motivation process and its organic development in interaction with a multiplicity of internal, social, and contextual factors (…) [and] a concern to theorize L2 motivation in ways that take account of the broader complexities of language learning and language use in the modern globalized world". Such a view of motivation in second or foreign language learning is reflective of two theoretical stances that have dominated research on this individual difference variable in recent years. One of them is complex dynamic systems (CDS) theory (e.g., Larsen-Freeman, 2015; Larsen-Freeman & Cameron, 2008), which allows viewing L2 motivation as a prime example of such a system, based on the assumption that it involves "(…) motivational conglomerates of motivational, cognitive, and emotional variables that form coherent patterns or amalgams that act as wholes" (Dörnyei, 2014b, p. 520). The other is the theory L2 motivation self system (Dörnyei, 2005, 2009, 2014c), comprising three components, that is *ideal L2 self* (i.e., representing aspirations concerning mastery of a given L2), *ought-to self* (i.e., reflective of expectations of others and the desire to ward off adverse consequences), and *L2 learning experience* (i.e., amalgams of internal and external influences on engagement in L2 learning), all of which are in a constant state of flux (Henry, 2015). This said, it has to be emphasized that research on motivational dynamics need not or perhaps even should not be grounded in a single theoretical position (cf. Pawlak, 2015), but, rather, it should involve different methodological approaches and employ a variety of data collection tools to allow as multifaceted and differentiated insights into this phenomenon as possible. The chapter contributes to this current line of inquiry by reporting on a study which, employing the research template known as retrodictive qualitative modeling (RQM), investigated the motivational trajectories of two Polish university students majoring in English.

2 Overview of Previous Research on Motivational Dynamics

Research on the temporal dimension of motivation can have as its aim exploring changes in this respect over longer periods of time, such as months, years or even decades, but it can also aspire to trace fluctuations in L2 motivation on much shorter timescales, such as days, minutes or even seconds, as the case might be with sequences of foreign language classes, single classes or the performance of specific language tasks. When it comes to the former line of inquiry, relevant studies are representative of the process-oriented period and they can be undertaken to provide insights into the changes in both the motives underlying the decision to initiate or persist in the process of language learning, or issues tied to what Dörnyei and Ottó (1998) refer to as *choice motivation*, and the level of engagement in that process along with the factors shaping this level, or what Dörnyei and Ottó (1998) term *executive motivation*. Irrespective of whether a particular study is intended to look into the former, the latter, or both aspects, its design differs considerably from that of traditional cross-sectional research into motivation which typically provides just a snapshot of reasons for learning or the intensity of motivated learning behavior at a given time. This is because the need to capture changes in these areas necessitates obtaining at least two, but preferably more, sets of data from the same participants at different points, such as the beginning and end of an academic year, the induction into and termination of a language program, or the onset of language learning and many years on completion of formal education in this respect, a task that may pose a formidable challenge due to inevitable attrition of the participants. In this kind of research, data can be collected by means of questionnaires, such as the *Attitude/Motivation Test Battery* (Gardner, 2004) or surveys tapping different facets of L2 motivational self system (e.g., Ryan, 2009; Taguchi, Magid, & Papi, 2009), which can represent very different views of motivation, interviews, diaries, other types of narratives as well as various combinations of such tools, with triangulation possibly constituting the best option. As regards research focusing on motivational dynamics over shorter periods of time, such as language lessons or learning tasks, it is typically, but by no means exclusively, conducted within the framework of CDS theory and represents the socio-dynamic period in the study of motivation. Since, with rare exceptions (e.g., falling in love at first sight with a foreigner or being offered a job of our dreams in a foreign land), the motives for learning a foreign language do not change dramatically from one day to the next, empirical investigations of this kind focus on the ups and downs in motivational intensity, often operationalized as interest, engagement or involvement, as well as the factors responsible for such fluctuations (Pawlak, 2017). While access to participants is less of a problem here, research of this kind is confronted with its own share of challenges which are related in the main to collecting the requisite data, particularly if it is conducted during naturally occurring classroom interaction or the performance of tasks that are an integral part of a lesson. Such data can be gathered, for example, by means of learners' self-ratings at predetermined time intervals in response to some auditory signal, a solution often employed by the present authors in their empirical investigations of motivation and one of its facets, willingness to communicate (e.g., Mystkowska-Wiertelak, 2016; Mystkowska-Wiertelak & Pawlak, 2017; Pawlak, 2012; Pawlak & Mystkowska-Wiertelak, 2015; Pawlak, Mystkowska-Wiertelak, & Bielak, 2014, 2016). This can be combined with post-class interviews, stimulated recall based on video recordings, questionnaires or immediate reports related to what transpired in a given class, or teacher-generated narratives concerning learners' motivation. Difficulties related to data collection can be ameliorated to some extent in laboratory studies, such as those using idiodynamic software which allows second-by-second measurement of attributes under investigation (e.g., MacIntyre & Legatto, 2011; MacIntyre & Serroul, 2015). This research, however, suffers from the obvious lack of ecological validity because it would be imprudent to assume that, however motivation is operationalized, patterns observed in performing tasks in artificial situations would in all cases hold for similar tasks in language classes, where a complex interplay of internal and external factors comes into play. In the present section, an attempt is made to provide a necessarily brief and selective overview of previous studies of the dynamic nature of motivation in learning foreign and second languages. Such empirical evidence will be presented, first, with respect to research examining long-term changes in motives and motivational intensity, second, in relation to empirical investigations of moment-by-moment fluctuation in engagement, and, third, with regard to studies taking advantage of retrodictive qualitative modeling, an approach that was embraced in the present study and can be seen as to some extent reconciling different timescales in exploring the temporal dimension of motivation.

In one of the first studies focusing on motivational dynamics, Koizumi and Matsuo (1993) examined changes in the attitudes and motivations of 296 seventh-grade students learning English as a foreign langue over the period of one school year, finding a decrease in this respect until the third or seventh month, followed by a period of relative stabilization. They also uncovered that, with the passage of time, participants became more realistic about their goals, those with initially high ability in English language were more likely to retain positive attitudes and motivation over time, and girls consistently outperformed boys on most attitudinal and motivational variables. A gradual drop in the levels of motivation in the course of time was later reported in a number of studies undertaken in different educational contexts. For example, Tachibana, Matsukawa and Zhong (1996) showed that both Chinese and Japanese students tended to lose interest in learning English as they moved from junior to high school, whereas Inbar, Donitsa-Schmidt and Shohamy (2001) provided evidence for a slight drop on all motivational dimensions for learners of Arabic in Israel. In another study, Williams, Burden and Lanvers (2004) demonstrated on the basis of data collected by means of questionnaires and interviews from 228 students in Great Britain that L2 motivation tended to decline from Grade 7 to Grade 9, with the caveat that, again, girls were more motivated than boys and all the participants were more eager to study German than French. Somewhat more nuanced results were reported by Gardner, Masgoret, Tennat, and Mihic (2004), who examined the integrative motivation of Canadian university students in an intermediate-level French course over the period of one academic year. While the findings were similar to those of previous research in that the attitudes and motivation deteriorated from the fall to the spring, they also observed that such changes were twice as marked in the case of situation-specific motives than general motives, with the patterns of change being mediated by achievement. There are also studies that have mainly focused on changes in the quality of L2 motivation in terms of learners' motives, goals, decisions and intentions rather than the magnitude of engagement. Ushioda (2001) conducted two interviews with 20 adult Irish learners of French, spaced 16 months apart, finding that during that period the participants were able to develop clearer goals with respect to the target language. Other researchers have explored the evolution of the nature of L2 motivation over much longer periods of time, going into two or more decades. Lim (2004), a Korean learner of English, for example, adopted an auto-biographical approach in investigating his motivation over a twenty-year period, providing evidence for changes from the integrative to the instrumental orientation, and interaction with the learning environments. Shoaib and Dörnyei (2005) used interviews with 25 language learners to examine factors shaping motivational change as well as temporal patterns emerging from such change over twenty years, identifying six recurring themes (e.g., maturation and a gradual increase in interest in L2 learning, a period when no progress was being made, a move into a new phase of life). More recently, Hsieh (2009) found in his study of two Taiwanese learners pursuing an M.A. in the US that a six-month study abroad experience led to changes in their self systems with respect to goals, attitudes and L2 self-images in response to the contextual challenges they encountered. The study by Nitta and Asano (2010), in turn, reported fluctuations in choice and executive motivation of Japanese students over one year, which could be attributed to an interplay of social and interpersonal variables (e.g., teaching style, group dynamics). Finally, also worth mentioning is the quantitative investigation by Piniel and Csizér (2015), who showed little fluctuation in motivation during a 14-week writing course taught to 21 Hungarian students majoring in English, with the ideal L2 self and motivated learning behavior tending to be more stable than the ought-to self and learning experience.

Empirical evidence concerning changes in L2 motivation in the course of lessons or tasks is much more tenuous, which is perhaps the corollary of the difficulties involved in collecting the requisite data in real-time. In what is perhaps the first classroom-based study of this kind, Pawlak (2012) explored fluctuations in 28 Polish senior high school students' motivation, operationalized as interest, involvement and persistence in the course of four regularly-scheduled lessons with the help of motivation grids which allowed self-assessment of involvement at five-minute intervals, questionnaires for teachers and learners, interviews with selected participants and detailed lesson plans. While no meaningful changes in motivational intensity were revealed between the classes, he reported some fluctuations in this respect within a lesson, which were tentatively attributed to "(…) not only the overall topic, the stage of the lesson or the task being performed, but also the place of this task in the overall lesson plan, the amount of novelty it involves, the phase of its execution, group dynamics, learner characteristics, as well as the priorities pursued by a group as a whole or individual students, with all of these internal and external variables constantly interacting (…)" (p. 273). Similar methodology was subsequently used in two research projects which were also conducted in the Polish context and involved senior high school students, but in both cases changes in motivational intensity from one lesson to the next and within single lessons were much more pronounced. Pawlak et al. (2014) investigated motivational change in 38 students in three intact groups during four naturally-occurring English classes and while they linked the observed fluctuations to the focus of the lesson, the nature of tasks and their length, transitions between different lesson stages, the opportunity to cooperate with others, and the relevance of what was being done to final examinations, they conceded that other factors must have been at play, such as, for example, individual difference variables, group dynamics, or rapport with the teacher. Kruk (2016), in turn, collected data during a total of 121 lessons in four intact groups over one semester, thereby considerably extending the longitudinal nature of this kind of research. He reported changes in motivation within and between lessons, but also periods of stability, which, however, were preceded or followed by abrupt decreases or increases in learner involvement, with the detected patterns being ascribed to a set of interrelated factors, including the lesson (e.g., topic, task, coursebook), the learners (e.g., age, ability, fatigue), and the school (e.g., the schedule). Motivational dynamics in the classroom was also the focus of the study carried out by Waninge, Dörnyei, and de Bot (2014), which involved 4 Dutch secondary school learners in six sections of German and Spanish lessons over the period of two weeks and in which the data were collected by means of classroom observations, questionnaires and the so-called motometers that enabled learners to indicate their level of motivation on a scale from 0 to 100 at five-minute intervals. As was the case with the studies mentioned above, the analysis provided evidence for "(…) considerable ups and downs and shifts within the learners' motivational state within single classroom sessions" (p. 719), but these alternated with periods of relative stability in the case of some of the participants, trends that were ascribed to a constellation of individual and contextual factors. Of interest here is also the laboratory study by MacIntyre and Serroul (2015), who applied idiodynamic software (see above) with the purpose of tracing changes in approach and avoidance motivation of 12 undergraduate Canadian university-level learners of French in the performance of eight tasks. They found that variation in motivational ratings was a function of task difficulty but was mediated by a combination of cognitive and affective reactions (i.e., approach and avoidance motivation, perceived competence, anxiety and willingness to communicate).

As regards studies drawing on retrodictive qualitative modeling (see a description below), these are still few and far between, for the simple reason that the methodology is relatively novel to the field of SLA and it is only beginning to be harnessed by researchers. While RQM can be applied in the investigation of various individual differences variables, such as learners' strategy use (Oxford, 2017) or teacher immunity (Hiver, 2016), it has first been employed in research on motivation. Chan et al. (2015) used RQM to investigate the motivational system's signature dynamics in the case of secondary school students in Hong Kong and, with the help of six English teachers, identified seven learner archetypes, that is: a highly competitive and motivated student with some negative emotions, an unmotivated student with lower-than-average English proficiency, a happy-go-lucky student with low English proficiency, a mediocre student with little L2 motivation, a motivated distressed student with low English proficiency, a "perfect" English learner, and an unmotivated student with poor English proficiency. While the procedure allowed valuable insights into motivational processes, the researchers emphasized some methodological challenges, connected, among other things, with difficulty in finding students exactly fitting the archetypes, the need to include other data collection tools apart from interviews or problems involved in determining the nature of signature dynamics. In a more recent study, Kikuchi (2017) employed RQM to trace the motivational trajectories of 20 Japanese university freshmen over a ten-month period with a view to investigating the role of various motivators and demotivators inside and outside the classroom. Five distinct types were identified, with each of them following a different motivational pattern, viewing different factors as motivating and demotivating, and responding differently to contextual influences. Given the paucity of research on L2 motivation that would rely on RQM as well as its limited scope in terms of geographical location, educational level and program type, the study reported below aimed to make a contribution to this fledgling line of inquiry by identifying learner archetypes in Polish university students majoring in English and examining the development of motivational processes over time in the case of two of them representing quite diverse motivational systems.

3 The Study

Before the aims, design and findings of the study are presented, three important caveats are in order. First, the study is part of a larger-scale research project and even though, out of necessity, it makes references to its overall results with respect to the established archetypes, it focuses on motivational processes of only two English majors. Second, while RQM guided the collection and analysis of the data and this methodology was devised as a way of investigating complex dynamic systems, the research project is not grounded in CDS theory and does not attempt to interpret the findings within this framework, which is in line with the conviction that researching motivational dynamics should by no means be confined to a single theoretical position. Third, the main point of reference in the analysis of the data was the theory of L2 motivational self system and the key concepts it comprises, similarly to previous studies of L2 motivation conducted by one of the authors (Pawlak, 2016a, b).

3.1 Aims and Research Questions

The study was aimed to identify typical patterns among Polish university students majoring in English with respect to their motivation systems, to examine the motivational trajectories in the learning histories of selected students that led to the emergence of these patterns, and to uncover factors responsible for such motivational dynamics. Importantly, it investigated changes in the participants' motivation both in terms of the motives driving them to study the target language, or choice motivation, the intensity of their motivated learning behaviors, which can be equated with executive motivation, and, to some extent, their reflections on and evaluation of previous learning, or motivational retrospection (Dörnyei & Ottó, 1998). More precisely, the following research questions were addressed:

1. What archetypes can be identified among English majors with respect to motivational structure?
2. What are the patterns for the development of these motivational systems in the learning histories of two students?
3. What factors are responsible for the dynamic character of these motivational processes?

3.2 Participants

There were two groups of participants in the study, that is the teachers who identified archetypes among the students they taught in practical English classes and seven prototypical learners with whom interviews were conducted. When it comes to the former, most of them were experienced lecturers in the Faculty of Philology in a local Polish university, holding M.A. and Ph.D. degrees in English, who ran different components of an intensive course in English in a three-year B.A. program in English (e.g., grammar, speaking, writing). As regards the latter, they were enrolled in year 2 and 3 of the B.A. program which included the English course mentioned above, classes in linguistics, applied linguistics, foreign language pedagogy, history, literature and culture, and a number of electives, such as diploma seminars, most of which were taught through the target language.

As mentioned above, only two students are the focus of the analysis presented below and therefore more information is in order about these individuals, with the caveat that their real names are not revealed and pseudonyms are used instead.

Anna, the first of the two participants, was 22 years old, she was interested in literature, film and culture, she had been learning English for 15 years at the time of the study and also reported learning or having learnt German, Russian and French, the last of these on her own. The other student, Mark, was 23 years of age, he was interested in English, music, movies and basketball, he had been learning English for 18 years and German for 10 years. It should be noted that he was truly fascinated with American culture and way of life and it was his dream to live in the US, with Scotland and the Scottish accent being other sources of fascination.

3.3 Procedures, Data Collection and Analysis

As elucidated above, the study employed the research procedure known as retrodictive qualitative modeling, which is only beginning to be applied to research on individual differences in language learning. Although a detailed discussion of this research template falls beyond the scope of this chapter and can be found in other publications (Chan et al., 2015; Dörnyei, 2014a), the idea is grounded in CDS theory and is aimed to pinpoint and analyze typical dynamic outcome patterns in learner motivation, understood as a complex dynamic system. According to Dörnyei (2014a, p. 90), "[t]his template aims to offer a systematic method of describing how the salient components within a dynamic system interact with each other to create unique development paths—or 'signature dynamics'—that lead to system-specific outcomes as opposed to other possible outcomes". This shares the assumptions underlying the empirical investigations reported earlier, namely that motivational processes occur on different timescales, different motives and goals can get the upper hand at different stages in language learning (e.g., integrative vs. instrumental, long-term or short-term), such changes are closely intertwined with fluctuations in motivational intensity, and both the choices made and the level of engagement hinge on amalgams of internal and external influences. However, it turns the traditional way of conducting research on its head by, first, examining the outcomes, or identifying learner archetypes in a given class or instructional setting, and, only at a later stage, examining the motivational trajectories that have led to the emergence of such outcomes. The application of RQM involves a three-step procedure as follows: (1) identification of salient student types in a particular group with the help of quantitative or qualitative procedures, such as cluster analysis, Q methodology (Irie, 2014), or social categorization, (2) identification of specific students who best fit in with the established archetypes and can thus be viewed as prototypical; such critical case sampling (Dörnyei, 2007) is followed by one or more semi-structured interviews, and (3) identification of the significant components of the motivational structure and the developmental patterns responsible for its emergence through qualitative analysis of the interview data. What should be underscored is that although the sequence of stages is rigid, the specific procedures employed at each of them are bound to vary from one study to another, depending on the number of participants, instructional contexts as well as researchers' preferences.

In line with this template, the research project of which the present study is part consisted of three distinct phases. First, six teachers formed a focus group with the aim of establishing the archetypes within the entire student population attending the B.A. program in the Faculty of Philology. This involved a number of discussions in the whole group as well as in pairs, both in face-to-face meetings and e-mail exchanges, which, following the procedure adopted by Chan et al. (2015), focused on cognitive, affective, motivational and behavioral aspects of the students' profiles. This resulted in the identification of seven student archetypes with respect to motivational systems, described by means of adjectives and nouns, as well as initial selection of 2-4 prototypical students that were representative of each archetype. In the second phase, critical case sampling took place as the teachers finally agreed on individuals that constituted the best fit for one of the archetypes, the selected students were requested to produce graphical representations of their self-perceived motivation to learn English over their learning histories, and they took part in semi-structured interviews which lasted from 35–70 min, depending on the extent to which a student was willing to share his or her experience. The interviews were conducted by four researchers, they were held in Polish to ascertain that the participants could precisely express their thoughts and feelings, and all of them were audio-recorded. In each case, the key point of reference was the motivation graph drawn by each participant, and, yet again, the themes revolved around cognitive, emotional, motivational and behavioral issues. When it comes to specific questions, at the outset they concerned general matters (e.g., interests) but also touched on critical episodes in the development of L2 motivation, which was followed by queries regarding clear-cut trends evident in the graphs, and, in the concluding part, motivating and demotivating factors as well as visions of themselves the students had as users of English in the future. In the final stage, the interviews were transcribed and subjected to qualitative content analysis, which was aimed to pinpoint the main components of the motivational systems and chart the developmental patterns which accounted for current motivational processes. As clarified above, in what follows such analysis will be presented for only two participants who, in the view of the researchers, could be assumed to differ quite considerably in regard to their motivational systems and trajectories that could be credited with generating them.

3.4   Findings

For the sake of clarity, the results of the study will be presented in two subsections: first, with respect to the seven archetypes identified by the focus group teachers, and, second, with regard to the two learner types selected for detailed analysis in this study, the cases of Anna and Mark. In the presentation of the two cases, the motivational profiles will be described at the outset, which will be followed by the discussion of the motivational trajectories and the factors shaping them.

3.4.1 Student Archetypes

The discussions conducted by the six focus group teachers, which, as was elucidated earlier, revolved around a combination of cognitive, affective, motivational and behavioral issues, led, after much deliberation, to the identification of seven archetypes in the population of English majors enrolled in the B.A. program. These archetypes were as follows:

- A 1: A motivated, eager and positive student with relatively low proficiency in English.
- A 2: A motivated student with considerable anxiety and low proficiency in English.
- A 3: A motivated, conscientious and diligent student with high proficiency in English.
- A 4: A poorly motivated and unambitious student with knowledge gaps, displaying traits of high self-confidence/esteem.
- A 5: A student with little motivation and a natural ability to communicate.
- A 6: A motivated and proficient student with some negative behavior.
- A 7: An unmotivated, withdrawn student with relatively low English proficiency.

Since detailed discussion of all the seven motivational profiles together with the processes that led to their emergence would far exceed the confines of this chapter, a decision was made to undertake such analysis in relation to two archetypes. These are A3, standing for an English major that is highly motivated, diligent and possesses high proficiency in the target language, and A5, representing a student whose motivation is limited but who is at the same time endowed with a knack for communication in a foreign language. The decision to focus on these two types of students stemmed from the fact that they to some extent represented two opposing ends of the continuum with respect to their motivational systems, that is high versus low motivation and diligence versus natural ability, with the proficiency level being more or less comparable, at least with respect to communicative skills. In what follows, the motivational trajectories of Anna and Mark, students viewed as prototypical for the two archetypes, will be analyzed.

3.4.2 Motivational Profiles and Trajectories of the Two Prototypical Students

As regards aspects of Anna's motivational profile that emerged from the discussions among the focus group teachers and resulted in nominating her as a prototypical manifestation of A3, the most important of them was that she was perceived as a motivated individual, strongly focused on attaining the goals that she set for herself. In cognitive terms, she was seen as a conscientious, diligent student, who was always willing to excel in class and worked hard at home, qualities that were in all likelihood responsible for her high proficiency in English. She exhibited high

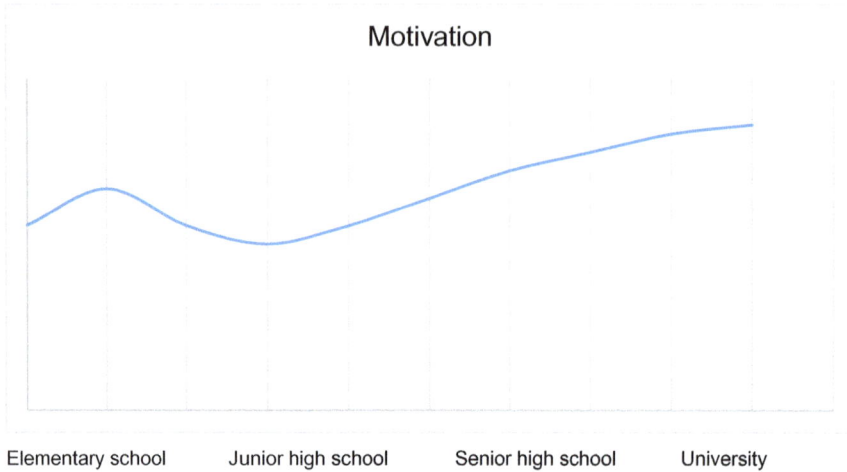

Fig. 1 Anna's motivational trajectory

self-esteem, was self-confident, serious, calm and relaxed, and at the same time curious about things which were covered in class, well-organized and willing to cooperate with others. As she admitted in the interview, she made all the decisions concerning learning English on her own, she never had the opportunity to get the benefit of private tutoring and her parents were not involved in the process. All of this indicates that it is her ideal self rather than different aspects of her ought-to self that account for her desire to master the target language. She has a clear vision of herself as a proficient speaker of English, someone working as a teacher as she enjoys it a lot and perhaps doing a Ph.D. in English.

As illustrated in Fig. 1, which depicts Anna's motivational trajectory from elementary school, when her adventure with English began, to the last year in the B.A. program, when the study was conducted, her motivation to learn English fluctuated to some extent over that time although a consistent upward trend is visible on graduation from junior high school. The first thing that can be observed from the graph is that her motivation at the beginning of elementary school was relatively low but then began two increase gradually, a change that can be attributed to the substitution of the teacher. As she commented, the teacher in the first grade was a "bad teacher",[1] both in terms of the kind of instruction provided and personal traits, which engendered fear in everyone, and only when she was replaced in grade 2 did "real learning begin" and the motivation start to grow, although the focus remained on learning rules and the development of explicit knowledge. Apart from the change of the teacher, an important stimulus for learning at that time was a presentation that she attended on innovative ways of learning, in particular with

---

[1]All the translations of the excerpts from the interview included in this chapter were made by the researchers.

respect to vocabulary, as this was the time when she recognized the utility of word cards, a strategy that she has been using ever since. As she emphasized, even in elementary school she was capable of self-assessment and was proud of the fact that she could excel in vocabulary learning in her class and, on the whole, she could feel that she was making more progress. This spike in motivation, however, began to gradually wear off as she entered junior high school, a situation which was, once again, attributable to the attitude of her teacher. More specifically, that teacher was young and inexperienced, treating the students as her peers and dedicated most of the class to gossiping about irrelevant matters rather than actual teaching. As a result, Anna was becoming increasingly bored and acutely aware of the lack of progress, which impelled her to do exercises on her own while others were wasting their time or simply waiting for the lesson to end. Still, she felt disappointed and more and more discouraged since she did not have an "authority" to fall back on, because homework assignments were not checked and tests were not administered. She was not convinced by the teacher's assurances that her English was improving by the day as she had a feeling that she was wasting her time attending school classes and a fail would have been more motivating than giving up on the students.

The situation started to change once again with the transition from junior to senior high school, which can perhaps be attributed to the fact that, thanks to her own hard work and doing numerous tests, she passed the final exam with flying colors. In fact, her results were not only so superior that was she placed in the most advanced group but also served as a benchmark for assigning other students to different levels in terms of their proficiency in English. Enthralled as she was, the very first class in senior high came as a shock because the teacher spoke English all the time and she had the feeling that she was the only one that could not follow because of the low level of English instruction in junior high school. However, she was not ready to give up and decided to "clench her teeth", carefully examining the materials used in class, searching for other sources on things that she could not understand, using the Internet to get in touch with people from other countries, as well as getting more and more cognizant of her errors because of regular use of a dictionary. At the same time she was fully aware of the progress that she was making because of the expertise and attitude of her teacher who was competent and demanding, spoke English all the time, was always prepared and made sure that the lessons were varied and interesting. A tangible sign of her growing mastery of English was the fact that she could talk to people from abroad and make herself understood, something that was confirmed when she went with her family to Prague, successfully ordering food or asking directions, achievements that made her proud of herself.

Despite these successes and shows of confidence, she intended to study Polish rather than English philology on completion of senior high school, a dream that she could not achieve for economic reasons, a situation which led to disappointment, frustration and a conviction that she was missing something important. In the end, however, she did not regret her decision to study English philology because as a result she was able to meet passionate and dedicated teachers, individuals that motivated and inspired her, which resulted in satisfaction and the belief that she was constantly developing both linguistically and intellectually. All of this happened despite a major setback that she suffered in the first year when she attended a plenary at an international conference organized by her institution, could not understand much of what the native speaker was saying and burst into tears. However, this event had a motivating rather than a demotivating effect and resulted in her considerably greater involvement in the process of learning English, which translated not only into her hard work in the courses she attended but also into her efforts to seek out opportunities for using English outside the classroom, participate in extra-curricular activities and be among students who volunteered to help out with the organization of future conferences.

As can be seen from the analysis of Anna's motivational trajectory, a constellation of factors resulted in the emergence of her motivational profile that she manifested as a student in the last year of a B.A. program in English. On the one hand, it was her personal qualities, such as diligence, determination and perseverance, that resulted in her positive approach to the goals that she set for herself, and, on the other, it was the environment, both with respect to teachers and everyday life circumstances that guided the choices she made and had an impact on her involvement and engagement. What is important, however, these external influences, even when negative, not only did not dissuade her for pursuing her goals, but caused her to grin and bear it, and, in fact, in the long run, fueled her motivation to learn English and to diminish the distance between her current abilities and skills, and her vision of herself in the future, or her ideal L2 self.

Moving on to Mark as a prototypical student representing archetype A5 (little motivation but a natural ability to communicate), the focus group teachers saw him as unmotivated mainly because he was usually unprepared for classes and was uninvolved in them. This was evident on both affective and behavioral planes, as he openly displayed boredom and lack of interest in what was going on and refused to cooperate with the teacher and other students in his group, in some cases manifesting a rather unfriendly attitude. At the same time, the teachers regarded him as intelligent and they admitted that he was quite proficient in English, which they attributed to the fact that he relied on the knowledge and skills gained in senior high school and these were sufficient to successfully meet the demands of the course. While Mark, similarly to Anna, seems to have formed a clear vision of himself as a user of English in the future, not only is this vision different but the sources of motivation are dissimilar as well since he places store on what others think about him rather than what he thinks about himself. In other words, while his ideal L2 self seems to be critical in driving his efforts, the fuel for its realization is external and seems to reside in the extent to which other people admire him and are ready to follow his example.

As can be seen from Mark's motivational trajectory, graphically represented in Fig. 2, he started learning English in kindergarten but it was just one hour a week and instruction took the form of game activities, with the effect that he was not even aware that he was learning and it is not really possible to talk about motivation at that time. The situation began to change with transition to elementary school because he soon noticed that he was top of his class in English, the teacher kept

Kindergarten Elementary school Junior high school Senior high school University

Fig. 2 Mark's motivational trajectory

heaping praise on him, singled him out as a role model and encouraged him to take part in competitions. Mark loved the recognition he received and enjoyed being rewarded to the point of becoming somewhat conceited, with his motivation being resultative in nature, and being bred by his accomplishments and a constant desire to excel. When he went to junior high school, however, he was in for a rather unpleasant surprise as it turned out that other kids easily outperformed him, his grades dropped considerably and he realized that he may not have learnt as much in elementary school as he thought. A crucial episode which dramatically changed his opinion about his ability in English was a grammar test at the beginning of the first year which he failed, an event that surprised and stunned him because it was the first fail grade he had ever received. As a result he developed a negative attitude towards the teacher who was, in his view, very strict, mainly focused on grammar and paid little attention to whether or not someone had rich vocabulary or was good in communication. Entire lessons were devoted to doing grammar exercises in Xerox copies brought by the teacher and evaluation was predominantly grammar-based, with 90% of the grades resulting from grammar tests. In the words of Mark, "she tortured us with grammar. It was a nightmare". He could not resist the feeling that his mastery of English was being blatantly underestimated and that the merely satisfactory (3 on a scale from 1 to 6) grade that he was awarded at the end of the school year did not do justice to his true abilities. He commented: "I had the impression that she was convinced I didn't know English and I didn't know grammar, and that was it. All the time I tried to prove, show I could communicate but it was pointless". Still he wished he had learned more in elementary school as this could have allowed him to avoid the problems he faced. Although he admitted that he did learn a lot at the time, he was not involved in classroom activities and he did not seek opportunities for out-of-class communication, because he had to cram a lot for other subjects and, by his own admission, he is not "very hard-working by nature". He did not get much support from his parents during this period because they did not seem to be concerned about him and attributed his lower grades to age problems. Looking back on learning English in junior high school, Mark insisted that he was still highly motivated to learn English and pinned the blame for the setbacks on the teacher. As he said during the interview, "the teacher was such that I could not do anything".

His lack of involvement and reliance on what he had learned previously continued into senior high school where his L2 motivation was stable and moderate, and he, once again, "rested on his laurels". There was a crucial difference in comparison with junior high school, however, since, although he felt that he could have invested more effort and his grades could have been better, as was the case in elementary school, Mark was again given as an example to his peers and earned their admiration, which served as a powerful motivator. When problems appeared, they were one more time related to insufficient knowledge of grammar which apparently was his Achilles' heel. Once again, he was not very happy with his teacher who apparently did not pay attention to students and did not care much about them, but, much more importantly, failed to ensure ample opportunities for communicative practice, mainly focusing on various aspects of the linguistic system. In his view, teachers, including his English teacher, generated a lot of anxiety and stress in connection with the school-leaving examination, which may have been excessive given the challenge that this exam posed in reality, but had a very motivating effect on everyone. In contrast to junior high school, the parents were much more supportive at this stage, especially the father, and, to quote Mark, "(…) they liked that I was good in English and it was motivating". Still, as he pointed out, had he a chance to go back to senior high school, he would have done much more to excel and stand out as this would have provided fuel for his motivation. Most importantly perhaps, it was at that time that he was beginning to form a vivid and concrete vision of himself in the future as someone going to the USA where he had a family, preferably Miami and Syracuse, and using English on an daily basis to communicate with native speakers. Although Mark did not comment on it in his interview, it was probably this vision that propelled him to take up English studies, a decision that was encouraged by his father.

Marks' comments concerning his motivation at the university and the factors influencing it were much more extensive than those of Anna's. First and foremost, he emphasized a major rise in motivation as he enrolled in the program, which he credited to the new context in which he had to function, enthusiastic teachers, the support of the parents, but also a tangible ideal self in the target language as someone having a job requiring regular use of English. This did not mean that he was still the best, as was the case in elementary and senior high school, as he had to repeat the second year and in general was not satisfied with his performance. While he was critical of some courses, such as British literature, where "there was too much information, problems were beginning to accumulate and in the end I got lost", he experienced a major shock because other students were much less competitive than in junior and senior high school, they did not compare their grades with each other and they were focused on their own progress. In the course of his studies Mark became much more cognizant of the fact that learning a foreign language requires commitment, regular hard work and perseverance, things that were hard to come by, though, considering the fact that he was living in the dorm with all of its distractions. It is also interesting to point out that while he still cherished his senior high school vision of going to the USA, doubts started to appear, triggered by a growing realization that a diploma in English did not constitute guarantee of employment, whether in Poland or abroad. At the same time, he was full of admiration for those who had the courage to turn over a new leaf, leave everything behind and start a new life in a foreign land, which to some extent indicates that his vision of a user of English in the USA was still valid. What should be stressed is the fact that he was of the opinion that, although he did not have many opportunities to shine, his motivation was the highest at the university, and he was in fact ashamed when thinking of the opportunities that he may have wasted at previous educational levels.

Looking at Mark's motivational trajectory, its seems clear that, in comparison to Anna, instead of deriving his strength from within himself, he was in obvious need of acceptance and admiration from others, which might testify to his extraverted personality. Even though it is still clearly possible to talk about the impact of an ideal rather than ought-to self, the vision was conditioned by the opinions of others that he more or less wittingly held in high esteem, mainly his teachers. However, this was only one source of his motivation because he also had a clear vision of what he wanted to do in the future, that is going to the US and communicating with native speakers, a goal that seemed to be distinct from the positive or negative evaluation that he may have received from his instructors. What should also be noted is the fact that his own assessment of L2 motivation was drastically disparate from that of the six focus group teachers, because he was apparently very motivated to learn English and quite cognizant of the mistakes he may have made, even if this did not show during the classes he attended.

4　Discussion

As shown in the analysis provided above, the application of RMQ yielded valuable insights into the L2 motivational self systems and processes of English majors and in-depth interviews with two of them offered evidence for temporal variation in L2 motivation and shed valuable light on factors that brought about such fluctuations. When it comes to the first research question, the procedure allowed for the identification of seven archetypes, characterized by quite distinct motivational patterns, which only to some extent overlapped those established in other studies using RMQ (e.g., Chan et al., 2015; Kikuchi, 2017), which should not come as a surprise given the differences in culture, age, educational level, type of program and overall proficiency. What should be emphasized, however, is that reaching a consensus on student types turned out to pose a formidable challenge, and, similarly to Chan et al. (2015), it was even more difficult to pinpoint students that would have constituted a perfect match for each of them. In fact, several candidates were identified in each case and the participating teachers were not unanimous about the final choices, which may indicate that the discussions should have been augmented with observations, learner narratives or interviews with more potential candidates.

Moving on to the second research question, the interview data together with the graphs produced by the students, provided unambiguous evidence for changes in their L2 motivational systems, both with respect to motives guiding them, levels of engagement, reflection on various aspects of the process of learning as well as visions of themselves as users of English in the future, or their ideal L2 selves. It should be stressed that although Anna and Mark represented two disparate archetypes, their motivational paths did not deviate from each other as much as could have been expected. In both cases, there was a visible spike in motivation in elementary school, followed by a dip in junior high school, which, incidentally, may indicate that there are problems with foreign language instruction at this level, and then yet another increase which has continued into the B.A. program. The only difference is connected with the fact that while Anna's motivation began to climb steadily since she entered senior high school and this tendency has been maintained to the present day, in the case of Mark it remained stable for a longer period of time and only towards the end of senior high school could an upward trend be observed. Due to the nature of the data, it is not possible to compare the actual levels of engagement of the two students but it is clear that they have created vivid, if quite different, visions as users of English in the future and they are determined to move towards these ideal L2 selves, a fact that is understandable but by no means can be taken for granted in the case of English majors. What should alert teachers and researchers alike are the pitfalls of developing unfounded or downright false notions about the motivation of learners or research participants. This is because, unless we assume that he wished to paint a positive picture of himself in the interview, Mark was quite highly motivated, which stood in stark contrast to the archetype to which he was assigned, and his apparent lack of engagement in class may have stemmed from his disapproval of the instructional practices applied rather than his reluctance to study English. This goes to show how deceiving appearances can be and provides an additional argument for basing decisions about archetypes and prototypical learners representing them on more solid grounds than just the impressions or preconceived judgments of teachers.

With respect to the last research question, the factors that triggered changes in motivation were not dramatically different for the two students, being both internal and external in nature, although the consequences they produced were surely not the same. One such crucial influence was the teacher as a key element of learning experience, both in regard to his or her attitude, personality, involvement and the nature of instruction provided, which speaks to the fact that while school classes in and of themselves are insufficient to ensure mastery of a foreign language, they play an immense role in motivating or demotivating learners. As the two motivational trajectories demonstrate, they have the power to drastically alter learners' involvement in the process of language learning, towards more positive and enthusiastic, as was the case with Anna when her first teacher in elementary school was substituted, or more negative and indifferent, as when Mark's communicative skills were ignored after he started attending junior high school. Two other important factors, admittedly much more so in the case of Mark than Anna, are peers and parents, as the former can become a kind of an audience in front of which one's language abilities can be displayed and the latter can provide the necessary support or, alternatively, fail to do so. Yet another pivotal influence on L2 motivation turned out to be critical moments in the learning histories of both learners, not as much the positive ones as those unpleasant that constituted a rude awakening, such as difficulty in understanding the teacher, a failed grammar test or inability to follow a plenary at a conference. What matters, though, was the response to these influences which was heavily dependent on the two students' personality, a variable that in some cases trumped the impact of other factors. While Anna was introverted, had an internal locus of control and internal attributions, which allowed her to persevere despite all the setbacks she may have experienced, Mark was visibly extraverted, exhibited an external locus of control and external attributions, craving admiration and praise as well as easily doubting his abilities in the face of adversity (see Ehrman, Leaver, & Oxford, 2003, for discussion of these concepts). Although they appear to have made the right choice in studying English philology and can envisage a well-defined path ahead of them, their personalities still play a critical role, which is evident, for example, in the fact that Mark has more misgivings about his future than Anna. What also shaped the motivational trajectories of the students was motivational retrospection, which appeared to have positive consequences for Anna, but less so for Mark, who, instead of looking to the future, ruminated excessively on what he could have done differently in the past.

5 Conclusion

The present chapter has presented partial results of what is, to the best knowledge of the authors, the first attempt to apply retrodictive qualitative modeling to the study of L2 motivation in the Polish educational context. Although the focus has been on the motivational trajectories of only two English majors representing two different archetypes with respect to motivational systems, the study constitutes an important contribution to the scant existing literature on the application of RQM to research on motivation and focuses on contexts, proficiency levels and programs that have not yet been examined with the help of this procedure. Obviously, for the picture to become more complete, the analysis of the motivational trajectories of the remaining students is necessary. However, even at this early stage it appears warranted to assume that the process of identifying archetypes and selecting students that fit them best should draw on more reliable data sources than outcomes of discussions among teachers that are somewhat inevitably tinted by their impressions about learners, founded on one-off occurrences or erroneous judgments and thus failing to do justice to reality. For this reason, as postulated by Chan et al. (2015), future research should employ additional data collection tools, such as observations, interviews with past teachers or analyses of available documentation, but also ensure that interviews are conducted with a greater number of candidates for a given archetype so that the best possible fit can be achieved. A separate issue is the extent to which findings of such research can inform everyday classroom pedagogy, in this case the manner in which the intensive course in English is planned and taught in the B.A. program. While suggestions of this kind can only be tentative at this juncture, it would appear that awareness of motivational profiles would enable teachers to better cater to the needs of individual students and, to refer to another novel line of inquiry in motivational research, to be better able to generate in them what has come to be known as *directed motivational currents*, or periods of intense involvement that can support long-term motivation to learn a foreign language (Dörnyei, Henry, & Muir, 2016). Given this potential, there is surely a need for more research utilizing RQM, with the important caveat that such empirical investigations do not have to be confined to the theoretical perspective from which this set of empirical procedures has originated.

Acknowledgements The authors would like to take this opportunity to thank the focus group teachers and the students who participated in the study, but in particular our friends and colleagues from State University of Applied Sciences in Konin, Poland, who were involved in the research project that yielded data for the study described in this chapter: Dr. Jakub Bielak, Dr. Marek Derenowski, Dr. Katarzyna Papaja and Dr. Bartosz Wolski.

References

Chan, L., Dörnyei, Z., & Henry, A. (2015). Learner archetypes and signature dynamics in the language classroom: A retrodictive qualitative approach to studying L2 motivation. In Z. Dörnyei, P. D. MacIntyre, & A. Henry (Eds.), *Motivational dynamics in language learning* (pp. 238–259). Bristol, Buffalo and Toronto: Multilingual Matters.

Dörnyei, Z. (2005). *The psychology of the language learner: Individual differences in second language acquisition*. Mahwah, NJ: Lawrence Erlbaum.

Dörnyei, Z. (2007). *Research methods in applied linguistics*. Oxford: Oxford University Press.

Dörnyei, Z. (2009). The L2 motivational self system. In Z. Dörnyei & E. Ushioda (Eds.), *Motivation, language identity and the self* (pp. 9–42). Bristol, Buffalo and Toronto: Multilingual Matters.

Dörnyei, Z. (2014a). Researching complex dynamic systems: 'Retrodictive qualitative modelling' in the language classroom. *Language Teaching, 47*, 80–91.

Dörnyei, Z. (2014b). Future self-guides and vision. In K. Csizér & M. Magid (Eds.), *The impact of self-concept on language learning* (pp. 7–18). Bristol, Buffalo and Toronto: Multilingual Matters.

Dörnyei, Z. (2014c). Motivation in second language learning. In M. Celce-Murcia, D. M. Brinton, & M. A. Snow (Eds.), *Teaching English as a second or foreign language* (4th ed., pp. 518–531). Boston, MA: National Geographic Learning/Cengage Learning.

Dörnyei, Z., Henry, A., & Muir, C. (2016). *Motivational currents in language learning: Frameworks for focused interventions*. New York: Routledge.

Dörnyei, Z., MacIntyre, P., & Henry, A. (2015). *Motivational dynamics in language learning*. Bristol, Buffalo and Toronto: Multilingual Matters.

Dörnyei, Z., & Ottó, I. (1998). Motivation in action: A process model of motivation. *Working Papers in Applied Linguistics, 4,* 43–69.

Dörnyei, Z., & Ryan, S. (2015). *The psychology of the language learner revisited.* New York and London: Routledge.

Dörnyei, Z., & Ushioda, E. (2011). *Teaching and researching motivation* (2nd ed.). Harlow: Pearson Education.

Ehrman, M. E., Leaver, B. L., & Oxford, R. (2003). A brief overview of individual differences in second language learning. *System, 31*(3), 313–330.

Gardner, R. C. (2004). *Attitude/motivation test battery: International AMTB research project.* Canada: The University of Western Ontario.

Gardner, R. C., Masgoret, A.-M., Tennant, J., & Mihic, L. (2004). Integrative motivation: Changes during a year-long intermediate-level language course. *Language Learning, 81,* 344–362.

Henry, A. (2015). The dynamics of possible selves. In Z. Dörnyei, P. D. MacIntyre, & A. Henry (Eds.), 2015. *Motivational dynamics in language learning* (pp. 83–94). Bristol, Buffalo and Toronto: Multilingual Matters.

Hiver, P. V. (2016) *Tracing the signature dynamics of language teacher immunity.* Ph.D. thesis, University of Nottingham.

Hsieh, Ch-N. (2009). L2 learners' self-appraisal of motivational changes over time. *Issues in Applied Linguistics, 17,* 3–26.

Inbar, O., Donitsa-Schmidt, S., & Shohamy, E. (2001). Students' motivation as a function of language learning: The teaching of Arabic in Israel. In Z. Dörnyei & R. Schmidt (Eds.), *Motivation and second language acquisition* (pp. 297–311). Honolulu, HI: University of Hawaii Press.

Irie, K. (2014). Q methodology for post-social-turn research in SLA. *Studies in Second Language Learning and Teaching, 4,* 13–32.

Kikuchi, K. (2017). Reexamining demotivators and motivators: A longitudinal study of Japanese freshmen's dynamic system in an EFL context. *Innovation in Language Learning and Teaching, 11,* 124–145.

Koizumi, R., & Matsuo, K. (1993). A longitudinal study of attitudes and motivation in learning English among Japanese seventh grade students. *Japanese Psychological Research, 35,* 1–11.

Kruk, M. (2016). Temporal fluctuations in foreign language motivation: Results of a longitudinal study. *Iranian Journal of Language Teaching Research, 4,* 1–17.

Larsen-Freeman, D. (2015). Ten 'lessons' from Complex Dynamic Systems Theory: What is on offer? In Z. Dörnyei, P. D. MacIntyre, & A. Henry (Eds.), *Motivational dynamics in language learning* (pp. 11–19). Bristol, Buffalo and Toronto: Multilingual Matters.

Larsen-Freeman, D., & Cameron, L. (2008). *Complex systems and applied linguistics.* Oxford: Oxford University Press.

Lim, H. Y. (2004). The interaction of motivation, perception, and environment: One EFL learner's experience. *Hong Kong Journal of Applied Linguistics, 7*(2), 91–106.

MacIntyre, P. D., & Legatto, J. J. (2011). A dynamic system approach to willingness to communicate: Developing an idiodynamic method to capture rapidly changing affect. *Applied Linguistics, 32,* 149–171.

MacIntyre, P. D., & Serroul, A. (2015). Motivation on a per-second timescale. Examining approach-avoidance motivation during L2 task performance. In Z. Dörnyei, P. D. MacIntyre, & A. Henry (Eds.), *Motivational dynamics in language learning* (pp. 109–138). Bristol, Buffalo and Toronto: Multilingual Matters.

Mystkowska-Wiertelak, A. (2016). Dynamics of classroom WTC: Results of a semester study. *Studies in Second Language Learning and Teaching, 6,* 651–676.

Mystkowska-Wiertelak, A., & Pawlak, M. (2017). *Willingness to communicate in instructed second language acquisition: Combining a micro- and macro-perspective.* Bristol: Multilingual Matters.

Nitta, R., & Asano, R. (2010). Understanding motivational changes in EFL classrooms. In A. M. Stoke (Ed.), *JALT 2009 Conference Proceedings* (pp. 186–196). Tokyo: JALT.

Oxford, R. L. (2017). *Teaching and researching language learning strategies: Self-regulation in context.* London and New York: Routledge.

Pawlak, M. (2012). The dynamic nature of motivation in language learning: A classroom perspective. *Studies in Second Language Learning and Teaching, 2,* 249–278.

Pawlak, M. (2015). Review of Zoltán Dörnyei, Peter D. MacIntyre, and Alastair Henry's Motivational dynamics in language learning. *Studies in Second Language Learning and Teaching, 5,* 707–713.

Pawlak, M. (2016a). Investigating language learning motivation from an ideal language-self perspective: The case of English majors in Poland. In D. Gałajda, P. Zakrajewski, & M. Pawlak (Eds.), *Researching second language acquisition from a psycholinguistic perspective. Studies in honor of Danuta Gabryś-Barker* (pp. 63–59). Heidelberg and New York: Springer.

Pawlak, M. (2016b). Another look at the L2 motivational self system of Polish students majoring in English: Insights from diary data. *Theory and Practice of Second Language Acquisition, 2* (2), 9–26.

Pawlak, M. (2017). Dynamiczny charakter motywacji w nauce języka obcego. Perspektywy badawcze [The dynamic nature of motivation in learning a foreign language: Research directions]. In A. Stolarczyk-Gembiak & M. Woźnicka (Eds.), *Zbliżenia: Językoznawstwo – translatologia [Encounters: Linguistics – translatology]* (pp. 115–128). Konin: Wydawnictwo PWSZ w Koninie.

Pawlak, M., & Mystkowska-Wiertelak, A. (2015). Investigating the dynamic nature of L2 willingness to communicate. *System, 50,* 1–9.

Pawlak, M., Mystkowska-Wiertelak, A., & Bielak, J. (2014). Another look at temporal variation in language learning motivation: Results of a study. In M. Pawlak & L. Aronin (Eds.), *Essential topics in applied linguistics and multilingualism. Studies in honor of David Singleton* (pp. 89–109). Heidelberg and New York: Springer.

Pawlak, M., Mystkowska-Wiertelak, A., & Bielak, J. (2016). Investigating the nature of classroom WTC: A micro-perspective. *Language Teaching Research, 20*(5), 654–671. doi:10.1177/ 1362168815609615.

Piniel, K., & Csizér, K. (2015). Changes in motivation, anxiety and self-efficacy during the course of an academic writing seminar. In Z. Dörnyei, P. D. MacIntyre, & A. Henry (Eds.), *Motivational dynamics in language learning* (pp. 164–194). Bristol, Buffalo and Toronto: Multilingual Matters.

Ryan, S. (2009). Self and identity in L2 motivation in Japan: The ideal L2 self and Japanese learners of English. In Z. Dörnyei & E. Ushioda (Eds.), *Motivation, language identity and the L2 self* (pp. 98–119). Bristol: Multilingual Matters.

Shoaib, A., & Dörnyei, Z. (2005). Affect in life-long learning: Exploring L2 motivation as a dynamic process. In P. Benson & D. Nunan (Eds.), *Learners' stories: Difference and diversity in language learning* (pp. 22–41). Cambridge: Cambridge University Press.

Tachibana, Y., Matskukawa, R., & Zhong, Q. X. (1996). Attitudes and motivation for learning English: A cross-national comparison of Japanese and Chinese high school students. *Psychological Reports, 79,* 691–700.

Taguchi, T., Magid, M., & Papi, M. (2009). The L2 motivational self system among Japanese, Chinese and Iranian learners of English: A comparative study. In Z. Dörnyei & E. Ushioda (Eds.), *Motivation, language identity and the L2 self* (pp. 120–143). Bristol: Multilingual Matters.

Ushioda, E. (2001). Motivation as a socially mediated process. In Z. Dörnyei & R. Schmidt (Eds.), *Motivation and second language acquisition* (pp. 91–124). Honolulu, HI: University of Hawaii Press.

Ushioda, E., & Dörnyei, Z. (2012). Motivation. In S. M. Gass & A. Mackey (Eds.), *The Routledge handbook of second language acquisition* (pp. 396–409). London and New York: Routledge.

Waninge, F., Dörnyei, Z., & de Bot, K. (2014). Motivational dynamics in language learning: Change, stability, and context. *Modern Language Journal, 89,* 704–723.

Williams, M., & Burden, R. (1997). *Psychology for language teachers*. Cambridge: Cambridge University Press.

Williams, M., Burden, R., & Lanvers, U. (2002). 'French is the language of love and stuff': Student perceptions of issues related to motivation in learning a foreign language. *British Educational Research Journal, 28,* 503–528.

Author Biographies

Mirosław Pawlak is Professor of English at the Faculty of Philology, State University of Applied Sciences, Konin, Poland, and the Department of English Studies, Faculty of Pedagogy and Fine Arts in Kalisz, Adam Mickiewicz University, Kalisz, Poland. He received his doctoral and post-doctoral degrees as well as his full professorship from Adam Mickiewicz University, Poznań, Poland. His main areas of interest are SLA theory and research, form-focused instruction, corrective feedback, classroom discourse, learner autonomy, learning strategies, grammar learning strategies, motivation, willingness to communicate and pronunciation teaching. His recent publications include *The place of form-focused instruction in the foreign language classroom* (2006, Adam Mickiewicz University Press), *Production-oriented and comprehension-based grammar teaching in the foreign language classroom* (co-authored with Anna Mystkowska-Wiertelak, 2012, Springer), *Error correction in the foreign language classroom: Reconsidering the issues* (2014, Springer), *Applying cognitive grammar in the foreign language classroom: Teaching English tense and aspect* (co-authored with Jakub Bielak, 2013, Springer), *Willingness to communicate in instructed second language acquisition: Combining a macro- and micro-perspective* (co-authored with Anna Mystkowska-Wiertelak, 2017, Multilingual Matters), and numerous edited collections. Mirosław Pawlak is the Editor-in-Chief of the journals *Studies in Second Language Learning and Teaching, Konin Language Studies,* and the book series *Second Language Learning and Teaching.*

Anna Mystkowska-Wiertelak is Assistant Professor at the Department of English Studies of the Faculty of Pedagogy and Fine Arts of Adam Mickiewicz University, Poznań/Kalisz, Poland as well as Senior Lecturer at the Faculty of Philology of State University of Applied Sciences, Konin, Poland. Her main interests comprise, apart from teacher education, second language acquisition theory and research, language learning strategies, learner autonomy, form-focused instruction, willingness to communicate, and motivation. Her recent publications include *Production-oriented and comprehension-based grammar teaching in the foreign language classroom* (with Mirosław Pawlak, Springer, 2012) and *Willingness to communicate in instructed second language acquisition* (with Mirosław Pawlak, Multilingual Matters, 2017).

Trilingual Learners' Awareness of the Role of L1 in Learning Target Language Grammar

Aleksandra Wach

Abstract The role of the L1 in learning a target language has recently been reconsidered in the context of both L2 and multilingual learning and teaching, and researchers now see it as a vital resource for enriching and facilitating the process of constructing the system of another language in a learner's mind. The L1 can serve as a useful cognitive basis for understanding how a grammatical system works in another language and for discovering form-meaning connections. In the case of multilingual learning, the role of the L1 appears to be even more complex because the interplay among all the languages known to the learner appears to impact the learning processes. The study reported in this chapter looks into the perceptions of trilingual learners about the role of the L1 (Polish) in learning L2 English and L3 Russian grammar. Ninety-four learners (university students) participated in the study, in which the research tool used was a questionnaire consisting of open-ended questions. The elicited data revealed high levels of awareness among the participants about the usefulness of the L1 in learning the grammatical system of the target languages, and, in particular, about differences between its role in learning English and Russian, and the suitability and efficiency of translation as a grammar learning strategy.

Keywords Learning grammar · Multilingual learners · L1, L2, L3, English · Russian

1 Introduction

The last two decades have seen renewed interest in the role of learners' native language (the L1) in learning additional languages, both in bilingual (learning an L2) and multilingual (learning an L3 and subsequent languages) settings. This trend is visible in a reconsideration of the effects of crosslinguistic influence, or language

A. Wach (✉)
Adam Mickiewicz University, Poznań, Poland
e-mail: waleks@wa.amu.edu.pl

© Springer International Publishing AG 2018
M. Pawlak and A. Mystkowska-Wiertelak (eds.), *Challenges of Second and Foreign Language Education in a Globalized World*, Second Language Learning and Teaching, DOI 10.1007/978-3-319-66975-5_13

transfer, reflected in the recent literature (Arabski & Wojtaszek, 2016; Odlin, 2016; Tolentino & Tokowicz, 2011). The scope of investigation arising from these new perspectives on transfer is much wider than in previous studies, encompassing such issues as conceptual and pragmatic transfer (Cummins, 2007), although crosslinguistic influence in learning L2 grammar has also been a recent field of inquiry (Izquierdo & Collins, 2008; Trenkic, Milkovic, & Altmann, 2014). A number of arguments for the facilitative role of the L1 have been made in the literature, among them the assertion that it provides an important cognitive basis for L2 learning. Within this line of reasoning, the L1 is being increasingly appreciated as a "reference system" (Stern, 1992, p. 283) facilitating L2 learning, and as a relevant "Language Acquisition Support System" (Butzkamm, 2003, p. 29). The L1 is thus recognized as a source of prior conceptual knowledge about language structure and communication, and a foundation upon which new linguistic knowledge can be constructed. Referring to the L1 and making crosslinguistic comparisons also enhance metalinguistic knowledge and awareness in L2 learners, which contributes to the development of their overall language competence and sensitivity to linguistic forms (Butzkamm & Caldwell, 2009; Gozdawa-Gołębiowski, 2003; James, 1996).

The role of the L1 is equally important, yet considerably more intricate, in the process of L3 learning. Learning more than one foreign language is believed to share some characteristics of L2 acquisition, but there are vital differences, including the generally greater complexity of multilingual learning, which justifies making it an independent field of study (Cenoz, 2013; De Angelis, 2007; Sanz, Park, & Lado, 2015). Investigations into transfer in multilingual learning point to both L1-L3 and L2-L3 transfer effects, guided by language typology and psychotypology, L2 status, levels of proficiency, L1 metalinguistic knowledge, and other factors (De Bot & Jaensch, 2015; Schepens, van der Slik & van Hout, 2016; Tsang, 2015). The role of the L1 as a source of metalinguistic knowledge and awareness is also a valid area of L3 research. Multilinguals are believed to display higher levels of capacity in these areas than bilinguals due to the larger repertoires of linguistic resources in their minds, resulting from a prior knowledge of at least two languages (the L1 and the L2) and greater experience in learning languages (Falk, Lindqvist, & Bartel, 2015; Jessner, 2008, 2014). Angelovska and Hahn (2015) point to enhanced crosslinguistic awareness in multilingual learners, which enables them to make effective use of comparisons across the languages they know.

Previous work has mainly focused on the effects of L1-L2-L3 similarities and differences on acquisition, and psycholinguistic processes triggered by crosslinguistic connections, largely neglecting, however, learners' accounts on their own experiences of learning additional languages and their opinions about the role that the L1 plays in these processes. With this in mind, the present research aims to explore trilingual learners' awareness about the role of the L1 in learning L2 and L3 grammar. First, however, the current perspective on the L1 in L2 learning, as well as in the learning of L3 grammar, will be discussed on the basis of a literature review.

2 Literature Review

2.1 The Role of the L1 in Learning Another Language: A Current Perspective

The role of a learner's native language (L1) in learning and teaching foreign languages (the L2) has recently been reconsidered after being rejected as detrimental to L2 development within naturalistic approaches and largely neglected within purely communicative ones. For over two decades now, the findings of extensive research have pointed to an important role of the L1 as a foundation for the developing foreign language systems (Butzkamm, 2003; Butzkamm & Caldwell, 2009; Cook, 2010; Hall & Cook, 2012; Littlewood & Yu, 2011).

Renewed interest in crosslinguistic influence in SLA is one of the threads of current research into the role of the L1. Odlin (2016) re-examines the notion of language transfer in relation to the Contrastive Analysis Hypothesis from the perspective of contemporary psycholinguistic study of L2 and multilingual acquisition. Cummins (2007) surveys the different types of crosslinguistic influence addressed by current research, such as those related to the transfer of conceptual elements, pragmatic aspects of language use, phonological awareness, and metacognitive and metalinguistic strategies. His discussion reveals that the scope of recent transfer studies is much broader than in those with a behaviorist orientation. In the recent literature there are also numerous examples of research investigating the role and effects of L1 transfer on the processes and effectiveness of learning foreign language grammar, which indicates that this line of inquiry has also gained popularity in recent years. For example, Chan (2004) found that L1 transfer was responsible for a large proportion of grammatical errors made by learners at lower- and higher-proficiency levels, although in the case of the former, interference was more prevalent. Izquierdo and Collins (2008) traced the effects of L1-L2 similarity on the acquisition of L2 forms, observing that greater L1-L2 similarity allowed learners to manage the formal aspects of structures with greater efficiency, while learners with a typologically different L1 relied more on semantic aspects of grammatical constructions. Trenkic, Milkovic and Altmann (2014) investigated the influence of L1 transfer on L2 grammar processing, noting considerable differences between its effects on comprehension and production. All of the researchers mentioned above posited that explicit instruction or guidance involving crosslinguistic comparisons would be recommended in order to counter the effects of interference and to ease the process of understanding how the system of the new language operates. In needs to be stressed that the studies outlined in this section involved adult L2 learners, because at least a certain level of language awareness is required in the investigated processes.

In the recent literature, a number of arguments have been made backing the claim that the L1 is an important cognitive resource in learning other languages, most of which are derived from the constructivist principle of facilitating the learning of new knowledge with reference to previously possessed knowledge (Brooks-Lewis, 2009; Cummins, 2007). As stated by Hall and Cook (2012, p. 291), "prior knowledge and the learners' own language provide a cognitive framework through which new knowledge is constructed and regulated". According to one important argument within this reasoning, the L1 is a source of conceptual and metalinguistic knowledge about communication processes, parts of speech, form-meaning connections, and so on. Having already acquired one language and the ability to use it with high levels of accuracy and fluency, a learner is well-equipped to approach the task of learning another language. The knowledge that they possess aids them significantly in making discoveries about the structure and use of a new language, even if there are considerable L1-L2 differences in the forms and functions of structures. It also helps them notice and understand form-meaning correspondences in the new grammatical system (Butzkamm & Caldwell, 2009; Corder, 1992).

Referring to the L1 and making use of crosslinguistic comparisons can also lead to enhanced linguistic and metalinguistic awareness in learners. James (1996, p. 139) explains that foreign language learners develop a certain kind of intuition on the basis of L1-L2 connections, which he calls "Cross-linguistic Intuition (XLI)". This intuition is responsible, for example, for making procedural choices concerning which L1 elements can be transferred to the L2. On the other hand, "Cross-linguistic Awareness (XLA)" is declarative and metacognitive, and helps learners use L2 forms on the basis of their metacognitions about language in general. Horst, White and Bell (2010) state that metalinguistic awareness is influenced by such factors as crosslinguistic comparisons and provides a useful basis for the development of overall language competence.

Gozdawa-Gołębiowski (2003) and Zojer (2009) point out that increased metalinguistic awareness can lead, in turn, to enhanced reflectivity about how language (both the L1 and additional languages) is structured and about form-meaning connections, and can contribute to higher levels of sensitivity to numerous linguistic phenomena, which usually results in stronger intrinsic motivation and more effective learning. Additionally, Brooks-Lewis (2009) and Littlewood (2014) stress the affective benefits of using the L1 in the processes of learning and teaching additional languages, suggesting that relying on a familiar system gives learners a feeling of security and confidence, and a sense of ownership over their learning. For many learners being able to fully understand foreign language input is an important condition for becoming predisposed to the acquisition of new, often complicated, grammatical material. As observed by Deller and Rinvolucri (2002, p. 28), "[g]rammr becomes much less frightening and much more accessible if students are allowed and encouraged to notice the similarities and differences between their own language and English". Butzkamm and Caldwell (2009), in turn, provide numerous examples of learners' accounts of their feelings of alienation and frustration caused by a teacher's reliance on L2 exclusivity, with little or no regard for learners' lack of comprehension.

Although there has been extensive research on learners' attitudes toward teachers' use of the L1 in the classroom, research on learners' beliefs about the usefulness of the L1 in learning another language has been scarce. One example of such a study is Liao's (2006) investigation into learners' opinions about translation as a learning strategy, conducted on 351 Taiwanese college students learning English. A high reliance on translation was revealed, and a number of advantages of translation were highlighted, including enhanced comprehension of input, improved remembering of vocabulary, a better understanding of grammar, higher levels of production in the L2, and lower levels of anxiety in the process of learning. Although similar frequencies of the use of translation were reported across different proficiency groups, more proficient learners demonstrated better awareness of its benefits and constraints. In Scheffler's (2013) study, 45 Polish secondary school learners of English participated in lessons which included grammar-translation as well as monolingual, communicative consciousness-raising activities, and evaluated the usefulness of such activities for their learning. Their opinions about the utility and interest of the two different kinds of activities were similar. Highlighting L1-L2 differences, providing direct examples, and bringing novelty to classroom activities were among the advantages of translation listed by the learners.

2.2 The Role of Learners' L1 in the Learning of L3 Grammar

Over the last two decades, as noted by De Angelis (2017), research into multilingual learners has become a necessity for the obvious practical reason that there are few monolingual learners of an L2; most learners of a foreign language have already learned a first foreign language (usually English). This "multilingual turn" in language education has been caused by increasing globalization, transnational mobility, and the use of computer technologies (Cenoz & Gorter, 2015). Although there are numerous similarities between L2 and L3 acquisition, the major differences between them have led researchers to conclude that multilingualism is not just "an additive extension of bilingualism" (Cabrelli Amaro, Flynn, & Rothman, 2012, p. 2), and L3 learning needs to be treated as a specific and separate field of inquiry.

The phenomenon of crosslinguistic influence in learning additional languages (the third and any subsequent languages, referred here as the L3) by multilingual learners indicates the importance of the role of the L1. Although research into multilingual processing is relatively recent, it has been discovered by researchers (De Bot & Jaensch, 2015; Ringbom, 2007; Sanz et al., 2015) that the phenomenon of transfer in multilingual users is considerably more complex than in the case of bilinguals because all the languages known are subject to mutual influence in a multilingual mind. The L1 influences the learning of additional languages, but non-native languages also influence one another. De Angelis (2007, p. 136) calls this kind of transfer, which "can occur when two or more languages interact with one another and concur in influencing the target language," "combined" crosslinguistic influence. Interestingly, Cenoz and Garter (2015) point out that multilingual research, unlike SLA research, tends to focus on transfer phenomena as a means of facilitating language learning, rather than a source of interference, acknowledging that "the languages learners have in their linguistic repertoire can be used as a resource when learning additional languages" (p. 7). Naturally, as is the case with bilingual transfer, interlingual (L1-L3, L2-L3) similarity leads to facilitated L3 acquisition (Cenoz, 2013). This is in line with the Typological Primacy Model devised by Rothman (2011, 2015), according to which L3 acquisition is aided by those features of the previously learned languages which seem to be the most appropriate in a given situation. Transfer is guided by "structural similarities at an underlying level of linguistic competence across the three languages" (Rothman, 2015, p. 183). Therefore, L3 research stresses the important role of language typology (especially the L1-L2-L3 distance) and psychotypology [defined by Kellermann (1979) as a perceived distance between languages] in multilingual learning.

De Angelis (2007), however, notes that although learners tend to rely on the typologically closer language in L3 learning, multilingual transfer undergoes numerous other influences. Sanz et al. (2015) point to the privileged role of the L1 during L3 learning and use; their study participants, during the initial stages of L3 acquisition, relied on the most prominent L1 features in L3 sentence processing. Other factors, however, also seem to play a role in crosslinguistic influence in L3 learning. The status of the L2 is of relevance here; as was discovered by Bardel and Falk (2007), transfer from the L2 can block positive L1 transfer if the target feature exists in the L1 and L3, but not in the L2. De Bot and Jaensch (2015) and Tsang (2015) found that learners' L1, L2 and L3 proficiency levels are among the factors influencing transfer effects in L3 learning. Falk et al. (2015) observed that the level of metalinguistic knowledge, understood as "the conscious knowledge of the linguistic rules of a particular language" (p. 227), in learners' L1 was a factor influencing transfer to the L3. It was found that the extent of explicit L1 metalinguistic knowledge played an important role in L3 acquisition. Schepens et al. (2016) pointed to individual variables in learners, such as age, gender, intelligence, motivation, and the length and quality of formal education, as contributing to multilingual transfer.

Another point worth considering when discussing the role of the L1 in L3 learning is the effects of prior linguistic knowledge (resulting from knowing the L1 and the L2) on learners' metalinguistic knowledge and awareness. These capacities "are assumed to play an important role for the development of multilingualism and the learning of new languages" (Falk et al., 2015, p. 229), and they are believed to be better developed in multilingual than bilingual learners. In fact, according to Jessner (2014), metalinguistic awareness is "one, or even the key factor in multilingual learning" (p. 175). The high level of metalinguistic knowledge and awareness in L3 learners results from a more extensive repertoire of linguistic resources in their minds, their contact with multiple languages, and experience in foreign language learning, and seems to be confirmed by research. For example, Gibson and Hufeisen (2011) found that in a sample of multilingual L1 German learners of between 2 and 5 different foreign languages, the more experienced ones showed an enhanced ability to identify and correct preposition errors in English. The results were interpreted as an indication that more experienced multilinguals displayed more efficient use of metalinguistic strategies and higher levels of sensitivity to the severity of errors. Rutgers and Evans (2015) conducted a longitudinal study on trilingual (L1 Dutch, L2 English) and bilingual (L1 Dutch) learners of L3 German. Although the results did not point to clear metalinguistic advantages of trilingual over bilingual learners, they revealed higher levels of "functional language awareness" in L3 learners, as well as more positive attitudes toward language learning. Tsang (2015) compared linguistic perception between trilingual (L1 Chinese, L2 English, L3 French) and bilingual (L1 Chinese, L2 English) learners, and found that the knowledge of the L3 had an influence on the perceptions of linguistic features in the L1 and L2. The researcher concluded that trilingual learners demonstrated higher levels of linguistic sensitivity and metalinguistic awareness than bilingual ones. Angelovska and Hahn (2015) highlight a closely related concept, crosslinguistic awareness, which they define as "a mental ability which develops through focusing attention on and reflecting upon language(s) in use and through establishing similarities and differences among the languages in one's multilingual mind" (p. 187), as a particularly crucial factor in learning L3 grammar. In their study, they investigated L3 learners' ability to consciously make use of L1 and L2 resources. The participants had different L1 backgrounds, and were L2 German and L3 English learners. They displayed an awareness of both L1-L3 and L2-L3 influence in L3 learning, as evidenced by their contrasting and comparing grammar features across languages, and making explicit references to the L1 and L2 in learning tasks based on a discovery-based method.

Finally, it needs to be stressed that enhanced metalinguistic awareness in multilingual learners can lead to more effective use of language learning strategies, resulting from their more elaborate learning experience. As a result, as suggested by Nayak, Hansen, Krueger and McLaughlin (1990), L3 learners often display higher levels of awareness of factors which make them learn more effectively, and can select learning strategies and available linguistic and non-linguistic resources in a more efficient manner. Similarly, Cenoz (2013, p. 73) stresses that the skills and strategies developed for L2 learning are "reactivated and adapted" in an L3 context, and that learners often acknowledge using prior languages as a basis for L3 learning. According to Gabryś-Barker (2013), multilingual learners are capable of transferring their learning skills and strategies to the learning of different languages, which gives them an advantage over L2 learners, and De Angelis (2007) notes that the linguistic information possessed by L3 learners can help them formulate hypotheses about language forms and devise effective strategies on the basis of crosslinguistic comparisons.

3 The Study

3.1 Aims

The main aim of the study was to investigate trilingual learners' awareness of the role of the L1 in learning foreign languages. More specifically, it aimed to gather their opinions about the facilitative role of L1 Polish in learning the grammar of L2 English and L3 Russian, with a special emphasis on differences between the usefulness of L1 Polish in learning English and Russian grammar. Finally, the study investigated the participants' experience in the use of translation as a strategy in learning English and Russian.

3.2 Method

3.2.1 Participants

Ninety-four students of English-Russian Philology at Adam Mickiewicz University in Poznań participated in the study. They were in their 1st and 2nd years of a B.A. program, and their average age was 19.5. Although they majored in both English and Russian, the sample's proficiency levels in these languages differed considerably; for English, the proficiency was roughly at the B1/B2 level, according to the common reference levels described by the Council of Europe (2001), while for Russian it was A1/A2, with the mean length of previous learning being 11 and 1.5 years, respectively.

3.2.2 Data Collection Instrument and Data Analysis

The present study makes use of a subset of data from a larger investigation, based on a questionnaire that included Likert-type and open-ended questions, and interviews. This analysis focuses only on the following four open-ended questions from the questionnaire:

1. Is the L1 helpful in learning foreign languages? Why/Why not?
2. Do you think referring to your L1 (Polish) is useful in understanding the form and meaning of foreign language grammatical structures? Why/Why not?
3. Is there a difference between how helpful Polish is in learning English and Russian grammar?
4. When you learn foreign language grammar on your own, do you translate sentences/structures? Do you find it helpful?

The language of the questionnaire, and of the responses provided by the participants, was English. The elicited qualitative data were used to create a textual database, which underwent subsequent analysis using Atlas.ti software according to the general procedures outlined in Creswell (2014, pp. 195–196). Predominant themes related to the research aims were identified, and the raw data were grouped and coded, leading to a synthesis of the participants' comments about the relevant topics. In order to detect patterns in the responses, the data units (relevant quotes selected from the questionnaires) were quantified, as suggested by Friedman (2012, p. 182). In the following section, both the frequencies of responses within given categories and their illustrations in the form of participants' quotations will be presented.

3.3   Results

3.3.1   Perceptions About the Usefulness of the L1 in Learning Additional Languages

The answers given to questions about the usefulness of the L1 in learning foreign languages were grouped under three headings, outlined in Table 1. As can be seen from the quantification of the answers, while 40% of the students generally considered the L1 to be an important resource in foreign language learning, most of them (45%) did not give a definite answer.

Most of the arguments given by those who claimed that the L1 is helpful in learning the L2 pointed to the L1 as a basis for any other language processing. This is illustrated by the following quotes: "Yes, it's very useful. It's the language I know best, so I will always refer to it; Your native language is a kind of anchor for foreign languages". Others frequently underscored the interconnections among languages, making the following statements: "In fact, all languages, native and foreign, are useful when learning another language"; "Comparing languages helps to create some connections in the brain". Interestingly, vocabulary was the only area referred to when answering this question. "Polish words often help me remember Russian or even English words" is an example of frequently made comments.

As can be seen in Table 1, relatively few students (about 15%) gave a negative answer to this question. Their arguments were mainly linked to crosslinguistic differences which, according to the respondents, make L2 and L3 learning more difficult. This is evident in the following examples of quotes: "No. Each language is different, so languages shouldn't be mixed; Polish makes it more difficult to

Table 1 Frequency of answers to the question: "Is the L1 helpful in learning foreign languages?"

Category of answers	N (94)	%
1. L1 is helpful in learning foreign languages	38	40.42
2. L1 is not helpful in learning foreign languages	14	14.89
3. It depends	42	44.68

remember words in foreign languages, because words are never the same"; "No, comparing languages is tricky. I switch my brain off from Polish when I learn Russian or English".

Comments revealing a lack of univocal opinions on the facilitative role of the L1 in L2/L3 learning constituted the highest percentage of answers (45%). Most of the respondents stressed that the role of the L1 strongly depends on the foreign language, as exemplified by the following quotes: "It depends what language we're talking about, because the situation looks very different for different languages"; "It can be very useful in learning some languages, but it can also disturb in learning". Again, the lexical area was most frequently used to illustrate the point: "It is generally useful, but we have to remember about false friends. You wouldn't like to feed anyone in Russia with a carpet, would you?" In this example, the semantic dissimilarity between *kawior* (Pol.) and *ковёр* (Rus.) was referred to.

The following question was more specific, because it concerned the usefulness of the L1 in the learning of foreign language grammar. According to the data in Table 2, the highest percentage of respondents (48%) acknowledged the facilitative role of the L1 in understanding the form and meaning of L2/L3 grammatical structures, while 11% gave negative answers. Forty-two percent of the participants found it difficult to unequivocally answer this question.

Those who said that the L1 is helpful in learning foreign language grammar provided a number of justifications for their opinions. Most of these were related to the enhanced attention to grammatical patterns that cross-linguistic comparisons stimulate, and, as a result, an easier understanding of target language grammar structures. The following quotes illustrate this: "By distinguishing differences and similarities we remember the patterns in the new language more effectively"; "Comparing languages involves dividing structures into chunks, which can be good for understanding how they work"; "Referring to Polish helps me understand structures rather than learning them by heart". The participants also noted that L1-L2/L3 comparisons encourage a problem-solving, discovery-based approach toward working out foreign language grammar rules that helps them develop a deeper "feel" for L2/L3 grammar, and triggers associations between "what is known and what is new". Finally, some of the respondents mentioned the feeling of security that relying on the L1 can give: "Grammar is usually difficult, and using your mother tongue can give you a feeling that you understand it".

Among the 10 comments about a lack of positive influences on understanding L3 grammar, some referred to interference effects (e.g., "When referring to L1

Table 2 Frequency of answers to the question: "Do you think referring to the L1 (Polish) is useful in understanding the form and meaning of foreign language grammatical structures?"

Category of answers	N (94)	%
1. L1 is helpful in learning foreign language grammar	45	47.9
2. L1 is not helpful in learning foreign language grammar	10	10.6
3. It depends	39	41.5

students can copy structures and make mistakes"), while others stressed that the L1 disturbs naturalistic foreign language development, which should be limited to contextualized practice. Two students pointed out that basing on one's intuitions about L2/L3 grammar and thinking in the foreign language with no L1 mediation lead to a deeper understanding of structures.

Finally, 41% respondents stated that while the L1 could be a relevant basis for understanding the grammatical system of another language, there are three main factors that need to be considered. Learners' proficiency level was the most frequently mentioned factor; participants saw a role for the L1 at initial stages of learning, in particular, as exemplified by this quote: "L1 helps a lot, but only at the beginning, when the L2 grammar is a new system". Similarly, the complexity of structures was another factor mentioned: "It can be useful, but rather when we learn some very difficult constructions". Lastly, language typology was considered to influence the role of the L1 in understanding L2/L3 grammar. These comments focused mainly on the facilitative role of L1 Polish in learning Russian grammar ("It is useful in learning Slavic languages, but not in learning German or French"), but one respondent made a claim that detecting links between similar languages can lead to confusion.

The following question specifically addressed issues related to these comments, as it directly focused on differences between how helpful L1 Polish is in learning English and Russian grammar. As can be seen in Table 3, the vast majority of respondents (65%) believed that Polish plays a significant role in learning Russian, but not English. Two of the previously mentioned factors were listed in this category: L1-L2 similarity and the length of learning. The following two quotes aptly illustrate these points: "Russian grammar is very similar to Polish grammar, so Polish is very useful here"; and "Russian is a new language for me, so I need to refer to Polish to grasp its grammar more easily".

The second largest group of comments (19%) expressed a belief in the equally important role of L1 Polish in learning both languages. This point of view is exemplified by the following excerpt: "It's easier to learn Russian grammar because most structures are the same. But even if most structures in Polish and English are completely different, it is still possible to use those differences to understand English grammar". As can be seen, the student considered both similarities and differences to be conducive to comprehending how the grammatical system of another language works.

Table 3 Frequencies of answers to the question: "Is there a difference between how helpful Polish is in learning English and Russian grammar?"

Category of answers	N (94)	%
1. Polish helpful in learning Russian, but not English	61	64.9
2. Polish helpful in learning English, but not Russian	6	6.4
3. Polish helpful in learning both Russian and English	18	19.1
4. Polish helpful in learning neither Russian nor English	9	9.6

On the other hand, according to almost 10% of the respondents, L1 Polish was not helpful in understanding either Russian or English grammar. The students who made such comments referred mainly to the confusion caused by comparing grammatical systems ("Referring to Polish interrupts me, in learning both English and Russian. It makes me feel lost"), and a need to get maximum exposure and practice in the foreign language in order to learn it effectively.

Interestingly, six of the participants (6%) were of the opinion that L1 Polish is helpful in learning English, but not Russian grammar. All of them pointed to the danger of relying too much on a "misleading" similarity between two typologically close systems; this reasoning can be seen in the following quotation: "I use Polish-English rather than Polish-Russian comparisons because the Polish-Russian similarity is often confusing to me. Even if the form is similar, the meaning can be different".

Table 4 sums up the tallied responses to the question about the participants' practice in using translation as a grammar learning strategy and their opinions about its usefulness. As can be seen, a major part of the sample (54%) reported using translation in learning L2/L3 grammar and finding it a useful strategy. Thirty-four percent of the respondents acknowledged using translation, but made a provision that it depended on certain factors. Finally, 11 students (12%) stated that they did not make use of translation at all when learning the grammar of foreign languages.

It should be noted that a few students reported applying translation strategies very frequently; some of them used phrases such as "I always translate sentences", and even "It's the only way I learn foreign language grammar". A number of arguments were given by the respondents to justify their use of translation and its effectiveness. Its perceived role in providing clarity, or transparency, in L2/L3 foreign language material was definitely the most frequent rationale provided. This function is evident in the following quotes: "When I translate sentences, I can clearly see how a structure is constructed"; "When translating I explain it to myself in my own words so it's more clear to me". Some of the students stressed the role of translation in making the study of L2/L3 grammar more conscious and systematic: "(…) when I translate, I am focused on details, which makes my work more accurate". Others noted the beneficial role of the challenge posed by translation: "It requires time and effort, and the more time I spend on a particular exercise, the more I remember". Still others referred to the metacognitive role of translation in self-evaluation: "I use translation to confirm my understanding of a rule".

Those who reported using translation, but only under certain circumstances, mentioned that it depended on the language being studied (most students stated that

Table 4 Frequencies of answers to the question: "When you learn foreign language grammar on your own, do you translate sentences/structures? Do you find it helpful?"

Category of answers	N (94)	%
1. I use translation in learning grammar, and generally find it useful	51	54.3
2. I use translation, but only under certain circumstances	32	34
3. I don't use translation in learning grammar	11	11.7

they translate when learning Russian: "I have to translate Russian sentences, because I barely understand anything") and the level of difficulty of a specific grammar structure, with difficult material requiring more translation. These were the most frequently provided answers.

The opponents of translation as a learning strategy mainly pointed to its limited effect on acquiring foreign language structures. They preferred intensive opportunities to hear and use the foreign language. The following quote aptly illustrates this point of view: "It's better to find examples of using a given structure in literature, movies, press etc., and it gives you fluency in using new forms and creating sentences". One student stated that translation disturbs the process of developing the ability to think in a foreign language, and thus it should be avoided; another explained that they did not make use of translation because they did not learn grammar in a formal way, focusing instead on holistic comprehension of input.

4 Discussion

It can be seen on the basis of the research data that a definite majority of the participants either believed in the positive role of the L1 in learning foreign languages or openly expressed the opinion that there are constraints on its usefulness, and were able to list and further discuss them. The views were well-balanced; while convictions about the definitely supportive role of the L1 were prevalent, caution was also voiced about its facilitative role under all conditions. The constraints listed by the participants concerned language typology and proficiency levels, the two factors most frequently discussed in the literature (Cenoz, 2013; Tsang, 2015), which points to their awareness of transfer phenomena and the role of language similarities and differences in foreign language learning.

Interestingly, the participants' opinions about the facilitative role of the L1 were even more positive in relation to learning the grammar of L2 English and L3 Russian. A high reliance on systematic, explicit learning of grammar was revealed, and the students seemed to be very well aware of the role that making references to the L1 plays in this process. Therefore, it can be concluded that they displayed high levels of awareness of the L1 as an important cognitive resource specifically in making sense of L2 and L3 structures. This could be detected from the comments they made and the examples they provided about their own experience and practice. The participants reported making deliberate use of crosslinguistic comparisons, breaking foreign language sentences into chunks and analyzing them, and referring to the L1 in order to fully understand the form and meaning of foreign language structures. Reflections stimulated by crosslinguistic comparisons, so frequently cited by the students, are a clear sign of their metalinguistic awareness. Similarly, reservations voiced about the utility of referring to the L1 in certain situations (depending on the language typology, the complexity of the structure, and the proficiency level) also point to the presence of this capacity in the sample.

Not surprisingly, most of the respondents saw the greatest justification for the use of L1 Polish in learning a typologically similar language, L3 Russian. Another reason indicated to was their limited proficiency in this language and the compensatory function that L1 resources play. This role of the L1 is also discussed in the literature, for example, by Iluk (2008), who sees referring to the L1 as alleviating the cognitive burden of dealing with difficult L2 tasks. However, one-fourth of the participants also claimed that L1 Polish played a role in their learning of L2 English, a typologically more distant language in which their proficiency was rather high. While some of them believed that the L1 is useful for learning both languages, a few students, interestingly, decided that the similarities between Polish and Russian can lead to confusion, and therefore references to Polish make more sense in the learning of English.

The participants' awareness of the role of the L1 was also evident in their opinions about, and accounts of, the use of translation strategies in learning the grammar of English and Russian. It is important to note that translation as a learning strategy appeared to be very popular among the participants. Altogether, almost 90% of them reported making use of translation. Over half of the respondents considered it to be an efficient strategy, while others, although admitting to using it, could see its limitations. Again, the positive opinions pointed to translation being an adequate strategy for conscious, explicit, often analytic learning, which was highly appreciated by the participants.

Recapitulating, it can be stated that the study participants, trilingual university students of L2 English and L3 Russian, demonstrated high levels of awareness of the role of the L1 in learning foreign language grammar. In the answers provided to the questionnaire, they listed and explained a number of functions of the L1 in L2/L3 learning, at the same being cautious of its possible negative effects. The study results, however, do not make it possible to state univocally that this awareness was a result of being trilingual, as there was no comparison with a group of bilingual learners. This is one limitation of the study. Another one concerns the limited number of questions and the self-report character of the tool.

However, despite its limitations, the study offers insight into the metacognition of trilingual learners and allows suggesting certain practical implications. Hofer (2015, p. 15) concludes that the skills and abilities developed by L3 learners "form part of a larger metasystem which develops in trilingual and multilingual learners and which is not available to the monolingual speaker or to learners of a second language", adding that metalinguistic development can be promoted through didactic activities. Jessner (2008) and Hofer (2015) thus suggest the introduction of pedagogic procedures that expose and sensitize learners to the structure of all the languages they know (the L1, L2, L3) by consciously building on their existing linguistic knowledge. This can be done by conducting crosslinguistic comparisons, stimulating reflection on similarities and differences they notice, and by training learners in the use of learning strategies involving L1 and L2 resources.

5 Conclusions

The study aimed to investigate trilingual learners' awareness of the role of the L1 in learning foreign languages, the L2 and the L3. On the basis of the elicited data, it can be concluded that the participants revealed high levels of awareness and sensitivity in terms of crosslinguistic comparisons and the possibility of using crosslinguistic information in their learning. The L1 was admitted to be an important point of reference in understanding the form and meaning of grammatical structures in the target languages. Although its facilitative role was primarily stressed in relation to learning L3 Russian because of the L1-L3 typological similarity and the participants' proficiency level, interestingly, the benefits of the L1 in learning L2 English were also acknowledged. The reflections expressed by the respondents and the examples of learning strategies provided revealed deliberate utilization of the L1 as a tool in making sense of the L2 and L3 systems. Generally, the arguments provided by the participants seemed to indicate that they were conscious learners, highly aware of whether and why the L1 could assist their L2 and L3 learning.

References

Angelovska, T., & Hahn, A. (2015). Raising language awareness for learning and teaching L3 grammar. In A. Benati, C. Laval, & M. J. Arche (Eds.), *The grammar dimension in instructed second language learning* (pp. 185–206). London and New York: Bloomsbury.

Arabski, J., & Wojtaszek, A. (2016). Contemporary perspectives on crosslinguistic influence. In R. Alonso Alonso (Ed.), *Crosslinguistic influence in second language acquisition* (pp. 215–224). Bristol: Multilingual Matters.

Bardel, C., & Falk, Y. (2007). The role of the second language in third language acquisition. The case of Germanic syntax. *Second Language Research, 23*(4), 459–484. doi:10.1177/0267658307080557.

Brooks-Lewis, K. A. (2009). Adult learners' perceptions of the incorporation of their L1 in foreign language teaching and learning. *Applied Linguistics, 30*(2), 216–235. doi:10.1093/applin/amn051.

Butzkamm, W. (2003). We only learn language once. The role of the mother tongue in FL classrooms: Death of a dogma. *Language Learning Journal, 28,* 29–39. doi:10.1080/09571730385200181.

Butzkamm, W., & Caldwell, J. (2009). *The bilingual reform: A paradigm shift in foreign language teaching.* Tübingen: Narr.

Cabrelli Amaro, J., Flynn, S., & Rothman, J. (2012). Introduction: Third language (L3) acquisition in adulthood. In J. Cabrelli Amaro, S. Flynn, & J. Rothman (Eds.), *Third language acquisition in adulthood* (pp. 1–6). Amsterdam/Philadelphia: John Benjamins Publishing Company.

Cenoz, J. (2013). The influence of bilingualism on third language acquisition: Focus on multilingualism. *Language Teaching, 46*(1), 71–86. doi:10.1017/S0261444811000218.

Cenoz, J., & Gorter, D. (2015). Towards a holistic approach in the study of multilingual education. In J. Cenoz & D. Gorter (Eds.), *Multilingual education: Between language learning and translanguaging* (pp. 1–15). Cambridge: Cambridge University Press.

Chan, A. (2004). Syntactic transfer: Evidence from the interlanguage of Hong Kong Chinese ESL learners. *Modern Language Journal, 88,* 56–74. doi:10.1111/j.0026-7902.2004.00218.x.

Cook, G. (2010). *Translation in language teaching: An argument for reassessment.* Oxford: Oxford University Press.

Corder, S. P. (1992). A role for the mother tongue. In S. Gass & L. Selinker (Eds.), *Language transfer in language learning* (pp. 18–31). Amsterdam: John Benjamins.

Council of Europe. (2001). *Common European framework of reference for languages: Learning, teaching, assessment.* Cambridge: Cambridge University Press.

Cresswell, J. W. (2014). *Research design: Qualitative, quantitative, and mixed methods approaches* (4th ed.). Thousand Oaks: SAGE Publications.

Cummins, J. (2007). Rethinking monolingual instructional strategies in multilingual classrooms. *Canadian Journal of Applied Linguistics, 10*(2), 221–240. Retrieved from https://journals.lib. unb.ca/index.php/CJAL/article/view/19743/21428.

De Angelis, G. (2007). *Third or additional language learning.* Clevedon: Multilingual Matters.

De Angelis, G. (2017). Dealing with multilingualism in quantitative research. In J. McKinley & H. Rose (Eds.), *Doing research in applied linguistics* (pp. 91–100). London and New York: Routledge.

De Bot, K., & Jaensch, C. (2015). What is special about L3 processing? *Bilingualism: Language and Cognition, 18,* 130–144. doi:10.1017/S1366728913000448.

Deller, S., & Rinvolucri, M. (2002). *Using the mother tongue: Making the most of the learner's language.* London: Delta Publishing.

Falk, Y., Lindqvist, C, & Bardel, C. (2015). The role of L1 explicit metalinguistic knowledge in L3 oral production at the initial state. *Bilingualism: Language and Cognition, 18*(2), 227–235. doi:10.1017/S1366728913000552.

Friedman, D. A. (2012). How to collect and analyze qualitative data. In A. Mackey & S. Gass (Eds.), *Research methods in second language acquisition: A practical guide* (pp. 180–200). Malden, MA: Blackwell Publishing.

Gabryś-Barker, D. (2013). The role of transfer of learning in multilingual instruction and development. In D. Gabryś-Barker & J. Mydla (Eds.), *English studies at the University of Silesia: Forty years on* (pp. 67–83). Katowice: Wydawnictwo Uniwersytetu Śląskiego.

Gibson, M., & Hufeisen, B. (2011). Perception of preposition errors in semantically correct versus erroneous contexts by multilingual advanced English as a foreign language learners: Measuring metalinguistic awareness. In G. De Angelis & J. M. Dewaele (Eds.), *New trends in crosslinguistic influence and multilingualism research* (pp. 74–85). Clevedon: Multilingual Matters.

Gozdawa-Gołębiowski, R. (2003). *Interlanguage formation: A study of the triggering mechanisms.* Warszawa: Instytut Anglistyki Uniwersytetu Warszawskiego.

Hall, G., & Cook, G. (2012). Own-language use in language teaching and learning. *Language Teaching, 45*(3), 271–308. doi:10.1017/S0261444812000067.

Hofer, B. (2015). *On the dynamics of early multilingualism: A psycholinguistic study.* Berlin: de Gruyter.

Horst, M., White, J., & Bell, P. (2010). First and second language knowledge in the language classroom. *International Journal of Bilingualism, 14*(3), 331–349. doi:10.1177/1367006910367848.

Iluk, J. (2008). Tłumaczyć czy nie tłumaczyć na lekcjach języka obcego. *Języki Obce w Szkole, 5,* 32–41.

Izquierdo, J., & Collins, L. (2008). The facilitative role of L1 influence in tense-aspect marking: A comparison of Hispanophone and Anglophone learners of French. *Modern Language Journal, 92*(3), 350–368. doi:10.1111/j.1540-4781.2008.00751.x.

James, C. (1996). A cross-linguistic approach to language awareness. *Language Awareness, 5*(3–4), 138–148. doi:10.1080/09658416.1996.9959903.

Jessner, U. (2008). Teaching third languages: Findings, trends and challenges. *Language Teaching, 41*(1), 15–56. doi:10.1017/S0261444807004739.

Jessner, U. (2014). On multilingual awareness or why the multilingual learner is a specific language learner. In M. Pawlak & L. Aronin (Eds.), *Essential topics in applied linguistics and multilingualism* (pp. 175–184). Cham: Springer.

Kellerman, E. (1979). Transfer and non-transfer: Where we are now. *Studies in Second Language Acquisition, 2*(1), 37–57. doi:10.1017/S0272263100000942.

Liao, P. (2006). EFL Learners' beliefs about and strategy use of translation in English learning. *RELC Journal, 37*(2), 191–215. doi:10.1177/0033688206067428.

Littlewood, W. (2014). Communication-oriented language teaching: Where are we now? Where do we go from here? *Language Teaching, 47*(3), 349–362. doi:10.1017/S0261444812000134.

Littlewood, W., & Yu, B. (2011). First language and target language in the foreign language classroom. *Language Teaching, 44*(1), 64–77. doi:10.1017/S0261444809990310.

Nayak, N., Hansen, N., Krueger, N., & McLaughlin, B. (1990). Language-learning strategies in monolingual and multilingual adults. *Language Learning, 40*(2), 221–244. doi:10.1111/j.1467-1770.1990.tb01334.x.

Odlin, T. (2016). Was there really ever a Contrastive Analysis Hypothesis? In R. Alonso Alonso (Ed.), *Crosslinguistic influence in second language acquisition* (pp. 1–23). Bristol: Multilingual Matters.

Ringbom, H. (2007). *Cross-linguistic similarity in foreign language learning.* Clevedon: Multilingual Matters.

Rothman, J. (2011). L3 syntactic transfer selectivity and typological determinacy: The Typological Primacy Model. *Second Language Research, 27,* 107–128. doi:10.1177/0267658310386439.

Rothman, J. (2015). Linguistic and cognitive motivations for the Typological Primacy Model (TPM) of third language (L3) transfer: Timing of acquisition and proficiency considered. *Bilingualism: Language and Cognition, 18*(2), 179–190. doi:10.1017/S136672891300059X.

Rutgers, D., & Evans, M. (2015). Bilingual education and L3 learning: metalinguistic advantage or not? *International Journal of Bilingual Education and Bilingualism.* doi:10.1080/13670050.2015.1103698.

Sanz, C., Park, H. I., & Lado, B. (2015). A functional approach to cross-linguistic influence in ab initio L3 acquisition. *Bilingualism: Language and Cognition, 18*(2), 236–251. doi:10.1017/S1366728914000285.

Scheffler, P. (2013). Learners' perceptions of grammar-translation as consciousness raising. *Language Awareness, 22*(3), 255–269. doi:10.1080/09658416.2012.703673.

Schepens, J., van der Slik, F., & van Hout, R. (2016). L1 and L2 distance effects in learning L3 Dutch. *Language Learning, 66*(1), 224–256. doi:10.1111/lang.12150.

Stern, H. H. (1992). *Issues and options in language teaching.* Oxford: Oxford University Press.

Tolentino, L. C., & Tokowicz, N. (2011). Across languages, space, and time: A review of the role of cross-language similarity in L2 (morpho)syntactic processing as revealed by fMRI and ERP. *Studies in Second Language Acquisition, 33*(1), 91–125. doi:10.1017/S0272263110000549.

Trenkic, D., Mirkovic, J., & Altmann, G. (2014). Real-time grammar processing by native and non-native speakers: Constructions unique to the second language. *Bilingualism: Language and Cognition, 17*(2), 237–257. doi:10.1017/S1366728913000321.

Tsang, W. L. (2015). Learning more, perceiving more? A comparison of L1 Cantonese-L2 English-L3 French speakers and L1 Cantonese-L2 English speakers in Hong Kong. *International Journal of Multilingualism, 12*(3), 312–337. doi:10.1080/14790718.2014.961470.

Zojer, H. (2009). The methodological potential of translation in Second Language Acquisition: Re-evaluating translation as a teaching tool. In W. Arnd, T. Harden, & A. R. de Oliveira Harden (Eds.), *Translation in second language learning and teaching* (pp. 31–51). Oxford and Bern: Peter Lang.

Author Biography

Aleksandra Wach, Ph.D. works as an Assistant Professor at the Faculty of English, Adam Mickiewicz University, Poznań, Poland. Apart from teaching English as a foreign language at university level, she conducts EFL didactics courses and is involved in training pre-service and in-service English teachers. Her current professional interests include: EFL teacher training, the use of learners' L1 in learning and teaching the L2, and learning and teaching EFL grammar.

The Effect of Strategy Instruction on English Majors' Use of Affective Strategies and Anxiety Levels

Jakub Bielak

Abstract The chapter reports a mixed-methods quasi-experimental study extending over one year which investigated the effects of strategy instruction (SI) aimed at anxiety reduction on affective strategy use, and language and test anxiety levels. Strategy use and anxiety levels were investigated not only in general terms (self-reported anxiety levels in a given type of situation, self-reported frequency of strategy use) but also in relation to two implementations of an actual oral English exam (self-reported anxiety and use of strategies before, during and after an oral English exam). The participants were English majors in a small Polish university (N = 23). The tools used were language learning strategy use surveys including *Strategy Inventory for Language Learning* (Oxford, 1990), *Reactions to Tests* (Sarason, 1984; a test anxiety survey), *Foreign Language Classroom Anxiety Scale* (Horwitz, Horwitz, & Cope, 1986), and anxometers (1-item 1–10 scales for measuring state anxiety). The results indicate that affective SI results in greater affective strategy use as well as the use of a larger range of strategies in general and in relation to the actual language exam when it is properly contextualized. An unequivocal reduction in anxiety levels as a result of SI was not detected possibly due to an insufficient amount of treatment and a small number of highly-anxious learners in the sample, with only some indications of an anxiety-reducing effect.

Keywords Language learning strategies · Affective strategies · Strategy instruction · Language anxiety · Test anxiety

J. Bielak (✉)
Adam Mickiewicz University, Poznań, Kalisz, Poland
e-mail: kubabogu@amu.edu.pl

J. Bielak
State University of Applied Sciences, Konin, Poland

© Springer International Publishing AG 2018   227
M. Pawlak and A. Mystkowska-Wiertelak (eds.), *Challenges of Second and Foreign Language Education in a Globalized World*, Second Language Learning and Teaching, DOI 10.1007/978-3-319-66975-5_14

1   Introduction

One of the obstacles to successful language learning are negative emotional responses to situations and challenges commonly encountered in language education. Anxiety in the more specific guises of language and test anxiety (LA and TA) is one of the best studied of these negative reactions. Their experience by language learners is especially common in assessment situations such as language tests and gives rise to test performance not realistically reflecting true abilities and proficiency. It may therefore for ethical and educational reasons make sense to try to minimize their incidence in test-like situations. It may be done, among other things, by enrolling learners in anxiety-reduction programs involving interventions focusing on learners' cognition, affect and study skills (Hembree, 1988; Kralova, Skorvagova, Tirpakova, & Markechova, 2017; Zeidner, 1998). An intuitively appealing way of curbing negative affect such as anxiety and perhaps also boosting positive emotions (cf. Dewaele & MacIntyre, 2014) is the introduction of elements of such interventions into the teaching of affective strategies for language learning. The reason is that if language students learn to utilize anxiety reduction techniques as part of their strategic repertoires, they may benefit from self-improved emotions in the long term. The purpose of the present study was the investigation of the effect of affective strategy instruction (SI) on English majors' use of affective strategies and their anxiety levels, with anxiety understood both as a situation-specific trait (TA and LA) and a state occurring in a highly stressful exam situation. In the Polish context in which the study was conducted, the use of emotion-regulation strategies targeting excessive levels of anxiety is very much needed given the anxiety-inducing test-centeredness of the educational system which is rarely mitigated by any measures of anxiety reduction.

2   Overview of Previous Research

This overview of previous research covers LA, TA, language learning strategies (LLSs) and SI.

2.1   *Language Anxiety and Test Anxiety*

Although TA and LA are alike in some respects such as the physiological arousal manifesting their occurrence, they are generally researched as separate constructs. However, some confusion exists in the field concerning the relations between them. According to Horwitz (2010, 2016, 2017), some authors have misinterpreted the early seminal research on LA (Horwitz, Horwitz, & Cope) "to mean that FLA [foreign language anxiety] is composed of CA [communication apprehension], FNE [fear of negative evaluation], and TA rather than as simply being related to them" (Horwitz, 2010, p. 158). Of another important early study (Horwitz, 1986), Horwitz (2016) recently wrote that "importantly, (...) [it] established that language anxiety is independent of related anxieties including trait anxiety, communication apprehension, test anxiety, and fear of negative evaluation" (p. 933). Despite the sometimes conflicting research results concerning the two anxieties, it seems safe to conclude that they tend to correlate, especially when the TA under investigation is not general TA but TA specifically related to taking language tests. This is manifested for example in the composition of the *Foreign Language Classroom Anxiety Scale* (Horwitz et al., 1986), which includes three items directly related to language tests.

Like other situation-specific anxieties, TA may be experienced on the emotional, cognitive, physiological and behavioral levels; its uniqueness lies in the fact that it sets in when one faces the possibility of failing a test or exam (Zeidner, 1998). Thus, such reactions to tests and exams as tension, fast heartbeat, increased perspiration, worrisome, intrusive and chaotic thoughts, and behavior unrelated to the task are the possible manifestations of TA (Cizek & Burg, 2006; Spielberger, Anton, & Bedell, 1976; Spielberger & Vagg, 1995). TA is generally thought to be negative as it prevents test-takers from demonstrating their full potential during tests. TA, when construed in relation to language tests, is one correlate of LA, which was originally defined by Horwitz et al. (1986) as "a distinct complex of self-perceptions, beliefs, feelings and behaviors related to classroom language learning arising from the uniqueness of the language learning process" (p. 128). One important characteristic of this process, especially until high proficiency is achieved, is the difficulty or near-impossibility of self-expression. However, LA is thought to be unique and distinct from other anxieties such as TA or general anxiety, which were earlier thought to form its basis (MacIntyre, 2017). Research has documented a relationship between LA and less success in language learning and communication (e.g., Aida, 1994; Dewaele, 2007; Gardner & MacIntyre, 1993; Horwitz, Horwitz, & Cope 1986; Woodrow, 2006). A likely cause is that LA interferes with cognitive processing including the processing of linguistic input and output (MacIntyre & Gardner, 1994). Both anxiety types have more often been investigated as relatively stable traits, but they may also be conceptualized and studied as states occurring for limited periods in actual situations (MacIntyre, 2007; Zeidner, 1998).

Researchers have been interested in interventions aimed at reducing both types of anxiety, but much more so with respect to TA. This anxiety type can be successfully reduced by means of interventions focused on learners' emotions (e.g., relaxation training), cognition (e.g., boosting perceptions of self-competence) and study and test-taking skills (e.g., test-taking strategy instruction). For example, Weems et al. (2009) offered a 5-week combination of relaxation training, psychoeducation about TA and activities aimed at boosting self-efficacy beliefs and study and test-taking skills to 30 highly test-anxious 9th graders formerly exposed to Hurricane Katrina and found that this intervention reduced their TA and improved academic performance. The general effectiveness of TA-reduction interventions has been confirmed by meta-analyses such as Ergene (2003) and von der Embse, Barterian, and Segool (2013). Studies examining deliberate reduction of LA are much less numerous. They have mostly focused on specific instructional options such as particular forms of corrective feedback (Lee, 2016) or "computerized pronunciation practice" (Shams, 2005) which are supposed to lead to LA reduction. In addition, literature offers calls for creating anxiety-free class-rooms by adopting a commonsense approach to teaching (e.g., not flooding learners with too much material) and evaluation (e.g., introduction of peer evaluation) (cf. Young, 1999). However, there are almost no studies of dedicated interventions aimed at LA reduction. A rare recent quasi-experimental study of this kind is Kralova et al. (2017). They exposed 22 college students to 18 h of "psycho-social training", which "is a non-therapeutic intervention program of active social learning (Hupkova, 2011) that should help individuals cope with stressful situations by developing their social abilities (sensitivity, assertiveness, empathy, communication and cooperation)" (p. 52). This intervention coupled with intensive English pro-nunciation practice resulted in significant foreign language pronunciation anxiety reduction and pronunciation quality gains. The present project is intended as a contribution to the study of the little-researched issue of the effectiveness of interventions targeted at the reduction of LA (rather than other anxiety types; however, given the possible links between LA and TA mentioned earlier, the effect on TA was also investigated). In particular, it aims to do so by investigating the effectiveness of affective SI involving elements of emotion-focused and other types of therapy in anxiety reduction.

2.2   LLSs and SI

LLSs have been variously defined over the years. They will be understood here as cognitive and physical activities consciously utilized by language learners in their learning effort (cf. Cohen, 2014). There are many classifications of LLSs both in general (O'Malley & Chamot, 1990; Oxford, 1990) and in relation to specific language skills and subsystems, such as reading and grammar (e.g., Oxford, 1990, 2017; Pawlak, 2010; Sheorey & Mokhtari, 2001). Here, generally, Oxford's (1990) division of LLSs into memory, cognitive, compensation, metacognitive, social and affective strategies will be employed because Oxford's (1990) instrument for measuring strategy use was exploited in the present study (see Sect. 4.4). However, the "meta-" dimension will additionally be applied to affective strategies, as pro-posed in Oxford's (2011, 2017) later publications. Affective strategies, which are of special interest in this chapter, are used to manage the emotions, beliefs and atti-tudes for successful language learning (Oxford, 1990, 2011, 2017), and their examples include lowering one's anxiety and encouraging oneself in relation to language learning, as well as meta-affective strategies related to general organization (planning, monitoring, evaluating, etc.) of affective strategy use. SI is teaching LLSs taking into account learning styles and learner strategies currently used; the learner should notice the relationship between his/her preferred learning style and the strategies used to perform specific tasks (Cohen, 2014). There are several models of SI (e.g., Grenfell & Harris, 1999; Macaro, 2001; Oxford, 1990) which carefully detail the steps necessary for its success. Also, it has been recently stressed that SI should be situated and contextualized with due consideration given to tailoring it to its cultural, institutional and social environment (Oxford, 2011; Oxford & Amerstorfer, in press). Numerous studies have offered evidence that SI may improve learners' use of strategies (e.g., Atay & Ozbulgan, 2007; De Silva & Graham, 2015; Sarafianou & Gavriilidou, 2015), performance with respect to a range of language skills (e.g., Cohen, 2014; De Silva, 2015; Iwai, 2006; Manoli, Papadopoulou, & Metallidou, 2016; Vandergrift & Tafaghodatari, 2010) and learner autonomy (Nguyen & Gu, 2013). What is more, Plonsky's (2011) meta-analysis of 61 experimental and quasi-experimental studies concerning the impact of SI revealed a mild, yet hard-to-ignore effect. Importantly, Plonsky correctly noted that generally SI research tends to ignore social and affective strategies. The present study, which investigates the effects of teaching affective strategies on language learners' strategy use by applying a quasi-experimental design, attempts to contribute to this neglected research area.

In fact, the number of studies concerning affective SI is small, and they have rendered mixed results. In Chaury's (2015) meta-analysis SI including affective strategies appeared to improve reading comprehension. Affective SI did not raise oral test scores in English in Rossiter's (2003) study, and Chan (2014) reported that affective SI combined with the teaching of other strategies did not improve proficiency test scores. Rossiter's (2003) explanation of the lack of effect for the affective SI group in comparison with the control group was that both groups enjoyed relaxed and friendly atmosphere generated by teachers. However, it also appears that high-anxiety learners are more responsive to affective SI in comparison to low-anxiety learners (Bielak & Mystkowska-Wiertelak, in press; Parra, 2010). Given the small number of studies and their inconclusive results, the effectiveness of affective SI requires further research. One possible avenue of research is testing the usefulness of affective SI for improving strategy use and anxiety reduction in learners of English whose proficiency is repeatedly evaluated by a relatively high-stakes test. This is what the present study set out to do.

3 Research Questions

This chapter addresses the underresearched area of affective SI and its possible effects on anxiety. The following are the research questions (RQs) of the present quasi-experimental study:

RQ1   Does SI result in more frequent use of affective strategies?
RQ2   Does SI result in greater use of affective strategies in relation to an oral English-as-a-foreign-language (EFL) exam?
RQ3   Does SI result in the use of a greater range of affective strategies?
RQ4   Does SI result in lower levels of anxiety?

RQ1 and RQ2 should be clearly distinguished. RQ1 concerns general use of strategies self-reported by participants (as if they were answering the question "How often do you use particular strategies?"). RQ2 pertains to the use of strategies reported by participants in relation to two implementations of an actual EFL exam they took twice in the course of the study (as if they were answering the question: "Which strategies did you use before, during and after this exam and how much?").

4 Method

4.1 Participants

The study participants were 23 Year 1 and 2 English majors (9 males, 14 females) in a small Polish university. Their mean age was 21.6, ranging from 20 to 25. The mean time of their English instruction prior to the study was 12.0 years (range: 4–16 years). On a 2–5 scale, they self-assessed their general English proficiency at 3.95 and their speaking skill at 3.80.

The participants were taking university classes in three groups. Two of them, including 15 participants, were designated as an experimental group for the purposes of the study. One, with 8 participants, constituted a control group. The groups were comparable with respect to the means listed in the previous paragraph.

The participants were involved in the study on a voluntary basis. Nonetheless, in recognition of their effort, they were rewarded with bonus points contributing to their final grades in two university courses. However, their participation did not affect their EFL course grades or exam scores.

4.2 Exam

At the end of every academic year the English majors participating in the study take a final EFL exam which includes a speaking component. This part is an oral proficiency test in the form of a 10-min interview with two examiners during which testees answer questions concerning diverse general-interest topics covered in EFL classes throughout the year. Failure of this relatively high-stakes EFL exam may hinder promotion to the next year of university study or postpone graduation. During the exam, analytic scoring is used with a focus on pronunciation, grammar, vocabulary, and communicative efficiency/fluency.

4.3 Treatment

The treatment used in the present study was affective SI with elements of cognition- and emotion-focused anxiety reduction interventions and lasted approximately six hours. Although it was based mostly on several activities included in Gregersen and MacIntyre (2014) and a TED talk (online video) by Cuddy (2012), it was generally delivered in Polish.

The SI treatment generally followed the steps suggested by the SI models mentioned in the literature review. The participants were thus first informed of the existence of affective strategies that may be applied in language learning, especially in relation to stressful oral language exams. They also brainstormed and discussed ways of coping with anxiety provoked by such exams. A lot of strategies were modeled for them and subjected to practice. Among them were the following elements of therapy: systematic desensitization (Wolpe, 1958), relaxation techniques and cognitive restructuring.

Systematic desensitization aimed at "unlearning" anxiety induced by oral language tests. Participants created several vivid descriptions of situations connected with speaking exams which trigger their anxiety. Subsequently, they arranged them on a scale from the weakest to the strongest anxiety triggers. Because systematic desensitization was intertwined with the teaching of relaxation techniques, the participants were taught to use autogenic relaxation (relaxation of the mind and body coming "from within" and achieved by imagining peaceful places, repetition of soothing words, etc.), progressive muscle relaxation (effected by tensing different muscle groups for several seconds and then relaxing them for about half a minute), and visualization accompanied by activating other senses (vividly imagining one's presence and sensory experience in a peaceful environment). After relaxation practice, the participants were informed that the aim of desensitization is to be able to realistically imagine one's anxiety triggers without actually experiencing anxiety. Therefore, they practiced relaxation by means of one technique or another, and directly afterwards they read the graphic descriptions of anxiety triggers of their creation with an attempt to stay free of anxiety. Cognitive restructuring, another element of therapy included in the treatment, consisted in attempts to eliminate harmful views such as the one that the examiners of the EFL exam are keen on spotting errors and meting out poor grades.

The elements of therapy just described were taught together with and portrayed as components of a range of related affective strategies. In addition, the strategy of assuming confidence-boosting and stress-reducing body postures before stressful events, which is likely to have an anxiety-reducing effect and thus improve the outcomes of such events (Cuddy, 2012), was included in the intervention.

The treatment is described in greater detail in Bielak and Mystkowska-Wiertelak (in press), and the above account draws on this source. Although it included elements of behavioral and cognitive therapy, it may still be viewed as being in essence affective SI because the participants were encouraged to view the therapeutic elements as tools they may use on their own in a flexible manner in a range of situations and encouraged to do so. It is important to note that even though the strategies taught may be applied in relation to a variety of language use/learning situations, the participants were constantly reminded that their oral EFL exam is a prime example of such a situation. This is in line with the SI models mentioned above as they endorse teaching learners to transfer strategies to new contexts and tasks.

Meta-affective strategies (i.e., paying attention to, planning for, organizing and obtaining resources for, and monitoring and evaluating for affect; Oxford, 2011) were also subject to treatment to a certain extent. The participants were for example encouraged to pay attention to and plan their emotions. Therefore, in the present chapter the terms *affective SI* and *affective strategies* also cover a certain amount of meta-affective SI and use, which is justified given Oxford's (2017) insistence that strategies should not be rigidly compartmentalized.

4.4   Instruments

Data for the study was collected by means of several instruments. The first tool was the *Strategy Inventory for Language Learning* (SILL; Oxford, 1990), a well-known 5-point Likert scale focusing on the frequency of use of memory, cognitive, metacognitive, compensation, affective and social strategies. A slightly modified 50-item version was used which referred to English rather than a random second language. The reliability was satisfactory for the second administration only (Cronbach's alphas = 0.80 and 0.86 for the first and second administration, respectively). The participants were also asked (in Polish) to list additional strategies not included in the SILL which they used to "get rid of stress/anxiety related to speaking English and to foster positive emotions".

The next tool was the *Survey of Exam-Related EFL Affective Strategies* (SEREAS; Bielak and Mystkowska-Wiertelak, in press), which includes seven 4-point Likert scale items concerning affective strategy use some time and immediately before, during, and immediately after the final EFL exam. The items relate to the strategies/tactics which were subject to the study intervention (e.g., "I tried to feel the right emotions" and "I tried to somehow plan my emotions"). The anchors were 1 (*not at all true of me*) and 4 (*very true of me*). Reliability was acceptable (Cronbach alphas = 0.29 and 0.80 for the first and second administration, respectively). Additionally, the SEREAS included one open-ended item asking for listing additional strategies employed before, during and after the EFL exam "in order to experience favorable emotions (low level of stress/anxiety, self-confidence, self-efficacy, etc.)".

Another tool was *Reactions to Tests* (RTT; Sarason, 1984), one of the TA scales often used by psychologists (Zeidner, 1998). This 40-item 4-point Likert scale survey views TA in terms of four components, that is tension, worry, test-irrelevant thinking and bodily reactions, with 10 items devoted to each. The anchors are 1 (*not at all typical of me*) and 4 (*very typical of me*). The original scale was slightly modified to reflect the focus of the study on oral language tests rather than tests in general. The RTT scores were highly reliable (Cronbach's alphas = 0.90 and 0.92 for the first and second administration, respectively).

Yet another measure was the *Foreign Language Classroom Anxiety Scale* (FLCAS; Horwitz et al., 1986), a 33-item 5-point Likert scale tool which views LA in terms of its three "correlates": fear of communication, fear of negative evaluation and TA. It is worth noting, though, that only three items relate to TA, with the majority corresponding to the other two constructs. The anchors are 1 (*strongly agree*) and 5 (*strongly disagree*). The scores for this tool were highly reliable (Cronbach's alphas = 0.86 and 0.91 for the first and second administration, respectively).

The last measure were three anxometers, or "anxiety thermometers", similar to those used by MacIntyre and Gardner (1991), which are 1-item visual analog scales measuring state anxiety (SA) on a scale from 1 to 10. In particular, they tapped participants' subjective ratings of anxiety experienced immediately before, during and immediately after the EFL exam. For this reason, it may be assumed that the SA measured was to a large extent linked to TA and LA in the sense that its repeated occurrence gives rise to the establishment of the trait-like situation-specific anxieties.

The original English versions of the SILL and FLCAS were used because their language is relatively simple. Given the participants' English proficiency levels, the other tools were translated into or written in Polish to eliminate the possibility of misunderstanding. Similarly, the respondents provided all answers in their mother tongue, which was intended to ensure insightful comments not impoverished by insufficient command of English.

4.5   Procedure

The schedule of data collection, intervention and EFL exam is presented in Table 1. It should be noted that the procedure of this quasi-experimental study spanned the whole calendar year, beginning at the end of one academic year and finishing at the close of the next. At the end of the first year of their study, in June 2015 (Time 1a), the participants took the EFL exam, which was in the form of a 10-min interview of each individual testee conducted by two examiners. After the interview, the participants left the examination room for a few minutes so that the examiners could discuss their performance and calculate the final grades. Simultaneously, immediately after the exam and therefore with the levels of anxiety experienced and the strategies used immediately before, during, and just after the exam fresh in their memories, the participants filled in the anxometers and SEREAS. Next, the participants re-entered the examination room, submitted the questionnaire forms and were given customary after-exam feedback including the final grade. At the very beginning of the next academic year, their second year of study as English majors,

Table 1 The procedure of the study

Time	Activity
Time 1a (June 2015, the day of the EFL exam for freshmen)	EFL exam (interview)
	Anxometers, SEREAS
	EFL exam (announcement of grade and scores)
Time 1b (October 2015)	Cross-sectional measurement: SILL, RTT, FLCAS
October 2015–June 2016	Treatment: affective SI (experimental group)/Activities related to learner beliefs and completion of surveys related to a different study (control group)
Time 2a (June 2016, the day of the EFL exam for sophomores)	See the procedures for Time 1a
Time 2b (June 2016, two weeks after Time 2a)	Cross-sectional measurement: SILL, RTT, FLCAS

in October 2015 (Time 1b), the participants completed the remaining surveys, that is, the SILL, RTT and FLCAS.

The affective SI intervention was conducted by the present author, the participants' university teacher. It was done during nine university classes dispersed throughout the academic year and took approximately six hours in every subgroup of the experimental group (see Sect. 4.1). Simultaneously, the control group took part in several activities related to learner beliefs, which concerned the difficulty of the language they were learning and in which the hazards of holding extreme beliefs were emphasized, and completed a number of surveys required for a different study concerning anxiety experienced during language tests. After the above-mentioned SI/other activities, at the end of their sophomore year in June 2016 (Time 2a), the participants took another EFL exam, with the testing and data collection sequence identical to the one used at Time 1a. Two weeks later, at Time 2b (still in June 2016), the second administration of the SILL, RTT and FLCAS took place.

4.6   Data Analysis

To reveal general patterns, the quantitative data is first presented in the form of descriptive statistics. Because the data were not normally distributed, to address RQs 1, 2 and 4, non-parametric inferential statistics tests were used. In particular, to investigate the possible effects of the treatment on participants' strategy use and anxiety in the two groups, Mann-Whitney U tests and Wilcoxon signed ranks tests were applied to determine the statistical significance or otherwise of the between- and within-group differences, respectively.

Effect sizes were calculated for all the inferential statistics. The power and therefore the results of statistical significance testing depend to a large extent on sample sizes, which, for practical reasons, were rather small in the present study, especially in the case of the control group, which included only eight participants.

Effect sizes, which do not depend on group sizes and which show the strength of relationships between variables, may sometimes be a preferred indicator of the "practical significance" of an effect (Larson-Hall, 2010, pp. 114–115). Therefore, in this study the effect size measure r^2 belonging to the r *family* (Rosenthal, 1994) is reported. It shows how much the independent and dependent variables co-vary, which reveals what percentage of the variance of the dependent variable is explained by the independent variable.

Given the small sizes of the groups, the use of strategy types listed in the SILL other than the affective ones is included in the analysis in order to provide an additional point of reference for the examination of affective strategy use. This is done despite the fact that the RQs do not concern the use of strategy types other than the affective ones. It seems justified given the fact that in a study by Bielak and Mystkowska-Wiertelak (in press) a significant increase in the use of many strategy types not targeted by the SI intervention was detected from pre- to post-self-reports. If a similar pattern were to occur in the present study, the influence of extraneous variables such as exposure to SI in some university classes on the use of affective strategies would be highly possible.

Qualitative data were content analyzed in search of affective strategies used by the participants by the researcher and his colleague. Any disagreements in classification were resolved through discussion and reference to the relevant literature.

5   Results

5.1   The Effect of the SI Intervention on the Use of Strategies: Quantitative Results

Table 2 includes descriptive statistics of the SILL- and SEREAS-measured strategy use for the two groups before (Time 1) and after (Time 2)[1] the SI intervention, as well as the mean increases/falls in strategy use and the general indications of the results of within-group significance testing.

Before the intervention, almost all the strategy types included in the SILL were used with medium frequency (2.5–3.4; Oxford & Burry-Stock, 1995) by the two groups, with the exception of affective strategies, which were used with low frequency ($M = 2.43$, slightly below the medium frequency threshold) by the experimental group, and the compensation strategies, used with high frequency ($M = 3.56$, slightly above the medium frequency limit) by the control group. The

---

[1]In the presentation of the results, the terms *Time 1* and *Time 2* are used to refer to the pre- and post-intervention survey scores. Differentiation into Times 1a and 2a on the one hand and Times 1b and 2b on the other is not essential here and may be easily determined with reference to Table 1 depending on the survey discussed.

Table 2 Strategy use before (Time 1) and after (Time 2) the intervention and within-group significance testing

Strategies	Experimental group (n = 15)					Control group (n = 8)				
	Time 1		Time 2		Increase/fall	Time 1		Time 2		Increase/fall
	M	SD	M	SD	(M)	M	SD	M	SD	(M)
Memory (SILL)	2.67	0.41	2.66	0.57	−0.01	2.90	0.52	2.67	0.41	−0.23
Cognitive (SILL)	3.30	0.55	3.46	0.68	0.16	3.30	0.30	3.14	0.55	−0.16
Compensation (SILL)	3.06	0.79	3.34	0.73	0.28	3.56	0.44	3.06	0.79	−0.50
Metacognitive (SILL)	3.49	0.36	3.28	0.77	−0.21	3.19	0.53	3.49	0.36	0.30
Affective (SILL)	2.43	0.49	2.84	0.50	0.41**	2.75	0.51	2.43	0.49	−0.32
Social (SILL)	3.26	0.75	3.16	0.92	−0.10	3.67	0.67	3.26	0.75	−0.41
Affective (SEREAS)	2.32	0.46	2.92	0.60	0.60**	2.53	0.30	2.37	0.79	−0.16

Note **$p < 0.01$

affective strategies were used the least frequently in comparison to other strategy types in both groups. Similarly to the affective strategies included in the SILL, the affective strategies used in relation to the exam (measured by the SEREAS) were used by both groups only to a moderate extent: The mean scores fell in the middle of the 4-point scale, between the scores of 2.00 and 3.00. Thus, the medium or even below-medium use of affective strategies at Time 1 pointed to the potential usefulness of the SI offered in the study's intervention.

Obviously, of special interest for this study is the application of affective strategies, whose use prior to and post the SI is additionally shown in Figs. 1 and 2. In comparison to all the other strategies used by both groups, the use of these strategies increased the most in the experimental group from Time 1 to Time 2. In particular, in this group the frequency of affective strategy use measured by the SILL increased by 0.41 and reached the medium level, and the use of the SEREAS-measured EFL-exam-related affective strategies by 0.60. As Figs. 1 and 2 illustrate, the use of these strategies in the control group actually fell, by 0.32 and 0.16, respectively, with the SILL-measured affective strategies being as a consequence used with low frequency at Time 2. All the other increases in either group

Fig. 1 Affective strategy use (SILL)

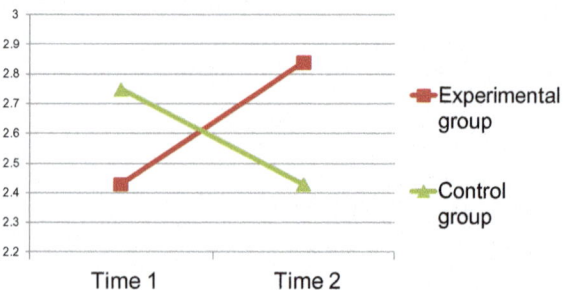

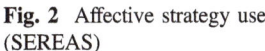
Fig. 2 Affective strategy use (SEREAS)

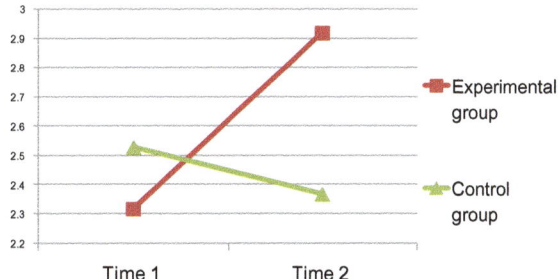

were considerably lower than those for the affective strategies in the experimental group (the closest one was by 0.30 for the use of metacognitive strategies by the controls), with the use of many other strategy types in both groups experiencing rather negligible increases or even falls.

A series of Mann-Whitney U tests did not reveal any significant differences between the two groups in the use of any strategy types prior to SI, including the SILL-measured $(Z = -1.69, \ p = 0.10, \ r^2 = 0.12)$ and the SEREAS-tapped $(Z = -1.50, \ p = 0.15, \ r^2 = 0.09)$ affective strategies. Somewhat surprisingly, given the considerable increases mentioned above and the within-group tests discussed in what follows, no significant affective strategy use differences between the groups were discovered at Time 2, either (SILL: $Z = -1.07, p = 0.29, r^2 = 0.05$; SEREAS: $Z = -1.57, p = 0.13, r^2 = 0.10$). What may go some way towards explaining this is the fact that the control group used the SILL-measured affective strategies more often than the experimental group at Time 1, with the r^2 effect size of 0.12 being medium according to Cohen's (1987) tentative guidelines,[2] while at Time 2 the experimental group used these strategies more often than the controls (see the statistics in the previous sentence), with the effect size of 0.05 being small. These data show that the medium effect size for Group with respect to the SILL-measured affective strategies existing at Time 1 in favor of the controls disappeared by Time 2. Thus, possibly, the between-group difference in the use of affective strategies in favor of the controls at Time 1 revealed by the medium effect size rather than statistical significance may have been responsible for the absence of a significant difference between the groups at Time 2 despite the experimental group's increased use of the strategies in question. It should be noted that despite the controls' somewhat greater use of the affective strategies in comparison with the experimental group at Time 1, the ceiling effect for the former preventing their increased strategy use at Time 2 is unlikely given that their use of affective strategies at Time 1 was merely medium.

In addition to the investigation of the between-group differences, the within-group changes in the use of the strategy types over time were also examined

---

[2]Cohen's (1987) guidelines for the interpretation of r^2 effect sizes that were used are as follows: small effect = 0.01, medium effect = 0.09, large effect = 0.25.

to further explore the possible effects of the treatment. The Wilcoxon signed ranks tests revealed only two significant differences, which occurred in the experimental group and were characterized by very large effect sizes. These were the increases in SILL-measured ($Z = -3.14$, $p < 0.01$, $r^2 = 0.70$) and SEREAS-measured ($Z = -3.11$, $p < 0.01$, $r^2 = 0.69$) affective strategy use mentioned above. When it comes to the other differences in strategy use over time, although none were statistically significant, a few were characterized by medium effect sizes, the highest reaching 0.17. However, they did not concern the use of affective strategies used by the control group, the effect sizes for all of them were far lower than those for affective strategies used by the experimental group, and some of them demonstrated falls rather than increases in strategy use. All of this suggests that only the increases in the use of affective strategies by the experimental group were relatively strong.

5.2   The Effect of the SI Intervention on the Use of Strategies: Qualitative Results

Tables 3 and 4 present the general strategies and particular tactics used by the participants in the two groups before and after the intervention. Table 3 focuses on general self-reported strategies used to reduce anxiety and generate positive emotions. Table 4 includes the strategies which the participants reported as used in relation to the two implementations of the actual EFL exam at the end of their first and second year at university. Of particular interest are those strategies and tactics which were used at Time 2 and not at Time 1 by members of particular groups as at least some of them were presumably introduced into the participants' strategic repertoires as a result of the intervention. These strategies are given in italics in Tables 3 and 4.

With respect to general strategy use (Table 3) the following strategies and tactics were used in the experimental group after the intervention, but not before it: *breathing exercises* (3 participants), *progressive muscle relaxation* (2), *talking to friends, jokes* (2), *assertive body postures and facial expressions* (2), *techniques from the intervention* (it is not clear which ones) and *cognitive restructuring: imagining that one has to do a penalty shot in football; that "one will manage and that the examiners are OK"* (2), and *focusing on the task and language (rather than on emotions)* (2). The following were used in the same group only at Time 2 in relation to the EFL exam (Table 4) *eating* (2), *progressive muscle relaxation* (2), *visualization* (1), *massage* (1), *cognitive restructuring: imagining that one has to do a penalty shot in football; that "one will manage and that the examiners are OK"* (2), *cherishing one's language successes* (1), and *talking about emotions* (1).

With respect to general strategy use (Table 3), the following strategies and tactics were used in the control group after the intervention, but not before it: *talking to friends, jokes* (1), *doing something else* (1), *smiling* (1), and *focusing on*

Table 3 General use of affective strategies and tactics before (Time 1) and after (Time 2) the intervention (in brackets there are numbers of participants using particular strategies)

Experimental group	Control group
Time 1	
• Self-encouragement to speak despite errors (8) • Preparation, practice (5) • Relaxation (3): thinking about something else (2), doing something else (2), music (1), eating (1) • Positive thinking (3) • Desensitization: imagining oneself talk to boost self-confidence (1) • Cognitive restructuring: repeating to oneself that errors are not so important (1) • Cherishing one's language successes (1) • Comparing one's errors with the errors of others (1) • Compensation strategies (1)	• Self-encouragement to speak despite errors (4) • Relaxation (3): thinking about something else (2), music (1), visualization (1), breathing exercises (1) • Positive thinking (2) • Preparation, practice (1) • Cherishing one's language successes (1) and other successes (1)
Time 2	
• Relaxation (9): doing something else (5), *breathing exercises (3), progressive muscle relaxation (2), talking to friends, jokes (2), assertive body postures and facial expressions (2), techniques from the intervention (1),* thinking about something else (1), music (1), eating (1) • Preparation, practice (6) • Self-encouragement to speak despite errors (4) • Positive thinking (3) • *Cognitive restructuring: imagining that one has to do a penalty shot in football; that "one will manage and that the examiners are OK" (2)* • *Focusing on the task and language (rather than on emotions) (2)* • Cherishing one's language successes (1)	• Relaxation (6): music (3), thinking about something else (1), *talking to friends, jokes (1), doing something else (1), smiling (1)* • Self-encouragement to speak despite errors (1) • Positive thinking (1) • Preparation, practice (1) • *Focusing on the task (1)*

the task (1). Just one tactic was used in the same group only at Time 2 in relation to the EFL exam (Table 4), namely *preparation, practice* (2).

Some of the strategies and tactics disappeared from Time 1 to Time 2 from the use by one group or another, but they were much less numerous than the "new" ones used by the experimental group and the "disappearance rate" was very similar for both groups. This is taken to reflect natural use of some strategies to the exclusion of others at particular times.

Table 4 EFL exam-related use of affective strategies and tactics before (Time 1) and after (Time 2) the intervention (in brackets there are numbers of participants using particular strategies)

Experimental group	Control group
Time 1	
• Relaxation (14): talking to friends, jokes (6), breathing exercises (5), pacing along the corridor (2), music (2), doing something else (2), autogenic relaxation (1), thinking about something else (1), closing eyes (1), sleeping well (1), long shower (1) • Positive thinking (4) • Focusing on the task and language (2) • Preparation, practice (1) • Talking about the exam (1) • Trying to control emotions (1)	• Relaxation (7): talking to friends, jokes (3), breathing exercises (2), thinking about something else (2), doing something else (2), music (1), coffee (1), tranquilizer (1), beer (1) • Focusing on the task and language (1) • Positive thinking (1) • Cognitive restructuring: repeating to oneself that the exam may be retaken (1) • Cherishing one's language successes (1) • Talking about the exam (1)
Time 2	
• Relaxation (12): talking to friends, jokes (8), music (6), breathing exercises (5), *eating* (2), *progressive muscle relaxation* (2), *visualization* (1), autogenic relaxation (1), thinking about something else (1), doing something else (1), *massage* (1), nap (1), hot shower (1) • *Cognitive restructuring: imagining that one has to do a penalty shot in football; that "one will manage and that the examiners are OK"* (2) • Focusing on the task and language (rather than on emotions) (2) • Preparation, practice (1) • Positive thinking (1) • *Cherishing one's language successes* (1) • Talking about the exam (1) • *Talking about emotions* (1)	• Relaxation (7): music (2), thinking about something else (2), talking to friends, jokes (1), breathing exercises (1), doing something else (1) • Positive thinking (3) • *Preparation, practice* (2) • Cherishing one's language successes (1) • Talking about the exam (1)

5.3 The Effect of the SI Intervention on Anxiety

Table 5 includes the descriptive statistics of the anxiety scores obtained at Times 1 and 2, as well as the mean increases/falls in anxiety and the general indications of the results of within-group significance testing. The levels of TA measured by the RTT ($N = 23$, $M = 2.20$) and LA measured by the FLCAS ($N = 23$, $M = 2.87$) before the intervention were similar to those obtained in earlier studies of a similar population (Pawlak, 2011; Bielak & Mystkowska-Wiertelak, in press). This means that, as expected, the participants displayed moderate levels of anxiety.

The anxiety scores for the two groups at Time 1 were comparable, with the exception of the SA-during-the-exam score, which was by 1.42 higher for the experimental group. This difference was largely eliminated by the decrease in this

Table 5 Anxiety before (Time 1) and after (Time 2) the intervention with within-group significance testing

Anxiety types	Experimental group (n = 15)					Control group (n = 8)				
	Time 1		Time 2		Increase/fall (M)	Time 1		Time 2		Increase/fall (M)
	M	SD	M	SD		M	SD	M	SD	
TA	2.15	0.35	2.20	0.48	0.05	2.29	0.47	2.23	0.48	−0.06
LA#	3.12	0.58	2.90	0.61	−0.22*	3.13	0.45	3.09	0.44	−0.04
SA (before exam)	7.40	1.55	6.13	2.03	−1.27*	7.25	2.55	4.88	2.03	−2.37*
SA (during exam)	6.67	2.50	5.67	2.38	−1.00*	5.25	3.06	5.25	2.25	0.00
SA (after exam)	3.73	2.66	2.10	0.76	−1.63*	3.75	2.76	3.88	1.81	0.13

Note TA Test anxiety; LA Language anxiety; SA State anxiety
#The FLCAS means were adjusted to ensure uniform directionality
*$p < 0.05$

anxiety in the experimental group by 1.00 by Time 2, compared to no change in this SA score for the controls. Two more decreases in the anxiety of the participants in the experimental condition were quite large and exceeded 1.00, that is those in SA before (by 1.27) and after the exam (by 1.63). Only one comparable decrease (by 2.37) occurred in the control group for SA before the exam. It should be noted that none of the large decreases concerned the TA and LA trait anxieties.

Mann-Whitney U tests did not reveal any significant differences between the groups at Time 1 (TA: $Z = -0.93$, $p = 0.35$, $r^2 = 0.03$; LA: $Z = -0.25$, $p = 0.82$, $r^2 = 0.00$; SA [before exam]: $Z = -0.20$, $p = 0.87$, $r^2 = 0.00$; SA [during exam]: $Z = -1.10$, $p = 0.29$, $r^2 = 0.05$; SA [after exam]: $Z = -0.00$, $p = 1.00$, $r^2 = 0.00$). At Time 2 most of the between group differences were not significant, either (TA: $Z = -0.19$, $p = 0.87$, $r^2 = 0.00$; LA: $Z = -0.80$, $p = 0.42$, $r^2 = 0.02$; SA [before exam]: $Z = -1.17$, $p = 0.26$, $r^2 = 0.05$; SA [during exam]: $Z = -0.36$, $p = 0.72$, $r^2 = 0.00$), but the one in SA after the exam, when the experimental group was less anxious than the control group, was in fact significant ($Z = -2.40$, $p < 0.05$, $r^2 = 0.25$), with a large effect size. This seems to be the result of the treatment as in the case of the experimental group several within-group differences concerning anxiety decreases over time were registered, including SA after the exam (LA: $Z = -2.10$, $p < 0.05$, $r^2 = 0.29$; SA [before exam]: $Z = -2.37$, $p < 0.05$, $r^2 = 0.43$; SA [during exam]: $Z = -2.21$, $p < 0.05$, $r^2 = 0.54$; SA [after exam]: $Z = -2.16$, $p < 0.05$, $r^2 = 0.39$). All of these differences were characterized by very large effect sizes. In the case of the controls, only one such within-group-anxiety-decrease difference was registered (SA [before exam]: $Z = -1.97$, $p < 0.05$, $r^2 = 0.48$), also with a large effect size. This anxiety reduction was probably the effect of the participant's greater familiarity with the exam procedures in their sophomore year compared to the exam one year before.

6 Discussion

The first two research questions (RQ1: Does SI result in more frequent use of affective strategies?; RQ2: Does SI result in greater use of affective strategies in relation to an oral EFL exam?) concerned the effect of affective SI on the general frequency of affective strategy use and the intensity of their use in relation to a particular EFL exam. The results indicate that the SI intervention did indeed bring about the expected benefit of increased use of affective strategies not only in terms of general frequency but also before, during and after a relatively important EFL exam. What supports this interpretation is the fact that the use of other strategy types included in the SILL did not increase as substantially as the use of affective strategies. This makes the possibility of the effect of extraneous factors other than the SI intervention rather unlikely, contrary to what was found in another study involving a similar intervention (Bielak & Mystkowska-Wiertelak, in press). The results thus contribute to the body of research which has confirmed the moderate effectiveness of SI in general (Plonsky, 2011) and in terms of greater or better strategy use in particular (e.g., De Silva & Graham, 2015; Sarafianou & Gavriilidou, 2015). Specifically, the study has demonstrated the teachability of the strategy type, the teaching of which has rarely been investigated in relation to language learning, that is affective strategies (Plonsky, 2011). It has done so with respect to a particular context of a university English department in Poland, where EFL testing is generally highly anxiety-inducing, thus joining in the trend of contextualizing strategy use research (Oxford, 2011; Oxford & Amerstorfer, in press).

The third research question (RQ3: Does SI result in the use of a greater range of affective strategies?) concerned the effect of affective SI on the range of strategies used and was investigated through qualitative analysis. It is clear from the qualitative data presented in Sect. 5.2 that the experimental group used a much greater range of affective strategies than the control group after the intervention, both in absolute numbers and in terms of "new" strategies not used before the intervention. The difference in absolute numbers is especially telling in the case of strategy use in relation to the actual EFL exam because before the intervention the numbers of strategies used were comparable for the two groups while the list of the strategies used at Time 2 by the experimental group is almost twice as long. Importantly, a lot of the "new" strategies used by the experimental group at Time 2 such as progressive muscle relaxation, assuming assertive body postures or talking about emotions were specifically introduced and quite intensively practiced in the treatment. Admittedly, they were used by small numbers of participants; this seems natural, though, because the ones using them were probably the most anxious ones (Bielak & Mystkowska-Wiertelak, in press). The control group did not introduce these strategies at Time 2, which supports the finding that, similarly to SI concerning other strategy types (Atay & Ozbulgan, 2007), affective SI is effective in increasing learners' range of affective strategies.

The present study has in fact shown that there is a "demand" for affective SI, at least among the more highly anxious learners, in the exam-centered milieu of the Polish educational system, and in university language departments in particular. Why else would some participants embrace the new strategies and tactics after the intervention, especially when dealing with the anxiety-provoking, actual exam? The point is that they reported using the strategies introduced in the intervention not only generally (as if perfunctorily saying: "I use the strategies with X frequency") but also "in the heat of the battle" of an actual, highly stressful language exam, which makes their self-reports highly plausible. As Cohen (2014) writes, "once learners move away from actual instances of language learning or language use behavior, they may also tend to become less accurate about their strategy behavior (Cohen, 1987)". In focusing on the range of affective strategies used by participants, the present study has also moved beyond the examination of the mere frequency of strategy use, thus responding to the calls to do so (Cohen, 2014; Oxford, 2011).

It should be admitted that the intervention did not result in the use of some strategies (e.g., the use of desensitization) introduced in the treatment. It is possible that desensitization is too time-consuming to be used frequently in a strategic manner and should only be part of therapeutic interventions, which is one implication of the present study concerning the make-up of affective SI.

The fourth research question (RQ4: Does SI result in lower levels of anxiety?) looked at the effect of the affective SI treatment on participants' anxiety (TA, LA and SA). It cannot be unequivocally concluded from the study's quantitative results that the intervention and the use of strategies it has brought about reduced the experimental participants' anxiety. The reason is that the intervention clearly affected the significance and size of the difference between the groups from pre- to post-treatment only with respect to SA after the EFL exam, to the exclusion of other SAs as well as TA and LA. However, the after-exam-SA significant large-sized between-group difference revealing anxiety reduction in the experimental group and the more numerous large-sized decreases in LA and SA of the experimental group (three such decreases) compared to the control group (one such decrease) constitute some, relatively weak and preliminary, evidence for the effectiveness of affective SI of the sort implemented in the study for anxiety reduction. Research clearly shows that various therapeutic and non-therapeutic interventions may reduce the levels of anxiety (Hembree, 1988; Kralova et al., 2017; Zeidner, 1998); the relative weakness of the evidence obtained in this study may have resulted from the fact the treatment was not very extensive (it lasted approximately 6 h) in comparison to many other studies of anxiety reduction interventions (e.g., Faber, 2010; Kralova et al., 2017). Also, as affective SI focused on anxiety reduction meets the needs of and therefore affects mostly highly-anxious learners rather than low-anxiety ones (Bielak & Mystkowska-Wiertelak, in press), the small group sizes and the probably small number of anxious learners may have prevented the manifestation of its anxiety-reducing effects in the present study. Further research is needed to investigate the role of affective SI in anxiety reduction.

7   Conclusions

The present quasi-experimental study has contributed to the still small body of research on the effects of affective SI. The finding that such SI results in greater affective strategy use in the context of an educational system heavily focused on anxiety-provoking language testing such as the Polish one is good news to language teachers, who in the absence of dedicated learning-to-learn programs might include some affective SI in their everyday teaching practice. However, contrary to the present study, this should rather be done in the target language so that the time devoted to affective SI is not wasted for low-anxiety learners who simply do not need such strategies. If SI transpires in the target language, such learners may still benefit from it languagewise, especially given the fact that emotions are a popular topic in the foreign language classroom. The study has also exposed the need for more research concerning the links between affective SI and test and language anxiety; it is still not clear to what extent such SI directly translates into the mitigation of negative affect.

In closing, a few limitations of the present study will be mentioned with a view to eliminating them from further research. An obvious limitation is the small sample, especially the number of participants in the control group, which has resulted from high participant mortality in a study spanning the whole academic year. Another limitation is that strategies for positive emotions were not really investigated due to their absence from the SILL and SEREAS and their relative neglect by the participants in the open-ended parts of the surveys. With the growing interest in positive emotions in relation to language learning (Dewaele & MacIntyre, 2014, 2016; MacIntyre, Gregersen, & Mercer, 2016) new instruments with a greater focus on positive emotions, such as the one designed by Gkonou and Oxford (2016), should be increasingly used in individual differences and strategy research. Another limitation is that the study focuses only on the effects of SI viewed as products (strategy use and anxiety) and neglects the effects on the learning process (e.g., greater concentration and improved attitudes to FL learning; Chen, 2007), the investigation of which might be a particularly interesting endeavor given the lack of an unequivocal effect of SI on anxiety in the present study.

Acknowledgements I thank the anonymous reviewer as well as the editors of this volume for their insightful comments which helped improve the chapter. Obviously, I take full responsibility for the errors which remain.

References

Aida, Y. (1994). Examination of Horwitz, Horwitz, and Cope's construct of foreign language anxiety: The case of students of Japanese. *Modern Language Journal, 78,* 155–168.

Atay, D., & Ozbulgan, C. (2007). Memory strategy instruction, contextual learning and ESP vocabulary recall. *English for Specific Purposes, 26,* 39–51. doi:10.1016/j.esp.2006.01.002.

Bielak, J., & Mystkowska-Wiertelak, A. (in press). Investigating English majors' affective and meta-affective strategy use, test anxiety, and strategy training. In R. Oxford & C. Amerstorfer (Eds.), *Situating strategy use: Language learning strategies and individual learner characteristics*. London: Bloomsbury.

Chan, M. L. (2014). Strategy instruction for Macao EFL students. *American Journal of Educational Research, 2,* 990–1004. doi:10.12691/education-2-11-1.

Chaury, P. (2015). The effects of strategy instruction on reading comprehension in English as a foreign language. *Concordia Working Papers in Applied Linguistics, 6.* Retrieved from http://doe.concordia.ca/copal/documents/1_Chaury_Patrick.pdf.

Chen, Y. (2007). Learning to learn: The impact of strategy training. *ELT Journal, 61*(1), 20–29. doi:10.1093/elt/ccl041.

Cizek, G., & Burg, S. (2006). *Addressing test anxiety in a high stakes environment.* Thousand Oaks, CA: Corwin.

Cohen, J. (1987). *Statistical power analysis for the behavioral sciences* (2nd ed.) Hillsdale, NJ: Lawrence Erlbaum.

Cohen, A. D. (2014). *Strategies in learning and using a second language* (2nd ed.). Abingdon: Routledge.

Cuddy, A. (2012). *Your body language shapes who you are: TEDtalks.* Video file. http://www.ted.com/talks/amy_cuddy_your_body_language_shapes_who_you_are. Accessed January 23, 2014.

De Silva, R. (2015). Writing strategy instruction: Its impact on writing in a second language for academic purposes. *Language Teaching Research, 19*(3), 301–323.

De Silva, R., & Graham, S. (2015). The effects of strategy instruction on writing strategy use for students of different proficiency levels. *System, 53,* 47–59.

Dewaele, J.-M. (2007). The effect of multilingualism, sociobiographical, and situational factors on communicative anxiety and foreign language anxiety of mature language learners. *International Journal of Bilingualism, 11,* 391–409.

Dewaele, J.-M., & MacIntyre, P. D. (2014). Two faces of Janus? Anxiety and enjoyment in the foreign language classroom. *Studies in Second Language Learning and Teaching, 4,* 237–274.

Dewaele, J.-M., & MacIntyre, P. D. (2016). Foreign language enjoyment and foreign language classroom anxiety: The right and left feet of the language learner. In P. D. MacIntyre, T. Gregersen, & S. Mercer (Eds.), *Positive psychology in SLA* (pp. 193–214). Bristol: Multilingual Matters.

Ergene, T. (2003). Effective interventions on test anxiety reduction. *School Psychology International, 24*(3), 313–328.

Faber, G. (2010). Enhancing orthographic competencies and reducing domain-specific test anxiety: The systematic use of algorithmic and self-instructional task formats in remedial spelling training. *International Journal of Special Education, 25,* 78–88.

Gardner, R. C., & MacIntyre, P. D. (1993). A Student's contributions to second language learning: Part II. Affective variables. *Language Teaching, 26,* 1–11.

Gkonou, Ch., & Oxford, R. L. (2016). Managing Your Emotions for Language Learning Questionnaire. Version 4.1. In R. L. Oxford (Ed.), *Teaching and researching language learning strategies* (pp. 317–33). New York: Routledge.

Gregersen, T., & MacIntyre, P. D. (2014). *Capitalizing on language learners' individuality: From premise to practice.* Clevedon: Multilingual Matters.

Grenfell, M., & Harris, V. (1999). *Modern languages and learning strategies: In theory and practice.* London: Routledge.

Hembree, R. (1988). Correlates, causes, effects, and treatment of test anxiety. *Review of Educational Research, 58,* 47–77.

Hupkova, M. (2011). *Developing social abilities in helping professions.* Bratislava: Iris.

Kralova, Z., Skorvagova, E., Tirpakova, A., & Markechova, D. (2017). Reducing student teachers' foreign language pronunciation anxiety through psycho-social training. *System, 65,* 49–60.

Horwitz, E. K. (2010). Foreign and second language anxiety. *Language Teaching, 43*(2), 154–167. doi:10.1017/S026144480999036X.

Horwitz, E. K. (2016). Reflections on Horwitz (1986). Preliminary evidence for the validity and reliability of a foreign language anxiety scale. *TESOL Quarterly, 50,* 932–935. doi:10.1002/tesq.295.

Horwitz, E. K. (2017). On the misreading of Horwitz, Horwitz, and Cope (1986) and the need to balance anxiety research and the experiences of anxious language learners. In C. Gkonou, M. Daubney, & J.-M. Dewaele (Eds.), *New insights into language anxiety: Theory, research and educational implications [Kindle version].* Clevedon: Multilingual Matters.

Horwitz, E. K., Horwitz, M. B., & Cope, J. (1986). Foreign language classroom anxiety. *Modern Language Journal, 70,* 125–132.

Iwai, C. (2006). *Linguistic and pedagogical values of teaching communication strategies: Integrating the notion of communication strategies with studies of second language acquisition.* Hiroshima, Japan: Hiroshima City University.

Larson-Hall, J. (2010). *A guide to doing statistics in second language research using SPSS.* New York: Routledge.

Lee, E. J. (2016). Reducing international graduate students' language anxiety through oral pronunciation corrections. *System, 56,* 78–95.

Macaro, E. (2001). Learning strategies in second and foreign language classrooms. London: Continuum.

MacIntyre, P. D. (2007). Willingness to communicate in the second language: Understanding the decision to speak as a volitional process. *Modern Language Journal, 91,* 564–576.

MacIntyre, P. D. (2017). An overview of language anxiety research and trends in its development. In C. Gkonou, M. Daubney, & J.-M. Dewaele (Eds.), *New insights into language anxiety: Theory, research and educational implications* (pp. 11–30). Clevedon: Multilingual Matters.

MacIntyre, P. D., & Gardner, R. C. (1991). Language anxiety: Its relationship to other anxieties and to the processing in native and second languages. *Language Learning, 41,* 513–534.

MacIntyre, P. D., & Gardner, R. C. (1994). The subtle effects of language anxiety on cognitive processing in the second language. *Language Learning, 44,* 283–305.

MacIntyre, P. D., Gregersen, T., & Mercer, S. (Eds.). (2016). *Positive psychology in SLA.* Bristol: Multilingual Matters.

Manoli, P., Papadopoulou, M., & Metallidou, P. (2016). Investigating the immediate and delayed effects of multiple-reading strategy instruction in primary EFL classrooms. *System, 56,* 54–65.

Nguyen, L. T. C., & Gu, Y. (2013). Strategy-based instruction: A learner-focused approach to developing learner autonomy. *Language Teaching Research, 17*(1), 9–30.

O'Malley, J. M., & Chamot, A. U. (1990). *Learning strategies in second language acquisition.* Cambridge: Cambridge University Press.

Oxford, R. L. (1990). *Language learning strategies: What every teacher should know.* Boston: Heinle & Heinle.

Oxford, R. L. (2011). *Teaching and researching language learning strategies.* Harlow: Longman.

Oxford, R. L. (2017). *Teaching and researching language learning strategies: Self-regulation in context* (2nd ed.). New York: Routledge.

Oxford, R. L., & Amerstorfer, C. M. (Eds.). (in press). *Language learning strategies and individual learner characteristics: Situating strategy use in diverse contexts.* Bloomsbury.

Oxford, R. L., & Burry-Stock, J. L. (1995). Assessing the use of language learning strategies worldwide with the ESL/EFL version of the Strategy Inventory for Language Learning (SILL). *System, 23,* 153–175.

Parra, Y. J. F. (2010). Explicit teaching of socio-affective language learning strategies to beginner EFL students. *Íkala, revista de lenguaje y cultura, 15,* 145–169.

Pawlak, M. (2010). Designing and piloting a tool for the measurement of the use of pronunciation learning strategies. *Research in Language, 8,* 189–202.

Pawlak, M. (2011). Anxiety as a factor influencing the use of language learning strategies. In M. Pawlak (Ed.), *Extending the boundaries of research on second language learning and teaching* (pp. 149–165). Heidelberg: Springer.

Plonsky, L. (2011). The effectiveness of second language strategy instruction: A meta-analysis. *Language Learning, 61,* 993–1038.

Rosenthal, R. (1994). Parametric measures of effect size. In H. Cooper & L. V. Hedges (Eds.), *The handbook of research synthesis* (pp. 231–244). New York: Russell Sage Foundation.

Rossiter, M. J. (2003). The effects of affective strategy training in the ESL classroom. *TESL-EJ, 7* (2). Retrieved from http://www.tesl-ej.org/wordpress/issues/volume7/ej26/ej26a2/.

Sarafianou, A., & Gavriilidou, Z. (2015). The effect of strategy-based instruction on strategy use by upper-secondary Greek students of EFL. *Electronic Journal of Foreign Language Teaching, 12*(1), 21–34.

Sarason, I. G. (1984). Stress, anxiety, and cognitive interference: Reactions to tests. *Journal of Personality and Social Psychology, 46,* 929–938.

Shams, A. N. (2005). *The use of computerized pronunciation practice in the reduction of foreign language classroom anxiety* (Doctoral dissertation). Florida State University, Tallahassee, USA.

Sheorey, R., & Mokhtari, K. (2001). Differences in the metacognitive awareness of reading strategies among native and non-native readers. *System, 29,* 431–449.

Spielberger, Ch. D, Anton, W. D., & Bedell, J. (1976). The nature and treatment of test anxiety. In M. Zuckermann & Ch. D Spielberger (Eds.), *Emotions and anxiety: New concepts, methods, and applications* (pp. 317–344). Hillsdale, NJ: Erlbaum.

Spielberger, Ch. D., & Vagg, P. R. (1995). Test anxiety: A transactional process. In Ch. D. Spielberger & P. R. Vagg (Eds.), *Test anxiety: Theory, assessment, and treatment* (pp. 3–14). Washington, DC: Taylor & Francis.

Vandergrift, L., & Tafaghodatari, M. H. (2010). Teaching L2 learners how to listen does make a Difference: An empirical study. *Language Learning, 60,* 470–497.

von der Embse, N., Barterian, J., & Segool, N. (2013). Test anxiety interventions for children and adolescents: A systematic review of treatment studies from 2000–2010. *Psychology in the Schools, 50,* 57–71. doi:10.1002/pits.21660.

Weems, C. F., Taylor, L. K., Costa, N. M., Marks, A. B., Romano, D. M., Verrett, S. L., & Brown, D. M. (2009). Effect of a school-based test anxiety intervention in ethnic minority youth exposed to Hurricane Katrina. *Journal of Applied Developmental Psychology, 30,* 218–226. doi:10.1016/j.appdev.2008.11.005.

Wolpe, J. (1958). *Psychotherapy by reciprocal inhibition.* Stanford, CA: Stanford University Press.

Woodrow, L. (2006). Anxiety and speaking English as a second language. *RELC Journal, 37,* 308–328.

Young, D. J. (Ed.). (1999). *Affect in foreign language and second language learning: A practical guide to creating a low anxiety classroom atmosphere.* Boston: McGraw-Hill.

Zeidner, M. (1998). *Test anxiety: The state of the art.* New York: Kluwer.

Author Biography

Jakub Bielak, Ph.D. is Assistant Professor in the Department of English Studies, Adam Mickiewicz University, Poznań/Kalisz, Poland and Senior Lecturer at State University of Applied Sciences, Konin, Poland. He has done research into applied cognitive linguistics, form-focused instruction and individual differences in language learning. He has authored and co-authored one book and several articles in journals and edited volumes, and co-edited two edited volumes.

Characteristics of Good Foreign Language Educators Across Cultural Boundaries

Marek Derenowski

Abstract Identifying the characteristics of high-quality foreign language teachers has been a matter that has occupied researchers and teacher trainers for decades, resulting in an assortment of diverse sets of qualities presented in various publications. However, these sets of characteristics differ depending on the cultural context they exist in. The role and position of a teacher are closely linked to existing cultural values which impact the ways educators and students are supposed to behave. Furthermore, educational objectives are often perceived in diverse ways. Nevertheless, the author of this article strongly believes that despite flagrant culture-related differences, there exist culture-indifferent characteristics of effective teachers which may be either transferred between cultures or rediscovered in one's native cultural reality. Therefore, the first part of the chapter tackles Western and Eastern educational philosophies and the most striking, culture-based differences between foreign language teacher characteristics in Eastern and Western cultures. The study described in the following section aimed at identifying the characteristics of good foreign language teachers that pertain to every cultural environment or that may transcend from one culture to another. The data was gathered with the use of interviews. The final section contains conclusions and suggestions for further research.

Keywords Good language teacher · Reflectivity · Motivation · Teacher development · Cultural differences

1 Introduction

Identifying the characteristics of good foreign language teachers has occupied researchers and teacher trainers for decades, resulting in an assortment of diverse traits. However, these sets of good foreign language teacher characteristics are not

M. Derenowski (✉)
State University of Applied Sciences, Konin, Poland
e-mail: derenosiu73@gmail.com

© Springer International Publishing AG 2018   251
M. Pawlak and A. Mystkowska-Wiertelak (eds.), *Challenges of Second and Foreign Language Education in a Globalized World*, Second Language Learning and Teaching, DOI 10.1007/978-3-319-66975-5_15

entirely homogenous and are undoubtedly influenced by cultural context. Sheorey (2006) points out that the studies on teacher and learner role expectations revealed that educators and their learners who come from different cultures have different expectations about their roles in a foreign language classroom. The role and position of a teacher are linked to existing cultural values which influence the ways teachers and students are expected to behave. For example, American educators and students expressed similar opinions on their respective roles, whereas the role expectations of Japanese students and their American professors differed to a large extent. Furthermore, educational objectives are often perceived in diverse ways. While in some cultures the objective of education is to develop a critical mind, in others a critical mind is viewed as unnecessary. In these countries students are supposed to try to learn as much as possible from the older generation and only when young people are fully initiated may they express their own ideas (Wursten & Jacobs, 2013). However, the author strongly believes that despite flagrant culture-related differences, there exist culture-indifferent good foreign language teacher characteristics which may either exist in one's native culture or may be transferred from one culture to another. Therefore, on the one hand, the chapter touches upon most striking, culture-based differences between foreign language teacher characteristics in Eastern and Western cultures. On the other hand, it aims at identifying the successful foreign language teacher characteristics that subsist in every cultural environment or that may be transferred from one culture to another.

2   Western and Eastern Educational Philosophies

It seems evident that different places have their own different cultures. Generally, Western philosophy of education comprises two major schools and has its roots in Athens, Rome and Judeo-Christianity, whereas Eastern philosophy derives from Islam, Confucianism, Taoism and Mahayana Buddhism. Eastern and Western cultures have distinct differences in their ways of developing and shaping an individual in terms of skills and attitudes. Consequently, different cultures have different philosophies, which may result in different ways of educating the next generations (Hassan, Jamaludin, Sulaiman, & Baki, 2017). When both schools are compared, it may be concluded that Western cultures since ancient Greeks such as Plato, Aristotle and Socrates have stressed active learning and rational thinking, whereas Eastern cultures based on Islam, Buddhism, Confucianism, Hinduism and Taoism have focused on more passive learning (Onn, 2009).

These cultural differences can be observed when one of Hofstede's (1997) culture dimensions, *power distance*, is taken into consideration. Power distance may be understood as the extent to which less powerful members of society accept the fact that power is distributed unequally. As a result, in *high power-distance* cultures everybody has his or her rightful place in society and old age and status are respected. Conversely, in *low power-distance cultures* people try to look younger and more powerful. Countries like the US, Canada, the UK, all Scandinavian

Table 1 Implications of Power Distance on teaching (Wustern & Jacobs, 2013, p. 8)

Low	High
Student centered. Focus on initiative	Teacher centered. Focus on order
Teacher expects students to initiate communication	Students expect teacher to initiate communication
Teacher expects students to find their own ways	Student expects teacher to show ways
Students allowed to contradict and criticize	Teacher never contradicted nor criticized
Effectiveness results from two-way communication	Effectiveness results from the excellence of teachers

countries and the Netherlands score low on the power distance index and are more likely to accept empowerment, matrix management or flat organizations (Wursten & Jacobs, 2013). Implications of power distance on teaching have been summarized in Table 1.

As Richards and Lockhart (1994) point out, "Western education focuses more on individual learner autonomy and creativity, which has its implications for the roles that educator perform. Firstly, the teacher is expected to facilitate and encourage independent learning. His or her primarily role is of a facilitator who helps students identify their own ways of learning and work independently" (p. 106). According to Lin, Brantmeier and Bruhn (2008), learners of the Western education philosophy appear to be active participants of the learning process, since teaching and learning are not teacher-centered, and concentrate more on active involvement of learners in the classroom. Furthermore, autonomy encourages learners to be active in giving and sharing ideas. A similar opinion is presented by Thornton and McEntee (1995), according to whom, learners are encouraged to take control over their own learning and express their talents and skills by problem-solving, which may be considered as one of the basic requirements for learners' critical mental development.

Compared to Western education, Eastern education philosophy holds on to the concept of teaching where students receive full knowledge from teachers inside the classroom. Learners receive knowledge in a rigid way as they only seem to learn and study straight from their teachers. For example, learners are not educated or even required to do anything, as most of the materials are provided by educators. Students are not trained or encouraged to voice their own views and beliefs, either. In certain cases, learners are not allowed to even respond to the questions posed by the teacher, as the questions are meant rhetorical questions (Lin et al., 2008). Consequently, a good educator needs to be consistent in delivering ideas, teaching and maintaining a good relationship with children. In addition, Eastern education is more systematic with a standardized syllabus and timetable (Aminuddin & Syuhada, 2010; Gurney, 2007).

China, which is considered a collectivistic or interdependent, high-context society, may be considered as a good example of Eastern culture educational philosophy. This high-context society is a hierarchical and traditional. Furthermore, in a high-context society group honor and interpersonal harmony are of utmost importance. In an interdependent society, the concepts of shame and honor are much more important than they are in low-context, individualized societies; being humiliated or losing face before the group can be worse than death in some cases (Cohen, 1997). A similar viewpoint is presented by Jianhua (2017), who writes that since self-effacement is a trait traditionally valued in many Eastern cultures, Chinese students tend to wait to participate, unless otherwise requested by the teacher. Having attention drawn to, for example, a name put on the board for misbehaving can bring considerable distress. Students have been socialized to listen more than to speak, to speak in a soft voice, and to be modest in dress and behavior (Biggs, 1996; Bond, 1991). Chinese teacher-student interaction is predominantly hierarchical, with teachers overseeing learners. Therefore, teachers in Chinese culture are accorded a higher status than teachers in Western cultures. Chinese learners may be confused by the informality between American teachers and students as they expect considerable structure and organization. An opposite point of view has been presented by an Australian student studying in Shanghai, who remarked that he found it problematic with Chinese teachers that they never do any real teacher training courses and all they do is follow the book. What is more, students are not allowed to talk and the only thing they must do is listen (Baruth & Manning, 1992; Chan & Chan, 2005; Derenowski, 2011).

The philosophy of education and the approach towards schooling undoubtedly influence the roles that educators perform. In Western cultures the role of a teacher is more of a "facilitator" rather than "knowledge provider". Teachers are often responsible for helping and guiding their learners in the learning process rather than teaching them what to do. In this way, students are given the opportunity to take control of their own learning. Educators are also responsible for supporting and encouraging students in self-management and in controlling their own learning process. In the classroom, learners share more responsibility in their leaning process and evaluation, and assessment is conducted to highlight their capability. In contrast, teachers in Eastern education are seen as "knowledge providers" and students act as "knowledge receivers". As a result, students depend on teachers, show less initiative, refuse to think or generate new ideas. Teachers need to make sure that their students are well-equipped with sufficient knowledge and skills to prepare them for the future (Hussin, 1996; Teel & DeBruin-Parecki, 2001).

In Eastern cultures the concept of the "perfect" educator has existed for centuries. The expression *first born* used by Shakespeare could be easily translated into Japanese by the word *sensei*, which is composed of two characters, *sen*, meaning previous or before and *sei*, meaning birth or life. A sensei, therefore, is someone who has been *born before* you in the system you are studying and is senior to you, or as can be written in Shakespearian terms *your better* (http://www.dragon-tsunami.org/Dtimes/Pages). A sensei is a teacher whose position is based on age, wisdom, and experience. Consecutively, there exists an implication of respected stature for a character who holds the title. Most senseis are considered to be life-long guides who provide students with physical, mental and even sometimes spiritual training. It is also appropriate to use the term for teachers in educational institutions and many other student-teacher relationships. Its English equivalent is *gentleman*, or more commonly *mister*. In Western cultures different shades of meaning in terms such as "teacher", "educator", "instructor", "mentor", or even "master" can be distinguished. However, in the Japanese language the term *sensei* is not only restricted to function as a counterpart of a teacher. It is often associated with transmitting knowledge to learners or rather disciples who are usually of younger age (http://www.aikiweb.com/language/goldsbury1.html).

Therefore, Japan and its educational system may be considered as an Eastern model of education where students learn to obey (Kristof, 1995). The managerial role of Japanese teachers is unquestionable and results from historical and social traditions. Accordingly, teachers are always seen as controllers and assessors, whose status should never be undermined. Japanese teachers are an essential element in the success story because Japanese society entrusts major responsibilities to teachers and expects much from them. It confers high social status and economic rewards but also subjects teachers to constant public scrutiny. Because Japanese culture views school as a moral community and a basic training ground for becoming a good citizen, teachers are held responsible for moral education and character development, and for instilling fundamental Japanese values, attitudes, and living habits in students at all levels. These responsibilities are equal in importance to the academic roles of developing motivation and helping students meet the high academic standards required for success in secondary school and university entrance examinations. Therefore, educators are expected to infuse cultural values throughout school activities and to be concerned about students' lives both in and out of school. Furthermore, their efforts and influence often extend into home and community (www.members.tripod.com/h_javora/jed4).

The roles teachers are expected to perform undoubtedly reflect the relationship between educators and their learners. Teachers should treat students as partners and express concern. Therefore, in Western cultures students have a good rapport with their teachers. This is highly encouraged, as a trusting relationship between a teacher and student minimizes antagonism and maximizes mutual understanding. Good interpersonal connections influence students' learning outcomes and enhance the quality of their learning. A good example of such a relationship can be found among American teachers and students who are equal participants in teaching-learning processes. Students are encouraged to be critical thinkers and to question the authority of teachers (Gao & Liu, 2013). Furthermore, American educators are predominantly concerned with the learners' expectations and interests. As Auerbach (2001) writes, "Americans tend to go to extremes to lay much stress on the students' interest and unfavorably push the teacher far down in the corner" (p. 277). What is more, in American culture educators feel that they should adjust the learning environment to their students' needs. Hence, Western students may not know how to respect their teachers as they lack knowledge on social etiquette when they speak to the elderly, and see everyone as friends. For instance, some of them call their teachers, parents and elderly by their names, just like calling a friend. It may show friendliness, but it may also show impoliteness (LeTendre, 1999).

In Eastern cultures, on the other hand, the teacher-student relationship is a position of trust in which the teacher is in a situation of authority and the student is obliged to comply with the legal directives of the adult. The specificity of this relationship results from the fact that in many Eastern and Southeastern cultures, Confucian ideals, which include respect for elders, deferred gratification, and discipline, still exert strong influence. Unlike in some Western cultures, most parents teach their children to value educational achievement, respect authority, feel responsibility for relatives, and show self-control. Parents tend to view school failure as a lack of will, and as a result, increase parental restrictions. In comparison to Western learners, Asian children tend to be more dependent, conforming, and willing to place family welfare over individual wishes (Aminuddin & Syuhada, 2010; Chory & McCroskey, 1999; Jianhua, 2017; Joyce, 2008).

3 Study

3.1 Aim of the Study

Despite obvious culture-based differences, there seems to exist a set of culture-indifferent efficient foreign language teacher characteristics which may be either transferred between cultures or rediscovered in one's native cultural reality. Therefore, this small scale, pilot study aims at identifying some of these successful foreign language teacher characteristics which exist in Western and Eastern educational cultures alike or which should be transmitted from one cultural educational context to another.

3.2 Participants

The study included 18 Polish second-year students from State University of Applied Sciences in Konin, Poland. There were 14 female students and 4 male students. All of them had over 15 years of English language learning practice and their level, according to the *Common European framework for reference* was B2. Additionally, these students had been enrolled in a teacher training specialization which comprised three hundred hours of language teaching methodology and over two hundred hours of teaching practice, during which they not only observed other teachers, but also conducted lessons on their own. Another group of participants included nine Turkish Erasmus exchange students who were studying in Konin during the winter semester. Their command of English was somewhere between B1 and B2. After coming back to Turkey they all wanted to continue their teacher training program and become teachers of English. Finally, the study included a small group of Chinese students attending a teacher training course at the

Northeastern University in Boston. This group consisted of six female pre-service teachers who had been studying at the pedagogical faculty in the USA for the last seven months.

3.3 Instruments and Procedures

The study was designed as a pilot study and should be considered as an introduction to a larger, longitudinal study. Therefore, it included only a group interview which was used to obtain the necessary data. Polish and Turkish students were asked to participate in four group interviews conducted by the researcher. Three groups consisted of seven students and one group comprised six interviewees. Furthermore, each group included both Turkish and Polish students. During each interview the researcher asked questions about the characteristics of good language teachers in Polish and Turkish educational contexts and how culture influenced these characteristics. Moreover, the respondents were asked about the roles teachers performed in the foreign language classroom. Most of the time, the students were active and did not need encouragement to express their opinions. Only occasionally did the researcher have to direct the discussion towards the topic of the study. During each of the four interviews the researcher made notes and wrote down additional comments offered by the students. The last group of participants took part in a similar interview conducted by an experienced educator teaching at the Northeastern University in Boston. During an online meeting he received detailed instructions and explanations of what the aim of the study was and arranged one group interview during his classes. The obtained data was sent to the researcher with additional comments from the teacher. All the data were analyzed in order to find reoccurring opinions concerning good foreign language teacher characteristics and the influence of culture on these traits.

3.4 Results of the Study and Discussion

During the interviews students provided the researcher with a set of a good foreign language teacher characteristics. Some of these characteristics were mentioned by members in every group, while others were mentioned only by the respondents in particular groups. Sometimes the students used synonyms to describe the same teacher characteristic. In such a case, the researcher selected the most often mentioned feature, reduced the responses to three categories, and labeled them with one word. These labels included *friendliness, enthusiasm*, and *flexible mind*. Two of these traits, enthusiasm and flexible mind, were mentioned by members of every group as existing in every cultural context. Additionally, the respondents pointed to friendliness as a characteristic which apparently was more present in Polish and Turkish contexts. The last feature, labeled as *unassuming nature*, was pointed out

Table 2 Characteristics of a good foreign language teacher

Polish group—18 students	Turkish group—9 students	Chinese group—6 students
Friendliness—15	Enthusiasm—8	Flexible mind—5
Enthusiasm—13	Friendliness—7	Enthusiasm—5
Flexible mind—11	Flexible mind—7	Unassuming nature—4
Professionalism—9	Fairness—5	Strictness—3
Fairness—8	Professionalism—4	Good language conduct—3

only by Chinese students. Frequency of occurrence was the predominant criterion with the exception of the last attribute (unassuming nature) which was selected as a unique feature mentioned only by members of one culture. Table 2 contains five of the most frequent responses in every group, together with the number of students who mentioned them during the interviews.

The feature labeled as *friendliness* included synonyms such as kindliness, sympathy, openness, and sociability. *Enthusiasm* was also understood as passion, excitement, pleasure, or eagerness. Words such as creativity, flexibility, resourcefulness, and imagination were treated as synonymous with *flexible mind*. Finally, *unassuming nature* was used literally by two respondents, whereas one student talked about *humbleness* and another used the term *modesty*.

3.4.1 Enthusiasm

Enthusiasm is a state of mind that inspires people to complete the task at hand, regardless of the difficulty of the challenge. It is fundamental in developing a positive and supportive atmosphere in a foreign language classroom. When students see an enthusiastic educator, they tend to be more willing and motivated to continue their language practice. Every time a teacher enters the classroom, his or her enthusiasm will determine whether the students will succeed or fail. A good instructor perceives each lesson as the most important to conduct, despite being tired or having to confront his or her personal problems outside the classroom (daringtolivefully.com/enthusiasm).

Enthusiasm for language teaching should be one of the predominant features of a foreign language teacher, and, according to Tauber and Mester (1994), "teacher enthusiasm plays a central role in holding students' attention, generating students' interest, and developing students' positive attitudes toward learning. Highly enthusiastic teachers are highly expressive in vocal delivery, gestures, body movement, and overall energy level. All of these are crucial ingredients that, in turn contribute to greater student achievement" (p. 11). Educators need to be passionate about what they are teaching and, as Leblanc (1998) says, good teaching is as much about passion as it is about reason. Furthermore, it is about caring for the craft, being passionate, and most important of all, conveying that passion to everyone, most importantly to students. His opinion is supported by Patrick, Hisley, and Kempler

(2010), who argue that enthusiasm has the most powerful and positive impact on student learning. Similar opinions have been expressed by the participants:

> I need my teacher to be enthusiastic. His or her enthusiasm makes me more involved in the lesson. It makes me more motivated and positive. Teacher enthusiasm increases my enthusiasm and I am willing to be more active during my foreign language lessons (Polish student).

> In Turkey teachers are not often enthusiastic during lessons. I wish they were more enthusiastic while conducting lessons because it makes learners more enthusiastic about their learning. I know sometimes it is difficult to show enthusiasm during lessons, but even a small attempt from the teacher could change learners' attitudes (Turkish student).

However, enthusiasm as a teaching tool has often been questioned and perceived as evoking artificiality or lack of seriousness about the educational endeavor. However, some educators state that this is not what enthusiasm is about, as they refer to it as allowing to convey the true zest for learning. Furthermore, a set of creative devices which include *vocal animation*, defined as greater vocal vigor and using voice as a signpost drawing students to the most important elements in the commentary, may be found. Other devices encompass *physical animation* (i.e., eye contact, facial expressions, gestures, postural changes), *using the classroom space, humor, role playing,* or *suspense and surprise.* All of these do not require additional effort, but rather expect the teacher to reflect on his or her everyday classroom behavior (www.psychologicalscience.org).

3.4.2 Flexible Mind

Martial arts *sensei* Morihei Ueshiba (1992) wrote that there are many paths leading to the top of Mont Fuji, but there is only one summit. Consequently, foreign language teachers, regardless of their cultural background, encounter a variety of pupils who differ in their learning abilities, motivation, personalities, openness to critique, patience, etc. In order to merge them into one, efficient entity they need to have a "flexible mind". According to Eastern philosophy, the root cause of frustration, irritation, anger and sadness is an inflexible mind or a person that holds onto the way he or she wished things were and the ideas with which he or she was comfortable with. Therefore, developing a flexible mind is a way of becoming contented with occurring changes. When facing a major disruption, it is wrong to hold onto the old and comfortable ways. Changes should not be considered as negative because they are just different and could be good if one embraces them and perceives them as an opportunity (http://zenhabits.net/flex/). Flexibility of mind allows teachers to develop a repertoire of efficient teaching techniques. This truth extends to foreign language teaching and any other subject:

> Teachers need to be creative while conducting classes. Creativity makes lessons more interesting and involving for the learners. Furthermore, sometimes unpredictable things may happen during lessons, and creative teachers will cope with them effortlessly (Chinese students).

I consider "flexible mind" as an essential good language teacher characteristic. Only creative teachers can inspire students and conduct lessons during which learners are not bored. Flexible educators are able to adjust to various circumstances and deal with unpredictable situations in the classroom (Turkish student).

During observations, seminars and workshops inexperienced teachers often gravitate towards the comforting thought that there is only one way to teach foreign languages, the "best way", the "right way". The idea that "one way fits all" not only thwarts language teachers' professional development, but also harms our students, who enter the school environment with varying levels of readiness to learn, different ways to learn, different motivations, skills, interests, personalities, anxieties, expectations, and so on. A teacher with a flexible mind acknowledges and appreciates these differences, and adjusts teaching practices in order to meet the needs of his or her students. Furthermore, an educator with a flexible mind challenges students without the stressful component of encountering unchanging educational expectations. He or she may achieve it by providing them with the opportunity to progress at their own pace, so they may successfully reach their individual educational goals when they are ready to do so (www.friends-school.org/about-the-flexible-classroom).

Such a mindset may be perceived as a challenge for some educators. However, having a flexible mind may be indispensable for efficient teaching. A similar concept has been introduced by Spiro, Feltovich, Jacobson and Coulson (1992), who wrote about *cognitive flexibility*, defined as "the ability to represent knowledge from different conceptual and case perspectives and then, when the knowledge must later be used, the ability to construct from those different conceptual and case representations a knowledge ensemble tailored to the needs of the understanding or problem-solving situation at hand" (p. 58). Such a statement has been supported by an opinion expressed by one of the respondents:

Teachers with flexible minds challenge learners with activities that demand unconventional approach and extra effort. Learners are faced with problem-solving based activities and need to incorporate unconventional solutions (Polish student).

Furthermore, as Leblanc (1998) writes, good teaching is about not always having a fixed agenda and being inflexible, but being flexible, fluid, experimenting, and having confidence to react and adjust to changing circumstances. He continues by saying that good teaching is about getting only 10 percent of what you wanted to achieve in the classroom and still feeling good about it. Good teaching is about deviating from a lesson plan when there is more and better learning elsewhere. It is about finding a creative balance between controller and facilitator. Efficient teachers migrate between these poles at all times, depending on the circumstances as they know where they need to be and when.

Perceiving instructional flexibility as variability of teaching performance, Joyce and Hodges (1981) introduced *instructional flexibility training* for elementary school teachers, in order to help them develop a repertoire of teaching techniques for finding effective themes around which they could build instructional continuity. The authors strongly believe that in order to select the most appropriate methods, teachers need to know how to use the knowledge of the learner, subject matter and the society. However, one of the problems present during their study was the absence of an agreed-upon definition of flexibility in teaching. Joyce and Hodges (1981) argued that flexibility is the essence of effective teaching. Yet, their definition of flexibility refers to ever expanding repertoires of teaching strategies, emphasizing the teacher's adaptive actions to students' needs and portraying the teacher as the instructional leader in the classroom. By contrast, Erickson (1982) claimed that teachers and students are both improvising situational variations within and around socioculturally prescribed thematic material in class, something that was later called *disciplined improvisation* (Sawyer, 2004).

3.4.3 Friendliness and Kindliness

The classroom climate positively influenced by the teacher has a major impact on learners' motivation and attitude towards learning. Therefore, for teachers, having been equipped with pedagogical and professional characteristics would not be enough to establish a positive, learnable, and teachable classroom climate. Factors that best facilitate learning are considered to be the ones that are described as being purposeful, task-oriented, relaxed, warm, supportive, and having a sense of humor in an integrated sense (Kumaravadivelu, 1992). Furthermore, as Açkgöz (2005) claims, research indicates that certain personality characteristics influence student evaluations of teachers. From the students' points of view, teacher-expressive characteristics such as warmth, enthusiasm, and extroversion apparently separate effective from ineffective teachers. Students seem to have similar opinions concerning teacher friendliness:

> Friendly teachers make learning more pleasurable and enjoyable. I cannot imagine my teacher not to be friendly towards me and my friends. With friendly teachers classroom atmosphere is positive and encourages learners to actively participate in teacher generated activities (Polish student).

> I always enjoy teachers who can create a friendly atmosphere in the classroom. However, I sometimes feel that some teachers are reluctant towards acting in a more friendly way because they are afraid to lose their respect. It is obviously not true. Students prefer to work with friendly teachers because positive learning atmosphere is an essential factor in foreign language learning (Polish student).

According to Aultman, Williams-Johnson and Schutz (2009), teacher-student relationship is widely recognized as being important to student motivation, intellectual development, and achievement as well as to an overall supportive and safe classroom environment that encourages learning. Additionally, the importance teachers place on developing positive personal relationships with their students has been suggested as one aspect of effectiveness and expertise in teaching (Carr, 2005).

An effective teacher-student relationship cultivates engaging pedagogical conversations that hold the interest and imagination of learners and serve to enhance students' lives (Carr, 2005). Personal interest in students may help teachers find ways to bring them into these important conversations. Much of the literature on teacher-student relationships has focused on the role of caring (Noblit, 1993; Wright, 2004), where the ethic of care privileges the emotional connections between a teacher and a student as well as emphasizes the significance of the reciprocal nature of the relationships between educators and their students. Thus, caring and the resulting shared "power" can manifest itself in student success and teacher satisfaction (Graham, West, & Schaller, 1992; Marlowe, 2006).

Teachers and students have described caring relationships as being composed of several different basic concepts such as time, dialogue, sensitivity, respect, acting in the best interest of the other, being there, caring as feeling and doing, and reciprocity (Gomez, Allen & Clinton, 2004). Furthermore, researchers suggest that engaging in the process of establishing and maintaining caring relationships requires considerable emotional work and investment of self. For example, teachers may choose to display motivational enthusiasm and excitement when teaching, spend personal time on behalf of a student, or even mask anger when upset with a student (Aultman, Williams-Johnson & Schutz, 2009).

Komorowska (1999) claims that good language teacher characteristics may be estimated with respect to interaction with learners. Of great importance is the teacher's friendliness and kindliness, his or her support given to a student in difficult social and domestic situations, teacher's loyalty and his or her discretion in relation to students' private and family matters. Good teachers more often praise than criticize. It does not always have to be an encouraging remark, but a nonverbal signal, such as a smile, clapping or nodding since all positive emotions enhance learning and memorizing new language features. In addition, spontaneity, gestures, mimes, walking around the classroom, body language were observed in good language teachers. Good teachers more often and more vividly reacted to students' utterances, expressing at the same time their feelings and emotions.

Nevertheless, according to Fontana (1988), a teacher-student relationship requires utmost caution, as it should be devoid of emotions. Relying too much on the relationship with learners, teachers may appear unfair or not objective enough. To achieve greater cooperation and mutual understanding with students, it is necessary for a good teacher to establish clear rules at the very beginning of the language course (Komorowska, 1999). Some teachers find their work and investment of self emotionally and physically draining, leading to fatigue and frustration with their careers. As a result, they may create their own boundaries that help them deal with situations in the classroom while limiting their emotional involvement and feelings of burnout (Hargreaves, 2001).

3.4.4 Unassuming Nature

As Eliot (1927) wrote: "Humility is the most difficult of all virtues to achieve; nothing dies harder than the desire to think well of oneself" (p. 8). According to Miyamoto (1645), "poor teaching, or teaching with the wrong motivation, will only lead to poor technique" (p. 34). A humble teacher is not concerned with rewards or praises but rather with the progress or promotion of his or her learners. Furthermore, modest teachers are predominantly concerned with the advancement of learners, often at the expense of their own time and energy. If a student receives an award, an unassuming teacher will not look to take tribute. Such an approach is difficult on two levels, personal and professional. In Western societies where fortune favors the strong, being humble is often seen as a weakness.

Additionally, educators often become too self-confident and proud, which is defined by *Merriam-Webster dictionary* as: "a feeling that you are more important or better than other people". It seems easy to come across people who have an inflated perception of their wisdom, skills, and abilities. However, such over-confidence and arrogance may often be demotivating. Moreover, negative pride prevents people from acknowledging human vulnerabilities that exist in everyone. Unfortunately, it seems that overconfidence is present among teachers who become well-versed and self-assured in their teaching. In Western cultures educators often seem so assured of their own authority that humility is completely absent from their perspective on teaching, while others seem to have translated humility into denial of their right to critically assess a student's response (Hare, 1993). When there is a lack of humility teachers believe they are never wrong or should not be challenged by their learners. Freire writes (2017):

> It feels good to be in control, and it feels good to win. If teachers aren't careful, they can take advantage of their experience, education, and superior communication skills and overpower children. An articulate, educated teacher, can defeat a learner during a classroom discussion in the same way an adult basketball coach can defeat a child during a basketball practice. And just as a too-enthusiastic, overpowering coach can deflate the enthusiasm of children playing sports, so too a too-enthusiastic, overpowering teacher can deflate the enthusiasm of learners (http://www.radicallearners.com/humility/).

Furthermore, if the teacher wants to stay humble, he or she needs to understand that a great amount of knowledge does not result in omnipotence. Therefore, humble teachers should be able to objectively analyze their performance and in order to do so they need to become "change agents". "The need here therefore, is for teachers to become more self-aware with regard to their beliefs and the ways in which they make sense of the world, particularly with regard to their views about education and how those views themselves come to be shaped" (Williams & Burden, 1997, p. 53). A similar opinion has been expressed by a Chinese student who said:

> Teachers need to stay humble in their work. They need to acknowledge their strengths and weaknesses in order to become more reflective educators. Self-awareness helps teachers to notice what they do wrong and introduce changes in their teaching. At the same time, teachers can reinforce their positive classroom behaviors (Chinese student).

Reflectivity is more characteristic of Eastern cultures. However, in any culture becoming critically reflective involves gaining awareness of the fact that educators are responsible for their own beliefs and behaviors. In more practical terms, it means that educators should engage in systematic and social forms of inquiry that examine the origin and consequences of everyday teaching. As Ueshiba (1992) wrote, "[c]ontemplate the workings of the world, listen to the words of the wise and take all that is good as your own. With this as your base, open your own door to truth. Do not overlook the truth that is right before you (…) Also learn from holy books and wise people. Everything should be your teacher" (p. 26).

Contrastingly, when teachers are too humble, they fail to critically assess their students' answers. Therefore, teachers need to be aware that students have the capability of becoming critical thinkers and are able to assess what they have been taught. Although humility cannot be taught, it can be nurtured and cherished in school. "It can be seen in the eyes of our learners, in their self-possession and engagement, and in the respectful relationships educators have with colleagues, students' families, and communities. In the times of hubris and shameless self-promotion, humility seems to be an essential quality for teachers to have" (kigurai.wordpress.com). In Eastern cultures, martial art masters are constantly practicing and are always open to the wisdom of others. It is a true virtue of a *sensei* to be the master and apprentice at the same time. Mastering martial arts is a never-ending endeavor and only people who are humble will be able to successfully follow the path of wisdom. The same truth applies to every form of teaching.

4   Conclusions and Suggestions for Further Research

Throughout the whole life people constantly learn, develop and transform, as change is imprinted into every human life. Therefore, it should be considered not as an encumbrance, but, rather, as an opportunity to introduce enhancements. Personal transformation, regardless of the cultural background, influences our professional careers, and even despite some palpable cultural differences, a set of apparently culture-indifferent qualities may be identified and transmitted into almost every educational context. On the other hand, the question remains if it is feasible to create a "culture free" efficient educational system which other cultures can simply adopt what has been successful in another country. The answer is that cultural values and norms are often deeply rooted in societies and are very consistent over time. For that reason, it might be at least difficult to adopt new ideas if they do not fit the context of a particular cultural value system. Obviously, it does not mean that people cannot learn from each other, but it might be naïve to think that best practices in a specific culture can be automatically copied and adopted in another culture. Therefore, what educators need is to find a way to "translate" from one culture value system to another and to increase awareness of their own and other cultures. This heightened awareness may eventually result in adopting new values in their teaching practices. Teachers also need to develop their intercultural sensitivity and increase their tolerance and openness towards otherness. As Suzuki (2009) once said: "Without accepting the fact that everything changes, we cannot find perfect composure. But unfortunately, although it is true, it is difficult for us to accept it. Because we cannot accept the truth of transience, we suffer" (p. 91).

According to the respondents in the study, there are teacher characteristics which exist in every culture such as *enthusiasm* and *flexible mind*. However, other characteristics have been perceived as more culture-bound and not always present in a particular cultural context. *Unassuming nature* was considered as a more Eastern trait, whereas *friendliness* was perceived as a more Western culture characteristic, often absent in Eastern education. However, the study included only thirty-three representatives from three countries who participated in group interviews. Undoubtedly, a more extensive study is needed that would encompass more participants from diverse cultural backgrounds and generate more data.

References

Ackgöz, F. (2005). A study on teacher characteristics and their effects on students' attitudes. *The Reading Matrix, 5*(2), 103–143.

Aminuddin, H., & Syuhada, N. (2010). Approaches and values in two gigantic educational philosophies: East and West. *Online Educational Research Journal, 1,* 1–15.

Auerbach, E. (2001). Yes but …: Problematizing participatory ESL pedagogy. In P. Campbell & B. Burnaby (Eds.), *Participatory practices in adult education* (pp. 267–307). Mahwah, NY: Lawrence Erlbaum.

Aultman, L., Williams-Johnson, M., & Schutz, P. (2009). Boundary dilemmas in teacher-student relationships: Struggling with the line. *Teacher and Teacher Education, 25,* 636–637.

Baruth, L. G., & Manning, M. L. (1992). *Multicultural education of children and adolescents.* Needham Heights, MA: Allyn and Bacon.

Biggs, J. B. (1996). Learning, schooling, and socialization: A Chinese solution to a Western problem. In S. Lau (Ed.), *Growing up the Chinese way: Chinese child and adolescent development* (pp. 147–167). Hong Kong: The Chinese University Press.

Bond, M. H. (1991). *Beyond the Chinese face: Insights from psychology.* Hong Kong: Oxford University Press.

Carr, D. (2005). Personal and interpersonal relationships in education and teaching: A virtual ethical perspective. *British Journal of Educational Studies, 53*(3), 255–271.

Chan, K. L., & Chan, C. L. W. (2005). Chinese culture, social work education and research. *International Social Work, 48*(4), 381–389.

Chory, R. M., & McCroskey, J. C. (1999). The relationship between teacher management communication style and affective learning. *Communication Quarterly, 27,* 1–12.

Cohen, R. (1997). *Negotiating across cultures: Communications obstacles in international diplomacy.* Washington DC: US Institute of Peace Press.

Derenowski, M. (2011). *Reflective teachers in the modern educational context.* Konin: PWSZ Konin Press.

Elliot, T. S. (1927). *Shakespeare and the stoicism of Seneca. Selected essays* (pp. 126–140). London: Faber.

Erickson, F. (1982). Classroom discourse as improvisation: Relationships between academic task structure and social participation structure in lessons. In L. C. Wilkinson (Ed.), *Communicating in the classroom* (pp. 153–181). New York: Academic Press.

Fontana, D. (1988). *Psychology for teachers.* UK: Palgrave Macmillan.

Freire, J. (2017, June 28). Retrieved from http://www.radicallearners.com/humility.

Gao, M., & Liu, Q. (2013). Personality traits of effective teachers represented in the narratives of American and Chinese preservice teachers: A cross-cultural comparison. *International Journal of Humanities and Social Science, 3*(2), 84–95.

Gomez, M. L., Allen, A., & Clinton, K. (2004). Cultural models of care in teaching: a case study of one pre-service secondary teacher. *Teaching and Teacher Education, 20,* 473–488.

Graham, E. E., West, R., & Schaller, K. A. (1992). The association between the relational teaching approach and job satisfaction. *Communication Reports, 5,* 11–22.

Gurney, P. (2007). Five factors for effective teaching. *New Zealand Journal of Teacher's Work, 4* (2), 89–98.

Hare, W. (1993). Humility as a virtue in teaching. *Journal of Philosophy of Education, 26*(2), 227–236.

Hargreaves, A. (2001). Emotional geographies of teaching. *Teachers College Records, 103*(6), 1056–1080.

Hassan, A. Jamaludin, J. Sulaiman, & Baki, R. (2017, June 28). *Western and eastern educational philosophies.* Retrieved from https://ivc.instructure.com/files/6886.

Hofstede, G. (1997). *Cultures and organizations: Software of the mind.* New York: McGraw-Hill.

Hussin, S. (1996). *Pendidikan Di Malaysia: Sejarah, Sistem, dan Falsafah.* Kuala Lumpur: Dewan Bahasa dan Pustaka.

Jianhua, F. (2017, June 28). Asian-american children: What teachers should know. *ERIC Digest.* Retrieved from http://www.ericdigests.org.

Joyce, L. (2017, June 28). *The difference between Western and Eastern education: Education system in need of change?* Retrieved from www.oerj.org.

Joyce, B., & Hodges, R. (1981). Flexibility and repertoire. In B. Joyce, L., Peck, & C. Brown (Eds.), *Flexibility in teaching* (pp. 280–2990). New York: Longman.

Komorowska, H. (1999). *Metodyka nauczania języków obcych [Methodology of foreign language teaching].* Warszawa: WSiP.

Kristof, N. (1995). Japan's schools: Safe, clean, not so much fun. New York Times. Retrieved from: www.nytimes.com/1995/07/18/world/japan-s-schools-safe-clean-not-so-much-fun.html.

Kumaravadivelu, B. (1992). Macrostrategies for the second/foreign language teacher. *Modern Language Journal, 76*(1), 41–49.

Leblanc, R. (2017, June 28). Good teaching: The top ten requirements. *The Teaching Professor, 12* (6). Retrieved from http://www.catholiceducation.org.

LeTendre, G. K. (1999). *Competitor or Ally? Japan's Role in American Educational Debates.* New York: Taylor & Francis.

Lin, J., Brantmeier, E., & Bruhn, C. (2008). *Transforming education for peace.* North Carolina: Information Age Publishing.

Marlowe, M. (2006). Torey Hayden's teacher lore: A pedagogy of caring. *Journal of Education for Teaching, 32*(1), 93–103.

Miamoto, M. (2016). *Go Rin No Sho [The book of five rings].* CreateSpace Publishing.

Noblit, G. W. (1993). Power and caring. *American Educational Research Journal, 30*(1), 23–38.

Onn, C. M. (2009). *Lifelong learning/education policy and career design/human resource development—the Singapore experience.* Singapore: The Singapore Association for Continuing Education.

Patrick, B., Hisley, J., & Kempler, T. (2010). What's everybody so excited about? The effects of teacher enthusiasm on student intrinsic motivation and vitality. *The Effective Educator, 68*(4), 74–93.

Richards, J. C., & Lockhart, C. (1994). *Reflective teaching in second language classrooms.* New York: Cambridge University Press.

Sawyer, R. K. (2004). Creative teaching: Collaborative discussion as disciplined improvisation. *Educational Researcher, 33,* 12–20.

Sheorey, R. (2006). *Learning and teaching English in India.* New Delhi: SAGE.

Spiro, R. J., Feltovich, P. J., Jacobson, M. J., & Coulson, R. L. (1992). Cognitive flexibility, constructivism, and hypertext: Random access instruction for advanced knowledge acquisition in ill-structured domains. In T. M. Duffy & D. H. Jonassen (Eds.), *Constructivism and the technology of instruction: A conversation* (pp. 57–76). Hillsdale, NJ: Lawerence Erlbaum.

Suzuki, S. (2009). *Not always so: Practicing the true spirit of Zen.* San Francisco: Harper Collins.

Tauber, R. T., & Mester, C. S. (1994). *Acting lessons for teachers: Using performance skills in the classroom*. Westport, CN: Praeger.

Teel, K., & DeBruin-Parecki, A. (2001). *Making school count: Promoting urban student motivation and success*. New York: Routledge.

Thornton, L., & McEntee, M. (1995). Learner centered schools as a mindset, and the connection with mindfulness and multiculturalism. *Theory Into Practice, 34*(4), 250–257.

Ueshiba, M. (1992). *The art of peace*. Boston: Shambhala Publishing.

Williams, M., & Burden, R. L. (1997). *Psychology for teachers*. Cambridge: Cambridge University Press.

Wright, R. (2004). Care as the 'heart' of prison teaching. *The Journal of Correctional Education, 55*(3), 191–209.

Wursten, H., & Jacobs, C. (2013). The impact of culture on education. Can we introduce best practices in education across countries? *ITIM International, 1*, 1–28.

Internet Sources

http://www.dragon-tsunami.org/Dtimes/Pages. Access date 05 March 2017.

http://www.aikiweb.com/language/goldsbury1.html. Access date 05 March 2017.

http://zenhabits.net/flex. Access date 05 March 2017.

http://www.friends-school.org/about-the-flexible-classroom. Access date 05 March 2017.

http://www.psychologicalscience.org. Access date 05 March 2017.

http://www.kigurai.wordpress.com. Access date 05 March 2017.

http://www.members.tripod.com/h_javora/jed4. Access date 05 March 2017.

http//www.daringtolivefully.com/enthusiasm. Access date 05 March 2017.

Author Biography

Marek Derenowski received his Ph.D. in applied linguistics from Adam Mickiewicz University in Poznań, Poland. He is a teacher and a teacher educator working at the Department of English Studies of Faculty of Pedagogy and Fine Arts of Adam Mickiewicz University (Kalisz, Poland). He also works at Faculty of Philology at State University of Applied Sciences, Konin, Poland. His major interest is in teacher education and professional development, the place of target language culture in the foreign language education as well as learner and teacher autonomy and reflectivity.

Part III
Challenges of Teacher Education and Development

The Contribution of Metaphor to University Students' Explicit Knowledge About ELT Methodology

Joanna Zawodniak and Mariusz Kruk

Abstract The aim of this study is to examine the relationship between metaphor and a group of English students' awareness of and engagement with various ELT methodology issues (feedback, induction, error, etc.). The study, conducted among 27 EFL students of English philology, was based on the triangular approach intended to yield both quantitative and qualitative data from a questionnaire and an argumentative paragraph. The analysis of obtained results reveals ontological correspondence between the concrete source domains from which the respondents derived their comments and the abstract target domains referring to various ELT concepts that they tried to explore and understand. An overall conclusion is that the conceptual and linguistic layers of metaphor can be viewed as a constructive tool for transforming language students' implicit beliefs and assumptions into the explicit and thus more meaningfully as well as effectively exploited system of knowledge about L2 pedagogy ideas and principles.

Keywords Conceptual metaphor · Linguistic metaphor · Ontological mapping · Source domain · Target domain · ELT methodology

1 Introduction

Around two decades ago metaphor became one of the key concepts of applied linguistics opening new areas of the EFL classroom and offering promising opportunities for the meaningful learning and teaching of the target language (Cameron, 1999; Chen, 2003; de Guerrero & Villamil, 2000; Komorowska, 2010; Littlemore, 2004). Etymologically traced back to Latin *metaphora* and Greek μεταφορά, the term *metaphor* can be characterized as an implied comparison

J. Zawodniak (✉) · M. Kruk
University of Zielona Góra, Zielona Góra, Poland
e-mail: j.zawodniak@in.uz.zgora.pl

M. Kruk
e-mail: mkanglik@gmail.com

© Springer International Publishing AG 2018   271
M. Pawlak and A. Mystkowska-Wiertelak (eds.), *Challenges of Second and Foreign Language Education in a Globalized World*, Second Language Learning and Teaching, DOI 10.1007/978-3-319-66975-5_16

referring to a figure of speech in which the sense of one word is transferred to another word. Metaphor can also be specified as "a central", verbally, nonverbally and/or graphically operated "tool of our cognitive apparatus" that is conducive to an imaginative way of describing things and that contributes to an understanding of the nature of language and thought (Long & Richards, 1999, p. x).

For most of the previous century metaphor was studied in relation to cognition, without too many attempts to focus on its linguistic features which were viewed as playing a minor role in the formal study of language (Searle, 1979). However, more recent research provides justification for considering metaphor as a phenomenon of both language and thought, and highlights the need to create frameworks that would concurrently link it to the cognitive and the socio-cultural (Drew & Holt, 1988; Edwards, 1997; Gao & Meng, 2010). In a similar vein, the present paper adopts a language-in-use approach to metaphor for the purpose of examining the relationship between its conceptual and linguistic levels with respect to the opportunities for metaphorical reasoning to generate metaphorical expressions meant to enhance English philology students' understanding of certain ELT methodology issues. The empirical part of the paper is preceded by a brief discussion of stereotyped views on metaphor, Lakoff and Johnson's Conceptual Metaphor Theory and influential metaphors pertaining to language and thought.

2   Literature Review

2.1   Common Misconceptions About Metaphor

In light of some of the traditional beliefs enumerated below, metaphor exists in the realm of figurative language mainly found in literature and thus having little in common with the mundane realities of life on the one hand and with sophisticated terminology used in various disciplines on the other (Reddy, 1979):

- Metaphor is primarily a product of poetic imagination, a kind of rhetorical quirk.
- Everyday language is literal, not metaphorical.
- The definitions used in grammar are never metaphorical.

These assumptions, based on the already discarded literal vs. metaphorical distinction (Lakoff, 1993), have been addressed in the Lakoff and Johnson's (1980) theory discussed in the next section.

2.2   The Conceptual Metaphor Theory

In their seminal Conceptual Metaphor Theory (CMT) Lakoff and Johnson (1980) argue against a traditional understanding of metaphor as a device associated with and reserved for acts of literary creation. This very understanding is synonymous with perceiving metaphor as a fancy, ornamental and thus unnecessary addition to the language used on an everyday basis (Gao & Meng, 2010). Contrary to that, Lakoff and Johnson's (1980) findings reveal that metaphor is an inseparable component of our lives, including language, thought and action.[1] Reddy (1993) goes a step further claiming that everyday English is a highly metaphorical language, which might not be so obvious until it is exemplified with the Shakespearean "All the world's a stage" (Brissenden, 1993) or the pop culture "It's raining men" (Jabara & Shaffer, 1979), both of them functioning as commonplace statements.

The fundamental premise of CMT is that the locus of metaphor is thought, hence Lakoff and Johnson's (1980) reference to and emphasis on the dominance of thought over language. The said authors elaborate on metaphor as comprising conceptual mappings and metaphorical expressions (linguistic metaphors) alike. Conceptual mappings constitute the deep-structure level of metaphor and stretch from the source domain including literal entities, characteristics, phenomena and relations to the target domain that is comprised of abstract and thus more complex and ambiguous ideas.[2] There are ontological correspondences between the source domain and the target domain, that is, the relationships between particular items and processes within the target domain reflect the ones which take place in the source domain. Finally, these correspondences are realized at the linguistic surface level of metaphorical expressions, meaning that entities and processes in the target domain undergo the lexicalization via expressions derived from its source counterpart (Deignan, 2005; Littlemore & Low, 2006) (see Fig. 1).

The mapping across the conceptual source and target domains enables language users to understand the abstract entities and attributes of the latter with reliance on the physical ones included in the former (Aronin & Politis, 2015). Metaphor paves the way for familiarizing with, contemplating and discussing difficult and emotionally dense experiences. Consequently, it leads one to grasp a target domain-specific idea with the help of source domain-triggered associative links (Deignan, 2005). To prove that metaphors pervade human life through a wide range of expressions drawn from the source domain, Lakoff and Johnson (1980) provide the example of metaphorical concept which is ARGUMENT IS WAR. Consequently, they establish the ontological connection between the source-domain concept of war and the target-domain concept of argument, the abstract properties of which are descriptively explained in terms of the former's characteristics encompassing gaining and losing grounds,

---

[1]Lakoff and Johnson were not the first to underline the ubiquitous character of metaphor, the fact having been indicated around twenty-four centuries ago by Aristotle (Grube, 1958) and nearly half a century ago by Richards (1936).

[2]Other authors refer to the ideas of *source domain* and *target domain* using different terminology, like Richards (1936, as cited in Way, 1994, p. 5) and Perrine (1971), who distinguish between *vehicle* and *tenor (topic)*, and Black (1993), who renames the two categories as *focus (secondary subject)* and *frame (primary subject)*.

Fig. 1 The graphical
representation of the
conceptual metaphor theory
(the authors' own design)

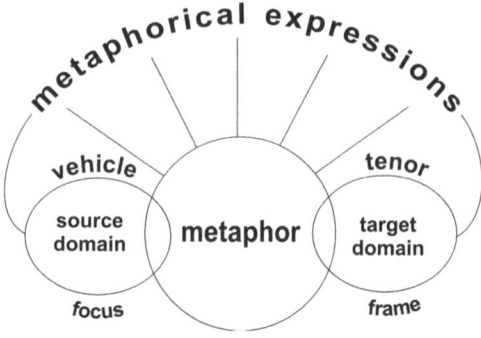

Fig. 2 The
teaching-as-journey mapping
(the authors' own design)

taking a new line of attack, using strategies or abandoning an indefensible position. Lakoff (1993) also discusses the LOVE IS A JOURNEY metaphor which the present authors have decided to move in the applied linguistic direction and propose the TEACHING IS A JOURNEY mapping (see Fig. 2). The complex and multidimensional concept of teaching has been, therefore, explained as a process requiring traveler-like abilities to take risks, cope with various adverse circumstances and develop a satisfying itinerary.

Lakoff and Johnson's (1980) primary interest in the conceptual content of metaphor followed by other authors' (Gibbs, 1994; Kövecses & Szabó, 1996) reflections drawing on the cognitive semantics approach and findings obtained from laboratory experiments led to the under-emphasizing of metaphor as positioned within the goal-oriented, context-dependent paradigm.[3] Hence the need to explore the applied linguistic and thus language-in-use dimension of metaphor with the dynamic interaction between its primary and secondary layers.

---

[3]The 20th-century authors' preoccupation with the thought level of metaphor was preceded by a more language-in-use, interactional and discourse-oriented stance revealed by Aristotle in the fourth century B.C. as well as by Vico and Teasauro in the 17th/18th centuries (Aristotle, 367-347 BC, 335-322 BC [1991]; Grube, 1958; Cooper, 1986).

2.3 Language and Thought in Metaphor

One of the above-mentioned stereotyped assumptions that needs to be revisited in this paper is that the definitions taken advantage of in grammar have nothing in common with metaphor (Lakoff, 1993). Lakoff (1993) questions it on similar grounds as in the case of the other two assumptions (see Sect. 2.1.) and argues that metaphorical interpretation is not a mere result of applying certain algorithmic operations to the literal meaning.

Following this path of reasoning, the present authors would like to discuss several selected definitions of language and mind which appear to be their metaphorical interpretations. For example, de Saussure (1966, cited in Hussein & Abushihab, 2014, p. 60) explains the symbolic functioning of language with regard to a game of chess in which the value of the pieces depends on where they are placed on the chessboard; similarly, every single linguistic term can be valued in relation to other terms which "move (…) into nonliteral meaning combinations" (de Saussure, 1959, cited in Jensen, 2006, p. 42). Chomsky (1968) defines language as an innate faculty of human mind, while one of his followers, Pinker (1994) claims that human beings have an instinct for language just like spiders have an instinct enabling them to spin webs. A definition of human mind which deserves attention was formulated by Locke (1690) [1999] referring to it as a receptive blank slate or a white sheet of paper that will be gradually filled with characters and ideas as a result of an individual's growing experience. One cannot but acknowledge that the aforementioned definitions are metaphorical as they establish an ontological link between the abstract target domains of language and mind, and the concrete source domains like a game of chess or a blank slate.

Going into further detail, quite a few complex processes pertaining to SLA and ELT methodology have been addressed in a metaphorical way, like language acquisition patterns (*u-shaped behavior, telegraphic speech*), learner errors (*the Monitor, fossilization, backsliding*) L2 classroom of activities (*warm-ups, brain-switching activities, information-gap activities*), strategies (*approximation, code-switching, skimming, anchoring, pegword method*) or kinds of teacher assistance (*scaffolding, roughly/finely tuned input*). A metaphorical handling of those very often ambiguous and multi-faceted phenomena contributes to the understanding of their essence as, for instance, in the case of *fossilization* which is a term standing for the process of stopping to learn certain rules and incorporating incorrect L2 forms into the learner's competence, or in the case of *code-switching*, which stands for a complex act of systematically using two or more languages in the same sentence or utterance (Brown, 2000; Levine, 2011). This, once again, shows that metaphor helps "to see many issues in a new, unusual light" (Komorowska, 2010, p. 58), thus opening language learners to new experiences based on perceiving abstract notions through the filter of concrete entities.

3   Method

3.1   Aim of the Study

The aim of the study was to examine the place of metaphor in enhancing the EFL students' understanding of certain English language teaching and learning concepts with regard to the relationship between the target domain of methodological terms and the source domain of the subjects' lexicalized conceptualizations of these terms.

3.2   Participants

The participants of the study were 27 second-year students of English philology at the University of Zielona Góra in Poland. Of the 27 participants 21 (18 females and 3 males) were regular and 6 (5 females and 1 male) were part-time students. They were approximately 21 years old. All of the students chose the teaching special-ization and intended to enter the teaching profession and become teachers of English. The proficiency level represented by the study participants could be described as somewhere between B1 and B2, as specified in the levels laid out in the *Common European framework of reference for languages*.

3.3   Data Collection and Analysis

The data were collected by means of a structured questionnaire (see Appendix) divided into two parts. Part one comprised five closed questions based on a five-point Likert scale (1—*strongly disagree*, 5—*strongly agree*) tapping into the respondents' acceptance levels in relation to the metaphorical definitions of five English language teaching and learning concepts. These concepts included: *method* (e.g., "Method is a small cake taken from a pile of cakes"), *error* (e.g., "Error is a hole in the whole"), *feedback* (e.g., "Feedback is smaller or bigger treats given to students"), *writing* (e.g., "Writing is drawing your thoughts for others to see") and *induction* (e.g., "Induction is like a bridge which connects students to new knowledge"). Each ELT methodology-related concept involved six definitions. It should be noted that all those definitions were derived from another questionnaire administered a year earlier to a group of 118 students of English philology recruited from three different aca-demic centers in Poland, including Zielona Góra, Poznań and Wrocław. It aimed at examining the EFL teaching profession from a metaphorical perspective, one of the subjects' tasks being the provision of metaphorical definitions of the aforementioned concepts. The present authors decided to select the most interesting and original definitions, and investigate their potential to enhance the understanding of certain areas of ELT methodology in another group of students. As far as part two of the questionnaire is concerned, it included one open-ended question asking the subjects to choose one of their fellow students' definitions (from part one) they strongly agree with and develop it into a 300-word explanatory description.

The gathered data were subjected to quantitative and qualitative analysis. The former encompassed calculating means and standard deviations for all the questions requiring numerical responses (i.e., the Likert scale items) and counting the number of definitions the study participants chose to comment on, while the latter involved reading and rereading the descriptions of the definitions selected by the respondents. The first reading allowed the researchers to get familiarized with the participants' descriptions and gave them a vantage point over the responses. Then, the researchers reviewed the students' descriptions to identify metaphors, discussing all inconsistent cases. Differences in interpretation were few and a consensus was reached in all instances.

4   Findings

4.1   Part 1 of the Questionnaire: The Definitions that Earned the Highest and the Lowest Score

When it comes to the quantitative analysis of the first part of the questionnaire and its first concept, namely, *method*, the results showed that the participants favored the following definitions of the notion: "the meal which, according to our experience, will be the best in getting rid of hunger" ($M = 3.52$, $SD = 0.94$) and "a key used to fasten the screw" ($M = 3.48$, $SD = 0.85$). Conversely, the students' least favorite definitions of the said concept were: "a material with which a path is covered (asphalt, cobblestones)" ($M = 2.67$, $SD = 1.00$) and "a small cake taken from a pile of cakes" ($M = 2.93$, $SD = 1.00$). As for the concept of *error*, the highest means were determined for such definitions as: "a wrong step on the right path" ($M = 3.70$, $SD = 0.95$) and "a slight wound, but when it is healed, it makes us stronger" ($M = 3.63$, $SD = 1.15$). Items with the lowest means were as follows: "an agent provocateur trying to mislead us" ($M = 2.63$, $SD = 1.01$) and "a hole in the whole" ($M = 3.19$, $SD = 1.30$). As far as the concept of *feedback* is concerned, the students were in favor of the following definitions: "a book of wisdom, something to focus on" ($M = 3.56$, $SD = 1.05$) and "a boomerang that comes from the teacher or the student" ($M = 3.44$, $SD = 1.12$). In contrast, they regarded "a conversation between a pirate and an officer" ($M = 2.52$, $SD = 1.12$) and "smaller or bigger treats given to students" ($M = 2.85$, $SD = 1.10$) as the least favorite definitions of the concept of feedback. As regards the notion of *writing*, the highest means were calculated in the case of the following two items: "opportunity to make an error, notice it and correct it" ($M = 4.04$, $SD = 0.81$) and "drawing your thoughts for others to see" ($M = 3.78$, $SD = 1.22$). Definitions with the lowest means were as follows: "it is like sowing seeds in the soil" ($M = 3.07$, $SD = 1.04$) and "a skill making soldiers more patient and giving them a chance to practice planning skills" ($M = 3.38$, $SD = 1.20$).

Finally, in the case of *induction* the highest means were determined for such definitions as: "moving from small things to a bigger deal" ($M = 4.00$, $SD = 0.92$) and "discovery of something special" ($M = 3.85$, $SD = 0.99$). The lowest means were received by the following items: "a genealogical tree—we go from the general term 'family' to our ancestors" ($M = 3.12$, $SD = 1.14$) and "building a house stylistically matching furniture that we already possess" ($M = 3.15$, $SD = 1.08$).

4.2 Part 2 of the Questionnaire: The Definitions Chosen and Commented on by the Respondents[4]

As regards the second part of the questionnaire, that is, the part asking the study participants to select one of the definitions they strongly agreed with and develop it into an explanatory description, the majority of the students chose definitions related to the concepts of *writing* and *error* (11 and 9 respectively). In addition, definitions regarding the concepts of *method* were selected by three students, *induction* by three and *feedback* by only one participant.

When it comes to the concept of *writing*, the most frequently chosen and commented on definitions concerned writing as an "opportunity to make an error, notice it and correct it" (six students) and "making the impermanent permanent; creating things that did not physically exist before" (two students). The qualitative analysis of the data showed that the students considered writing as an "ideal idea" to convey the essence of one's own soul "while putting liquid thoughts onto the paper", the action of "taking a photo of a beautiful view to remember", or "a bridge between our minds and other people". In addition, the students described writing in terms of a discussion with oneself or as a journey to the writer's inside or an invitation for others to see the writer's world. The concept of writing was also perceived as the act of creation of "our personality once again" and written words were compared by one of the students with "multifoliate roses". The study participants referred to writing as a tool for saving invisible thoughts and reflection ("while writing you need to think about every sentence you make and after you finish your work you have to check"). Moreover, they regarded writing as a tool for "catching the fleeting moments", broadening one's horizons and exchanging written work with a classmate. The analysis of the data also revealed some references to literature, for example, to William Shakespeare and Hamlet's famous "to be or not to be" soliloquy which inspired one of the respondents to wonder whether it is worthwhile to foster the development of writing skills in the era of new technologies. That same subject made a handful of philosophical comments on writing as leaving room for understated ideas difficult to grasp by a wide audience in a way similar to how Søren Kierkegaard, Immanuel Kant or Friedrich Nietzsche unveiled their thoughts only to a narrow circle of readers and followers.

---

[4]The respondents' original spelling and grammar have been preserved.

As regards the concept of *error*, the most often selected and commented on definition was "a slight wound, but when it is healed, it make us stronger" (six students). For the study participants, errors were the evidence of learning and they comprehended them as a detour, that is, a small stop before returning to the right path, or as a mental scar that makes students more experienced. One participant claimed that as long as students make errors, there are concepts they need to wrap their heads around. Yet another student observed the relationship between students who have made an error and broken-hearted people:

> It's the same with someone who is broken-hearted. After a while this person wound disappear, forget about the past and move on. And he/she is ready to meet someone new. In language we also at first feel bad when we make mistakes, we are ashamed of them because we would like to pass those errors and talk perfectly from the beginning. When some time passes we realize that we needed these mistakes without them our language skills wouldn't have improved. We would still be on the same level and as a broken-hearted person we forget about our past and move on.

As far as the concept of *method* is concerned, it was compared with the role of a balanced diet in L2 classroom or it was referred to as a gun or a grenade intended to solve different problems:

> (...) when we have a lot of methods, we only choose one (or two) that is the most matching for us. The same situation is when we choose a cake—we have a lot of cakes and we choose only one that tastes best for us.

> (...) sometimes one method is suitable just to a particular problem, like grenades are most useful in running the building and guns are more suitable to shoot the enemies. In studying it is very similar.

Finally, the analysis of the data revealed that although some of the students referred to the concepts of *induction* and *feedback*, the comments they made were not exactly to the point.

5 Discussion

As regards the quantitative data gathered from the first part of the questionnaire, the respondents' judgments about the most/the least convincing definitions of five applied linguistic concepts revealed certain patterns of reasoning analyzed below.

Concerning the notion of *method*, most of the students seemed to have understood it either as a way in which the teacher could satisfy their curiosity (getting rid of hunger) or as an opportunity for overcoming problems encountered in the language classroom (fastening the screw). At the same time, they did not favor or presumably did not grasp the idea of method as one of many tools of the teacher's trade which need to be carefully selected (a small cake chosen from a pile). This shows that the subjects approached the concept in question from a perspective of their own expectations rather than with respect to the art and/or a craft of teaching. Referring to the concept of *error*, it was perceived by the majority as a natural part of learner language (Corder, 1967; Selinker, 1972) which, although problematic ("a wrong step"), pushes its development forward "on the right path". Simultaneously, the respondents revealed little acceptance of a traditional view of error as a negative phenomenon ("agent provocateur") inhibiting the learning process. When it comes to the concept of *feedback*, for the most part, the students opted for understanding it as a reciprocal process ("a boomerang") that can be profited from by the learners and by the teacher alike. Consequently, the respondents seemed to have de-emphasized the military connotation indicating a competitive relationship between the teacher (an officer) and his/her students (pirates). In the same vein, they questioned the superordinate role of the teacher as the one deciding about giving "smaller or bigger treats to students". As for the notion of *writing*, the subjects turned out to have paid attention to two important aspects of the process, namely that it enables language users to reflect on their work and improve it by noticing and correcting possible errors and that it can be a self-expressive kind of work acquainting potential readers with the writer's thoughts. They once again did not show much appreciation for the military associations nor did they approve of a definition highlighting writing as agricultural work. As far as the concept of *induction* is concerned, it was mainly perceived it in terms of discovery learning that proceeds from the particular to the general ("form small things to a bigger deal"), while the students quite rightly did not favor the reference to induction as a genealogical tree since, regardless of how interesting it is, it has more in common with deduction ("moving from the general term 'family' to our ancestors") than with induction.

Regarding the qualitative data culled from the second part of the questionnaire, it has to be noted that most of the respondents decided to elaborate on the definitions of writing and error, whereas only a few chose to concentrate on the notions of method, induction and feedback. A possible explanation might be that, relying on the present authors' own observations and teaching experience, the three least frequently discussed concepts pose certain difficulties to EFL students who tend to confuse method with technique and strategy, induction with deduction and feedback with reinforcement (this was the case with the descriptions of induction and feedback provided by the participants in this study). Although in all likelihood, the subjects possessed the receptive knowledge about the said terms, as was shown by their choices of the most/the least convincing definitions, they did not appear to be ready to attend to them on a productive basis.

Concerning the respondents' dealing with the concepts of method, error and writing, they managed to derive from the concrete source domain entities created by their fellow students a year earlier new and very often interesting linguistic metaphors, by means of which they reached the target domain of abstract ELT methodology terms (see Fig. 3). The very point of departure for the students' mappings from the source domain to the target domain that helped to fuel the emergence of metaphorical expressions were, therefore, the definitions offered to them at the outset of the study. Those definitions led the students to pay more conscious attention to the above-mentioned applied linguistic concepts, thus making them subject to closer scrutiny. In this way, their student peers' metaphorical interpretations of the notions in question inspired them to create their

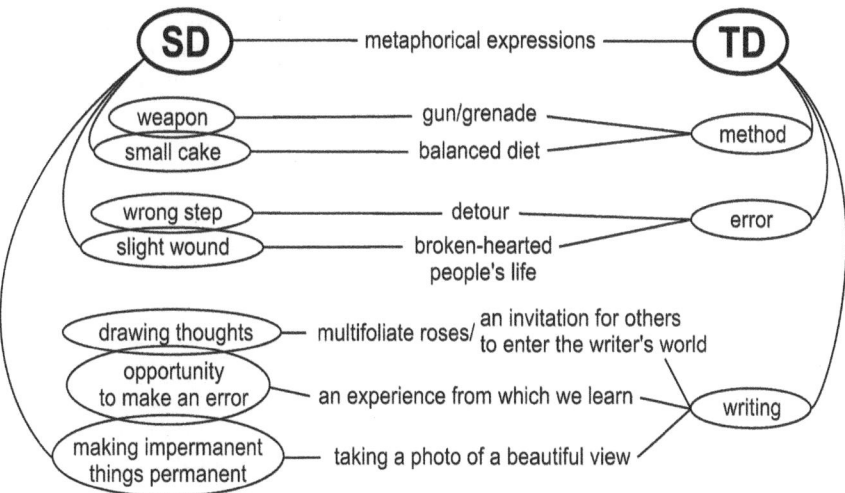

Fig. 3 The subjects' source domain-driven lexicalization of target domain ideas (the present authors' own design)

own linguistic metaphors that would be better suited to their own line of thinking. As a result, the subjects came up with a number of such expressions as, for example, "only one [cake] that tastes best", "[o]ur meal should (…) contain proteins, carbohydrates and vegetables" (method); "[w]hen you get hurt, you are depressed", "[i]f you experience a breakup in your life, you will be smarter in the future" (error); "an ideal idea", "a photo of a beautiful view", "multifoliate roses", "skills to survive", "dignity that the paper gives to the writer" (writing). All those and other linguistic metaphors used by the students in their descriptions seemed to have enabled them to approach the target domain of particular ELT methodology concepts and thus understand them in a broader and more explicit way. It was observed that metaphorical expressions made it possible for many subjects to engage in more or less detailed, logically handled discussions of the concepts under investigation in terms of real-world problems, as in the example referring to coping with errors as broken-hearted people cope with the emotional suffering ("In language we also at first feel bad when we make mistakes, we are ashamed of them because we would like to [...] talk perfectly from the beginning. When some time passes, we realize that we needed these mistakes"). The respondents' own metaphorical expressions also turned out to instigate them to reflect on the links between analyzed concepts and other L2 classroom-specific factors and processes including self-correction and peer correction, L2 learning experience, creativity, anxiety, language skills, age groups, sensory styles, strategy use (note-taking, repetition), learner needs, learner differences, memory and brain functioning. For instance, a few students tried to compare writing and speaking, giving the reasons for which the former is, in their opinion, a more difficult skill to learn, while two other respondents made reference to the history of writing and our ancestors' attempts "to convey knowledge from one generation to another" as well as to literature and philosophy. There were also comments on the importance of classifying errors, attempts to discuss written errors and complaints that some teachers do not allow their students to self-correct. Finally, one respondent discussed the advantages and disadvantages of being visual and auditory learners.

6 Conclusions

Summing up, the metaphorical definitions encouraged the subjects in this study to develop their own mappings from the source domain of concrete entities (e.g., weapon, cake, wound, hole, formalin, drawing) to the target domain of such ELT methodology concepts as method, error and writing. The mappings appeared to be a springboard for the respondents' reflections on the essence of those concepts and their role in the language classroom which was better understood when discussed in terms of the source domain items. The linguistic metaphors that the students created invited them to go into greater detail, use related terminology and investigate the said issues from different perspectives (e.g., cause-and-effect relationships, personality factors, learning preferences, learner needs). However, it has to be noted that out of five concepts metaphorical definitions failed to do their work in the case of two (feedback, induction) which, as has been mentioned above, EFL students find particularly problematic. Metaphorically speaking, the majority of the subjects' descriptions oscillating between the source domain and target domain items turned out to be a stimulating, magical journey to their own knowledge about ELT methodology, which experience helped refresh and systematize it as well as make it more explicit, thus contributing to deeper, interest-arousing understanding of some of its components.

Appendix ELT Methodology in Metaphor—An Inquiry

Date:
Circle what applies to you.
Gender: Male/Female
Year of study: 1st   2nd   3rd   4th   5th
Type of study: Day/Evening

(I) *The statements given below are your fellow students' metaphorical definitions of a few ELT methodology-related concepts. Please rank them, showing the degree to which you agree/disagree with them.*

Strongly disagree	Disagree	Neither agree nor disagree	Agree	Strongly agree
1	2	3	4	5

(1) Method

(a) weapon used to overcome problems and engage soldiers' minds;

1   2   3   4   5

(b) a key used to fasten the screw;

1   2   3   4   5

(c) the meal which, according to our experience, will be the best in getting rid of hunger;

1   2   3   4   5

(d) a material with which a path is covered (asphalt, cobblestones);

1   2   3   4   5

(e) a ball that you have to put into the basket;

1   2   3   4   5

(f) a small cake taken from a pile of cakes.

1   2   3   4   5

(2) Error

(a) a wrong step on the right path;

1   2   3   4   5

(b) a slight wound, but when it is healed, it makes us stronger;

1   2   3   4   5

(c) falling down on a bumpy road, but getting up quickly;

1   2   3   4   5

(d) a weed that needs to be removed as quickly as possible;

1   2   3   4   5

(e) an agent provocateur trying to mislead us;

1   2   3   4   5

(f) a hole in the whole.

1   2   3   4   5

(3) Feedback

(a) a book of wisdom, something to focus on;

1   2   3   4   5

(b) a conversation between a pirate and an officer;

1   2   3   4   5

(c) a boomerang that comes from the teacher or the student;

1   2   3   4   5

(d) a morale increasing talk;

1   2   3   4   5

(e) a reflection in the mirror;

1   2   3   4   5

(f) smaller or bigger treats given to students.

1   2   3   4   5

(4) Writing

(a) formalin which preserves knowledge;

1   2   3   4   5

(b) it is like sowing seeds in the soil;

1   2   3   4   5

(c) making the impermanent permanent; creating things that did not physically exist before;

1   2   3   4   5

(d) a skill making soldiers more patient and giving them a chance to practice planning skills;

1   2   3   4   5

(e) opportunity to make an error, notice it and correct it;

1   2   3   4   5

(f) drawing your thoughts for others to see.

1   2   3   4   5

(5) Induction

(a) a genealogical tree – we go from the general term 'family' to our ancestors;

1   2   3   4   5

(b) a hidden meaning;

1   2   3   4   5

(c) building a house stylistically matching furniture that we already possess;

1   2   3   4   5

(d) discovery of something special;

1   2   3   4   5

(e) moving from small things to a bigger deal;

1   2   3   4   5

(f) it is like a bridge which connects students to new knowledge.

1   2   3   4   5

(II) *Choose one of the definitions you strongly agree with and develop it into a 300-word explanatory description written in English; further metaphorical expressions are most welcome.*

References

Aristotle. (367-347 BC, 335-322 BC). *Rhetoric.* (H. Lawson-Tancred, Trans. 1991). London: Penguin.

Aronin, L., & Politis, V. (2015). Multilingualism as an edge. *Theory and Practice of Second Language Acquisition, 1*(1), 27–50.

Black, M. (1993). More about metaphor. In A. Ortony (Ed.), *Metaphor and thought* (pp. 19–41). New York: Cambridge University Press.

Brissenden, A. (Ed.). (1993). *The Oxford Shakespeare: As you like it.* Oxford: Oxford University Press.

Brown, H. D. (2000). *Principles of language learning and teaching.* White Plains, NY: Longman.

Cameron, L. (1999). Operationalizing 'metaphor' for applied linguistic research. In L. Cameron & G. Low (Eds.), *Researching and applying metaphor* (pp. 3–28). Cambridge: Cambridge University Press.

Chen, D. (2003). A classification system of metaphors about teaching. *Journal of Physical Education, Recreation, & Dance, 74,* 24–31.

Chomsky, N. (1968). *Language and mind.* New York: Harcourt, Brace & World.

Cooper, D. (1986). *Metaphor.* Oxford: Blackwell.

Corder, S. P. (1967). The significance of learners' errors. *International Review of Applied Linguistics, 5,* 161–170.

de Guerrero, M., & Villamil, O. S. (2000). Exploring ESL teachers' roles through metaphor analysis. *TESOL Quarterly, 34,* 341–351.

Deignan, A. (2005). *Metaphor and corpus linguistics.* Philadelphia: John Benjamins Publishing.

Drew, P., & Holt, E. (1988). Complainable matters: The use of idiomatic expressions in making complaints. *Social Problems, 35*(4), 398–417.

Edwards, D. (1997). *Discourse and cognition.* London: Sage.

Gao, L., & Meng, G. (2010). A study on the effect of metaphor awareness raising on Chinese EFL learners' vocabulary acquisition and retention. *Canadian Social Science, 6,* 110–124.

Gibbs, R. W. (1994). *The poetics of mind: Figurative thought, language and understanding.* New York: Cambridge University Press.

Grube, G. M. A. (1958). *Aristotle on poetry and style.* New York: Liberal Arts Press.

Hussein, B. A., & Abushihab, I. (2014). A critical review of Ferdinand de Saussure's linguistic theory. *Studies in Literature and Language, 8*(1), 57–61.

Jabara, P., & Shaffer, P. (1979). It's raining men [recorded by The Weather Girls]. On *It's raining men* [Vinyl]. New York, NY: Songs of Manhattan Island Music. (1982).

Jensen, D. (2006). Metaphors as a bridge to understanding educational and social contexts. *International Journal of Qualitative Methods, 5*(1), 36–54.

Komorowska, H. (2010). Metaphor in language education. In K. Szelest-Droździal & M. Pawlak (Eds.), *Psycholinguistic and sociolinguistic perspectives on second language learning and teaching* (pp. 57–72). Berlin Heidelberg: Springer.

Kövecses, Z., & Szabó, P. (1996). Idioms: A view from cognitive semantics. *Applied Linguistics, 17*(3), 326–355.

Lakoff, G. (1993). The contemporary theory of metaphor. In A. Ortony (Ed.), *Metaphor and thought* (pp. 202–251). New York: Cambridge University Press.

Lakoff, G., & Johnson, M. (1980). *Metaphors we live by.* Chicago: Chicago University Press.

Levine, G. S. (2011). *Code choice in the language classroom.* Bristol: Multilingual Matters.

Littlemore, J. (2004). Interpreting metaphors in the EFL classroom. *Les Cahiers de l'APLIUT, 23* (2), 57–70.

Littlemore, J., & Low, G. (2006). Metaphoric competence and communicative language ability. *Applied Linguistics, 27,* 268–294.

Locke, J. (1690) [1999]. *An essay concerning human understanding.* Philadelphia: The Pennsylvania State University.

Long, M. H., & Richards, J. C. (1999). Series editors' preface. In L. Cameron & G. Low (Eds.), *Researching and applying metaphor* (pp. x–xi). Cambridge: Cambridge University Press.

Perrine, L. (1971). Four forms of metaphor. *College English, 33,* 125–138.

Pinker, S. (1994). *The language instinct.* London: Penguin.

Reddy, M. J. (1979). The conduit metaphor: A case of frame conflict in our language about language. In A. Ortony (Ed.), *Metaphor and thought* (pp. 284–324). New York: Cambridge University Press.

Reddy, M. J. (1993). The conduit metaphor: A case of frame conflict in our language about language. In A. Ortony (Ed.), *Metaphor and thought* (pp. 164–201). New York: Cambridge University Press.

Richards, I. A. (1936/1979). *The philosophy of rhetoric.* Oxford: Oxford University Press.

Searle, J. (1979). Metaphor. In A. Ortony (Ed.), *Metaphor and thought* (pp. 92–123). New York: Cambridge University Press.

Selinker, L. (1972). Interlanguage. *International Review of Applied Linguistics, 10,* 201–231.

Way, E. (1994). *Knowledge representation and metaphor.* Oxford: Intellect.

Author Biographies

Joanna Zawodniak, Ph.D. is Associate Professor and Deputy Head at the Institute of Modern Languages at the University of Zielona Góra, Poland. Her major research interests involve metalinguistic awareness, print awareness, code-switching, socio-historical psychology in relation to L2 education, young learner SLA, metaphorical competence and boredom in the L2 classroom.

Mariusz Kruk, Ph.D. is Assistant Professor at the University of Zielona Góra, Poland. He studied Russian philology (Pedagogical University in Zielona Góra, Poland) and English philology (Adam Mickiewicz University, Kalisz, Poland). His main research interests include computer-assisted language learning, virtual worlds, learner autonomy, motivation, boredom and statistics in applied linguistics.

Is There a Place for "Sowing" in Second Language (L2) Education at the University Level? Neoliberal Tenets Under Scrutiny

Hadrian Lankiewicz

Abstract In recent years the prevalent opinion among educational policy makers is that academic institutions should be guided by the same principles as any other business unit. Corporate speak has pervaded the regulatory documents as well as management practices. The governing rule seems to be the ubiquitous accountability to guarantee "functional quality". The European Qualification Framework and its national equivalents have been intended to secure this end and create educational transparency in the era of enhanced mobility within the EU countries. However, the use of economic principles does not seem to translate easily into product quality (students' professional expertise and concurrent intellectual capacities), hence the growing criticism of measurement-oriented schooling [e.g., Biesta, 2010; Potulicka, 2010]. Invoking the concept of "sowing and reaping" put forth by van Lier (The ecology & semiotics of language learning. Kluwer, Dordrecht, 2004) in his ecological stance to education as well as the reflections of the Critical School, the article presents reflection on the consequences of neoliberal policy in education with a particular focus on the so-called L2 philological courses at Polish universities. Overall, commercialized language education is presented as falling short of expectations in social and academic terms as well as subverting dominant pedagogical reflection on autonomy in language teaching, reducing language teaching to mere skill training.

Keywords Neoliberalism · Commercialization · L2 teaching · Ecology of language learning · Autonomy · Critical perspective

H. Lankiewicz (✉)
University of Gdańsk, Gdańsk, Poland
e-mail: hadrian.lankiewicz@ug.edu.pl

© Springer International Publishing AG 2018
M. Pawlak and A. Mystkowska-Wiertelak (eds.), *Challenges of Second and Foreign Language Education in a Globalized World*, Second Language Learning and Teaching, DOI 10.1007/978-3-319-66975-5_17

1   Introduction

The very notion of "sowing" featuring in the title of this chapter has been incorporated from the publication of Leo van Lier (2004), in which he laid out the
foundation of his ecological and semiotic perception of language learning. The term
is used in the context of the criticism of bureaucratic educational policy "that fall
within the purview of standards, evaluations, performance reviews, accountability,
and standardized tests" (p. 12). Consequently, "sowing" exemplifies educational
practices, which stand in opposition to the aforementioned characteristics. The
eponymous term pertains to deeper and more lasting learning outcomes, not to be
easily measured on a day-to-day basis and, as the author posits, "the seeds lie
hidden beneath the surface, and may or may not bear fruit, at some unspecified time
in the future, in some unspecified way" (p. 12). Unfortunately, neoliberal educational practices are of a "reaping" kind, as the author defines them, and associated
with political expediency of immediate and tangible results to prove the efficiency
of the educational system. Such an approach, however, stands in opposition to
common sense and "the most firmly established research findings" (p. 11) since any
measurement which does not account for student differences, learning capacities,
contextual variability, or the simple fact that children learn in different ways and at
different rates will finally produce a false vision of reality and unwelcome unification. George W. Bush's slogan of "No child will be left behind" is presented by
van Lier as a spectacular example of such a short-sighted and unreliable
accountability-based educational policy, whose testing system produces a drop-out
rate of about 30% because it does not provide for the simple fact that English is not
a native language for all American students.

Ideas presented on the pages of van Lier's book cited above and his other
publications constituted an inspiration for my personal interest in the application of
the concept of "an ecosystem" to the field of language learning and language study
(see Lankiewicz, 2015), and, in my mind, may be easily applied to education in
general. Showing his dissatisfaction with the traditional way of doing research in
social sciences marked by the processes of induction and deduction, van Lier
resorts to chaos/complexity theories to call for an ecological way, which com-
pensates for prevailing levels of reductionism pertaining to context, data and
complexity (2004, p. 9) in doing science and ultimately applies it to language study
and language learning processes.

Thus, an ecological approach to language learning and teaching will constitute a
springboard for basic considerations in this paper. This stance basically involves a
shift of focus in language learning research from considering internal cognitive
factors to external (environmental) ones, which entails "looking at learning as a
socio-culturally defined phenomenon determined by the social and cultural macro
context and taking place in a socially, culturally and ecologically determined micro
context, for example, in the classroom" (Järvinen, 2009, p. 164). The immediate
corollary to language learning teaching of an ecological approach is that the language mindset is not finally the result of internal cognitive processing but rather the

product of interactions with the semiotic budget of the environment, including the fact that a remarkable part of cognition is done socially, on the "intermental plane" (Lankiewicz, 2015) during the communication process.

This fundamental line of thinking, enhanced by the so-called Critical School, which by nature is critical,[1] will be taken as a starting point for the critique of neoliberal educational polices at the tertiary level of language education and the ubiquitous system of accountability, which is supposed to guarantee quality and transparency of the educational systems across countries. In other words, the application of quality management system to education is to improve functional quality of educational institutions and their services to meet market needs and satisfy potential clients. Yet whether this functional quality secures product quality (students' intellectual capacities and their expertise) as well as educational processes has remained the subject of heated debates among scholars, educators and all other interested in the condition of education. Considerations in this chapter will be confined to the problems of language education pertaining to the so-called philological courses (B.A. and M.A. major in foreign languages) in Poland. The neoliberal entanglement of language education in Poland will be juxtaposed with the notion of quality and autonomy.

2 Neoliberalism

The notion of neoliberalism is frequently used to denote a recent, in particular after the market crash of 2008 (see Holborow, 2015), socio-political and economic shift based on the principles of *laissez faire*, standing for little or no government intervention in the transactions between individuals, which ultimately boils down to the promotion of profit-oriented tenets to any sphere of human activity. This tendency is accompanied by strong commercialization—perceiving relation between people and their actions in the prism of production processes with the alleged outcome in the form of some kind of product or service[2]—and globalization. In short, neoliberalism becomes the hallmark of late capitalism. Yet the term is mostly used by the critics of the so-called wild capitalism in a pejorative sense to signify "the lamentable spread of global capitalism and consumerism, as well as the equally

---

[1]The word "critical" may be used here in its different meanings: *axiological*—construed as protecting the smaller and the weaker to keep the ecological balance healthy; *Marxist*—"taking social inequality and social transformation as central"; *critical thinking*—based on humanist-cognitive egalitarianism; *social relevance*—evoking constructivism and contextualization, and *problematizing practice*—finding theoretical support in postoccidentalism and anarcho-particularism (see Lankiewicz, 2015, p. 79).

[2]Interestingly, even the services are referred to as products. Suffice it to notice how neoliberal ideology is reflected in the language use of the banking system. Banks no longer offer loans, instead their agents significantly use the term "product" offering credit services to their potential clients. For "creeping linguistic neoliberalism" see Mirowski (2013) or Holborow (2015).

deplorable demolition of the proactive welfare state" (Thorsen & Lie, 2007, p. 2) and, as argued further, it remains vague and disputable regarding to what degree it is the dominant ideology, "governing force" or world view shaping present-day reality.

There is, however, much equivocation pertaining to the use of the term in question as to what it really stands for and how much it evokes liberal practices and in what sense it diverges from them as the prefix *neo-* much suggest. As some authors maintain, "[t]he word [n]eoliberalism came into use at the end of the 19th century with a meaning completely different from the current one" (Vercelli, 2016). Originally, it had positive overtones to denote a moderate version of free market liberties with neoliberals suggesting "to divorce the freedom of individuals to compete in the marketplace from the freedom from state intervention" (Boas & Gans-Morse, 2009, p. 146, as cited in Vercelli, 2016) and arguing that "laissez-faire policy suffocates genuine competition favoring the progressive concentration of market power" (Gerber, 1994, p. 33, as cited in Vercelli, 2016). This meaning of neoliberalism is mostly associated with Germany and social liberalism or social market economy trying to legitimize government intervention as a way of securing *laissez faire* practices. Thus, putting it differently, this political ideology maintains that individual liberty, economic or otherwise, requires a level of social justice. In this sense, the neoliberal slant presented an attempt to search for the middle ground of the generic conflict between philosophies of classical liberalism and socialist planning, the so-called "third" or "middle" way.

In the 1970s the term underwent critical mutations and began to denote a more radical and *laissez-faire* capitalist set of ideas standing for market fundamentalism, with the Chilean coup d'etat of Pinochet being the critical moment for this new, negative connotation (see Boas & Gans-Morse, 2009; Vercelli, 2016). This was when the dictator and his government junta in the attempt to curb inflation decided to appoint technocrats (economic experts of the Chicago School of Economics background) to powerful positions in the government. They advocated strict free market polices including widespread deregulation and privatization as a viable alternative to government controlled economy of the deposed Chilean president Salvador Allende. The so-called ideas of "Chicago Boys" inspired by the teaching of, for example, Milton Friedman, a significant exponent of economic thinking, which today is associated with the neoliberalism characteristic of the government of Margaret Thatcher, for whom, parenthetically, Friedman worked as an advisor. This line of thinking has been gaining popularity among Western democracies, and dictating the political decisions of many developing post-communist countries, including Poland.

Although its etymological derivation remains equivocal, the meaning of neoliberalism alludes a distorted version of liberal tradition.[3] In a nutshell, neoliberalism embodies ideas promoting conservative (in its American meaning)

---

[3]For details regarding its continuity or discontinuity with the classical liberalism see Vercelli (2016, 2017).

economic principle of free trade with competition conceived of as the invisible hand to regulate the market. Hence those who question this term for the sake of obscurity use alternative notions of *neoconservatism* or *Washington consensus* to refer to the geopolitical reality of globalization processes after the 1980s. There is, however, one essential corollary of neoliberalism that makes this ideology very effective: it is its pervasive character, penetrating our postmodern existence. In other words, it is the ideology of the postmodern when "nature is gone for good" and "'culture' has become a veritable 'second nature'", as aptly concluded by Jameson (1991, p. 9). Commodification has become a lifestyle, marketization and economic rules have penetrated the most intimate spheres of everyday reality, with the latter one iron-ically becoming a *simulacrum* of its own: "the truth which conceals that there is none" (Baudrillard, 1981, p. 166). Extending Jameson's claim regarding the place of commodities in postmodern culture to the ideology underlying the relations which produce this reality, I assume that neoliberalism as such obtains the status of a monotheistic religion. In the post-communist era, which created a favorable ground for neoliberal ideas, anything collective and unaccountable is perceived as devilish. What matters is an individual whose value is measured by his or her productive capacity and an ability to adapt to market fluctuations. This rationality of contemporary capitalism permeates through all social levels and "tends to organize and structure not only the action of the rulers but also the conduct of the ruled" (Dardot & Laval, 2013, p. 9, as cited in Bori & Petanović, 2016, p. 155).

The "neoliberal church" is thus not congregational, its believers are approached individually via mass media channels and "real life"[4] situations. They remain genuinely unaware of what is being inculcated in them. One of the most subtle ways of controlling people is through language used in an indiscriminate way. It is via language that ideology seeps with impunity, making people unaware of the levels of manipulation they are exposed to. Not surprisingly, in recent years, neoliberal language and neoliberal principles have entered education. In a sense, legitimization of neoliberal ideology has been facilitated and neutralized and apparently restricts our liberty.

3   Neoliberal Language and Commercialization of Schooling

Critical linguistics and its extension, critical discourse analysis underscore the social constitution of language and the relationship between language, compre-hended as discursive practices, and developments in different social domains. Consequently, "[d]iscursive practices—through which texts are *produced* (created) and *consumed* (received and interpreted)—are viewed as an important form of

---

[4]The use of parenthesis is intentional here to underscore the doubtful nature of reality in the postmodern era.

social practice which contributes to the constitution of the social world including social identities and social relations" (Jorgensen & Phillips, 2002, p. 61). Critical thought in linguistics and social studies coincided with the spread of neoliberal ideas, far beyond economic setting; hence neoliberal language has received its due attention in the form of critique of dominant power relations. Discourse analysts explain how neoliberal language, with its derivatives such as corporate speak, financial language or management speak, has permeated many spheres of our lives and supports the ideological grip, in other words, how neoliberalism operates through language.

The phenomenon of "marketization of language", according to Holborow (2015, p. 1), is evident everywhere and conjecturally it may "reflect the apparent unassailable position of neoliberalism". Capitalizing on Mirowski's (2013, p. 117) "creeping linguistic neoliberalism", she claims the tightened relation between language and ideology. Uncritical use of economic vocabulary in a commonsensical way makes this ideology seep into different areas of our lives and constitutes proof of its hegemony in the Gramscian sense when the superstructure creates people's consciousness, as explained by Barrett (1991, p. 54): "Hegemony is best understood as *the organisation of consent*—the processes through which subordinated forms of consciousness are constructed without recourse to violence or coercion" (emphasis original). Assuming after Gramsci articulation of ideology in language, Holborow maintains that naturalized use of corporate speak (consensual power) masks its ideological workings. Hence, according to her, a level of critical language awareness unmasking power tensions may have a liberating potential and constitutes "the articulation of (…) new awareness" (p. 6). She further claims that, in the moment of crises, as it is the case after 2008, the ideological burden of language is more intensive since the ruling class seeks "to conserve and defend the existing structure" (Gramsci, 1971/1991, p. 400). Therefore "[t]he widespread presence of neoliberal ideology in language is one sign (…) of the concerted project for ideological hegemony on behalf of powerful social interests and therefore uncovering the ideological meanings in its use must also be part of the challenge to it" (Holborow, 2015, p. 7).

In contrast to the so-called "discursive turn," Holborow's study of the relation between neoliberalism and language restores the value of ideology as an analytical tool, which sets her analysis more in the Marxist tradition than the one of critical discourse analysis. Consequently, calling upon the social realm for the construction of discursive practices, she resolves to perceive language as a commodity, or a "technical skill amenable to managerial measurement" and "symbolic 'added value' to industrially produced resources" (p. 17), and additionally posits that the process of commodification has been extended to all, even most abstract, aspects of human behavior. Seeing language as an ideological medium, Holborow accentuates the dynamic nature of both of them. Researchers of neoliberal language see it not just as a domain over which neoliberalism holds a grip, or ideology inscribed in a language, but also as the way of sustaining and reproducing dominant ideology and an important tool to understand the very notion of neoliberalism and to highlight its constitutive contradictions (see Shin, 2016).

The study of neoliberal language and concurrent social practices allows to explicate the ways in which market rules pervade education and lead to its commodification. As Bori and Petanović (2016, p. 156) point out, from the beginning of "the 1970s onwards, in many countries which followed the US model, public administration has been substituted with managerialism, the state's role as a guarantor of the general welfare has been diminished, public education has been commodified, and the burden of social responsibility has been mostly placed onto the individuals". The actions of teachers, students and even school principals are subject to competition, a never-ending struggle in the economic sense in which knowledge, or rather skills, as I will argue further, are perceived as commodities offered by schools according to market rules of supply and demand.

Neoliberal ideology has successfully permeated university education calling into question some basic values traditionally associated with this institution (see Wąsikiewicz-Firlej, 2013 for further discussion). In the sense ascribed presently to educational institutions, derived from Latin, the word *universitas* stands for a corporate body or "community of teachers and scholars whose corporate existence had been recognized and sanctioned by civil or ecclesiastical authority or by both" ("universities"). Constitutive documents vested any institution of this type with certain civil liberties, academic freedom and autonomy, which effectively meant that this corporate organization was self-regulated (Colish, 1997, p. 267).

A ubiquitous entrepreneurial and consumerist approach enrooted in neoliberalism to social issues at the turn of the 20th and 21st century, introduced managerial models into academic institutions establishing "corporate universities (where) power is transferred from faculty to managers, economic justifications dominate, and the familiar 'bottom line' eclipses pedagogical or intellectual concerns" (Berg & Seeber, 2016, p. 10). At the moment of putting these words on paper, the Polish system of higher education is undergoing a radical reform. To a critical eye, neoliberal financial accountability is showing through new regulations and projects discussed as part of the reform, and all this with the alleged intention of raising the quality of education, efficiency of academics and intensification of research activities with the hope of going up in the world ranking lists, which Biesta (2010) perceives as part of the system of control incited by fear of being left behind. *Publish or perish*, the maxim shaping American well-donated universities is perceived as a remedy for Polish otherwise "lazy scholars", overloaded with reporting and doing extra hours in different places to earn a decent living. Some of the reform projects propose resignation from a traditional tenure system of building academic careers (even if according to the existing Polish regulations of higher education employment of academics is practically never permanent and its continuation is dependent on the fulfillment of contract academic criteria) by freelancing based on competitive projects financed by external institutions. Thereby, neoliberal insecurity of "*homo economicus*: the self-entrepreneurial, autonomous, and self-regulating individual" (Foucault, 2008, p. 226, as cited in Bori & Petanović, 2016, p. 155) is boldly entering the Ivory Tower.

The neoliberal obsession with mobility goes so far that some plans for reform foresee restrictions on the employment of the university's own graduates. The principle of doing a degree at one university and being employed by another gives no respect to the fact that scholars have their own families who cannot be moved from one place to another without repercussions. This neoliberal governmentality[5] does not only work out job insecurity; it also dehumanizes and objectifies people inculcating in them moral subjectivity—the need of constant "self-improvement" (Eleveld, 2009, as cited in Bori & Petanović, 2016, p. 155). The celebration of neoliberal entrepreneurial self and competition for acquiring new skills does not result in any stabilization or finding comfort in one's past achievements. For exponents of neoliberalism, stability is a taboo word to be confronted with a cliché that standing still is moving backwards. All this "functions to obscure the pain and misery of the precarity of work brought about by neoliberalism; instead of complaining about being laid off, people are told to welcome such challenges as an opportunity to improve themselves and live life to the fullest. In this sense, this subjective dimension is an important aspect of how neoliberalism commodifies even our deepest sense of belonging and identity" (Shin & Park, 2016, p. 445).

Another outcome of neoliberal educational policy is its corporatization (Urciuoli, 2010). This apparently applies to higher education, with the present Polish reform being a generic example. This policy is characterized by cost reductions, outcome orientations and self-direction, in a sense that each student is supposed to make a balance of his or her choices, abilities and motivations in such a way that it will meet market demands and bring tangible financial profits. Education is thus directed by an ethic of entrepreneurial self-management, stressing the fact that every person is his orher own product. Yet, as Shin (2016, p. 510) argues, "it is increasingly observed in the K-12 education sectors as well".

Indiscriminate application of market rules to education leads to the disintegration of schooling as a social realm, a community of committed individuals both on the part of teachers and students. The imposition of commercial values feeds competitive forces, of a Darwinian type, for which tradition, education quality and prestige (communal things) are not qualities per se; they are simple derivatives of the fight for survival and perceived as an aggregate of individual accountabilities (publication figures, indicators, indexes, and so on). They are tallied up in the form of estimates to be translated into economic terms—direct income and government subsidies. The survival of the fittest is additionally enhanced by job insecurity, precariousness of regulations and the threat of layoffs. This, as Bourdieu (1998) argues, is the result of neoliberal utopia of clinging to pure mathematical market logic and this ultimately leads to the destruction of collective structures. It suffices

---

[5]This Foucauldian term "is a neologism that combines 'government' and 'mentality' to study the links between the ways governments manage people's actions through techniques of domination and the ways people conduct their own behaviour through techniques of the self" (Bori & Petanović, 2016, p. 155).

to observe college and university life in Poland to draw similar conclusions. Not long ago an academic tenure was a prestigious position respected socially and recognized by "insiders" themselves during various events accompanying university life. Nowadays, this claim seems to be doubtful. Social events of the Academia are scarcely frequented by its members. Students, in turn, are not very much willing to contribute to the cultural life of their Alma Mater without and external incentive of the supervisor. No wonder, both parts calculate their potential investment against prospective profits. Bourdieu (1998) aptly maintains that the pervasive Darwinism, "with the cult of the winner, schooled in higher mathematics and bungee jumping, institutes the struggle of all against all and *cynicism* as the norm of all action and behavior" (emphasis original).

Last but not least, neoliberalism conceives of education as knowledge- and service-based economy enhanced by information dissemination resulting from the widespread use of information technologies (Vallima & Hoffman, 2008). The basic idea is fed by economic perception of knowledge as commodity or a key economic resource (Drucker, 1969). Although in social theory knowledge society is seen as fundamental for modern society consisting of well-informed citizens able to take effective and responsible actions, it seems that its educational purpose of producing aware citizens, democracy and equality has been taken over by its economic dimension. Critical discourse analysis elucidates how neoliberal ideas are reflected in education and how they result in commodification of learning and teaching as well as how they harness education into the reproduction processes through indoctrination (e.g., Giroux, 1983).

The tenets of neoliberal economy have become a founding principle for organizing educational institutions in such a way to make them "susceptible to corporate logic" (Shin, 2016, p. 511). Shin (2016), taking the example of South Korea, demonstrates an increased conflation between education and business and the emergence of education industry. Respectively, she maintains that "[i]n the discourses of corporate-driven educational reforms, the value of knowledge is highlighted and students are constructed as consumers, educational practices as services, faculty/teachers as employees or service providers, and education as resources or product. The accountability of education is thus determined by the ability to provide students with skills required in the labor market" (p. 511).

This commodification of education results in some spectacular businesslike behavior of schools and universities, which participate in an annual educational fair or operate abroad through transnational agencies. University performance is frequently measured by student mobility or so-called internationalization, which is the number of candidates coming from abroad as regular students, as well as by the figures of incoming and outgoing students for a short study period, within, for example, the Erasmus+ program. Business-like operation of higher education is equally visible in its functional structure; for example, curricula are to be endorsed by shareholders (organizational units showing interests in the education offer) or client satisfaction measurement in the form of evaluation surveys.

4 Neoliberalism and L2 Education

However questionable the notion of neoliberalism may be (see Vercelli, 2016, 2017), it is mostly presented as an ideological construct with drastic consequences for our contemporary lives. As mentioned before, the subtle ways for the reproduction of ideological mindsets are language and education. Critical linguistics and critical pedagogy respectively, try to account for the relations of power in the designated areas.

L2 language teaching constitutes a domain where neoliberal ideology has gained due consideration in recent research in applied linguistics. With the proviso that the latter discipline may be understood in its border sense, as an interdisciplinary field of researching real-life language problems, and the narrower one, identical to methodology of language teaching (see Richards & Rodgers, 2001, p. 46), there is no need to mention that neoliberal ideology has inspired both branches. Since language pedagogy is of focal attention here, it is necessary to admit that research on L2 teaching has been inspired both by the neoliberal mindset, as deconstructed and made visible by critical pedagogy (e.g., Bourdieu, 1983; Giroux, 1991; McLaren, 2013), and broadly conceived applied linguistics, including the one with a critical slant (e.g., Fairclough, 1989, 1992; Holborow, 2015). Direct criticism of neoliberal ideology in the field of L2 teaching may be exemplified by Block, Gray, and Holborow (2012), Bernstein, Hellmich, Katznelson, Shin, and Vinall (2015), Shin and Park (2016), Bori and Petanović (2016), and, with a particular focus on teaching English as a second language by Shin (2016) or Lankiewicz (2015). Problems related to the imprint of neoliberal ideology on L2 language learning and teaching will be considered in reference to two basic concepts presented in the conceptual continuum to account for their dialectal ecological complexity. These are *accountability versus quality* and *autonomy versus unification*, and they portray the mismatch between neoliberal rationale and its actual outcomes as communicated by the critiques of neoliberal educational practices and my personal observation as an academic teacher and a critical thinker.

4.1 Accountability Versus Quality

One of the crucial notions in any business unit is a quality management system which is supposed to be aligned with the organization's strategic mission and designed to secure its functional operations, product quality as well as customer satisfaction, all with the aim of sustainable development—prolonged balanced existence. The key word to guarantee high quality standards is *accountability* (responsibility or answerability) for actions, operations and products, both in the moral and economic sense. Neoliberal education reformers have adopted this basically economic term, borrowed from managing production lines (Potulicka, 2010, p. 178), making it one of the crucial tenets for governing educational institutions.

The narrowly construed accountability seems to lose its moral connotation and maintains only its market-related meaning. In the educational milieu, accountability measures include standardization, measurement and testing to secure individualism and competition (Hursh, 2005, p. 3).

On the tertiary level of academic education, accountability has received an additional spur since the application of the Bologna Process. Nowadays, there exist numerous regulations and institutional controls to guarantee good functional performance of universities and other schools of higher education. Some of them include: National Qualification Framework, internal reporting, or the system of national accreditation, saying nothing about parameterization (the system of reporting to the national government), which translates into subsidies (a tangible financial result). Language education has additionally been regulated by the *Common European framework of reference for languages*, constituting a guideline document for describing achievements of learners of foreign languages to make them verifiable and transparent across many European contexts. The aim of accountability measures was intended to tighten government control over nationally donated education, secure its quality and make the learning outcomes nationally and internationally comprehensible. The last objective is of importance for the European Common Market. Nonetheless, this system has received a remarkable load of criticisms on many accounts, for example, social, economic and political. Research in these fields demonstrates that testing and standardization fall short of their objectives, as they discriminate, lead to technocratic practices, and have a negative impact on students' critical abilities (see Potulicka, 2010).

Such an approach has drastic consequences for the quality of the so-called philology courses. Massive, market driven language education leads to reduction of curricula, teaching hours and general permissiveness regarding low academic requirements. Both teachers and students try to outwit the system, which is liable to multifarious manipulations. For example, an easy test raises accountability figures and pleases some less motivated students, resulting in high scores and inflation of grades (Cooper, 2009, p. 206, as cited in Potulicka, 2010, p. 182). This, in turn, satisfies school authorities since any student in the system translates easily into a tuition income for privately owned units, or a government subsidy for the state ones. In case of doubt, the financial aspect takes priority over quality. Consequently, what is on paper in the form of offered quality in terms of value and linguistic capital is not compatible with the quality of the product (student).

The application of verifiability and practicality of language courses results in students' resistance to academic courses requiring deep philosophical reflection on the nature of language such as, for example, translation theory. Treating philological studies as extended language courses, they refuse to learn anything which is not directly connected with skills development. Critics of neoliberalism admit that "[i]n this conceptual frame, every piece of knowledge one acquires can be interpreted and assessed as a skill, an aspect of oneself that can be considered productive by prospective employers. Skills thus become a form of self-marking, and students readily come to imagine themselves as bundles of skills" (Urciuoli, 2010, p. 162). Yet the failure to meet students' expectations has negative repercussions for the teacher (not being accountable to students' expectations, he or she is confronted with low evaluation of his or her teaching practice as expressed in surveys). Not groundlessly, philology courses are slowly losing their academic profiles in favor of practical ones. This fact is additionally supported by the neoliberal government in the claim that universities should educate for the market.

An academic, intellectual dimension of philological education seems to belong to the past. Neoliberal market needs tangible skills to be accounted for. Even academic language teaching is of a reaping kind, since there is little time for reflection, deep ecological teaching of a sowing kind with delayed outcomes (van Lier, 2004, p. 11). Although National Qualification Framework foresees method-ological reflection on doing linguistic research, my personal observation and research (Lankiewicz, 2013) allows me to claim that being a seminar tutor is a doubtful pleasure. Despite intensive guidance and monitoring, more and more students find it difficult to complete their diploma papers both in linguistic and intellectual terms. Potulicka (2010, p. 188) corroborates my allegations by citing research demonstrating that 44% of academic teachers are of the opinion that high school graduates are not prepared for further education, they neither possess ana-lytical skills nor are able to comprehend longer texts. Skill-oriented philological education disempowers students as potential candidates for Ph.D. university courses. In short, the neoliberal claims of self-improvement and responsibility for one's own progress disguise limited employability of poorly educated graduates.

My final remark pertaining to the issue of accountability versus quality of neoliberal linguistic education (yet not exhausting the issue) concerns the position of English as a foreign language. Globalization and the popularity of English makes English philology courses more popular than ever, which has an impact on the educational viability of minority languages. At a certain point in time even the Polish Ministry of Education opted for making this language an obligatory first foreign language in school curricula arguing that investing in other languages would be a waste of money. Neoliberal market dictates in academic language education stand in opposition to liberty, social justice and reduce university edu-cation to mere a skill training (Shin, 2016). Ironically, the so-called neoliberal knowledge society seems to be less and less knowledgeable than ever. Sound, sustainable development of communities necessitates a balanced approach. Van Lier, calling for a linguistic diversity, uses an ecological metaphor to accentuate the problem (2004, p. 50) by maintaining that "a monocultural ecosystem (basically, this would be a cultivated field) is extremely fragile and barren. Left to its own devices such a system explodes into diversity (…) or else remains barren". Language policy and neoliberal ideology surely impact minority languages (McEwan-Fujita, 2005). We can slowly experience the results of globalized market fuffering the nuisance of seeing the same products in the shops all around the world. We have to make sure that uniformity does make our linguistic heritage barren. Significant in this regard is Shin's (2016, p. 514) argument that language education industry is not only affected by neoliberalism but it also "assists in perpetuating the ideologies of neoliberalism" (Shin 2016, p. 514).

4.2 Autonomy Versus Uniformity

The concept of autonomous language learning has overshadowed earlier method-ological approaches and, as its proponents maintain, it has turned out that in the 21st century there is no way out of autonomy. It cannot be thought of as an alternative method but rather a constitutive concept of modern language pedagogy in the same way as the communicative approach was for the 20th century (Breen & Mann, 1997). Indeed a cursory review of language teaching literature warrants the claim that it has become a buzzword for educational policy makers, including regulatory documents of the European Union.

The main assumption behind autonomous language learning is the ability "to take charge of one's own learning" (Holec, 1981, p. 3), with students being able to define objectives and select contents, methods, monitor learning processes and evaluate their own progress. To make the idea more feasible and adjusted to the classroom context and account for the social character of language learning, a moderate version of the concept has been promoted. This semi-autonomy (Dickinson, 1987, p. 11) allows for autonomy development and counseling since it remains disputable whether it is an inherent ability of a human being or it needs some "training" (Smith, 2008, p. 386). All in all, literature on autonomy makes it explicit that the overall mission for developing autonomy in language learning is to produce better learners, better people and, ultimately, better citizens (see Benson & Voller, 1997, p. 3). Holec (1981, p. 1) places autonomy in the democratic tradition implying that the learning process is to result in the wholesome transformation of a person to be able "to act responsibly in running the affairs of the society in which he lives".

We may relate the definition of autonomy in education in general and language education in particular to the notion of subjectivity in its philosophical sense of being a subject as juxtaposed with an agent. Briefly, subjectivity in the critical, political dimension conceptualizes the idea of one wielding power over one's actions not to become an object of the actions of others and indirectly legitimizes an individual perception of reality and the search for personal subjective "truths". In this respect, promotion of language learning autonomy coincides with neoliberal "transformation of subjectivities". Shin and Park (2016) in their introduction to the special issue of the *Journal of Multilingual and Multicultural Development* dedi-cated to researching language and neoliberalism characterize the deeper level of neoliberal thought as laying emphasis "on individual responsibility, in which people are encouraged to take greater initiative regarding their lives and be accountable for their own choices (instead of relying on support of the state or solidarity of community)" (p. 444). This can be understood in terms of how subjects are governed, or, in terms of governmentality (Foucault, 1991). In this respect, Foucauldian neologism, constituting a combination of words "government" and "mentality", coined "to study the links between the ways governments manage people's actions through techniques of domination and the ways people conduct their own behavior through techniques of the self" (Bori & Petanović, 2016, p. 155), has its extension in the perception of autonomy in education.

Freedom in learning may be seen as part of neoliberal rationality of late capitalism in the educational realm, as a manifestation of hegemonic forces. In other words, autonomy in learning has been inscribed into a broader concept of subjectivation, ceding responsibility to individuals for the shape of their lives with government reaping the fruits of their endless self-development and adjustment to market conditions. In this sense "[n]eoliberal subjects are governed not by direct exercise of power and discipline over them through 'technologies of the self' (Foucault, 1997)—that is, set of practices that inculcate within individuals a willingness to conduct and manage themselves even in the absence of overt control" (Miller & Rose, 2008, as cited in Shin & Park, 2016, p. 444–445). Significantly, this freedom is only apparent since our positive liberty (see Vercelli, 2016, 2017)— autonomy standing for our potential—is determined by unintentional market conditions. To exemplify, my freedom as a researcher is conditioned by, for example, my access to online data bases, research funds, etc. Analogically, freedom in language learning may not only be the result of one's potential and willingness but may equally well be a derivative of somebody's socio-economic constitution.

In short, autonomy in language learning may well reproduce existing "class structure" and "reproduce unequal social relations" (Shin, 2016, p. 520). Additionally, the "construction of language as a skill, as claimed earlier, and the subsequent commodification of language learning and teaching as self-improvement becomes an indispensable mechanism in the neoliberal regime of human capital, which not only reflects neoliberal social transformations, but also reinforces them" (Shin & Park, 2016, p. 448).

Shin (2016), analyzing the Korean context, mentions "English Divide", referring to social polarization through voluntary quality education of English in the form of sojourn language courses in Canada as a way of self-direction which is to guarantee job security. The languages packages described by Shin on the one hand exemplify "deferential access to the linguistic capital" (p. 520), and, on the other, corporatization of language education. All this is done in the name self-management and seems to be well applicable to the Polish context of higher philological education. Philology courses offered by numerous educational institutions of different academic profiles function as business units, offering a language skill set in the form of a product, whose quality is to be guaranteed by the catchword "philology". Mass access to this education acts as a substitute for traditional language courses. Their potential candidates live under the delusion that graduation can be expected to upgrade their access to the global labor market. Well, in reality lamentable quality restricts employment possibilities to low-profile jobs and leads to anomalies such as, for example, a situation in which poorly educated language teachers are disempowered in confrontation with some students who beat the pants of them in terms of linguistic abilities. Free access to mass language education, apparently on highest level, does not liberate but "reproduces unequal social relations" (Shin, 2016, p. 520).

Shin (2016, p. 515) demonstrates how self-management reinforces existing inequality and how neoliberal "'self-management' obscures differential access to material and symbolic resources to develop the required skills among different social actors". Additionally, neoliberal discourse and the application of self-management tenets in the form of promoting personal responsibility for language education obscures how deeply it is intertwined with structures of class (Park, 2010, 2011, as cited in Shin, 2016, p. 520). "The analyses highlight ways in which the language learning industry not only interplays with but also actively shapes the ideologies of neoliberalism, by developing and selling packaged products that make the projects of self-management seem more achievable and desirable" (Shin, 2016, p. 509).

Even if European and national documents subscribe to the concept of autonomy in language learning, classroom reality is far from this. Very often neither students nor teachers manifest features defining autonomous language users and ultimately their potential activities are constrained by regulatory procedures. Shin and Park (2016, p. 448) evoking Block and Gray (2016) elucidate how "language teachers, as neoliberal workers, are increasingly subject to control over their profession and their training, and demonstrate that, contrary to the prevalent neoliberal myth of 'flexible self-manager' workers, the majority of labor under neoliberalism has actually become more routine, uniform, and predictable". Further, alluding to Bourdieu (1998), Shin and Park (2016, p. 450) put it differently and argue that "by equating English language learning with individual effort of self-improvement or self-management which is disconnected from external social structures, neoliberal logic mystifies interests and power that mediate individuals' access to language in the neoliberal regime of human capital development, and turns it to a belief system, as shared beliefs in private and public discourses".

The autonomy trend in language learning, being the outcome of general pedagogical reflection in the postmodern and post-method era as a form of learner-centered education is surely a great achievement in language teaching and learning, yet implemented indiscriminately may become an instrument for facilitating neoliberal ideology, as to a great extent it does. Self-management, the basic tenet of it, is well compatible with neoliberal discourse. Autonomy as pure theory is as dehistoricized (against the teaching tradition) as the "neoliberal faith" (Bourdieu, 1998), as both make themselves true and verifiable in the modern world and both present a big political project underway since education, no doubt, is a political act (Giroux, 2010), including language learning and teaching, which is not an apolitical activity. The ideological burden of it is manifested in various ways, not necessarily encompassing "the grand sweeping gestures of imperialism, language rights and globalization" (Pennycook, 2010, p. 10), but also presenting itself in "a form of politics that is grounded in local language activity" (p. 10). Thereby, an important aspect of autonomy is its critical, political level, which is offered in the concluding part the chapter as a way of transgressing uniform neoliberal mindset in language education.

5 Conclusion: Hope for Sowing?

Since this basically dark picture of Polish academic language education needs a counterpoint, instead of a traditional roundup, I have resolved to present a possible way of transgressing ubiquitous influence of neoliberalism, particularly in language education and I ironically argue that it can be done through a closer study of language.

Critical ecological thinking, drawing on the tradition of critical discourse analysis, critical pedagogy and critical linguistics, points out that language as living tissue and our discursive practices both shape and reflect the socio-political reality of human existence. As maintained by critical discourse analysts, "discourse is an important form of social practice which both reproduces and changes knowledge, identities and social relations including power relations, and at the same time is also shaped by other social practices and structures. Thus discourse is in a dialectical relationship with other social dimensions" (Jorgensen & Phillips, 2002, p. 65). Hence the level of language awareness of how language relates to power is essential for a better understanding of our social condition. Promoting critical awareness, Fairclough (1992) accentuates the need for problematization or de-naturalization of our language use so that it does not reproduce the *status quo* of power relations. Consequently, as Shin and Park (2016, p. 445) suggest, "if language occupies a central place in the way in which neoliberalism establishes itself as a dominant ideology, then (…) insights about language as socially grounded practice also lead to new understandings about neoliberalism (…) and thus "better understanding of the social and cultural grounding of language has much to offer to a more refined critique of neoliberalism" (p. 446).

In this regard, elsewhere I propose critical ecological language awareness as a necessary prerequisite of any language user, and in particular a language student in the era of neoliberal globalization and postmodern reality (Lankiewicz, 2015). This transversal skill may seem particularly indispensable for philology students and foreign language teachers so that they are not indiscriminate language users/learners of any language since the way one sees language influences the learning and teaching processes. To illustrate, if one is able to notice political tensions embedded in the language, he or she will try to look for strings attached and will not allow the language to do the thinking for him or her (Lankiewicz, 2015, p. 258). In this context, I propound the vision of a transformative language teacher (ecopedagogue) with a potential of raising the quality of life through critical language awareness. My claim seems to be compatible with that of Shin and Park (2016, p. 448), who, alluding to Bourdieu (1998), argue that "the 'skill-providing and skill-taking' mode of teacher preparation as represented in the policy and practices in the programs inevitably involves beliefs about what teaching and learning are, what it means to be a teacher, and what are the best ways to produce teachers [sic], thereby reinforcing the neoliberal regime. Nonetheless, the pervasiveness of skills discourse in the state and educational policy and institutional practices naturalizes particular practices as objective imperatives and renders people subject to the neoliberal belief system".

To summarize, relating directly to the question posed in the title, the sowing of philology courses may be regained in developing critical language awareness for a better understanding of the grip of neoliberalism and as a way of counteracting the neoliberal construct of the self in language learning, which results in the wrong positioning of oneself as a language user, language learner and ultimately a citizen.

References

Barrett, M. (1991). *The politics of truth. From Marx to Foucault.* Cambridge: Polity Press.

Baudrillard, J. (1981). Simulacra and simulations. In J. Baudrillard, M. Poster (Eds.), *Selected writings* (pp. 166–184). Stanford: Stanford University Press, 1988.

Benson, P., & Voller, P. (1997). Introduction: Autonomy and independence in language learning. In P. Benson & P. Voller (Eds.), *Autonomy and independence in language learning* (pp. 1–12). London and New York: Longman.

Berg, M., & Seeber, B. (2016). *The slow professor: Challenging the culture of speed in the academy.* Toronto: Toronto University Press.

Bernstein, K., Hellmich, E., Katznelson, N., Shin, J., & Vinall, K. (2015). Introduction to special issue: Critical perspectives on Neoliberalism in second/foreign language education. *L2 Journal, 7*(3), 3–14.

Biesta, G. J. J. (2010). *Good education in an age of measurement: Ethics, politics, and democracy.* London: Paradigm Publishers.

Block, D., & Gray, J. (2016). 'Just go away and do it and you get marks': The degradation of language teaching in neoliberal times. Researching language and neoliberalism. *Journal of Multilingual and Multicultural Development, 37*(5), 481–494.

Block, D., Gray, J., & Holborow, M. (2012). *Neoliberalism and applied linguistics.* London: Routledge.

Boas, T. C., & Gans-Morse, J. (2009). Neoliberalism: From new liberal philosophy to anti-liberal slogan. *Studies in Comparative International Development, 44,* 137–161.

Bori, P., & Petanović, J. (2016). Constructing the entrepreneurial-self: How Catalan textbooks present the neoliberal worker to their students. *Journal for Critical Education Policy Studies, 14*(3), 154–174.

Bourdieu, P. (1998). The essence of Neoliberalism. Le Monde Diplomatique. Retrieved from http://mondediplo.com/1998/12/08bourdieu

Colish, M. L. (1997). *Medieval foundations of the Western intellectual tradition, 400–1400.* New Haven: Yale University Press.

Cooper, Ch. (2009). Review essay: Neoliberalism, education and strategies of resistance. *Journal for Critical Education Policy Studies, 6*(2) http://www.jceps.com/wp-content/uploads/PDFs/6-2-11.pdf

Dardot, P., & Laval, C. (2013). *The new way of the world: On neoliberal society.* London: Verso Books.

Dickinson, L. (1987). *Self-instruction in language learning.* Cambridge: Cambridge University Press.

Drucker, P. F. (1969). *The age of discontinuity: Guidelines to our changing society.* New York, NY: Harper & Row.

Eleveld, A. (2009). Government through Freedom. The technology of the life cycle arrangement. In W. Zeydanlıoğlu & J. T. Parry (Eds.), *Rights, citizenship & torture: Perspectives on evil, law and the state* (pp. 167–189). Oxford: Inter-Disciplinary Press.

Fairclough, N. (1989). *Language and power.* London and New York: Longman.

Fairclough, N. (1992). *Critical language awareness.* London and New York: Longman.

Foucault, M. (1991). Governmentality. In G. Burchell, C. Gordon, & P. Miller (Eds.), *The foucault effect: Studies in governmentality* (pp. 87–104). London: Harvester Wheatsheaf.

Foucault, M. (1997). Technologies of the self. In P. Rabinow (Ed.), *Ethics: Subjectivity and truth* (pp. 223–319). New York: The New Press.

Foucault, M. (2008). *The birth of biopolitics: Lectures at the Collège de France, 1978–1979*. Basingstoke: Palgrave Macmillan.

Gerber, D. J. (1994). Constitutionalizing the economy: German neo-liberalism, competition law, and the 'New' Europe. *American Journal of Comparative Law, 42*(1), 25–84.

Giroux, H. (1983). *Theory and resistance in education: Towards a pedagogy for the opposition*. Westport: Bergin and Garvey.

Giroux, H. (1991). *Postmodern, feminism, and cultural politic: Redrawing educational boundaries*. Albany: State University of New York Press.

Giroux, H. (2010). Lessons from Paulo Freire. Chronicle of higher education, *57*(9). October 27. https://coms221–nstructionalcomm.wikispaces.com/file/view/Giroux,+h.+Lessons+From+Paulo+Freire.pdf

Gramsci, A. (1971/1991). *Selections from the prison notebooks*. London: Lawrence & Wishart.

Holborow, M. (2015). *Language and neoliberalism*. London and New York: Routledge.

Holec, H. (1981). *Autonomy in language learning*. Oxford: Pergamon. (First published 1979, Strasbourg: Council of Europe).

Hursh, D. (2005). Neo-liberalism, markets and accountability: Transforming education and undermining democracy in the United States and England. *Policy Futures in Education, 3*(1), 3–15.

Jameson, F. (1991). *Postmodernism or the cultural logic of late capitalism*. New York and Lodnon: Verso.

Järvinen, H. M. (2009). What has ecology to do with CLIL? An ecological approach in content and language integrated learning. In D. Marsh, P. Mehisto, & D. Wolff (Eds.), *CLIL practice: Perspectives from the field* (pp. 164–171). CCN: University of Jyväskylä, Jyväskylä, Finland.

Jorgensen, M., & Phillips, L. (2002). *Discourse analysis as theory and method*. London, Thousand Oaks and New Delhi: SAGE Publications.

Lankiewicz, H. (2013). Filologiczna praca licencjacka a rozwój kompetencji naukowych studenta [A philological B.A. thesis and the development of student academic skills]. *Neofilolog, 40*(1), 111–125.

Lankiewicz, H. (2015). *Teacher language awareness in the ecological perspective: A collaborative enquiry based on languaging*. Gdansk: Wydawnictwo Uniwersytetu Gdańskiego.

McEwan-Fujita, E. (2005). Neoliberalism and minority-language planning in the highlands and islands of Scotland. *International Journal of the Sociology of Language, 171*, 155–171.

McLaren, P. (2013). Seeds of resistance: Towards a revolutionary critical ecopedagogy. *Socialist Studies/Études socialistes, 9*(1), 83–108.

Miller, P., & Rose, N. (2008). *Governing the present: Administering economic, social and personal life*. Cambridge: Polity.

Mirowski, P. (2013). *Never let a serious crisis go to waste: How neoliberalism survived the financial crisis*. New York: Verso.

Park, J. S.-Y. (2010). Naturalization of competence and the neoliberal subject: Success stories of English language learning in the Korean conservative press. *Journal of Linguistic Anthropology, 20*(1), 22–38.

Park, J. S.-Y. (2011). The promise of English: Linguistic capital and the neoliberal worker in the South Korean job market. *International Journal of Bilingual Education and Bilingualism, 14*(4), 443–455.

Pennycook, A. (2010). Critical and alternative directions in applied linguistics. *Australian review of applied linguistics, 33*(2), 1–16.

Potulicka, E. (2010). Pedagogiczne koszty reform skoncentrowanych na standardach i testowaniu [Cost of pedagogical reform focused on standards and testing]. In E. Potulicka & J. Rutkowiak (Eds.), *Neoliberalne uwikłania edukacji [Neoliberal involvement in education]* (pp. 177–202). Kraków: Oficyna Wydawnicza Impuls.

Richards, J. C., & Rodgers, T. S. (2001). *Approaches and methods in language teaching.* Cambridge: Cambridge University Press.

Shin, H., & Park, J. S. (2016). Researching language and neoliberalism. *Journal of Multilingual and Multicultural Development, 37*(5), 443–452.

Shin, H. (2016). Language 'skills' and the neoliberal English education industry. *Journal of Multilingual and Multicultural Development, 37*(5), 509–522.

Smith, R. (2008). Key concepts in ELT: Learner autonomy. *ELT Journal, 62*(4), 395–397.

Thorsen, D. E., & Lie. A. (2007). What is neoliberalism? Department of Political Science University of Oslo. 2000 (WebCT), pp. 1–17. Working paper.

Universities. Encyclopædia Britannica (11th ed.). (1911). https://en.wikisource.org/wiki/1911_Encyclop%C3%A6dia_Britannica/Universities

Urciuoli, B. (2010). Neoliberal education: Preparing the student for the new workplace. In C. Greenhouse (Ed.), *Ethnographies of neoliberalism* (pp. 162–176). Philadelphia, PA: University of Pennsylvania Press.

Vallima, J., & Hoffman, D. (2008). Knowledge society discourse and higher education. *Higher Education, 56*(3), 265–285.

van Lier, L. (2004). *The ecology & semiotics of language learning.* Dordrecht: Kluwer.

Vercelli, A. (2016). On neoliberalism: Comments to Mirowski. Chapter one of his forthcoming books: *Crisis and sustainability. The delusion of free markets* (2017). A working paper retrieved form: https://www.ineteconomics.org/research/research-papers/on-neoliberalism-comments-to-mirowski

Vercelli, A. (2017). *Crisis and sustainability. The delusion of free markets.* London: Palgrave Macmillan.

Wąsikiewicz-Firlej, E. (2013). Pinnacles of learning or business-like organizations? Academic mission statements versus marketization of higher education. In A. Szczepaniak-Kozak & H. Lankiewicz (Eds.), *Creative potential of the word: from fiction to education* (pp. 85–103). Piła: Wydawnictwo PWSZ im. ST. Staszica w Pile.

Author Biography

Hadrian Lankiewicz, D. Litt. in applied linguistics and Ph.D. in literary studies, currently is Associate Professor in the Department of Applied Linguistics and Translation Studies of the University of Gdańsk, Poland. His scientific interests oscillate between history, American literature and applied linguistics, with the primary focus on language acquisition and foreign language teaching methodology. In recent years, his research has been inspired by the application of an ecological metaphor to the study of language and its learning. Drawing on the concept of multi-competence and political autonomy in the process of language learning, he has concentrated on issues of marginalization, empowerment and legitimization in the use of English as a foreign language.

The Dialogical Nature of Professional Identity: A Longitudinal Study of One EFL Teacher

Dorota Werbińska and Małgorzata Ekiert

Abstract Invoking two of Bakhtin's concepts, *voice* and *authoritative/persuasive* discourse, from his dialogical approach, the study in the present chapter attempts to show the construction of professional identity of one EFL teacher, highly regarded in her professional milieu and a former Ph.D. student of Krystyna Droździał-Szelest. The analysis of three in-depth interviews conducted within a period of sixteen years shows that the authoritative voice is present in the teacher throughout those years, that the authoritative voice (the imposed teacher's beliefs) can be modified, but not replaced, into persuasively internal (developed by the teacher) sub-voices, and that persuasively internal voices can be maintained. Some other conclusions of the study are also highlighted.

Keywords Professional identity · Longitudinal study · Bakhtin · Authoritative/persuasive voices

1 Introduction

Following the assumption that every act of language use reflects a particular time and space and that any speaker is a respondent to preceding utterances, both his own and others, the present article reports on a longitudinal study of an EFL teacher which was conducted over a period of 16 years. During that period the teacher was interviewed three times about her beliefs on different aspects of learning and teaching English. The collected data was used to trace the dialogical nature of her

D. Werbińska (✉) · M. Ekiert
Pomeranian University, Słupsk, Poland
e-mail: dorota.werbinska@apsl.edu.pl

M. Ekiert
e-mail: malgorzata.ekiert@apsl.edu.pl

© Springer International Publishing AG 2018
M. Pawlak and A. Mystkowska-Wiertelak (eds.), *Challenges of Second and Foreign Language Education in a Globalized World*, Second Language Learning and Teaching, DOI 10.1007/978-3-319-66975-5_18

evolving professional identity, as understood in Bakhtin's sense. In particular, the study aimed to examine whether some of the teacher's beliefs, understood as authoritative or persuasive voices, expressed by the teacher in any of the earlier interviews were maintained or modified (responded) in a later interview. As the participant in this study has always been deemed successful in her milieu by learners, their parents and her superiors, the article may contribute to the idea of the resourceful teacher's beliefs (Barkhuizen, 2017) rather than, as is often the case, looking at the participant from the perspective of teacher deficits. The study is also our modest response to Kalaja, Barcelos, Aro, and Ruohotie-Lyhty's (2016) call for more longitudinal discussions on teachers' beliefs and identities developed in local contexts of foreign language teaching.

2   Theoretical Background

Language teacher identity has been acknowledged in the literature only recently (Miller, 2009). Research on teacher identity draws on many theoretical approaches, especially those coming from psychology, sociology, general education and philosophy. Although it is hardly possible (and perhaps counterproductive) to generate a single definition of teacher identity, all contemporary teacher identity researchers agree on its development taking place all the time. The literature shows that identity is constantly being constructed and reconstructed as the teacher faces novel experiences, establishes new relations and makes decisions. One way to access a teacher's identity is through listening to her talking, as the content expressed in an in-depth interview reveals the identity of a concrete teacher through what she says about her work and herself, through what she chooses to describe or ignore, or through the meanings that she gives to her experiences.

The concept by which this study is informed is *the dialogical approach* contributed by the Bakhtin Circle. This approach concerns the relationship between utterances. It can be argued, however, that dialogue does not have to stand exclusively for an act of conversation between people, but can relate to interactions with the contexts in which individuals are located in a particular time and space. Aro (2016) posits that whenever people speak, they express intentions, evaluations, opinions, and emotions which have a social origin. Hence, as contexts—social and physical environments—determine what people learn, it is possible that the same people can hold contradictory beliefs, or "voices", to use Bakhtin's words, at different times in their lives, as beliefs are closely bound up with time and place.

Although some Bakhtin researchers treat heteroglossia and polyphony as synonymous, both terms are differentiated in Bakhtin's dialogical rhetoric. *Heteroglossia* can be understood as different languagedness, whereas *polyphony* as many-voicedness (Skidmore, 2016, p. 25). Although their meanings might sometimes overlap, the recognition of heteroglossia usually implies linguistic variations in terms of geographical, regional, socio-ideological diversity, as well as "shared language practices" (p. 33) or markers of social identity (p. 41). Polyphony, by contrast, refers to unique voices of individual people (p. 34), elements of improvisation, or willingness to depart from the script (p. 42) and follow their own thinking process.

Another dichotomy introduced by Bakhtin is that between *authoritative* versus *internally persuasive discourse*. *Authoritative discourse* refers to language use which is accepted unconditionally (Bakhtin's [1981, p. 342] "unconditional allegiance") and is not open to debate. *Internally persuasive discourse*, on the other hand, is open and "acknowledges the primacy of dialogue" (p. 155) or, like polyphony, reveals a departure from the script and a readiness to take into account various voices. In a way, authoritative discourses are stable, acknowledged as true, even termed as "languages of power" or "cultural capital" (Azar, Reza, Reza, & Reza, 2012, p. 4), whereas persuasive discourses are independent of authority, subject to modifications, not finite and, as Bakhtin (1981) puts it, "half ours and half someone else's", as they derive from people's understanding of events and relationships with others in their everyday lives.

Despite the recent popularity of language teacher professional identity in the literature, with two leading journals devoting special issues to this topic (e.g., *TESOL Quarterly*, 2016; *Modern Language Journal*, 2017), few studies have focused on investigating language teacher professional identity within a Bakhtinian conceptual framework. There are theoretical contributions related to the theory of Mikhail Bakhtin (e.g., Gieve & Miller, 2008; Golombek, 2011), studies on language learners that present the notions of Bakhtin's concerns (e.g., Dufva, 2006; Dufva & Aro, 2015; Harvey, 2017; Hosemfeld, 2006; Kramsch, 2001; Liaw & English, 2016; Róg, 2012; Werbińska, 2012), and yet there are few research projects on language teachers which would refer to the aspects addressed in the works of Bakhtin. Among those who have theorized language teacher identity in Bakhtinian understanding, the contributions of Kiernan (2010), Azar et al. (2012), Menard-Warwick (2014), and Hallman (2015) are worthy of mention here. Inspired by Bakhtin's notion of *chronotope*, Kiernan (2010) proposed the concept of spatio-temporal focus while exploring the construction of identity of "non-native" English and "foreign" native teachers in the Japanese context. The chronotopical nature of language teachers' identity construction was also studied by Azar et al. (2012), who showed that discourse type (authoritative/persuasive) and *chronotope* were key factors responsible for the construction of teachers' identities. Menard-Warwick's (2014) book chapter, "In dialogue with Bakhtin", like the whole monograph, explores the development of teacher identity through presenting teachers' voices with regard to the controversies around English as a global language. Finally, using a Bakhtinian perspective as a tool to gain insight into teacher identity, Hallman (2015) investigated one prospective language teacher's Teaching Philosophy Statement to investigate how she negotiated her teacher identity.

3 The Study

3.1 Aims

Three in-depth interviews made up the data for this study. The first interview was conducted in 2001. Its goal was to examine the beliefs of an EFL teacher highly regarded by her superiors, learners and their parents (Werbińska, 2004). The second interview took place almost ten years later (Werbińska, 2011) and focused on investigating whether the same teacher's earlier beliefs had stood the test of time. The format—a semi-structured interview—was the same in both the first and the second interview (see Appendix), which allowed for interactional and yet focused conversation. The third interview data was collected sixteen years after the first interview. The last interview aimed at investigating the teacher's beliefs from a wider perspective through looking at how her professional teacher identity had developed over the years. Starting with the question "Would you choose the same job again if you had the chance?",[1] followed by "Tell me what has happened to you as a language teacher since the time we met in 2011", the last interview was less structured than the previous two so as to see if the same "voices" (the teacher's beliefs), however unprompted, could be heard again. In a way, all interviews constituted a long dialogue of the teacher with herself, held at a different time and, therefore, a different socio-historic context. The specific research questions were:

1. Did the teacher express authoritative voices (beliefs) in the previous interviews that were maintained in the later interviews?
2. Did the teacher express authoritative voices (beliefs) in the previous interviews that were questioned and changed into internally persuasive voices in the later interviews?
3. Did the teacher express internally persuasive voices in the previous interviews that were developed in the later interviews?

3.2 Participant

The study is a longitudinal case study of ME, a female Polish teacher of English who has always been considered exceptional. Data collection began (the first interview) when she was a twenty-nine-year-old teacher in lower secondary school, a pre-service teacher trainer in a teacher training college and an examiner for secondary-school leaving examinations. In the second interview she was almost forty, working in the English departments of two universities. In addition, she worked as a part-time methodological adviser in a private language school and served as an expert on examination committees for language teacher job promotion

---

[1]The teacher did not hesitate for a single moment to provide a positive answer to this question.

examinations. In the third interview she was in her mid-forties, continuing her university language teaching and working at a private primary school as a part-time teacher. ME willingly agreed to take part in all the interviews and decided to use her true initials in all the subsequent publications.

3.3 Methodology

All the interviews with ME were audio-recorded, transcribed, translated from Polish into English and read through several times. The interviews were coded by themes which matched the research questions and addressed the authoritative voices that she maintained, authoritative voices that were questioned and modified into internally persuasive voices, and the internally persuasive voices that she developed. The interviews were conducted at a place convenient to ME. The first was held at ME's home, whereas the following two in town cafes. Each interview lasted over ninety minutes.

4 Findings

In this section, the data from all the three interviews is presented to get an overall picture of ME's beliefs, that is, the voices that were heard in each of them. The three subsections are matched with the three rounds of interviews, and the time of each interview is indicated in the title of each subsection. The three interviews are presented chronologically, from the earliest to the latest. At the beginning of each subsection, a short snapshot providing a hint of the socio-historic moment is offered to help the reader better grasp the context in which the interviews took place.

4.1 Interview I, Year 1, January 2000

The first interview took place when Poland was aspiring to become an EU member country. A decade after liberation from the communist regime, Poland was a country in which English enjoyed unprecedented popularity. There were shortages of English teachers due to the previous predominance of Russian as a second language in schools and the fact that those who graduated from English teacher training colleges often opted for job opportunities outside the education sector. This meant that English language lessons were sometimes taught by unqualified teachers. Teachers of other nationalities, including English native-speakers, were common in schools in larger towns or cities. As far as language teaching methodology was concerned, Communicative Language Teaching was thought to be the pinnacle of effective teaching. Creating a friendly classroom atmosphere, introducing language games and using English in the classroom were especially emphasized in the rhetoric of book publishers and teacher trainers of that time.

Of interest were the kinds of beliefs ME held concerning language, the syllabus, learning, teaching, the teaching profession and teacher metaphors. From the first interview it was clear that ME considered learning foreign languages as one of her main interests, and pronunciation was important, at least to be "comfortably intelligible", as she said quoting Kenworthy (1987). As for skills, she appeared to like teaching speaking most, signaling that language to her was primarily communication. Asked about the syllabus, ME responded that general aims were more important than specific aims, and that she always started her lessons by analyzing students' needs and interests, which were then included in her teaching program once external requirements had been satisfied. That was when she said that her lessons never relied on a coursebook exclusively, although a course book was always an invaluable teaching aid. ME also declared her interest in the latest developments in foreign language teaching at that time, as she encouraged her learners to be independent and reflective learners who would consciously employ learning strategies (the subject of her Ph.D. thesis[2] investigation, which she was preparing of her own free will rather than because of external pressures). ME said that she liked her job but she wished she had more time to prepare her classes better. She compared a foreign language teacher to an actor introducing realistic scenes. She said:

> I use a lot of authentic materials because I have to prepare them for real communication. This is how I see my role. I change the methods to attract the learners.

It could also be noted that she paid considerable attention to relations with pupils which were based on honesty, fairness and respect. The excerpts below illustrate this point:

> I'd like to spend more time with the students after class. But I realize that talking to some of them may give the impression that I am favoring them, which I try to avoid.

> My pupils are honest with me. They can tell me what they would like to change, what they don't like and, maybe that's why they never criticize me to other teachers. They can present their needs directly to me.

> A friendly and respectful learning atmosphere is best for language learning. Then they treat lessons as social meetings.

Upon analyzing the entirety of the first interview data, ME was labeled with the metaphor of a "friendly learner".[3] The term *learner* was used as she seemed to value the teacher's continuous professional development to which she often referred (participating in a significant number of courses, learning Italian, taking part in postgraduate studies, reading methodology books, writing her Ph.D.

---

[2]Krystyna Droździał-Szelest was ME's thesis supervisor.

[3]This study was part of a wider project in which each participating teacher was labeled with a metaphor reflecting her beliefs (for details, see Werbińska, 2004).

dissertation, experimenting with a variety of teaching techniques), whereas *friendly* stood for her friendly attitude to students focused on learner-centeredness with emphasis on their needs, autonomy, learning strategies, responsibility, cooperation and resourcefulness which, as she said, would be useful to them in the future.

As a matter of fact, she did not seem to have any major concerns aside from making her classes attractive enough for students to better motivate their language learning. Educated at a time when the communicative approach was at its height in post-communist Poland, she excelled in conducting "interesting lessons", which became a characteristic feature of her teaching. The wish she expressed at that time was only to have more time to prepare such lessons.

4.2   Interview II, Year 10, November 2011

The second interview was conducted over a decade later. At that time, Poland was probably one of the few EU countries that was successfully dealing with the world economic crisis, and English continued to be the most popular foreign language taught at all educational levels. Unlike ten years earlier, there were more restrictions concerning formal teacher qualifications, which meant that it was not possible for unqualified teachers to be employed in state schools. There was a new core curriculum, with high-stake examinations in language after each, except the first, educational level. The way language classes were conducted was still heavily dependent on the individual teacher's abilities, skills and motivation but increasingly teachers tended to focus their teaching on preparation for their learners' external tests. Native-speaker teachers, who were often not formally qualified to teach, now usually worked in the private sector.

The second interview with ME followed the same structure as the first one. She responded to questions about her beliefs concerning, as before, language, the syllabus, learning, teaching, the teaching profession and teacher metaphors.

What was the same?

Professional development still seemed to be significant for ME. She tried to keep abreast of new teaching trends, making, for example, information and communication technologies her newly-discovered passion or learning new languages, as, in her opinion, any teacher of a foreign language should possess a working knowledge of more than one language. She also wanted to have more practically-oriented teacher development courses organized by her university. This is what she said:

> What do we have now? Only a course on safety and hygiene at work. Nobody cares about sending us anywhere. If you didn't try to do something about the quality of your teaching yourself, nobody would care. Academic conferences are too theoretical.

ME's views were still focused on the learner. Communicative purposes came to the surface even more than in the first interview. She continued stressing the importance of teaching the four skills through introducing non-fabricated listening or reading texts, holding conversations with native speakers, or writing authentic texts, such as short text messages. This is what she said about her learning of Italian:

> I know all about different Englishes but since I started classes with an Italian native speaker I've seen a dramatic change in my progress. There is authentic communication with him. He isn't a trained teacher but I'm learning so much communicative language. I used to attend a language course conducted by a Polish teacher of Italian and I learned far less on that course.

ME still tried to promote learner autonomy and the image of a language learner as an independent, reflective, self-directed and autonomous individual. She expressed her belief that once the direction had been set by the teacher, learners would be able to regulate their own activities, thus simultaneously taking their first steps on their path to autonomy. In her first interview she expressed the opinion that general aims were more important than specific objectives. Now she referred to "long-term aims", which should provide a sense of direction. She explained that such aims were long-lasting, could guarantee a deep accumulation of knowledge and skills and could be personally cherished by learners since the investment in something over a long period of time, though it could undoubtedly cause frequent verification or questioning of its validity, would prove worthwhile for the learner if it resisted abandonment or modification. As was the case in the first interview, ME would have liked to have more time for the preparation of interesting classes and she again used the metaphor of a language teacher as an actor.

What was modified?

During the second interview ME presented herself as a teacher who had taken up several challenging tasks that had clearly played a role in the development of her teacher self. One of these challenges was the completion and successful defense of her doctoral dissertation, which had undoubtedly led to extensive reading on the researched topic resulting in more accurate interpretation of students' learning. This had probably contributed to her decision to write her own coursebook for the adult learners with whom she worked in the evenings. Moreover, she made computer technology a regular mark of her teaching, and even created her own IT-based language teaching programs. Far from merely consuming the methodological ideas created by others, ME tried to prove to herself that she was a teacher producing her own methodological knowledge, at least in the classes in which she taught. Although she had previously highlighted good rapport with all her students, in the second interview she named her "favorite" students, who were learners interested in what she did. Asked to elaborate on this, she referred to her students of English philology who, like herself, were fond of English and learning languages.

In the first interview the issue of assessment was hardly mentioned as ME merely remarked that she did not like giving bad grades. In the second interview, she explicitly stated that she disliked assessing students, principally due to their repeated requests for a change of grade, as several attempts or retakes were allowed by her university regulations. She explained:

I don't like assessing because they keep begging me to raise their grades. If I refuse to agree, they may even go too far and question my fairness. And I can't agree with this.

Her principal driving strategy had now become goal orientation, which she willingly tried to pass on to her students. The adopted targets indicated which road to follow, and simultaneously generated creativity, openness to novelty, and the ability to look at a problem from multiple perspectives. As these qualities are academic virtues promoted in scientific endeavors, their mention by ME as her life-guiding values revealed greater maturity than had been evident in the first interview.

Although aims were still important for ME's professional work, the priorities had changed in her personal hierarchy. When she was a school teacher, the most important aims had been those provided by the school, followed by language teaching trends, and ending with her own evaluations of what her learners needed. Now, what learners expected and what she felt they needed seemed on a par and even took precedence over school requirements or new teaching trends. That was why, unhappy with the available coursebooks and catering for mature learners, she decided to create her own materials which were more congruent with her learners' needs, such as their willingness to learn grammar, and better adapted to their perceptive abilities.

Primarily focused on her own classroom teaching in the first interview, she now commented on the context of English teaching in Poland and its responsibility for the gradual falling of standards in the profession. English language teaching as a profession was, in her opinion, still in its infancy in 2011. That was because, to her mind, it had become too easy to obtain teaching credentials in the mushrooming regional private institutions. This situation had brought about a fall in standards as too many badly-qualified, unmotivated and random students had entered the ranks of language teaching. Although the metaphor of the teacher as an actor was still used by ME, her understanding of the language teacher had changed. Now the teacher resembled a barometer that read the audience's (learners') feelings, needs and expectations, and adjusted her teaching accordingly.

For the sake of clarity, Table 1 presents ME's voices that remained stable and those which were modified over the lapse of over ten years. After the second interview it can be inferred that the most significant changes in ME's professional development concerned her goal orientation and, in particular, the use of technology. Other dimensions crucial for contemporary language learning and teaching discourse, such as fostering learner autonomy, seemed to have featured in her professional credo earlier. Goal orientation had already flickered in her revelations in the first interview, but it was the regular integration of technology into her English classes that had changed ME's mindset considerably. In a word, she gave the impression of a teacher who was an autonomous language user, a goal-oriented learner, a friendly communicator and, above all, a lesson innovator who made use of multiple technological possibilities. It was also during the second interview that ME explicitly expressed her uncertainty about student assessment.

Table 1 ME's beliefs in 2011

Beliefs (Voices) about:	Same as in 2000	Modified
Language	Interest in languages (learning Italian). Focus on communication and authenticity	Completion of writing a Ph.D. thesis in English
Learning	Promotion of learner autonomy	Focus on the teacher's role in the development of learner autonomy
Teaching	Variety of methods and teaching aids, Strategy training, Good rapport with students	Writing a book addressing her learners' needs Innovative IT applications Dislike of assessment
Profession	Professional development. Shortage of time	Goal-orientation Falling standards in the profession
Metaphors	Teacher as an actor	Teacher as an actor but for different reasons than before

4.3 Interview III, Year 16, February 2016

When the third interview with ME was conducted, English was still enjoying its popularity as the first foreign language in Poland. What had changed for English teachers, when compared with the socio-historic context of the second interview, was the more restricted number of job vacancies in state schools. What is more, the imminent educational reform with its planned liquidation of lower secondary schools meant that there would be even greater competition for securing tenured jobs in state schools. In contrast to the previous interviews, the third interview was unstructured and purposefully departed from the questions that had been used before. The intention was to see if the familiar former voices would reappear, even if the same questions were not asked. As in the previous interviews, the references to self-development (Interview I and Interview II), the language learner (Interview I and Interview II), goal-orientation (Interview II), assessment (Interview II), or the language teaching profession (Interview II) were continued, although enriched with new elements.

Professional development was an important common theme in the first two interviews. ME had mentioned participating in various teacher courses, reading teaching journals, experimenting with new techniques and performing various teacher-related jobs (an examiner, a teacher promotion expert, a methodological adviser, etc.) as important factors of becoming a language teacher. She always benefitted from them, as she said, "both practically and intellectually". In her last interview, however, she did not mention any external initiatives organized for teachers by others (e.g., being requested to become a teacher consultant or reading about other teachers' ideas) but emphasized teachers' own attempts to manage their professional development. Good cases in point were attending private lessons in French or teaching in primary school, in addition to being a university teacher, both taken up for the sake of professional learning.

> I did it for development, self-development. It's helped me a lot. Our postgraduate kindergarten teachers treat me differently. People who are like them, those who are practicing teachers at schools, who have similar challenges and problems, seem to be more respected. They stress this – "This lady knows, this teacher has practical knowledge". Partially, they have inspired me. There was an opportunity, I thought I could better prepare for classes and it really helped. This is some kind of knowledge we are not able to get without practice. You've got to test, see for yourself, reflect, analyze. I can now give them other examples, suggest other solutions, ask other questions, so I'm very pleased. This is my self-development, not related to theory. I'm working/I work at university, I'm expected to attend conferences but taking into consideration the courses that I'm teaching, I can gain more from this type of experience. It's more effective and, what to call it/how can I say, valuable for me. (...) I'm not afraid of challenges. Many people thought it (teaching in school) was a kind of degradation, but for me it was verification – I wanted to be more credible.

She also referred to her best language learner:

> I don't have a best learner. In the past we talked about the lower secondary school. It has changed now – each learner is a challenge for me. I have a different attitude to the blind student that I'm teaching. Difficult but I have to cope with it. I send her listening materials, I have problems with designing tests so that they can be on a good level and comparable with those for non-blind students but I'm learning.

ME had also developed her personal ideology about the language teacher's values. First of all, she seems to have understood what to strive for and what not to strive for:

> My real self and my ideal self? My ideal self is not long-term, an image created twenty years ago to which I'm heading. No. Something more related to the here, something short-termed, noticing things here and now and setting aims, fulfilling them as soon as possible. I don't remember I've ever had an ideal picture. (...) I often think that, irrespective of age and experience, I can do an assignment better than another person. In some other cases I can be equal to others and can exchange my ideas with those of others. But there is nobody I'd like to emulate holistically, maybe in one aspect that interests me.

Secondly, she found out what her own resources were:

> I'm not afraid of challenges. (...) I'm trying to be flexible. I find flexibility and creativity the most important qualities of a teacher. I am, sort of resistant to difficulties. I think this is very much related to burnout. Even if I have problems with documentation which seems to be mushrooming, lack of equipment, group atmosphere, and I don't know how to react to this, I never give up. This helps me with work, keeping going. There are crises but no burnout. A lot depends on external support. When there were problems with children at school, I was all alone. I consulted the principal, other teachers, a school psychologist – I was looking for answers. And it was parents that helped me the most. Someone might have thought – she is a university teacher and has so many problems. But I kept looking for new solutions. The principal even reacted differently when parents were on my side. And it turned out that other teachers had similar problems but they were afraid to talk aloud about them. No strategy of cooperation.

Or with assessment. I still have a problem with this. I have made a few experiments with self-assessment and peer assessment but they [students] assess others favorably hoping that others will assess them in the same way. And I'm still looking for something that will be satisfying for me and for them.

Thirdly, she knew what worked for her in terms of teacher practices:

My techniques depend on the learner. But what I always use or I'm trying to use are these connected with interaction, group work, more often pair work and I often change pairs. They must change places, cooperate with others, no matter if it is a lecture, a class, adults or children. Also short films or working with an image. (…) Also projects, an analysis of a software program where they have to log in, present its advantages and disadvantages. I know all of them, so I know what they are like. Even if students say nothing, I start asking and we start analyzing. They might say "I don't know this software", I reply, "It doesn't matter. You don't have to know it. When you start working, you'll have to work with different kinds of software, but you'll be able to adjust to it. When you start working for a firm, they check you and your knowledge of a concrete/particular type of? Software".

She also had definite notions about the English teaching profession in Poland:

In schools lessons are mostly course book-based. Students tell me "I won't manage, I've got to do one book task after another". (…) Native speakers are still being idealized, despite emigration but they are less needed in the classroom thanks to the access to the Internet. Learners are used to having direct contact with someone, at least in the form of input, podcasts, not necessarily interaction.

ME appeared to have found a secure image of herself as a language teacher:

I think problems with work don't concern me. I never look for a job, someone will always find me. If it turned out there was no place for me in one job, it shouldn't be hard to find a job in another educational institution. Especially that there are possibilities of working abroad as well. Maybe the age factor could eliminate me but not at school or university when you work with adults.

This professional security enabled her to author her own professional agency and develop her teaching although not all her colleagues approved of that:

In the primary school I was asked to prepare a diagnostic-placement test for 6-year-olds. I did it quite differently, not on paper, but as a PowerPoint presentation. I assumed that since it was to take place in the pastoral room, children could take it individually, even with their home room teacher. I waited for the response. Knowing who I was, they didn't dare to criticize. Only at the beginning some teacher or principal said, "Is it going to look like this?" Some other factors prevented their changing the groups. (…) I sometimes encounter surprise, laughter even, that all my lessons are in English. Most learners are not used to this, especially in large schools.

At the end of the interview, she was asked for a teacher metaphor, to which she responded:

The metaphor? Creativity and flexibility – this is what I associate with this job. After so many years I can say that a teacher is an actor, or rather a responsible artist. Responsible to herself, her duties, cooperating people – both the authorities and the students.

Clearly, the English teaching profession has become a primary part of ME's daily life; she knows what works for her, what works less, what she is good at and where she is heading.

5 Discussion

This study involved a narrative analysis of a foreign language teacher deemed effective by her learners, their parents, her colleagues and superiors during her sixteen years in the profession. Most studies have investigated "negative" factors impacting on teachers' identity change, such as challenging school reforms (e.g., Day, Elliot, & Kington, 2005; Lasky, 2005; van Veen, Sleegers, & van de Van, 2005; Liu & Xu, 2011), relocation (e.g., Perumal, 2015), uncooperative mentors (e.g., Burn, 2007; Smagorinsky, Cook, Moore, Jackson, & Fry, 2004; Trent, 2010), teacher redundancy (e.g., Bilgen & Richards, 2015), teacher dyslexia (e.g., Burns & Bell, 2011), to name but a few. This study is a story of success, or a story of a resourceful teacher, because ME has continued to be an excellent teacher for all those years.

Looking back at how she talked in her late twenties, her late thirties and her mid-forties, it is interesting to see how little she has actually changed over the years. The voices that were heard in Interview I were also prominent in Interview II. Despite their slight modification or enlargement (i.e., strategy training turned into the promotion of learner autonomy), they did appear in Interview III, as illustrated in Table 2. ME seems to have held on to her original ideas (authoritative voice) about teaching from the beginning. In the first interview she communicated her belief in learner-centeredness, an offshoot of CLT, and it seems that ME has never resigned from being a "friendly learner". The subordination of her teaching to learners' needs with the promotion of learner autonomy, the introduction of strategy training in her classes, the attention paid to being fair and the consideration of her students' needs have, in the long run, always been a mark of her teaching. Likewise, the emphasis placed on her own learning, be it formal or personally sought after, is also part of her active professional development approach.

As teacher professional learning and learner-centeredness in the classroom constitute the core of her professional identity, any developments of these philosophies are propelled by the context in which she happens to be. It can be said that she treats encounters with language learners as encounters with new experiences from which she learns valuable lessons. When she taught listening to a blind student, she experimented with creating different texts as if she wanted to gain knowledge about anything unfamiliar to her teaching repertoire. When she ran a course for postgraduate kindergarten teachers, she volunteered to teach in the primary school to become a more credible educator who could learn something for herself, as well. When the school principal asked her to prepare a diagnostic language test, she came up with an innovative PowerPoint-based visual test to check

Table 2 ME's beliefs in 2016

Beliefs (Voices) about:	Interview II versus Interview I Same	Interview II versus Interview I Modified	Interview III
Language	Focus on communication and authenticity Interest in languages (learning Italian) Extensive professional reading	Writing a Ph.D. thesis in English	Communication and authenticity Interest in languages (learning French)
Learning/Learner	Promotion of learner autonomy Good rapport with learners	Although fair to all learners, she prefers those who are interested in what she is interested	Learner independence. Preparation for real-life challenges Any learner of hers is her favorite
Teaching/Teacher	Strategy training, Variety of methods and teaching aids	Teacher intervention in the promotion of learner autonomy Writing a book addressing her own learners' needs Using IT Dislike of assessment	Teacher flexibility and creativity Experimenting with teaching methods Innovative IT applications Looking for a satisfying assessment form
Profession	Professional development Complaint about the shortage of time	Goal-orientation Complaint about the shortage of time Falling standards in the teaching profession	Short-terms dictated by context Complaint about shortage of time Complaint about teachers' overuse of course books
Metaphors	Teacher as an actor	Teacher as an actor but for different reasons	Teacher as a responsible artist

its usefulness. Clearly, ME makes active use of the affordances that the teaching context offers her.

As to the modifications to her "friendly learner" label, there are not many. The question about a good assessment technique asked in the second interview was still awaiting an answer in the last interview with her. She said, "I'm still looking for something that will satisfy me and my students", which shows that she was not pleased with techniques that only partially fulfilled her students' or her own criteria. This attempt at understanding what, in her opinion, "good assessment" involves, carries the potential for her transformation and results in the enrichment of teacher identity, as new queries—a new range of meanings—are introduced into her language.

It can be argued that ME's story is a story of a teacher who is confident and pleased with what she does, which certainly makes her appreciated in her work community. This, in turn, gives her an increased sense of agency, and this is probably why she is ready to take educational risks. She has developed a sense of conviction of the importance of fostering learners' needs and her own lifelong learning as the best ways to develop her teaching. These core beliefs of a language teacher already expressed and emulated at the beginning of her professional career provide her with important tools to continue working as a good language teacher. Although her teacher identity is relatively stable, it has not remained identical over the years. The contexts with their affordances have provided her with opportunities to "pick up" educational experiences and turn them into teacher development encounters. This also provided evidence that the environment plays a significant role in teacher identity negotiation, as the quality of experiences (their depth, diversity or uniqueness) influences how fast and how deeply a teacher's identity is affected. Yet without the teacher's agentic decisions to learn from the context, even a rich context could remain uninspiring.

As to the research questions, it can be inferred that ME's voices are both authoritatively formed and internally persuasive. For Bakhtin, an authoritative discourse is decontextualized, almost accepted as *sine qua non*, an imposition from without rather than within. By contrast, a persuasive discourse is open and still waiting for a response to possibly become an authoritative voice. In answering the first research question, it was found that there is a recurring authoritative voice throughout all three interviews. For ME, this is the belief in the success of the teacher who is bent on professional development as well as total acceptance of learners and all that is related to their language learning. The emphasis on these two elements is reflected in the "friendly learner" metaphor which was created for ME after the first interview, and which she confirmed in her responses in the following interviews. Within this authoritative voice, however, there are persuasively con-structed strands, the focus of the second research question. Originating from the contexts and the affordances they offer, persuasively formed voices do not replace the main authoritative discourse. Yet they contribute to ME's own attempts at designing more successful teaching strategies than previously used in order to better cater for learners' individual needs. This can be seen in what she says about assessment, her voluntary extra engagement in teaching English to a blind student, or her experimentation with IT in the primary school diagnostic test. In answering the third research question, concerning the maintenance of her persuasively formed voices, it is clear that ME's ideas on assessment are not yet satisfied. She is still experimenting with different assessment techniques, including students' self and peer assessment, clearly waiting for a solution that could fulfil, as she says, "her needs and those of her students". She is therefore in the process of becoming, as she has found her own voice which, for the time being, evaluates her provisional experiments with assessment negatively.

6 Conclusions

The study presented here was truly longitudinal, as it spanned over sixteen years. It examined the dialogical nature of professional identity of one successful English teacher invoking two Bakhtinian concepts: voice and authoritative/internally persuasive discourse. Although longitudinal studies like this one cannot be generalized to other contexts, we can learn the following from ME's story:

- Teacher beliefs making up her identity at the beginning of teaching career (her authoritative voice) can be reshaped (persuasively constructed) but not abandoned under the influence of teaching experience,
- Adopting and teaching by the maxim of a "friendly learner" (the authoritative discourse) can influence good relations with learners, earn the opinion of a good teacher, and impact on teacher agency.
- The teacher's agency expressed in the modification of the authoritative voice into an internally persuasive sub-voice can derive from the teacher's own sense of assurance and confidence in what she is doing if compared with other teachers.
- Using various context-based affordances can provide a good platform for teacher professional development.

Appendix

Questions in semi-structured Interviews I and II:

1. Beliefs about language:
   How does she perceive skills and subsystems?
   Is learning English more/less important, if compared to other subjects?
   What attitudes should successful learners present to learning as to learning a foreign language?
2. Beliefs about curriculum:
   What is the role of course books and teaching materials in her courses?
   How important are aims in teaching?
   How does she decide what she is going to teach?
   To what extent is her teaching based on learners' needs?
3. Beliefs about learning and learner:
   How does she define learning?
   What are the best ways of learning a language?

What kind of learners achieve success in language learning?
What roles do learners adopt in her classroom?
4. Beliefs about teaching and teacher:
How does she perceive her role in the classroom?
What teaching methods/techniques does she prefer?
What are the qualities of a good teacher?
What metaphor would she use to convey her understanding of "teacher"?
5. Beliefs about the language teaching profession:
What is her present attitude to teaching? Has she thought of changing her job?
What is the most pleasant/unpleasant in this job?

References

Aro, M. (2016). Authority versus experience: Dialogues on learner beliefs. In P. Kalaja, A. M. F. Barcelos, M. Aro, & M. Ruohotie-Lyhty (Eds.), *Beliefs, agency and identity in foreign language learning and teaching* (pp. 27–47). New York: Springer.

Azar, H. F., Reza, P., Reza, H. M., & Reza, A. S. M. (2012). The chronotopical nature of identity construction: Case studies of narrative identities of EFL teachers. *International Journal of Research Studies in Language Learning, 1*(1), 1–16.

Bakhtin, M. M. (1981). *The dialogic imagination. Four essays by M. M. Bakhtin*. USA: University of Texas Press Austin.

Barkhuizen, G. (2017). Language teacher identity research: An introduction. In G. Barkhuizen (Ed.), *Reflections on language teacher identity research* (pp. 1–11). New York-London: Routledge.

Bilgen, F. E., & Richards, K. (2015). Identity negotiations of TEFL teachers during a time of uncertainty and redundancy. In Y. L. Cheung, S. Ben Said, & K. Park (Eds.), *Advances and current trends in language teacher identity research* (pp. 61–73). London-New York: Routledge.

Burn, K. (2007). Professional knowledge and identity in a contested discipline: Challenges for student teachers and teacher educators. *Oxford Review of Education, 33*(4), 445–467.

Burns, E., & Bell, S. (2011). Narrative construction of professional teacher identity of teachers with dyslexia. *Teaching and Teacher Education, 27,* 952–960.

Day, C., Elliot, B., & Kington, A. (2005). Reform, standards and teacher identity: Challenges of sustaining commitment. *Teaching and Teacher Education, 21,* 563–577.

Dufva, H. (2006). Beliefs in dialogue: A Bakhtinian view. In P. Kalaja & A. M. F. Barcelos (Eds.), *Beliefs about SLA: New research approaches* (pp. 131–152). New York: Springer.

Dufva, H., & Aro, M. (2015). Dialogical view on language learners' agency: Connecting intrapersonal with interpersonal. In P. Deters, X. (A) Gao, E. R. Miller, & G. Vitanova (Eds.), *Theorizing and analyzing agency in second language learning* (pp. 37–53). Bristol: Multilingual Matters.

Gieve, S., & Miller, I. K. (2008). What do we mean by "quality of classroom life"? In S. Gieve & I. K. Miller (Eds.), *Understanding the language classroom* (pp. 8–46). Basingstoke: Palgrave Macmillan.

Golombek, P. R. (2011). Dynamic assessment in teacher education: Using dialogic video protocols to intervene in teacher thinking and activity. In K. E. Johnson & P. R. Golombek (Eds.), *Research on second language teacher education* (pp. 121–136). New York-London: Routledge.

Hallman, H. I. (2015). Teacher identity as dialogic response: A Bakhtinian perspective In Y. L. Cheung, S. Ben Said, & K. Park (Eds.), *Advances and current trends in language teacher identity research* (pp. 3–15). London-New York: Routledge.

Harvey, L. (2017). Language learning motivation as ideological becoming. *System, 65,* 69–77.

Hosemfeld, C. (2006). Evidence of emergent beliefs of a second language learner. In P. Kalaja & A. M. F. Barcelos (Eds.), *Beliefs about SLA: New research approaches* (pp. 37–54). New York: Springer.

Kalaja, P., Barcelos, A. M. F., Aro, M., & Ruohotie-Lyhty, M. (Eds.). (2016). *Beliefs, agency and identity in foreign language learning and teaching.* New York: Springer.

Kenworthy, J. (1987). *Teaching English pronunciation.* Harlow: Longman.

Kiernan, P. (2010). *Narrative identity in English language teaching.* Basingstoke: Palgrave Macmillan.

Kramsch, C. (2001). *Language and culture.* Oxford: Oxford University Press.

Lasky, S. (2005). A sociocultural approach to understanding teacher identity, agency and professional vulnerability in a context of secondary school reform. *Teaching and Teacher Education, 21,* 899–916.

Liaw, M. L., & English, K. (2016). Identity and addressivity in the 'Beyond These Walls' program. *System, 64,* 74–86.

Liu, Y., & Xu, Y. (2011). Inclusion or exclusion?: A narrative inquiry of a language teacher's identity experience in the "new work order" of competing pedagogies. *Teaching and Teacher Education, 27,* 589–597.

Menard-Warwick, J. (2014). *English language teachers on the discursive fault lines. Identities, ideologies and pedagogies.* Bristol: Multilingual Matters.

Miller, E. (2009). Teacher identity. In A. Burns & J. C. Richards (Eds.), *The Cambridge guide to second language teacher education* (pp. 172–181). Cambridge: Cambridge University Press.

Perumal, J. C. (2015). Critical pedagogies of place: Educators' personal and professional experiences of social (in)justice. *Teaching and Teacher Education, 45,* 25–32.

Róg, T. (2012). Bakhtinian dialogical principle as a philosophical rationale behind intercultural studies. In H. Lankiewicz & E. Wąsikiewicz-Firlej (Eds.), *Informed teaching* (pp. 69–80). Piła: Wydawnictwo PWSZ w Pile.

Skidmore, D. (2016). Dialogism and education. In Skidmore, D. & K. Murakami (Eds.), *Dialogic pedagogy. The importance of dialogue in teaching and learning* (pp. 17–47). Bristol: Multilingual Matters.

Smagorinsky, P., Cook, L. S., Moore, C., Jackson, A. Y., & Fry, P. G. (2004). Tensions in learning to teach. Accommodation and the development of a teaching identity. *Journal of Teacher Education, 55*(1), 8–24.

Trent, J. (2010). 'My two masters': Conflict, contestation, and identity construction within a teaching practicum. *Australian Journal of Teacher Education, 35*(7), 1–14.

van Veen, K., Sleegers, P., & van de Van, P. H. (2005). One teacher's identity, emotions, and commitment to change: A case into the cognitive-affective processes of a secondary school teacher in the context of reforms. *Teaching and Teacher Education, 21,* 917–934.

Werbińska, D. (2004). *Skuteczny nauczyciel języka obcego* [An effective foreign language teacher]. Warszawa: Wydawnictwo Fraszka Edukacyjna.

Werbińska, D. (2011). *Developing into an effective Polish teacher of English.* Słupsk: Wydawnictwo Naukowe Akademii Pomorskiej.

Werbińska, D. (2012). Akwizycja języka obcego w perspektywie studenta filologii: Badanie tożsamości językowej studenta w kontekście czasoprzestrzeni i heteroglosji [Foreign language learning from the point of view of a philology student: A study of a student's linguistic identity in the context of spacetime and heteroglossia]. Poznań: *Neofilolog, 39*(1), 55–81.

Author Biographies

Dorota Werbińska, Ph.D. works in the Institute of Modern Languages at Pomeranian University, Słupsk, Poland. Her main academic interests are within the field of language teacher education, both pre-service and in-service, in particular language teacher professional development, teacher beliefs and identity, the development of teacher reflexivity, and qualitative research. She is the author of 4 books on language teacher cognition, a co-editor of 2 collections and almost 60 articles, book chapters and reviews published nationally and internationally.

Małgorzata Ekiert, Ph.D. works in the Institute of Modern Languages at Pomeranian University, Słupsk, Poland. She received her doctorate from Poznań University. Her B.A., M.A. and doctoral theses focused on applied linguistics. She is a certified teacher and has taught in primary and secondary schools as well as worked as a foreign language teacher trainer. She took part in a pilot study aimed at introducing the *European language portfolio* in Polish middle schools. Her research interests include learner autonomy, learning strategies and educational technology. She gives courses in linguistics, methodology of English language teaching and language acquisition. She is the Erasmus coordinator at her institution.

Students Teachers' International Experience and Their Beliefs About Developing Intercultural Communicative Competence

Anna Czura

Abstract A thorough awareness of the role of intercultural communicative competence (ICC) and expertise in developing this construct in the classroom have become essential attributes of a foreign language teacher. The present study aims to explore whether the length of time pre-service teachers of English have spent abroad exerts any effect on their beliefs about ICC and their awareness of how this construct should be developed in the language classroom. The data was collected by means of a questionnaire consisting of both open- and closed-ended tasks conducted among students of English attending a teaching course at a large university in the south of Poland. The results indicate that despite some minor discrepancies in the understanding of ICC between the participants with different international experience, it is clear that in general the future teachers linked this concept to the ability to communicate cross-culturally. Still, regardless of the time spent abroad, the participants seemed to lack practical skills to develop this competence in the classroom context.

Keywords Intercultural experience · Culture contact · Intercultural (communicative) competence · Teacher beliefs · Initial teacher education · Intercultural language teaching

1 Introduction

At present learners are afforded numerous opportunities to communicate in a foreign language (L2), both with native and non-native speakers, be that during travels or through modern media. In the future, some learners may decide to study or live in a different country; some may be required to communicate cross-culturally on a daily basis in professional contexts. Therefore, it is not surprising that fostering intercultural communicative competence (ICC) has been treated as a fundamental

A. Czura (✉)
University of Wrocław, Wrocław, Poland
e-mail: anna.czura@uwr.edu.pl

© Springer International Publishing AG 2018
M. Pawlak and A. Mystkowska-Wiertelak (eds.), *Challenges of Second and Foreign Language Education in a Globalized World*, Second Language Learning and Teaching, DOI 10.1007/978-3-319-66975-5_19

327

objective of language education in Poland and other countries and, consequently, has become an object of interest in the research literature in the field of language learning and teaching (Corbett, 2003; Dervin & Liddicoat, 2013; Sercu, 2005).

Teachers' expertise and their own intercultural skills to a large extent affect the quality of intercultural teaching. Nowadays, L2 teachers need to assume a role of intercultural mediators whose task is to serve as guides and intermediaries between their own and the L2 culture(s). There is a volume of studies exploring teachers' beliefs about culture and the quality of developing intercultural competence in the classroom context (e.g., Larzén-Östermark, 2008; Oranje, 2016; Sercu, 2005; Young & Sachdev, 2011). Little is known, however, about whether and to what extent teachers' and student teachers' international experience affects the ability to employ pedagogical means to implement intercultural teaching in their own teaching context. As Byram (2015) points out, there is a clear difference between training teachers as regards intercultural language teaching and training them to develop their own ICC.

In view of this assertion, it seems compelling to investigate to what extent future English teachers' international experiences affect their beliefs concerning the concept of ICC. In particular, the present study explores whether the length of time student teachers have spent abroad affects their understanding of the concept of ICC and their beliefs as to how this construct should be attended to in the L2 classroom. The data was obtained by means of a questionnaire distributed among 74 undergraduate student teachers of English at one of the universities in the south of Poland. The questionnaire prompted the participants to formulate their own definition of ICC, decide on the importance of different aspects of culture teaching and express their understanding of ICC and the way it should be developed.

2 Culture and ICC in Language Education

This section outlines the theoretical underpinnings of ICC assumed in this chapter and used as the basis for further analysis. Today, in the era of globalization and extensive use of computer-mediated communication, the objective of language teaching is to prepare learners to communicate globally with speakers coming from diverse cultural and linguistic backgrounds. As a modern *lingua franca*, English is no longer perceived as a means of communicating with the target language community, but as a universal contact language. With this in mind, for the purposes of the study, ICC is understood as "the ability to communicate effectively in cross-cultural situations and to relate appropriately in a variety of cultural contexts" (Bennett & Bennett, 2004, p. 149).

The different definitions of culture that have evolved over the years have exerted a direct impact on the way it is perceived as an objective of language teaching. In more traditional approaches to the role of culture, characteristic of the Direct Method, Audiolingual Approach or even Communicative Approach, culture was perceived as a fixed and static entity attributable to one specific nation or ethnic group. Accordingly, the teaching of culture focused on passing on factual knowledge related to the history, geography and traditions of the target language countries. In contrast, in this chapter, culture is viewed to be of a more complex, dynamic and variable nature. Each nation, each ethic group and each community is deeply varied and, thus, "the focus has shifted from cultures as things to human beings as the social enactors of culture" (Dervin & Liddicoat, 2013, p. 6). In this light, it seems to be an oversimplification to try to explain any human behavior in terms of national or ethnic specificity; an oversimplification that often stems from biased preconceptions and stereotypical views of the "Other" (Dervin & Tournebise, 2013; Holliday, 2010). Nowadays, the non-essentialist approaches to interculturality advocating that the success of cross-cultural communication is conditional on the speakers' ability to negotiate the Self and Other (Dervin & Tournebise, 2013; Holliday, 2010) are preferred to the contrastive positions according to which cultures and people can be described in terms of clear-cut characteristics and dichotomies, for instance as individualistic versus collectivist, masculinity versus femininity or long-term versus short-term orientation (cf. Hofstede, 1991). This new stance by no means implies that teachers should give up on developing learners' knowledge of other countries and raising their awareness of cultural differences; to the contrary, the non-essentialist approaches assume that cultural elements should be viewed from a more practical perspective as tools which enable language learners to observe, interpret, relate and construct their own experiences in a variety of cross-cultural situations.

This shift in understanding of the role of culture has necessitated instructional changes in language pedagogy and traditional culture teaching is gradually giving way to intercultural teaching, which, as Byram (1997) and Risager (2005) note, consists in developing knowledge, skills and attitudes, and aims at enabling learners to communicate successfully and appropriately in a variety of contexts. This idea is detailed in Byram's (1997) influential educational model, which constitutes the basis of some elements of the instrument used in this study. The knowledge dimension refers to the awareness of history, culture and other sociocultural aspects of the community that help language learners understand the existence of differences between cultures and the impact of such differences on interpersonal communication. Additionally, truly intercultural speakers must be equipped with "skills of comparison, of interpreting and relating" (Byram, Gribkova, & Starkey, 2002, p. 12) which help them apply the knowledge of cross-cultural differences, social norms and conventions in effective communication, void of misunderstandings, stereotypes and culture clashes. The last element of Byram's (1997) model is focused on the importance of attitudes. Accordingly, the teacher's role is to develop tolerance, a sense of curiosity and openness towards other cultures so that students would be willing to suspend biased evaluations of other people and be able to accept intercultural differences. The development of such positive attitudes is not possible unless learners are able to critically evaluate their own culture in relation to that of other cultural groups. As can be seen, critical awareness of one's own cultural background is vital to becoming a competent intercultural speaker.

Another important contribution of the modern approaches to interculturality is the recognition of the role of language, which is viewed by Dervin and Liddicoat (2013, p. 8) as "the unnamed dimension of the intercultural". While learning a foreign language, one somehow automatically acquires a new identity and, as a result, a new stance towards one's own and other cultures (Lightbown & Spada, 1999; Pavlenko & Lantolf, 2000). However, language is perceived here not as a set of grammar structures and vocabulary items, but as a tool for conveying and interpreting meaning in the communication process. As Moloney and Harbon (2010, p. 281) accurately observe, a truly intercultural task "asks students to think and act appropriately within a growing knowledge of the culture within language". With this in mind, it can be said that there is a reciprocal relationship between language and intercultural teaching, and one element cannot go without the other (cf. Kramsch, 1993; Liddicoat, 2002; Liddicoat & Scarino, 2013; Sercu, 2005).

Even though the term *intercultural communicative competence* has not been explicitly referred to in the Polish national curriculum for foreign language teaching until 2017,[1] a more detailed analysis of the document reveals that interculturality is treated as an important learning objective at all levels of education. Both the old and the new national curricula posit that, apart from developing communicative language competence, the role of language education is to awaken learners' curiosity, promote tolerance and develop openness towards other cultures. Moreover, learners need to be acquainted with traditions, customs, rituals and everyday life habits typical of other cultures, including the target language culture. It can be concluded that fostering interculturality in Polish schools should ideally entail developing knowledge, skills and attitudes necessary to actively participate in social and cultural life. Consequently, the approach adopted in the national curriculum is to a large extent consonant with Michael Byram's (1997) conception of ICC.

3 The Role of International Experience in Teacher Education

According to Byram's (1991) assertion, one of the factors affecting the quality of intercultural language teaching is teachers' own international experience. In order to raise future teachers' intercultural awareness and enhance language skills, many organizations, including the European Commission and numerous institutions of teacher education, offer diverse mobility initiatives during which future L2 teachers have a chance to participate in academic classes, gain field experience and interact cross-culturally at personal, academic and professional levels.

Although the research literature on future teachers' international experience is rather scarce, the available studies report predominantly positive effects of such

---

[1]The new national curriculum for foreign language teaching is effective as of September 2017.

experiences on the development of ICC (Lee, 2009; Tang & Choi, 2004). A study of Hong Kong students' sojourn in New Zealand indicates that cross-cultural interactions in academic and social contexts contributed to an increase in the level of intercultural awareness, broader knowledge of the host country culture, greater sensitivity to cultural differences as well as raised critical awareness of their own culture (Lee, 2009). However, the positive impact of stays abroad on the level of ICC is not as straightforward as it might seem. A narrative account of a pre-service teacher of English who acted as a language assistant in France mentions a number of cultural misunderstandings and adaptation problems during her stay abroad. It appears that the development of ICC in a mobility context is conditional on such factors as the participants' personality, competence in the local language, initial level of ethnorelativism as well as the receptivity and openness of the host institution (Czura, 2017).

Kaplan (1989) indicates that the success of an L2 immersion program depends on the participants' initial level of L2 competence. And, indeed, since the reported studies focused on future L2 teachers with at least a communicative level of English proficiency, their stays abroad tended to have a positive impact on their language skills (Lee, 2009; Tang & Choi, 2004). Lee (2009) observed that on return to the home institution, the participants observed an improvement in the level of L2 competence. In particular, the students appreciated the exposure to different varieties, accents and registers of English. What is worth underlining, the participation in an immersion program made these student teachers aware of the intricate link between language and culture. Crew and Bodycott (2001) observed that the students who had tended to refrain from using English before the international program turned into active and willing to take linguistic risks communicators. However, in some cases, the language learning opportunity of an immersion program was not fully exploited. Lee (2009) and Barkhuizen and Feryok (2006) underline that when abroad some students tended to overuse their mother tongue in interaction with their peers, whereas the participants of Sutherland's study (2011) complained about having had little opportunity to communicate with native speakers in social and academic situations.

The student teachers who completed their field experience abroad appreciated the chance to learn about a new education system, to observe other teachers teaching and to be exposed to different teaching approaches and techniques (Czura & Pfingsthorn, 2016; Hepple, 2012). Pray and Marx (2010) observed that on return student teachers expressed more emphatic attitudes to the cultural and linguistic problems L2 learners may experience. Göbel and Helmke (2010), in their study conducted in the German context, reported a long-term impact of culture contact on the quality of culture teaching. It turned out that L2 teachers with more extensive culture contact tended to introduce intercultural and culture-related topics more readily than their less internationally experienced colleagues. The observations of the videotaped lessons additionally indicated that providing teachers with more specific directives for the intercultural lessons had a positive effect on the quality of their intercultural teaching and the choice of topics. On the other hand, the experience of an unfamiliar system of education may also result in the emergence of certain problems. Pray and Marx's (2010) note that the participants of a study abroad program referred to in their study formulated some misconceptions about language teaching, especially in terms of error correction and grammar teaching. Moreover, Chinese student teachers, when exposed to a system of education radically different from their own, developed conflicting teacher identities (Trent, 2011).

4 Research Methodology

4.1 Research Objectives

Taking into account the growing importance of developing ICC in a school context, the study aims to find answers to the following research question: Does the student teachers' international experience (length of stay abroad) affect their:

- understanding of the term *intercultural communicative competence*?
- understanding of the connection between language and the intercultural?
- beliefs as to how ICC should be developed in the L2 classroom?

Additionally, since in the questionnaire the student teachers were asked to provide information concerning the duration and type of their stays abroad, it will be attempted to outline the participants' engagement in different forms of learning mobility and study abroad initiatives.

4.2 Participants

The study involved 74 undergraduate students of English at a university in the south of Poland. The cohort consisted of 60 female and 14 male students aged 21–23. Except for 2 persons coming from Eastern Europe, all the participants were of Polish origin. All the participants had selected a Teaching English as a Foreign Language (TEFL) course, which consisted of lectures, tutorials and teaching practicum, in order to receive nationally acknowledged qualifications to teach English in primary and lower secondary schools. The data were collected after the completion of the fourth or sixth semester of a B.A. course. The main research instrument (see the next section) contained a few background questions concerning the duration of their stays abroad, self-assessment of their language skills and the inclusion of ICC-related topics in their teacher education courses. On the basis of the responses referring to the participants' transnational travels and the length of their stays in foreign countries, the sample was divided into four research groups:

- Gr1—48 participants whose stays abroad did not exceed one month. During such stays, lasting from a few days to 2 or 3 weeks, the student teachers usually went on holidays, visited their family or friends and, less frequently, participated in a language course abroad (2 persons) or in an international school exchange (also 2 persons).
- Gr2—12 participants who spent from one to three months abroad. The most common destinations turned out to be France, Germany, the United Kingdom and the USA. Apart from the stays for tourism purposes and family visits, some students in this group also took up temporary employment.
- Gr3—7 participants who spent from over three months to one year abroad. In this group two students studied from 5 to 10 months at a university in the UK as part of the Erasmus exchange program, one person took part in a work and travel program in the USA, and another person spent several summers working, travelling and visiting family in Ireland and Canada. The remaining persons spent from 3 to 5 months in Germany and the Netherlands; however, they failed to provide any specific information concerning their stays there.
- Gr4–7 participants who spent over one year abroad. Three persons lived approximately 5 years in the UK or Ireland. One participant moved to the UK with his or her family for one year and still visits the country on a regular basis, and one person spent over two years in two different non-English speaking countries. In the case of the non-Polish students, their study period in Poland is treated as the time spent abroad.

While the respondents who spent over one year abroad claimed to possess competence in English at the C1+ and C2 level, the remaining participants' self-assessment of their English skills oscillated around C1. Apart from a few student teachers who recalled discussing teaching cultural aspects in different English teaching methods, the vast majority of the respondents had not experienced any instruction on intercultural language teaching in the course of their studies.

4.3 Instrument and Procedures

The written questionnaire used as the main elicitation tool in the present study is to a large degree based on the instrument developed by Sercu (2005) and her collaborators in a study that aimed to investigate in-service L2 teachers' perceptions of culture teaching in eight different countries. The original instrument was modified in order to adapt it to the context of pre-service teacher education in Poland and translated into Polish. The questionnaire consisted of one open-ended and three closed-ended tasks. In the former, the respondents were asked to formulate their own definition of ICC. Next, they were to indicate what, in their opinion, is the appropriate ratio between language teaching and culture teaching. In the following task the participants put culture-related teaching objectives, referring to the knowledge, skills and attitudes, in order of their importance in L2 teaching. Finally, the last part of the questionnaire, which consisted of 19 Likert scale statements graded from 1 (*I strongly disagree*) to 5 (*I strongly agree*), intended to elicit the respondents' opinions about the feasibility of culture teaching and their beliefs on how ICC should be developed in L2 learners. The definitions provided in the open-ended task were content analyzed, whereas the statistical calculations were performed by means of SPSS 19.0. Since the TEFL course was normally selected by a small number of students, the data were collected over a period of three years and embraced all undergraduate student teachers who agreed to participate in this anonymous study. The introduction of a new TEFL program and syllabi in the institution where the research was conducted made it impossible to involve a larger number of respondents in the following years.

5 Results

Table 1 summarizes the main categories that emerged from the content analysis of the definitions of ICC formulated by the respondents in the four research groups. As some definitions were fairly complex and were thus attributable to several categories (e.g., they referred to both the ability to communicate and to the sociolinguistic aspects of language competence), it was decided to present them in percentage terms (rounded to the nearest whole number), which explains why the sum in each research group exceeds 100%.

The results indicate that about a half of the respondents in all groups tended to perceive ICC as the ability to communicate with individuals coming from diverse cultural and linguistic contexts. Whereas some participants provided rather succinct definitions, for example, "it's communication with people coming from different cultures[2]" (P68, Gr4), other respondents chose to formulate more elaborate responses and defined ICC as:

– "the ability to communicate with persons coming from different cultures, with different languages and systems of values" (P21, Gr3);
– "the ability to communicate with individuals of different nationalities, regardless of cultural differences" (P38, Gr1).

In the second most frequently mentioned category ICC was identified as the ability to apply "cultural elements" in effective communication with speakers of any origin. Depending on the author of the definition, the term "cultural elements" was either not explained at all or further referred to as: "the knowledge of the speaker's culture" (P59, Gr4), "differences in body language" (P28, Gr1) and "knowledge of polite forms, the ability to understand allusions and the origins of different situations" (P4, Gr1). The latter utterance was also assigned to the "Pragmatic and sociolinguistic competence" category, together with the following statements:

---

[2]All translations from Polish were made by the author of this chapter.

Table 1 Definitions of ICC provided by student teachers

Definitions of ICC	Gr1 (N = 48) (%)	Gr2 (N = 12) (%)	Gr3 (N = 7) (%)	Gr4 (N = 7) (%)
Communication with people from different cultural/linguistic backgrounds	46	50	57	43
Application of 'cultural elements' in effective communication	25	33	43	29
Knowledge of 'cultural elements' of the target language country and the ability to apply it in communication with native L2 speakers	17	8	–	–
Knowledge and awareness of L2 culture, history and traditions	–	8	14	14
Tolerance and openness	8	–	14	–
Pragmatic and sociolinguistic competence	10	–	–	14
Other	4	–	–	–
No answer	17	–	–	14

- "a speaker should know how to adjust his/her language to a specific situation (formal vs. informal, etc.)" (P51, Gr4);
- "an individual is well oriented in the pragmatics of a given language, understands the cultural codes that do not exist in the culture of his/her own native language" (P29, Gr1).

One person emphasized the need to raise language learners' awareness of cultural differences and defined ICC as "teaching about various cultural aspects and about differences between cultures. It's also teaching to communicate successfully in the face of these differences" (P18, Gr2). A small number of respondents in Gr1 and Gr3 additionally pointed to tolerance and openness to diversity as constituent elements of ICC. The apparent preference for the first two categories in all the groups indicates that for the majority of the respondents ICC is inherently linked to the ability to communicate with speakers of any language; this tendency was most pronounced in Gr3. The few respondents from Gr1 and Gr2 who limited ICC to the ability to communicate with native speakers of the target language offered the following definitions:

- "it's the ability to communicate with native speakers of the language in a way that is natural and acceptable to/for them" (P35, Gr1);
- "the knowledge of cultural elements of the target language country that help us to better understand and be more tolerant of its distinctiveness" (P64, Gr1).

Only single participants in Gr2, Gr3 and G4 understood ICC as the knowledge of different aspects of L2 culture, with no reference being made to the communicative aspects of this construct (e.g., "knowledge of culture and customs of the target language country" (P5, Gr2). As many as 8 respondents in Gr1 and 1 respondent in

Gr2 either left a blank space or explicitly stated that they did not understand the term in question.

Whereas most of the definitions were attributed to the first two categories and centered on communication, some inconsistencies can be observed with regard to the remaining categories in all research groups. The two persons from Gr4 who spent a longer period of time in an English-speaking country and still spend their holiday there tended to associate ICC with the target language culture and defined this term as "understanding the target language culture" (P67) and "the ability to communicate with native speakers of L2 and taking into account their culture, its applications and symbols" (P32).

Table 2 illustrates the respondents' answers to the second task, in which they were asked to indicate what percentage of teaching time, in their opinion, should be devoted to either language teaching or culture teaching. Regardless of the group, about a half of the respondents opted for the "80% language teaching—20% culture teaching" option. Some subtle differences between the research groups can be observed in the remaining answers. The respondents with more substantial international experience seemed to be slightly more inclined towards an integrated approach to language and culture teaching. In Gr1 and Gr2, in contrast, "60% language teaching—40% culture teaching" ratio appeared to be more popular than in the remaining two groups.

In the following step, the respondents ranked the objectives of culture teaching from the most (1) to the least (9) important. The rankings were established separately for each group on the basis of the median values. The results are illustrated in Table 3, in which, for the sake of clarity, the objectives were divided into three main categories: knowledge, attitudes and skills. In addition, any marked differences observed between the groups were underlined. The respondents univocally selected "developing the ability to communicate with individuals from different cultures" as the main objective of culture teaching. It is also clear that for most

Table 2 The respondents' perceptions of teaching time that should be devoted to language teaching and culture teaching in the L2 classroom

Role of culture in L2 classroom	Gr1 (%)	Gr2 (%)	Gr3 (%)	Gr4 (%)
100% language teaching—0% culture teaching	–	–	–	–
80% language teaching—20% culture teaching	52	50	57	57
60% language teaching—40% culture teaching	21	25	11	14
40% language teaching—60% culture teaching	–	–	–	–
20% language teaching—80% culture teaching	2	–	–	–
100% integrated language and culture teaching	21	25	28	28

Table 3 Culture teaching objectives in order of importance

Aspects of culture	Gr1	Gr2	Gr3	Gr4
Knowledge (informing the learners on...)				
Lifestyle and habits of the L2 community	4	4	4	6
Values and attitudes of L2 speakers	6	9	6	2
Literature, music and art of L2 country	7	5	8	3
Geography, history and political situation in L2 country	8	2	7	6
Attitudes				
Developing learners' tolerance and openness towards other nationalities and cultures	2	3	2	3
Skills (developing learners'...)				
Ability to communicative with individuals from different cultures	1	1	1	1
Understanding and empathy towards people from different cultural backgrounds	3	7	3	5
Ability to reflect on cultural differences	5	6	5	8
Ability to reflect on their own culture	9	8	9	9

respondents "developing learners' tolerance and openness towards other nationalities and cultures" was seen as more important than passing on factual knowledge about the target language culture. Gr2 seems to be an exception from this rule as the respondents considered "geography, history and political situation in L2 country" as second most important element of developing ICC, whereas the importance of developing understanding of and empathy towards people from different cultural backgrounds seemed to be relatively downplayed. It must be noted here, however, that in the case of these two points considerable variability among the respondents in Gr2 was observed. The groups considered "the ability to reflect on their own culture" as the least or the second least important component of intercultural skills. Whereas in the remaining categories the responses of Gr1, Gr2 and Gr3 were to a large extent comparable, Gr4 seemed to hold rather distinctive opinions in regard to a few categories. Most notable dissimilarities are visible in the knowledge dimension, in which Gr4 highlighted L2 speakers' values and attitudes as well as the knowledge of the target language literature, music and art as rather important. In contrast, these aspects were situated towards the bottom of the ranking in the remaining groups. Moreover, the respondents in Gr4 considered the ability to reflect on cultural differences as a rather unimportant aspect of culture teaching.

With the assumptions of normal distribution and homogeneity of variance met, one-way ANOVA was calculated to verify whether there were any statistically significant differences among the four research groups in the Likert-scale part of the questionnaire (Larson-Hall, 2010). With ANOVA $F_{(3.70)} = 2.193$ and $p = 0.097$ (at the $p < 0.05$ level) it can be stated that, statistically, there were no differences between the results obtained by the four groups in this part of the questionnaire. The distribution of mean results in the four research groups is presented in Fig. 1. It is

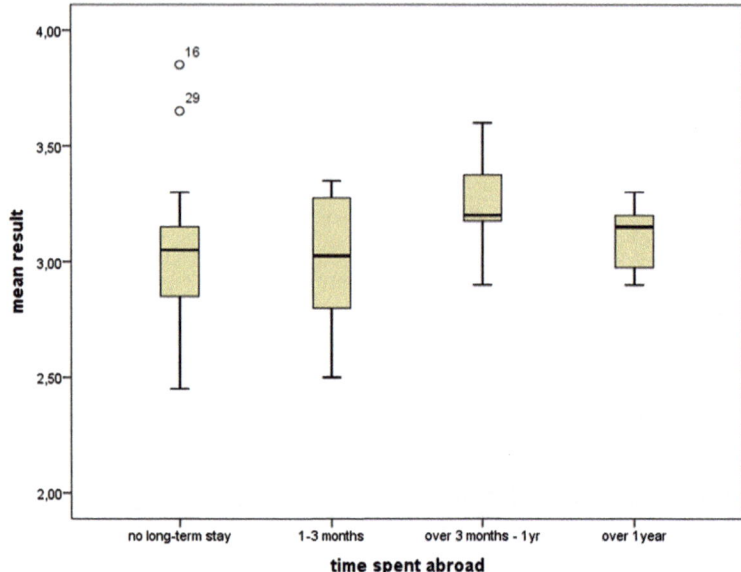

Fig. 1 Boxplot of Likert-scale questionnaire answers in the four research groups

clear that Gr3 and Gr4 are most homogeneous, while Gr2 appears to have larger variability than the other three samples.

Selected questionnaire items, divided by the author into two main categories, are summarized in Table 4. Since no statistically significant differences were observed between the four groups, the results are presented and analyzed collectively.With regard to the beliefs about the feasibility and the usefulness of developing ICC, the first three responses indicate that the participants were well aware that intercultural skills can be developed in the language classroom and that intercultural education can affect learners' attitudes. They also believed that intercultural education is not conditional on learners' level of L2 competence. In statement 10, the respondents agreed that teachers should present a realistic (as opposed to an idealized) picture of the target culture and society. Interestingly, the answers in statement 6 regarding the role of intercultural education in raising learners' awareness of their own cultural identity seemed to be at odds with the data presented in Table 3, where it was treated as the least prominent objective. Also, unlike illustrated in Table 2, in statement 8 the student teachers generally acknowledged the possibility of integrating language and culture teaching. Some dissonance is also visible in the case of statements 5 and 9—despite viewing intercultural teaching as an important element of L2 education, in practice, some respondents would be willing to sacrifice intercultural teaching to have more time for developing their learners' L2 skills.

Table 4 The analysis of selected questionnaire items

Student teacher's beliefs about:	Mean (SD)
The feasibility and the usefulness of developing ICC	
1. Intercultural skills cannot be developed at school	2.32 (1.02)
2. In a L2 classroom Ls can acquire cultural knowledge, but not intercultural skills	2.82 (1.16)
3. Intercultural education has no effect on S's attitudes	1.86 (0.94)
4. All learners should acquire ICC	3.36 (1.03)
5. In a language classroom, intercultural education is as important as language education	3.41 (1.15)
6. The aim of developing IC is raising Ls' awareness of their own culture and identity	3.22 (0.1)
7. Developing ICC in the classroom is possible only when Ls possess a high level of L2 competence	1.97 (0.81)
How to develop ICC	
8. Integrated teaching of language and culture is not possible.	1.65 (0.91)
9. In the case of a small number of hours devoted to L2 teaching, I will give up intercultural teaching to have more time to develop L2 skills	3.24 (1.19)
10. L2 teacher should present a realistic picture of the target culture and discuss also negative aspects of the target language culture and society	4.50 (0.76)
11. The best approach to intercultural teaching is an interdisciplinary approach	3.14 (0.8)
12. Teachers should compare different languages and cultures in a L2 classroom	3.14 (1.01)

6 Discussion

The results of the study indicate that there exist some minor differences between the student teachers with different cross-border experiences as regards their understanding of ICC and their awareness of culture teaching objectives in foreign language education. The future English teachers who had spent a longer period of time abroad more readily defined ICC as the ability to communicate cross-culturally and appeared slightly more fond of teaching approaches that assume full integration of culture and language. However, when asked about the practical aspects of developing this concept in the language classroom, these respondents were as confused as the student teachers with less substantial international experience. Interestingly, as illustrated in Tables 1 and 3, some participants from Gr4 seemed to stress the importance of the awareness of L2 speakers' values and attitudes and the factual knowledge of the target language culture. One possible explanation for such views is the fact that after living in an English-speaking country for a few years and being relatively proficient in the target language, the participants observed that closer integration with the L2 community depends to some extent on the speaker's nuanced knowledge of the target language literature, politics or pop culture, which makes it possible to understand jokes, allusions and cultural references encountered on a daily basis.

As mentioned earlier, student teachers' international experience failed to affect their beliefs about how ICC should be developed in a classroom context. In addition, some respondents in all research groups would consider devoting more time to developing language skills at the expense of culture teaching, which clearly shows that they did not fully understand the intricate relationship between language and culture. Bearing in mind the impact teachers' beliefs and subjective theories exert on their teaching practice (cf. Calderhead, 1996; Pajares, 1992), it can be assumed that student teachers who hold such inconsistent and at times distorted views of how to foster intercultural skills are hardly likely to succeed in developing ICC in their prospective learners.

The present study implies that as much as international experiences do not always automatically contribute to the development of intercultural competence (Jackson, 2010; Ward & Rana-Deuba, 1999), the experience of intercultural encounters during a stay abroad does not suffice to equip future teachers with professional expertise and skills that would facilitate successful intercultural teaching. These findings seem to be in conflict with the conclusions drawn by Göbel and Helmke (2010), who claimed that the extent of the teachers' culture contact had a positive impact on the quality of intercultural instruction. However, their article provided no information about the teachers' training and expertise in intercultural education and perhaps the German teachers had already been familiar with the concept of ICC, and the international experiences only further triggered their intercultural teaching skills. As the authors concluded, "[i]n order to realize the highly demanding goal of fostering intercultural competence among students, teachers evidently need more help and support. This support could be provided by more precise instructions within the textbooks and should be complemented by more comprehensive teacher training" (Göbel & Helmke, 2010, p. 1580).

In line with this assertion, the need for inclusion of intercultural modules in initial L2 teaching education is the main practical recommendation of the present study. Similar to other educational settings (see, e.g., Bektaş-Çetinkaya, 2014; Larzén-Östermark, 2009), one of the reasons for inadequate expertise of the pre-service teachers is the fact that teacher education programs offer insufficient guidelines on both theoretical and practical aspects of developing ICC. As Sercu (2005, p. 7) indicates, "it is very difficult to influence the conceptions of the practices of either experienced or beginning teachers". It seems therefore necessary that teacher education programs include modules aiming to raise pre-service teachers' awareness of what ICC really entails and equip them with practical techniques of implementing this concept in the classroom.

Although this observation does not refer to any research question, it is worth underlining here that in contrast to language teachers investigated in a number of earlier studies in Poland (e.g., Otwinowska-Kasztelanic, 2011; Sercu, 2005; Strzałka, 2005; Szczepaniak-Kozak, 2010), the respondents in the present study did not perceive ICC in terms of knowledge-related aspects. Their definitions and rankings of culture teaching objectives emphasized the ability to communicate cross-culturally and the attitudes of empathy, openness and tolerance as most vital elements of ICC. It is evident, however, that being able to define ICC in line with the acknowledged definitions and models of ICC (proposed, e.g., by Bennett & Bennett, 2004; Byram, 1997, 2003; Byram, Gribkova, & Starkey, 2002; Corbett, 2003) is not tantamount to knowing how to develop this construct in the classroom context.

Finally, it is worth analyzing the participants' involvement in mobility and study abroad initiatives. The data used to divide the student teachers into four research groups suggest that the vast majority of the participants have experienced only short-term stays in a foreign country. There is a group of students in Gr1 and Gr2 who recurrently travel abroad, mainly with the purpose of visiting family or undertaking temporary employment. It is worrying, however, that out of 74 participants, who are all majors in a philological discipline and who, out of their own volition, pursue a course qualifying them to become foreign language teachers, only two students have participated in the Erasmus exchange program. Future studies should set out to investigate why student teachers of a foreign language express so little interest in exchange schemes that are offered by their university and, as an immediate remedy, some attempts should be made to promote study abroad initiatives on a larger scale.

The surprisingly low mobility of the respondents resulted in large disproportions in the size of the research groups, which should be treated as a limitation of the study as the results cannot be regarded as fully representative. The second limitation is that the conclusions are based only on self-report questionnaires; hence, it should not be automatically assumed that the participants' actual teaching performance in the classroom would mirror the answers they provided. Future studies could complement these findings with the results of classroom observations of teachers with varying international experience.

7 Conclusions

Despite some minor discrepancies in the understanding of ICC that could be observed between the student teachers with different international experience, the results suggest that the majority of respondents linked this concept to the ability to communicate cross-culturally. On the other hand, it is also evident that the time spent abroad alone does not suffice for the emergence of adequate understanding and expertise in terms of the principles and techniques of intercultural language teaching. It is not intended here to downplay the role of culture contact. On the contrary, taking into account the advantages mobility programs and study abroad experiences bring at personal, linguistic, professional and intercultural levels, they should be encouraged as an important element of teacher education. However, sending students abroad should not be treated as a "golden solution" to the inadequacies of teacher education programs. International experiences may enhance future language teachers' level of ICC (Lee, 2009; Tang & Choi, 2004), but it does not mean that they will be able to transfer their intercultural skills to their future learners without being instructed how to do so. It is therefore necessary that initial teacher education courses offer explicit instruction on both theoretical and practical aspects of developing ICC in the foreign language classroom.

References

Barkhuizen, G., & Feryok, A. (2006). Pre-service teachers' perceptions of a short term international experience programme. *Asia-Pacific Journal of Teacher Education, 34*(1), 115–134.

Bektaş-Çetinkaya, Y. (2014). Extension of teacher knowledge: Developing the intercultural competence of pre-service foreign language teachers in Turkey. *Novitas-ROYAL (Research on Youth and Language), 8*(2), 153–168.

Bennett, J. M., & Bennett, M. J. (2004). Developing intercultural sensitivity. In J. M. Bennett, M. J. Bennett, & D. Landis (Eds.), *Handbook of intercultural training* (3rd ed., pp. 147–165). Thousand Oaks, CA: Sage.

Byram, M. (1991). Teaching culture and language: towards an integrated model. In D. Buttjes & M. Byram (Eds.), *Mediating languages and cultures: Towards an intercultural theory of foreign language education* (pp. 17–30). Clevedon: Multilingual Matters.

Byram, M. (1997). *Teaching and assessing intercultural communicative competence*. Clevedon: Multilingual Matters.

Byram, M. (2003). *Intercultural competence*. Strasbourg: Council of Europe.

Byram, M. (2015). Culture in foreign language learning–The implications for teachers and teacher training. In W. M. Chan, S. K. Bhatt, M. Nagami, & I. Walker (Eds.), *Culture and foreign language education: Insights from research and implications for the practice* (pp. 37–58). Berlin: De Gruyter Mouton.

Byram, M., Gribkova, B., & Starkey, H. (2002). *Developing the intercultural dimension in language teaching*. Strasbourg: Council of Europe.

Calderhead, J. (1996). Teachers: Beliefs and knowledge. In D. C. Berliner & R. C. Calfee (Eds.), *Handbook of educational psychology* (pp. 709–725). New York: Macmillan.

Corbett, J. B. (2003). *An intercultural approach to English language teaching*. Clevedon: Multilingual Matters.

Crew, V., & Bodycott, P. (2001). Reflections on short term study and residence abroad. In P. Bodycott & V. Crew (Eds.), *Language and cultural immersion—Perspectives on short term study and residence abroad* (pp. 141–150). Hong Kong: The Hong Kong Institute of Education.

Czura, A. (2017, June). *Me, myself and the 'other': Narrative accounts of integration during a teaching assistantship abroad*. Paper presented at the 17th International Conference of the International Association for Languages and Intercultural Communication, Edinburgh, UK.

Czura, A., & Pfingsthorn, J. (2016). The influence of a short-term international intensive programme on student teachers' perception of their future profession. *Anglica Wratislaviensia, 54*, 35–49.

Dervin, F., & Liddicoat, A. J. (2013). Introduction: Linguistics for intercultural education. In F. Dervin & A. J. Liddicoat (Eds.), *Linguistics for intercultural education* (pp. 1–25). Amsterdam: John Benjamins.

Dervin, F., & Tournebise, C. (2013). Turbulence in intercultural communication education (ICE): Does it affect higher education? *Intercultural Education, 24*(6), 532–543.

Göbel, K., & Helmke, A. (2010). Intercultural learning in English as foreign language instruction: The importance of teachers' intercultural experience and the usefulness of precise instructional directives. *Teaching and Teacher Education, 26*(8), 1571–1582. doi:10.1016/j.tate.2010.05.008.

Hepple, E. (2012). Questioning pedagogies: Hong Kong pre-service teachers' dialogic reflections on a transnational school experience. *Journal of Education for Teaching: International Research and Pedagogy, 38*(3), 309–322.

Hofstede, G. (1991). *Cultures and organizations: Software of the mind.* London: McGraw-Hill.

Holliday, A. (2010). *Intercultural communication and ideology.* London: Sage.

Jackson, J. (2010). *Intercultural journeys: From study to residence abroad.* Basingstoke, Hampshire: Palgrave Macmillan.

Kaplan, M. (1989). French in the community: A survey of language use abroad. *French Review, 63*(2), 290–301.

Kramsch, C. (1993). *Context and culture in language teaching.* Oxford: Oxford University Press.

Larson-Hall, J. (2010). *A guide to doing statistics in second language research using SPSS.* New York: Routledge.

Larzén-Östermark, E. (2008). The intercultural dimension in EFL-teaching: A study of conceptions among Finland-Swedish comprehensive school teachers. *Scandinavian Journal of Educational Research, 52*(5), 527–547. doi:10.1080/00313830802346405.

Larzén-Östermark, E. (2009). Language teacher education in Finland and the cultural dimension of foreign language teaching–a student teacher perspective. *European Journal of Teacher Education, 32*(4), 401–421.

Lee, J. F. K. (2009). ESL student teachers' perceptions of a short-term overseas immersion programme. *Teaching and Teacher Education, 25*(8), 1095–1104. doi:10.1016/j.tate.2009.03.004.

Liddicoat, A. J. (2002). Static and dynamic views of culture and intercultural language acquisition. *Babel, 36*(3), 4–11.

Liddicoat, A. J., & Scarino, A. (2013). *Intercultural language teaching and learning.* Malden, MA: Wiley-Blackwell.

Lightbown, P., & Spada, N. (1999). *How languages are learned.* Oxford, MA: Oxford University Press.

Moloney, R., & Harbon, L. (2010). Making intercultural language learning visible and assessable. *Proceedings of Intercultural Competence Conference* (vol. 1, pp. 281–303), August, 2010.

Oranje, J. M. (2016). *Intercultural communicative language teaching: Enhancing awareness and practice through cultural portfolio projects.* Unpublished doctoral thesis, University of Otago, Otago, New Zealand.

Otwinowska-Kasztelanic, A. (2011). Do we need to teach culture and how much culture do we need? In J. Arabski & A. Wojtaszek (Eds.), *Aspects of culture in second language acquisition and foreign language learning* (pp. 35–48). Berlin: Springer.

Pajares, M. (1992). Teachers' beliefs and educational research: Cleaning up a messy construct. *Review of Educational Research, 62,* 307–332.

Pavlenko, A., & Lantolf, J. (2000). Second language learning as participation and the (re)construction of selves. In J. P. Lantolf (Ed.), *Sociocultural theory and second language learning* (pp. 155–177). Oxford, MA: Oxford University Press.

Pray, L., & Marx, S. (2010). ESL teacher education abroad and at home: A cautionary tale. *The Teacher Educator, 45*(3), 216–229.

Risager, K. (2005). Foreword. In L. Sercu (Ed.), *Foreign language teachers and intercultural competence. An international investigation* (pp. vii–ix). Clevedon: Multilingual Matters.

Sercu, L. (Ed.). (2005). *Foreign language teachers and intercultural competence: An international investigation.* Clevedon: Multilingual Matters.

Strzałka, A. (2005). Preparing to teach culture in the English classroom and beyond. In M. Misztal & M. Trawiński (Eds.), *Studies in teacher education: Language, literature and culture* (pp. 98–104). Kraków: Wydawnictwo Naukowe Akademii Pedagogicznej.

Sutherland, M. L. (2011). *English language study abroad program: An investigation of Hong Kong pre-service teachers' experiences of a language immersion program.* Unpublished doctoral dissertation, Queensland University of Technology, Brisbane, Australia.

Szczepaniak-Kozak, A. (2010). Interkulturowa kompetencja komunikacyjna z perspektywy nauczyciela języka angielskiego [Intercultural communicative competence from the perspective of English language teachers]. In M. Mackiewicz (Ed.), *Kompetencja interkulturowa w teorii i praktyce edukacyjnej [Intercultural competence in theory and practice]* (pp. 125–136). Poznań: Wydawnictwo Wyższej Szkoły Biznesu.

Tang, S. Y. F., & Choi, P. L. (2004). The development of personal, intercultural and professional competence in international field experience in initial teacher education. *Asia Pacific Education Review, 5*(1), 50–63.

Trent, J. (2011). Learning, teaching, and constructing identities: ESL pre-service teacher experiences during a short-term international experience program. *Asia Pacific Journal of Education, 31*(2), 177–194.

Ward, C., & Rana-Deuba, A. (1999). Acculturation and adaptation revisited. *Journal of Cross-Cultural Psychology, 30*(4), 422–442.

Young, T. J., & Sachdev, I. (2011). Intercultural communicative competence: Exploring English language teachers' beliefs and practices. *Language Awareness, 20*(2), 81–98. doi:10.1080/09658416.2010.540328.

Author Biography

Anna Czura is Assistant Professor in the Institute of English Studies at the University of Wrocław, Poland. She was awarded a Ph.D. in linguistics in 2010 for her dissertation on the role of authentic assessment in developing learner autonomy in adolescent learners. In her research she is mainly interested in learner and teacher mobility, teacher education, intercultural competence, CLIL, language policy, language assessment and learner autonomy. She has been an expert of the European Centre for Modern Languages in Graz since 2013.

Printed by Printforce, the Netherlands